Lyrical B.
and Related

NEW RIVERSIDE EDITIONS

Series Editor for the British Volumes
Alan Richardson

Fictions of Empire: Heart of Darkness, Joseph Conrad; *The Man Who Would Be King*, Rudyard Kipling; and *The Beach of Falesá*, Robert Louis Stevenson
edited by John Kucich

Lyrical Ballads and Related Writings, William Wordsworth and Samuel Taylor Coleridge
edited by William Richey and Daniel Robinson

Making Humans: Frankenstein, Mary Shelley, and *The Island of Doctor Moreau*, H. G. Wells
edited by Judith Wilt

Sense and Sensibility, Jane Austen
edited by Beth Lau

Three Oriental Tales: History of Nourjahad, Frances Sheridan; *Vathek*, William Beckford; and *The Giaour*, Lord Byron
edited by Alan Richardson

Three Vampire Tales: Dracula, Bram Stoker; *Carmilla*, Sheridan LeFanu; and *The Vampyre*, John Polidori
edited by Anne Williams

Two Irish National Tales: Castle Rackrent, Maria Edgeworth, and *The Wild Irish Girl*, Sydney Owenson (Lady Morgan)
edited by James M. Smith

Wuthering Heights, Emily Brontë
edited by Diane Long Hoeveler

For a complete listing of our American and British New Riverside Editions, visit our web site at **http://college.hmco.com.**

NEW RIVERSIDE EDITIONS
Series Editor for the British Volumes
Alan Richardson, Boston College

WILLIAM WORDSWORTH
AND
SAMUEL TAYLOR COLERIDGE

Lyrical Ballads and Related Writings

*Complete Text with Introduction
Contexts • Reactions*

Edited by
William Richey

UNIVERSITY OF SOUTH CAROLINA

Daniel Robinson

WIDENER UNIVERSITY

Houghton Mifflin Company
BOSTON • NEW YORK

For Esther and Cynthia, Wendy and Sarah Margaret

Sponsoring Editor: Michael Gillespie
Editorial Associate: Bruce Cantley
Senior Project Editor: Tracy Patruno
Senior Cover Design Coordinator: Deborah Azerrad Savona
Manufacturing Manager: Florence Cadran
Marketing Manager: Cindy Graff Cohen

Cover image: © Corbis

Credits appear on page 459, which is a continuation of the copyright page.

Printed in the U.S.A.

Library of Congress Control Number: 2001090568
ISBN: 0-618-10732-0
2 3 4 5 6 7 8 9-QF-06 05 04 03 02

CONTENTS

ABOUT THIS SERIES
Alan Richardson

The Riverside imprint, stamped on a book's spine or printed on its title page, carries a special aura for anyone who loves and values books. As well it might: by the middle of the nineteenth century, Houghton Mifflin had already established the "Riverside" edition as an important presence in American publishing. The Riverside series of British poets brought trustworthy editions of Milton and Wordsworth, Spenser and Pope, and (then) lesser-known writers like Herbert, Vaughan, and Keats to a growing nation of readers. There was both a Riverside Shakespeare and a Riverside Chaucer by the century's end, titles that would be revived and recreated as the authoritative editions of the late twentieth century. Riverside editions of writers like Emerson, Hawthorne, Longfellow, and Thoreau helped establish the first canon of American literature. Early in the twentieth century, the Cambridge editions published by Houghton Mifflin at the Riverside Press made the complete works of dozens of British and American poets widely available in single-volume editions that can still be found in libraries and homes throughout the United States and beyond.

The Riverside Editions of the 1950s and 1960s brought attractive, affordable, and carefully edited versions of a range of British and American titles into the thriving new market for serious paperback literature. Prepared by leading scholars and critics of the time, the Riversides rapidly became known for their lively introductions, reliable texts, and lucid annotation. Though aimed primarily at the college market, the series was also created (as one editor put it) with the "general reader's private library" in mind. These were paperbacks to hold on to and read again, and the bookshelves of many a "private" library were brightened with the colorful spines of Riverside editions kept long after graduation.

Houghton Mifflin's New Riverside Editions now bring the combination of high editorial values and wide popular appeal long associated with the Riverside imprint into line with the changing needs and desires of twenty-first century students and general readers. Inaugurated in 2000 with the first set of American titles under the general editorship of Paul Lauter, the New Riversides reflect both the changing canons of literature in English and the greater emphasis on historical and cultural context that have helped a new generation of critics to extend and reenliven literary studies. The Series is not only concerned with keeping the classic works of British and American literature alive but grows as well out of the excitement that a broader range of literary texts and cultural reference points has brought to the classroom. Works by formerly marginalized authors, including women writers and writers of color, will find a place in the Series along with titles from the traditional canons that a succession of Riverside imprints helped establish beginning a century and a half ago. New Riverside titles will reflect the recent surge of interest in the connections among literary activity, historical change, and social and political issues, including slavery, abolition, and the construction of "race"; gender relations and the history of sexuality; the rise of the British Empire and of nationalisms on both sides of the Atlantic; and changing conceptions of nature and of the human.

The New Riverside Editions respond to recent changes in literary studies not only in the range of titles but also in the design of individual volumes. Issues and debates crucial to a book's author and original audience find voice in selections from contemporary writings of many kinds as well as in early reactions and reviews. Some volumes will place contemporary writers into dialogue, as with the pairing of Irish national tales by Maria Edgeworth and Sydney Owenson or of vampire stories by Bram Stoker and Sheridan Le Fanu. Other volumes provide alternative ways of constructing literary tradition, placing Mary Shelley's *Frankenstein* with H. G. Wells's *Island of Dr. Moreau*, or Lord Byron's *The Giaour*, an "Eastern Tale" in verse, with Frances Sheridan's *Nourjahad* and William Beckford's *Vathek*, its most important predecessors in Orientalist prose fiction. Chronologies, selections from major criticism, notes on textual history, and bibliographies will allow readers to go beyond the text and explore a given writer or issue in greater depth. Seasoned critics will find fresh new contexts and juxtapositions, and general readers will find intriguing new material to read alongside of familiar titles in an attractive format.

Houghton Mifflin's New Riverside Editions maintain the values of reliability and readability that have marked the Riverside name for well over a century. Each volume also provides something new — often unexpected — and each in a distinctive way. Freed from the predictable monotony and rigidity of a set template, editors can build their volumes around the special opportunities presented by a given title or set of related works. We hope that the resulting blend of innovative scholarship, creative format, and high production values will help the Riverside imprint continue to thrive well into the new century.

Lyrical Ballads
and Related Writings

Thomas Gainsborough, *The Cottage Door* (c. 1780)

INTRODUCTION
William Richey and Daniel Robinson

We have a tendency to romanticize Romanticism—to smooth away its rougher edges, to lighten its darker moods, and to ignore its more disturbing implications. Thus, while we expect a certain amount of cynicism and prickliness from early eighteenth-century writers dubbed "Neoclassical," such as Alexander Pope or Jonathan Swift, we typically attribute an abiding optimism and unfailing benevolence to Romantics such as William Wordsworth and Samuel Taylor Coleridge, who began writing late in the eighteenth century. To a casual observer then, Thomas Gainsborough's circa 1780 painting *The Cottage Door* (facing) might seem the very embodiment of Romantic values. With its depiction of man in harmony with nature and its idyllic representation of working-class life, the painting appears designed to inspire the kind of reverence for the natural world and appreciation of the commonplace that M. H. Abrams cites as two of the defining characteristics of the English Romantic movement (127–28). Moreover, its tender portrayal of a mother's love for her blooming, almost cherubic, children lends the painting a warm-hearted sentimentality that sharply distinguishes it from the cold rationality that we habitually associate with the earlier eighteenth century, the so-called Age of Reason.

But we would like to suggest with this edition of *Lyrical Ballads* that these sorts of equations and classifications are far too simplistic to reflect what was actually going on in 1798, the year in which *Lyrical Ballads* first appeared. In fact, we would argue that—far from mirroring Gainsborough's sentimental and idealized vision of the poor—*Lyrical Ballads* consistently seeks to strip away the pleasing illusions of late eighteenth-century art in order to reveal "things as they are." Admittedly, this is not the usual take on *Lyrical Ballads* as, influenced by Wordsworth's own comments in the 1800 and 1802 Prefaces, generations of scholars have asserted that what makes *Lyrical Ballads* such a watershed text is its use of a more colloquial,

1

less affected language ("the real language of men") and its unflinching focus on the poor and disenfranchised. Therefore, in contrast to Neoclassical poems such as Pope's *Rape of the Lock*, which chronicle the lives of the aristocracy in a highly ornate and formally sophisticated manner, *Lyrical Ballads* dares to exhibit the native dignity of "humble and rustic life" in a style accessible to the common people.

As with most generalizations of this type, there is some truth in this approach to *Lyrical Ballads*. Wordsworth's and Coleridge's language is simpler and more conversational than that of much poetry of its time, and their poems do often depict the poor in bold and highly sympathetic ways. Still, as Robert Mayo and others have pointed out, merely writing in simple language and describing "humble and rustic life" would hardly have struck late eighteenth-century readers as shocking or even unusual. After all, by the time Wordsworth wrote the Preface, George Crabbe had already reacted against the sentimental depictions of rustics in Oliver Goldsmith's *The Deserted Village*; Robert Burns had been writing for years in the real of language of Scotsmen; Joanna Baillie had argued that literary works should concentrate on "human nature in the middling and lower classes of society"; and such writers as Charlotte Smith and Robert Southey had been publishing poems about the poor in newspapers and literary magazines. Consequently—along with such critics as Mary Jacobus, Paul Sheats, and Heather Glen—we believe that what truly makes *Lyrical Ballads* an original and "experimental" book is how it daringly reworks the existing poetic conventions of the late eighteenth century, the period that Northrop Frye called the Age of Sensibility.[1] To borrow Wordsworth's own terminology from the 1798 Advertisement, *Lyrical Ballads* forces its readers to reevaluate their "own pre-established codes of decision" by imitating and parodying the very values and practices that its authors wished to subvert. Contrary to popular opinion then, *Lyrical Ballads* was far more a reaction against Sensibility than against Neoclassicism, and it is worth noting that the only poem Wordsworth singles out for attack in his famous Preface is a sonnet of Sensibility—Thomas Gray's "On the Death of Mr. Richard West"—not a poem by Pope or Samuel Johnson.[2]

A perfect example of how *Lyrical Ballads* challenges contemporary poetic practice is Wordsworth's "Simon Lee," a ballad that at first glance looks like one of the many other "humanitarian" poems written and published throughout the 1790s. Like *The Cottage Door* or the anonymous but com-

---

[1] See For Further Reading at the end of this volume.
[2] For more on how *Lyrical Ballads* responds to the Age of Sensibility, see the headnote to "Literary and Philosophical Backgrounds" in Part Two.

monly reprinted "The Beggar's Petition" (pages 294–95 in this volume), it seems to call up an affecting image of the lower classes in order to evoke a sympathetic response in its readers, thereby instilling in them an edifying message about the need for charity.[3] Upon closer inspection, however, it becomes clear that Wordsworth consistently refuses to sentimentalize his subject or to allow the usual sympathetic attachment between character and reader to develop. Instead, he employs a strategy of continual disruption, repeatedly pulling the rug out from under his readers. Throughout the first half of the poem, he veers wildly between Simon as he once was — a virile, almost legendary huntsman — and the pathetic, half-blind octogenarian he has become. In the third stanza, for instance, we hear both how "No man was so full of glee" and how he has survived all the former inhabitants of Ivor-hall ("Men, dogs, and horses, all are dead"). As a result, we are left uncertain as to how to respond to this tale. Is it a celebration of Simon's glory days, or is it — like "The Beggar's Petition" — a lament about what has befallen this unfortunate old man?

Then, just when the poem seems as if it might settle into a more consistently elegiac mode — lamenting how Simon has become so weak that he and his wife can barely farm a "scrap of land" — Wordsworth interrupts his already fractured narrative with this famous address to the reader:

> My gentle reader, I perceive
> How patiently you've waited,
> And I'm afraid that you expect
> Some tale will be related.
>
> O reader! had you in your mind
> Such stores as silent thought can bring,
> O gentle reader! you would find
> A tale in every thing.
> What more I have to say is short,
> I hope you'll kindly take it;
> It is no tale; but should you think,
> Perhaps a tale you'll make it.

Thus, if, in the previous two and a half stanzas, the reader had begun to muster the usual mawkish sympathy for this poor, old huntsman, the speaker's sudden intrusion instantly disperses that sentiment, injecting what seems a surprisingly wry note into this tale of decay and deprivation. The interruption, moreover, challenges the narrative expectations for the

---

[3] See the headnote to "Rustic and Humanitarian Poetry" in Part Two.

ballad form—solidified by the opening lines of the poem—by informing the "gentle" reader that he had better not expect the speaker to tell a story; rather, the speaker virtually defies the comfortable reader to find his own story grounded more firmly in the actual conditions faced by the poor rather than in some more sentimentalized image of poverty. Wordsworth shows the callowness of the reader's formal expectations and urges him to care about the poor old man without there having to be a remarkable story attached to him.

To conclude the ballad, Wordsworth subverts the norm one more time. Now the speaker himself encounters Simon Lee, and, after removing a stump that the old man had long been trying to uproot, he is "rewarded" in the following manner:

> —I've heard of hearts unkind, kind deeds
> With coldness still returning.
> Alas! the gratitude of men
> Has oftner left me mourning.

To some degree, these lines resemble what we would expect to see at the end of a typical humanitarian poem, as here the speaker seems to draw a moral from his encounter with the poor. But unlike "The Beggar's Petition," where an act of charity inoculates the benefactor against a similar fate ("give relief and Heav'n will bless your store"), the speaker now recognizes that there is no escape from Simon's fate for him or for anyone else. Therefore, rather than the rush of satisfaction that the speaker is expecting for his good deed, he is only brought face to face with the inevitability of human mortality and the impotence of charitable acts. Even after the stump is gone, Simon is still too weak to till his tiny "scrap of land," and so his gratitude merely serves as a pathetic reminder of how little the speaker has done. Indeed, far from resolving Simon's tragic situation, these lines merely reveal how intractable the problems of the poor and infirm are—how their misfortune is too severe, too deeply rooted, to be relieved by a single stroke. What emerges from the speaker's encounter is thus not so much a tale as a moment of introspection. Because the poem so deftly juxtaposes the narrative expectations for the ballad with a defiant lyrical resistance that redirects the emphasis to the speaker's own experience, "Simon Lee" is perhaps the definitive "lyrical ballad" in the collection, a ballad that tells no story but forces the reader to focus on this moment of lyrical insight. The poem seems to recognize, in its formal development, the oxymoronic nature of the very title of the book in which it appears.

Though different in both mood and subject matter from "Simon Lee," Coleridge's "Rime of the Ancyent Marinere" is no less a product of its time and no less devious in how it reworks an existing genre. Following the publication of Bishop Percy's *Reliques of Ancyent English Poetry* in 1765, imitations of medieval ballads became extremely popular in England and frequently were published in the literary magazines of the time. For readers in 1798, then, the antique setting, the archaic diction, and the supernatural happenings of Coleridge's poem would not have seemed at all surprising; these were standard equipment for a Gothic ballad. What is unusual about Coleridge's foray into this genre, however, is how he represents the supernatural.[4] In more conventional ballads, poets generally treat magical or supernatural events as if they are absolutely true. Gottfried Bürger's "Lenora" presents the appearance of the Grim Reaper and his spiriting away of the title character on a flying horse as if they were plain facts; M. G. Lewis's "Alonzo the Brave and Fair Imogine" concludes with a straightforward, if ghoulish, account of the lovers' ghostly revel. Despite the fanciful and improbable nature of these events, Lewis describes them all in unambiguous declarative sentences, and never does he qualify his statements with phrases like "legend has it that" or "I have heard it said."

Coleridge, however, consistently makes it difficult for his readers to suspend their disbelief. First he arouses their suspicions by doing something that is virtually unprecedented in the Gothic ballad tradition: He casts his poem largely as a first-person narrative—which is particularly remarkable since the speaker, for most of the poem, is a supernatural figure with a "glittering eye" and the power to arrest the more recognizably human wedding guest. Thus, in contrast to standard Gothic practice, where the narrator's testimony lends his sanction to the story he is telling, here no one corroborates the mariner's account. To use his own words, he has been "alone on a wide, wide sea." To make matters worse, the narrator that Coleridge chooses hardly inspires much confidence: A retired sailor who is well "past the middle of age of life," he is the very sort of person that Wordsworth uses in another lyrical ballad, "The Thorn," to epitomize someone "prone to superstition."[5] Even if we are inclined to believe this rather suspect source, Coleridge further challenges his credibility by having almost every supernatural event happen when the mariner and crew are asleep or unconscious. For instance, the first we hear of what Coleridge later calls "the Polar Spirit" occurs at line 127—just after the wind has ceased and the ship is stuck out in the middle of the ocean:

---

[4]In the *Monthly Review*, for instance, Charles Burney called it "the strangest story of a cock and bull that we ever saw on paper" and "a rhapsody of unintelligible wildness and incoherence." See "Contemporary Reviews" in Part Three.

[5]See the headnote to "The Ballad Revival" in Part Two.

And some *in dreams* assured were
  Of the Spirit that plagued us so:
Nine fathom deep he had follow'd us
  From the land of Mist and Snow. (ll. 127–30, emphasis added)

The sailors' dreams are hardly the most corroborative of evidence. These visions appear to just "some" of the crew—and apparently not even to the storyteller himself. Similarly, when the mariner does receive explanations for many of the poem's mysteries, it is only after he has fallen into a swoon, during which he overhears a conversation between two spirits. As a result, these seeming facts—that the mariner is doing penance for killing a bird dear to the Polar Spirit, that he has "penance more" to do, and so on—may all just be the product of a very vivid hallucination.[6]

Thus, like "Simon Lee," "The Rime of the Ancyent Marinere" does not invent a new genre or a new mode of literary discourse, but rather it re-examines an existing one, calling attention to its underlying assumptions and forcing the genre to serve other functions than it was originally designed to do. Whereas the primary objective of a ballad such as "Alonzo the Brave and Fair Imogine" is to evoke terror and astonishment in its readers, Coleridge psychologizes the Gothic ballad, showing more interest in the mind of the protagonist than in the fearful response of the reader (or wedding guest)—and, in the process, suggests that many of the poem's seemingly supernatural occurrences may well be the projections of his mariner's own guilty conscience.

Read in this way—that is, in relation to other late eighteenth-century Gothic ballads and to other "lyrical ballads" such as "The Thorn"—this all-too-famous poem starts to emerge from what Coleridge called "the film of familiarity." Conversely, if students come to poems such as "Simon Lee" and "The Rime of the Ancyent Marinere" with no knowledge of humanitarian poetry or Gothic ballads, they miss much of what made them so bold and original in 1798—how they work to undermine the conventions of their respective genres and to subvert the expectations of their original readership. As a result, students draw the natural but thoroughly inaccurate conclusion that Wordsworth and Coleridge invented these genres and modes of expression, a conclusion that does a disservice to the achieve-

---

[6]There is of course a major exception to this rule: the appearance of the Spectre ship—the one event that both defies logical explanation and occurs when the mariner and the crew are awake. However, given the fact that the mariner sees this ship after he's been stuck out on the ocean for days, with the sun beating down on his head, no water to drink nor food to eat, and a big, rotting bird hanging around his neck, a delusion is certainly not out of the question here, either.

ments both of *Lyrical Ballads* and of the very talented but often forgotten writers such as Joseph Warton and Charlotte Smith, who actually did carry out the rebellion against Neoclassicism. In short, since readers of this poetry and students of Romanticism in general are typically hearing one side of what was a highly complex and nuanced conversation, it is hardly surprising that they often fail to understand these sorts of distinctions.

Our goal in designing this edition of *Lyrical Ballads* has been to fill in these gaps in students' knowledge and to restore *Lyrical Ballads*, as much as possible, to its original context. In addition to sections devoted to the aesthetic, philosophical, and political backgrounds to *Lyrical Ballads*, we have included a generous sampling of late eighteenth-century verse to exemplify the kinds of poetry and literary trends to which Wordsworth and Coleridge were responding. After reading Charlotte Smith's "The Dead Beggar," Robert Southey's "The Idiot," and William Taylor's translation of Bürger's "Lenora," students will be able to see how truly "experimental" such poems as "Simon Lee," "The Idiot Boy," and "The Rime of the Ancyent Marinere" really are—and how strange and unsettling they must have seemed to readers in 1798. We also hope that the additional readings in this edition will provide scholars, undergraduate and graduate students, and general readers with useful and rewarding tools for appreciating *Lyrical Ballads* and its rich context.

Just as important, we have restored the texts of the *Lyrical Ballads* to their 1798 form, rather than doing what many editions and anthologies do, reprinting them in the later revised versions. *The Norton Anthology of English Literature*, for instance—the place where many readers encounter these poems for the first time—consistently selects these later versions as being more authoritative, without clearly indicating that these are not the texts that appeared in the *Lyrical Ballads'* first edition. Consequently, readers often come away with highly misleading impressions of what the 1798 volume was like—especially since these revisions filter out what was so vibrant and daring in the originally published versions.[7]

By reprinting the poems in their original form, this edition of *Lyrical Ballads* preserves the whimsy and sarcasm, the parody and startling shifts in perspective and tone—the very features that prompted Wordsworth to warn his readers in 1798 that they might well "look round for poetry and [. . .] be induced to enquire by what species of courtesy these attempts can be permitted to assume that title."

---

[7] See the revised versions of "Simon Lee" and "The Rime of the Ancient Mariner" in Part Three.

A NOTE ON THE TEXTS
William Richey and Daniel Robinson

Our general principle in reprinting texts has been to provide, when possible, the first published version. Because the primary aim of this volume is to show *Lyrical Ballads* in its context, we have preferred published versions of all texts over manuscript versions. Certainly, in the cases of Wordsworth and Coleridge, extensively annotated textual editions are widely available for those interested in the poets' own manuscripts, emendations, and revisions. This volume presents texts that were more available to the contemporary reading public. Our copytexts are cited in source notes at the beginning of each selection.

A notable exception is our selection of the London printing of *Lyrical Ballads* instead of the Bristol printing (both are considered the first edition); the London version, printed and published by Arch, is the more stable text due to the corrections, deletions, and additions that occurred during the printing of the Bristol version. The London printing, moreover, is the more widely circulated text. The differences between the two are not substantial (aside from the replacement of "Lewti" with "The Nightingale" in the London printing). Another significant instance where we have reprinted a later text than the first published form is our selection of the sixth edition of John Denham's *Coopers Hill*, which scholars long have accepted as the first authoritative printing. Our source notes at the beginning of each selection indicate the date of the selected texts; here we indicate, in the few other instances where we have used a later text, the first published version.

Except for the standardization of titles, we generally have retained the original spelling and punctuation. Such accidental features of the texts were usually in the hands of printers and, in most cases, do not affect greatly the reader's appreciation of the literature. We have resisted modernizing the texts in the hope of preserving something of their original flavor. We silently have emended the texts in the few instances where the original text, because of printers' errors or because of capricious eighteenth-century stylistic conventions, may present substantial difficulties in comprehension. Frequently this editing involves deleting excessive commas in the prose selections or adding quotation marks where the closing mark is missing. We also have changed the word *it's* to *its* when the original text makes it clear that the possessive pronoun is intended and provided glosses for unfamiliar terms. One additional feature of the poetic texts that a modern reader may find unfamiliar is the printing of metrical elisions such as "o'er" or "heal'd" to indicate an unpronounced syllable. We have preserved such spellings as essential to the meter. Conversely, words ending in *-ed* that are not elided usually are pronounced with an additional syllable, as in the liturgical pronunciation of the word *blessed*. The practice of printing elisions is consistent from the sixteenth through the nineteenth centuries, so we consider it an essential component of reading and appreciating the poetry of this time.

Part One

LYRICAL BALLADS,
WITH A FEW OTHER POEMS

LYRICAL BALLADS

> *. . . belovèd friend,*
> *When looking back thou seest, in clearer view*
> *Than any sweetest sight of yesterday,*
> *That summer when on Quantock's grassy hills*
> *Far ranging, and among the sylvan coombs,*
> *Thou in delicious words, with happy heart,*
> *Didst speak the vision of that ancient man,*
> *The bright-eyed Mariner, and rueful woes*
> *Didst utter of the Lady Christabel;*
> *And I, associate in such labour, walked*
> *Murmuring of him, who — joyous hap — was found,*
> *After the perils of his moonlight ride,*
> *Near the loud waterfall, or her who sate*
> *In misery near the miserable thorn. . . .*
>
> — *William Wordsworth,*
> The Prelude *(1805, 13.390 – 403)* [1]

So does William Wordsworth pay tribute to Samuel Taylor Coleridge and to the famous friendship that produced *Lyrical Ballads*. These lines from *The Prelude*, Wordsworth's personal epic written for Coleridge, also pay tribute to the place where they came to know one another as men and as poets. Writing in his *Biographia Literaria*, Coleridge describes the period from July 1797 to July 1798 as "the first year that Mr. Wordsworth and I were

---

[1] These lines are nearly identical in the 1850 version (14.394 – 409).

neighbours"—perhaps the only incontestable remark Coleridge makes here about the collaboration between himself and his fellow poet. Those familiar with the landscape of Somerset, near the Bristol Channel, may be impressed with the four-mile trek that Coleridge made on foot almost daily from his modest cottage at Nether Stowey across the Quantock hills to Alfoxden, the spacious residence of William and his sister Dorothy Wordsworth, and back home again to his wife and infant son. Nonetheless, Coleridge was a frequent visitor at Alfoxden, and it was during this time that the two poets conceived the plan for *Lyrical Ballads*. Moreover, it was the place itself that influenced the collaboration, for the hills overlooking the Bristol Channel became "the known and familiar landscape" upon which Wordsworth and Coleridge would found the poetic principles of the book. The character of the book, then, takes much from the county in which its poems were written and, for the most part, are set.

Wordsworth, at this time, was just emerging from a personal crisis, which resulted from two primary causes. The first was an ill-fated affair with a Frenchwoman, Annette Vallon, from whom he had separated in 1792. Although we remain uncertain about the exact details of this relationship and the reasons for Wordsworth's return to England only a few months before the birth of their daughter, Caroline, it is clear that this affair haunted him throughout the 1790s and may even have colored his depictions of forsaken women in such lyrical ballads as "The Thorn" and "The Mad Mother."[2] The other was his disillusionment over the course of the French Revolution. After having witnessed its early phases during his residence in France (1791–92), Wordsworth became an ardent supporter of the revolutionary cause, and, as his 1793 "Letter to the Bishop of Llandaff" reveals, he continued to defend it even after the September Massacres and the execution of the French king, Louis XVI, had horrified many of its initial sympathizers:

> What! have you so little knowledge of the nature of man as to be ignorant, that a time of revolution is not the season of true Liberty. Alas! the obstinacy & perversion of men is such that she is too often obliged to borrow the very arms of despotism to overthrow him, and in order to reign in peace must establish herself by violence. She deplores such stern necessity, but the safety of the people, her supreme law, is her consolation. (*Prose Works* 1.33–34)

---

[2] After reviewing the evidence and the interpretations of other Wordsworth biographers, Stephen Gill concludes that "there is simply no evidence on which to conjecture whether Wordsworth was deeply in love with Annette or, conversely, that his union with her was a short-lived passion which he was forced to take seriously only because she became pregnant" (65).

Gradually, though, the violence of the Reign of Terror, the increased militarism of the French Republic, the autocracy of the Directory (the government that replaced the Jacobins), and the rise of Napoleon Bonaparte dampened Wordsworth's enthusiasm and plunged him into a deep depression.[3]

By 1795, however, both his prospects and his state of mind had begun to brighten considerably. In that year, Wordsworth received a legacy of £900 from a deceased friend, Raisley Calvert, which would have a dramatic impact on his future. In practical terms, this money provided him with the financial security he needed to devote himself to his poetic calling; but, just as important, it enabled him to be reunited with his beloved sister, Dorothy. An unparalleled observer of the natural world and a writer of considerable talent herself, Dorothy Wordsworth served from 1795 until her brother's marriage in 1802 as his housekeeper, secretary, and confidant; she, more than anyone else, helped him recover from his prolonged depression. His sense of admiration and gratitude is obvious from the eloquent tribute that he pays her in *The Prelude:*

> And then it was
> That the belovèd woman in whose sight
> Those days were passed — now speaking in a voice
> Of sudden admonition like a brook
> That does but cross a lonely road; and now
> Seen, heard and felt, and caught at every turn,
> Companion never lost through many a league —
> Maintained for me a saving intercourse
> With my true self (for, though impaired, and changed
> Much, as it seemed, I was no further changed
> Than as a clouded, not a waning moon);
> She, in the midst of all, preserved me still
> A poet, made me seek beneath that name
> My office upon earth, and nowhere else. (1805, 10.334 – 47)

After living for a brief period at Racedown Lodge in North Dorset, William and Dorothy moved in 1797 to Alfoxden in Somerset to be closer to Coleridge where, in Coleridge's words, they became "three persons with one soul."

Like Wordsworth, Coleridge left Cambridge University largely uninspired and dabbled in radical politics connected with his initial revolutionary enthusiasm. Unlike Wordsworth, however, Coleridge had a family

---

[3] For more on the French Revolution, see the headnote to "Political Backgrounds" in Part Two. John Williams devotes a chapter of his *Wordsworth: Romantic Poetry and Revolution Politics* to the letter to Llandaff (55–68).

for whom to provide—he was married, somewhat incompatibly, to Sara Fricker—and had an infant son, Hartley.[4] As a result, Coleridge had to earn his living by lecturing and preaching and thus resented to some degree the luxuries the Wordsworths enjoyed at Alfoxden, "the mansion of my friend," which he compares in "Fears in Solitude" to his "own lowly cottage" (220–22). The growing friendship between the two men, however, more than compensated for the difference: it fueled their literary ambitions and inspired Coleridge to focus on poetry. Their frequent walking excursions among the hills overlooking the Bristol Channel and subsequent conversations concentrated the mind of each upon what Coleridge calls, in the *Biographia Literaria*, "the poetry of nature." Their common interest established, the two distinguished "the two cardinal points of poetry," which Coleridge famously describes as "the power of exciting the sympathy of the reader by a faithful adherence to the truth of nature, and the power of giving the interest of novelty by the modifying colors of the imagination." As he tells us, it was the "sudden charm" of "accidents of light and shade" upon the Quantock hills that urged the two poets to attempt combining these two poetic powers in one book, with Wordsworth devoting himself to subjects "chosen from ordinary life" and Coleridge to "incidents and agents [. . .] in part at least supernatural." Wordsworth similarly characterizes the initial aims of *Lyrical Ballads* in his 1802 Preface, suggesting that, whereas Coleridge's contributions were supposed to make the unreal or supernatural seem real, his were intended to portray the usual in an unusual manner, to give ordinary experience a fresh expression in the minds of their readers and to make it interesting by demonstrating in ordinary life "the primary laws of our nature."[5]

Poetic aspirations aside, however, the mechanics of the initial collaboration were greatly influenced by the personal and financial circumstances of the two men. In November 1797, Wordsworth and Coleridge were planning

---

[4]Coleridge's marriage grew out of the arrangements for the "Pantisocracy" colony, the utopian scheme that he and his friend Robert Southey were planning in the mid-1790s. Already engaged to Edith Fricker, Southey suggested to Coleridge that he propose to her older sister, Sara. Though the plans for Pantisocracy fell through, Coleridge nevertheless felt honor-bound to go ahead with the marriage. For more on Pantisocracy, see page 212.

[5]Wordsworth's and Coleridge's accounts of the origins and goals of *Lyrical Ballads* provide invaluable insight but tend to make the book seem more carefully planned and coherent than it actually was. See Mark Reed, "Wordsworth, Coleridge, and the 'Plan' of the *Lyrical Ballads.*" For more on the collaboration, see especially Stephen Maxfield Parrish's *The Art of the* Lyrical Ballads (34–79) and Richard Matlak's *The Poetry of Relationship: The Wordsworths and Coleridge, 1797–1800*, which also emphasizes the contribution of Dorothy Wordsworth to the poetic accomplishments of the two men.

an excursion to Linton to see the Valley of Stones, so they decided to write a poem together that might provide them with money for expenses.[6] Wordsworth had an idea for a poem about a sailor who kills an albatross, which he had gotten from reading a similar account in George Shelvocke's *A Voyage Round the World by the Way of the Great South Sea* (1726). Inspired by this incident as well as by a dream recounted to him by his neighbor John Cruikshank, Coleridge began writing, as a ballad, the poem that would become "The Rime of the Ancyent Marinere," since both poets were interested in the revival of that form—particularly in Thomas Percy's *Reliques of Ancient English Poetry* and William Taylor's then recent translations of Gottfried Bürger's ballads. As family friend Isabella Fenwick records, Wordsworth contributed a few lines and suggested the device of having the ship piloted by the dead seamen, but he realized that the poem was better suited to Coleridge's imagination and style, that he "could only have been a clog" on it (Curtis 3). Coleridge took over composition of the poem and finished it in March 1798.

During the writing of "The Ancyent Marinere," the rest of the volume took shape. Wordsworth says in the 1798 prefatory Advertisement that the two poets considered most of their efforts as poetic "experiments," but not in the typically apologetic sense that many contemporary poets attached to their innovations. Rather, the Advertisement boldly announces the volume as a challenge to contemporary tastes, an attempt to replace "the gaudiness and inane phraseology of many modern writers" with "the language of conversation in the middle and lower classes of society." Given the radical nature of this experiment, Wordsworth anticipates the "feelings of strangeness and aukwardness" that his readers might experience on reading these poems. Therefore, he urges his readers to "temper the rashness of decision"—at least until they have asked themselves "if [the poem] contains a natural delineation of human passions, human characters, and human incidents."

Of the two poets, Wordsworth was the more prolific, contributing the majority of poems that would make up *Lyrical Ballads*.[7] Some of these contributions—like "The Female Vagrant," an excerpt from his unpublished narrative poem "Salisbury Plain"—dated from earlier in the 1790s, but many were written in early 1798, including some of the most famous and memorable poems in the collection ("We Are Seven," "Anecdote for Fathers," "Goody Blake and Harry Gill," "Simon Lee," "The Idiot Boy," and

---

[6]This much of the story is corroborated by William Hazlitt in his memoir *My First Acquaintance with Poets* (1823).

[7]In this same period, Wordsworth also completed the long blank verse poem *The Ruined Cottage* and a prototypical "lyrical ballad" titled *Peter Bell* (which would not appear in print until 1819).

"The Thorn").[8] Wordsworth and Coleridge attempted a collaboration on the unfinished poem "The Three Graves," which did not appear in the book, and Coleridge revised one of Wordsworth's poems and published it under the title "Lewti; or the Circassian's Love Chant" in the *Morning Post* in April 1798. In keeping with the division of labor between the two poets, Coleridge began working on another Gothic ballad called "Christabel" for inclusion in *Lyrical Ballads* but became distracted by political intrigue surrounding a feared invasion of England by the French army via the Bristol Channel, resulting in the publication of a small volume that included "Fears in Solitude," "France: An Ode," and "Frost at Midnight."

Adding to this activity, Coleridge's literary efforts so impressed the wealthy Wedgwood family that they bestowed upon him a comfortable annuity, so he, too, could devote his time to his writing. This good fortune encouraged him to suggest to the Wordsworths, who had just learned that they would soon be turned out of Alfoxden because of what their landlord deemed some unsavory political connections, that they travel with him to Germany while he pursued the study of philosophy and religion at the highly esteemed University of Göttingen. Wordsworth, now less financially secure than he had been of late, needed to sell the poems he and Coleridge had been working on, in order to afford the trip. As Coleridge had no hope of completing "Christabel," he abandoned it, contributing instead "The Rime of the Ancyent Marinere" and two other pieces, "The Foster-Mother's Tale" and "The Dungeon," excerpted from his tragedy, *Osorio*.

Although he did not compose as many of the poems in the book as he had intended, Coleridge had an established connection with Bristol bookseller Joseph Cottle, who had published two volumes of Coleridge's poetry in 1796 and 1797, which paid off when Cottle accepted the new book for publication. Cottle preferred this collection over a proposed joint publication of Wordsworth's tragedy, *The Borderers*, and Coleridge's *Osorio*. After some negotiations between Cottle and the two poets, *Lyrical Ballads* went to press in May 1798, Wordsworth's now-famous "Tintern Abbey" being the last poem written for the volume. Since they deliberately omitted their names from the title page, Wordsworth and Coleridge soon thereafter withdrew "Lewti" because its prior publication in the *Morning Post* under the pseudonym Nicias Erythraeus compromised the anonymity of the volume.[9] In its place, they substituted Coleridge's "The Nightingale: A Conversational Poem." [10]

---

[8] See Mark L. Reed, *Wordsworth: The Chronology of the Early Years, 1770–1799*.

[9] Coleridge insisted on the anonymous publication, writing to Cottle that "Wordsworth's name is nothing" and that "to a large number of persons mine *stinks*" (*Letters* 1.412).

[10] Coleridge wrote to Humphry Davy two years later that "Christabel" (still unfinished) was ill suited to the concept of the *Lyrical Ballads* and thus would not appear in the second edition because of its fantastic character: "The poem was in direct opposition to the

Cottle printed several hundred copies of *Lyrical Ballads* in Bristol, perhaps as many as five hundred, but within two weeks sold the copyright to the London booksellers J. and A. Arch.[11] With the book on sale in London, the two poets left Somerset, where it was conceived. In September, leaving his wife and son in England, Coleridge departed with Wordsworth and his sister for Germany. *Lyrical Ballads* was published finally on 4 October 1798. Despite mixed reviews and slow initial sales, the slim volume of poems they left behind sold out within a year.

---

very purpose for which the Lyrical Ballads were published—viz—an experiment to see how far those passions, which alone give any value to extraordinary Incidents, were capable of interesting, in & for themselves, in the incidents of common Life" (*Letters* 1.631).

[11] D. F. Foxon years ago suggested that Southey, who had an advance copy of the book, warned Cottle that *Lyrical Ballads* would be an imminent failure, thus encouraging Cottle, with whom Southey had a business relationship, to dispose of the copyright (240). As his review shows, Southey was unimpressed with the volume (see pages 352–54 in Part Three). For more on the intricacies of the publishing history, see Foxon's article "The Printing of *Lyrical Ballads*, 1798."

Lyrical Ballads

with

A Few Other Poems

William Wordsworth
and
Samuel Taylor Coleridge

Advertisement[1]

It is the honourable characteristic of Poetry that its materials are to be found in every subject which can interest the human mind. The evidence of this fact is to be sought, not in the writings of Critics, but in those of Poets themselves.

The majority of the following poems are to be considered as experiments. They were written chiefly with a view to ascertain how far the language of conversation in the middle and lower classes of society is adapted to the purposes of poetic pleasure. Readers accustomed to the gaudiness and inane phraseology of many modern writers, if they persist in reading this book to its conclusion, will perhaps frequently have to struggle with feelings of strangeness and aukwardness: they will look round for poetry, and will be induced to enquire by what species of courtesy these attempts can be permitted to assume that title. It is desirable that such readers, for their own sakes, should not suffer the solitary word Poetry, a word of very disputed meaning, to stand in the way of their gratification; but that, while they are perusing this book, they should ask themselves if it contains a natural delineation of human passions, human characters, and human incidents; and if the answer be favourable to the author's wishes, that they should consent to be pleased in spite of that most dreadful enemy to our pleasures, our own pre-established codes of decision.

Readers of superior judgment may disapprove of the style in which many of these pieces are executed. It must be expected that many lines and phrases will not exactly suit their taste. It will perhaps appear to them, that wishing to avoid the prevalent fault of the day, the author has sometimes descended too low, and that many of his expressions are too familiar, and not of sufficient dignity. It is apprehended, that the more conversant the reader is with our elder writers, and with those in modern times who have been the most successful in painting manners and passions, the fewer complaints of this kind will he have to make.

An accurate taste in poetry, and in all the other arts, Sir Joshua Reynolds[2] has observed, is an acquired talent, which can only be produced by severe thought, and a long continued intercourse with the best models of composition. This is mentioned not with so ridiculous a purpose as to prevent the most inexperienced reader from judging for himself; but merely to

---

London: Arch, 1798.

[1] Wordsworth composed the Advertisement. [ED.]
[2] Joshua Reynolds (1723–92) was a noted English portrait painter and first president of the Royal Academy. [ED.]

temper the rashness of decision, and to suggest that if poetry be a subject on which much time has not been bestowed, the judgment may be erroneous, and that in many cases it necessarily will be so.

The tale of Goody Blake and Harry Gill is founded on a well-authenticated fact which happened in Warwickshire. Of the other poems in the collection, it may be proper to say that they are either absolute inventions of the author, or facts which took place within his personal observation or that of his friends. The poem of the Thorn, as the reader will soon discover, is not supposed to be spoken in the author's own person: the character of the loquacious narrator will sufficiently shew itself in the course of the story. The Rime of the Ancyent Marinere was professedly written in imitation of the style, as well as of the spirit of the elder poets; but with a few exceptions, the Author believes that the language adopted in it has been equally intelligible for these three last centuries. The lines entitled Expostulation and Reply, and those which follow, arose out of conversation with a friend[3] who was somewhat unreasonably attached to modern books of moral philosophy.

---

[3]The friend is William Hazlitt, who frequently visited Wordsworth and Coleridge in Somerset during 1797–98. [ED.]

The Rime of the Ancyent Marinere
in Seven Parts[1]

Argument

How a Ship having passed the Line was driven by Storms to the cold Country towards the South Pole; and how from thence she made her course to the tropical Latitude of the Great Pacific Ocean; and of the strange things that befell; and in what manner the Ancyent Marinere came back to his own Country.

I

It is an ancient Marinere,
    And he stoppeth one of three:
"By thy long grey beard and thy glittering eye
    "Now wherefore stoppest me?

5 "The Bridegroom's doors are open'd wide
    "And I am next of kin;
"The Guests are met, the Feast is set,—
    "May'st hear the merry din."

But still he holds the wedding-guest—
10   There was a Ship, quoth he—
"Nay, if thou'st got a laughsome tale,
    "Marinere! come with me."

He holds him with his skinny hand,
    Quoth he, there was a Ship—
15 "Now get thee hence, thou grey-beard Loon!
    "Or my Staff shall make thee skip."

---

the Line: the equator.

[1] By Coleridge. By the 1800 edition of *Lyrical Ballads*, Coleridge had already revised the poem substantially, eliminating many of its archaisms and adding the subtitle, "A Poet's Reverie." Over the next two decades, he continued tinkering with it, until in his 1817 volume of poems, *Sibylline Leaves*, he published the version that is familiar to most readers. This revised version is reprinted in "Reactions of Wordsworth and Coleridge" in Part Three.

    See also Wordsworth's "Note to 'The Ancient Mariner'" from the 1800 edition of *Lyrical Ballads* (389–90) and compare the 1798 version to two ballads that strongly influenced Coleridge: Thomas Percy's "The Wandering Jew" (242–46) and Bürger's "Lenora" (253–56). [ED.]

He holds him with his glittering eye —
   The wedding-guest stood still
And listens like a three year's child;
20   The Marinere hath his will.

The wedding-guest sate on a stone,
   He cannot chuse but hear:
And thus spake on that ancyent man,
   The bright-eyed Marinere.

25 The Ship was cheer'd, the Harbour clear'd —
   Merrily did we drop
Below the Kirk, below the Hill,
   Below the Light-house top.

The Sun came up upon the left,
30   Out of the Sea came he:
And he shone bright, and on the right
   Went down into the Sea.

Higher and higher every day,
   Till over the mast at noon —
35 The wedding-guest here beat his breast,
   For he heard the loud bassoon.

The Bride hath pac'd into the Hall,
   Red as a rose is she;
Nodding their heads before her goes
40   The merry Minstralsy.

The wedding-guest he beat his breast,
   Yet he cannot chuse but hear:
And thus spake on that ancyent Man,
   The bright-eyed Marinere.

45 Listen, Stranger! Storm and Wind,
   A Wind and Tempest strong!
For days and weeks it play'd us freaks —
   Like Chaff we drove along.

Listen, Stranger! Mist and Snow,
50   And it grew wond'rous cauld:

Kirk: church.
cauld: cold.

And Ice mast-high came floating by
    As green as Emerauld.

And thro' the drifts the snowy clifts
    Did send a dismal sheen;
55 Ne shapes of men ne beasts we ken—
    The Ice was all between.

The Ice was here, the Ice was there,
    The Ice was all around:
It crack'd and growl'd, and roar'd and howl'd—
60   Like noises of a swound.

At length did cross an Albatross,
    Thorough the Fog it came;
And an it were a Christian Soul,
    We hail'd it in God's name.

65 The Marineres gave it biscuit-worms,
    And round and round it flew:
The Ice did split with a Thunder-fit;
    The Helmsman steer'd us thro'.

And a good south wind sprung up behind,
70   The Albatross did follow;
And every day for food or play
    Came to the Marinere's hollo!

In mist or cloud on mast or shroud
    It perch'd for vespers nine,
75 Whiles all the night thro' fog-smoke white
    Glimmer'd the white moon-shine.

"God save thee, ancient Marinere!
    "From the fiends that plague thee thus—
"Why look'st thou so?"—with my Cross-bow
80   I shot the Albatross.

Ne . . . ne: neither, nor.
ken: recognized.
swound: tempest, tremor.
an: as if.
hollo: shout, call.
vespers: evening prayers.

II

The Sun came up upon the right,
　　Out of the Sea came he;
And broad as a weft upon the left
　　Went down into the Sea.

85 And the good south wind still blew behind,
　　But no sweet Bird did follow
Ne any day for food or play
　　Came to the Marinere's hollo!

And I had done an hellish thing
90　　And it would work 'em woe:
For all averr'd, I had kill'd the Bird
　　That made the Breeze to blow.

Ne dim ne red, like God's own head,
　　The glorious Sun uprist:
95 Then all averr'd, I had kill'd the Bird
　　That brought the fog and mist.
'Twas right, said they, such birds to slay
　　That bring the fog and mist.

The breezes blew, the white foam flew,
100　　The furrow follow'd free:
We were the first that ever burst
　　Into that silent Sea.

Down dropt the breeze, the Sails dropt down,
　　'Twas sad as sad could be
105 And we did speak only to break
　　The silence of the Sea.

All in a hot and copper sky
　　The bloody sun at noon,
Right up above the mast did stand,
110　　No bigger than the moon.

Day after day, day after day,
　　We stuck, ne breath ne motion,
As idle as a painted Ship
　　Upon a painted Ocean.

---

weft: a large flag used on ships for signaling distress.
furrow: the track of the ship through the water, indicating easy passage.

115 Water, water, every where
     And all the boards did shrink;
     Water, water, every where,
     Ne any drop to drink.

     The very deeps did rot: O Christ!
120   That ever this should be!
     Yea, slimy things did crawl with legs
     Upon the slimy Sea.

     About, about, in reel and rout
     The Death-fires danc'd at night;
125 The water, like a witch's oils,
     Burnt green and blue and white.

     And some in dreams assured were
     Of the Spirit that plagued us so:
     Nine fathom deep he had follow'd us
130   From the Land of Mist and Snow.

     And every tongue thro' utter drouth
     Was wither'd at the root;
     We could not speak no more than if
     We had been choked with soot.

135 Ah wel-a-day! what evil looks
     Had I from old and young;
     Instead of the Cross the Albatross
     About my neck was hung.

III

     I saw a something in the Sky
140   No bigger than my fist;
     At first it seem'd a little speck
     And then it seem'd a mist:
     It mov'd and mov'd, and took at last
     A certain shape, I wist.

145 A speck, a mist, a shape, I wist!
     And still it ner'd and ner'd;

---

drouth: thirst.
wist: believed.
ner'd: neared.

And, an it dodg'd a water-sprite,
    It plung'd and tack'd and veer'd.

With throat unslack'd, with black lips bak'd
150   Ne could we laugh, ne wail:
Then while thro' drouth all dumb they stood
I bit my arm and suck'd the blood
    And cry'd, A sail! a sail!

With throat unslack'd,[2] with black lips bak'd
155   Agape they hear'd me call:
Gramercy! they for joy did grin
And all at once their breath drew in
    As they were drinking all.

She doth not tack from side to side—
160   Hither to work us weal
Withouten wind, withouten tide
    She steddies with upright keel.

The western wave was all a flame,
    The day was well nigh done!
165 Almost upon the western wave
    Rested the broad bright Sun;
When that strange shape drove suddenly
    Betwixt us and the Sun.

And strait the Sun was fleck'd with bars
170   (Heaven's mother send us grace)
As if thro' a dungeon grate he peer'd
    With broad and burning face.

Alas! (thought I, and my heart beat loud)
    How fast she neres and neres!
175 Are those *her* Sails that glance in the Sun
    Like restless gossameres?

Are those *her* naked ribs, which fleck'd
    The sun that did behind them peer?

---

unslack'd: dry.
Gramercy!: God have mercy on us!
gossameres: gossamer, a sheer fabric.

[2] Although the mariner has moistened his mouth with his own blood, his thirst remains unquenched. [ED.]

And are these two all, all the crew,
₁₈₀   That woman and her fleshless Pheere?

His bones were black with many a crack,
    All black and bare, I ween;
Jet-black and bare, save where with rust
Of mouldy damps and charnel crust
₁₈₅   They're patch'd with purple and green.

Her lips are red, *her* looks are free,
    Her locks are yellow as gold:
Her skin is white as leprosy,
And she is far liker Death than he;
₁₉₀   Her flesh makes the still air cold.

The naked Hulk alongside came
    And the Twain were playing dice;
"The Game is done! I've won, I've won!"
    Quoth she, and whistled thrice.

₁₉₅ A gust of wind sterte up behind
    And whistled thro' his bones;
Thro' the holes of his eyes and the hole of his mouth
    Half-whistles and half-groans.

With never a whisper in the Sea
₂₀₀   Oft[3] darts the Spectre-ship;
While clombe above the Eastern bar
The horned Moon, with one bright Star
    Almost atween the tips.

One after one by the horned Moon
₂₀₅   (Listen, O Stranger! to me)
Each turn'd his face with a ghastly pang
    And curs'd me with his ee.

Four times fifty living men,
    With never a sigh or groan,

Pheere: mate or spouse.
ween: believe, think.
charnel: burial place.
sterte: started.
clombe: climbing.
ee: eye.

[3] From 1800 and after, the word *oft* is changed to *off*. [ED.]

210 With heavy thump, a lifeless lump
        They dropp'd down one by one.

    Their souls did from their bodies fly—
        They fled to bliss or woe;
    And every soul it pass'd me by,
215   Like the whiz of my Cross-bow.

IV

    "I fear thee, ancyent Marinere!
        "I fear thy skinny hand;
    "And thou art long and lank and brown
        "As is the ribb'd Sea-sand.

220 "I fear thee and thy glittering eye
        "And thy skinny hand so brown"—
    Fear not, fear not, thou wedding-guest!
        This body dropt not down.

    Alone, alone, all all alone
225   Alone on the wide wide Sea;
    And Christ would take no pity on
        My soul in agony.

    The many men so beautiful,
        And they all dead did lie!
230 And a million million slimy things
        Liv'd on—and so did I.

    I look'd upon the rotting Sea,
        And drew my eyes away;
    I look'd upon the eldritch deck,
235   And there the dead men lay.

    I look'd to Heaven, and try'd to pray;
        But or ever a prayer had gusht,
    A wicked whisper came and made
        My heart as dry as dust.

240 I clos'd my lids and kept them close,
        Till the balls like pulses beat;

---

eldritch: ghostly, horrific.

For the sky and the sea, and the sea and the sky
Lay like a load on my weary eye,
   And the dead were at my feet.

245 The cold sweat melted from their limbs,
   Ne rot, ne reek did they;
The look with which they look'd on me,
   Had never pass'd away.

An orphan's curse would drag to Hell
250   A spirit from on high:
But O! more horrible than that
   Is the curse in a dead man's eye!
Seven days, seven nights I saw that curse,
   And yet I could not die.

255 The moving Moon went up the sky
   And no where did abide:
Softly she was going up
   And a star or two beside —

Her beams bemock'd the sultry main
260   Like morning frosts yspread;
But where the ship's huge shadow lay,
The charmed water burnt alway
   A still and awful red.

Beyond the shadow of the ship
265   I watch'd the water-snakes:
They mov'd in tracks of shining white;
And when they rear'd, the elfish light
   Fell off in hoary flakes.

Within the shadow of the ship
270   I watch'd their rich attire:
Blue, glossy green, and velvet black
They coil'd and swam; and every track
   Was a flash of golden fire.

O happy living things! no tongue
275   Their beauty might declare:
A spring of love gusht from my heart,
   And I bless'd them unaware!
Sure my kind saint took pity on me,
   And I bless'd them unaware.

280 The self-same moment I could pray;
    And from my neck so free
The Albatross fell off, and sank
    Like lead into the sea.

V

O sleep, it is a gentle thing
285 Belov'd from pole to pole!
To Mary-queen the praise be yeven
She sent the gentle sleep from heaven
    That slid into my soul.

The silly buckets on the deck
290 That had so long remain'd,
I dreamt that they were fill'd with dew
And when I awoke it rain'd.

My lips were wet, my throat was cold,
    My garments all were dank;
295 Sure I had drunken in my dreams
    And still my body drank.

I mov'd and could not feel my limbs,
    I was so light, almost
I thought that I had died in sleep,
300 And was a blessed Ghost.

The roaring wind! it roar'd far off,
    It did not come anear;
But with its sound it shook the sails
    That were so thin and sere.

305 The upper air bursts into life,
    And a hundred fire-flags sheen
To and fro they are hurried about;
And to and fro, and in and out
    The stars dance on between.

Mary-queen: the Virgin Mary.
yeven: given.
silly: commonplace, simple.
sere: parched.

310 The coming wind doth roar more loud;
　　The sails do sigh, like sedge:
　　The rain pours down from one black cloud
　　　And the Moon is at its edge.

　　Hark! hark! the thick black cloud is cleft,
315　And the Moon is at its side:
　　Like waters shot from some high crag,
　　The lightning falls with never a jag
　　　A river steep and wide.

　　The strong wind reach'd the ship: it roar'd
320　And dropp'd down, like a stone!
　　Beneath the lightning and the moon
　　　The dead men gave a groan.

　　They groan'd, they stirr'd, they all uprose,
　　Ne spake, ne mov'd their eyes:
325 It had been strange, even in a dream
　　　To have seen those dead men rise.

　　The helmsman steerd, the ship mov'd on;
　　Yet never a breeze up-blew;
　　The Marineres all 'gan work the ropes,
330　Where they were wont to do:
　　They rais'd their limbs like lifeless tools —
　　　We were a ghastly crew.

　　The body of my brother's son
　　Stood by me knee to knee:
335 The body and I pull'd at one rope,
　　But he said nought to me —
　　And I quak'd to think of my own voice
　　　How frightful it would be!

　　The day-light dawn'd — they dropp'd their arms,
340　And cluster'd round the mast:
　　Sweet sounds rose slowly thro' their mouths
　　　And from their bodies pass'd.

　　Around, around, flew each sweet sound,
　　Then darted to the sun:

―――――――――

sedge: grass or rushes (when the wind blows upon them).

345 Slowly the sounds came back again
     Now mix'd, now one by one.

Sometimes a dropping from the sky
     I heard the Lavrock sing;
Sometimes all little birds that are
350 How they seem'd to fill the sea and air
     With their sweet jargoning,

And now 'twas like all instruments,
     Now like a lonely flute;
And now it is an angel's song
355   That makes the heavens be mute.

It ceas'd: yet still the sails made on
     A pleasant noise till noon,
A noise like of a hidden brook
     In the leafy month of June,
360 That to the sleeping woods all night
     Singeth a quiet tune.

Listen, O listen, thou Wedding-guest!
     "Marinere! thou hast thy will:
"For that, which comes out of thine eye, doth make
365   "My body and soul to be still."

Never sadder tale was told
     To a man of woman born:
Sadder and wiser thou wedding-guest!
     Thou'lt rise to morrow morn.

370 Never sadder tale was heard
     By a man of woman born:
The Marineres all return'd to work
     As silent as beforne.

The Marineres all 'gan pull the ropes,
375   But look at me they n'old:
Thought I, I am as thin as air —
     They cannot me behold.

Lavrock: skylark.
jargoning: singing, warbling.
n'old: would not.

Till noon we silently sail'd on
    Yet never a breeze did breathe:
380 Slowly and smoothly went the ship
    Mov'd onward from beneath.

Under the keel nine fathom deep
    From the land of mist and snow
The spirit slid: and it was He
385   That made the Ship to go.
The sails at noon left off their tune
    And the Ship stood still also.

The sun right up above the mast
    Had fix'd her to the ocean:
390 But in a minute she 'gan stir
    With a short uneasy motion—
Backwards and forwards half her length
    With a short uneasy motion.

Then, like a pawing horse let go,
395   She made a sudden bound:
It flung the blood into my head,
    And I fell into a swound.

How long in that same fit I lay,
    I have not to declare;
400 But ere my living life return'd,
    I heard and in my soul discern'd
    Two voices in the air,

"Is it he?" quoth one, "Is this the man?
    "By him who died on cross,
405 "With his cruel bow he lay'd full low
    "The harmless Albatross.

"The spirit who 'bideth by himself
    "In the land of mist and snow,
"He lov'd the bird that lov'd the man
410   "Who shot him with his bow."

The other was a softer voice,
    As soft as honey-dew:

---

swound: fainting fit, swoon (a different connotation here than in line 60).

Quoth he the man hath penance done,
    And penance more will do.

VI

FIRST VOICE
415 "But tell me, tell me! speak again,
    "Thy soft response renewing—
"What makes that ship drive on so fast?
    "What is the Ocean doing?"

SECOND VOICE
    "Still as a Slave before his Lord,
420   "The Ocean hath no blast:
    "His great bright eye most silently
      "Up to the moon is cast—

    "If he may know which way to go,
      "For she guides him smooth or grim.
425 "See, brother, see! how graciously
    "She looketh down on him."

FIRST VOICE
    "But why drives on that ship so fast
      "Withouten wave or wind?"

SECOND VOICE
    "The air is cut away before,
430   "And closes from behind.

    "Fly, brother, fly! more high, more high,
      "Or we shall be belated:
    "For slow and slow that ship will go,
      "When the Marinere's trance is abated."

435 I woke, and we were sailing on
    As in a gentle weather:
'Twas night, calm night, the moon was high;
    The dead men stood together.

All stood together on the deck,
440   For a charnel-dungeon fitter:
All fix'd on me their stony eyes
    That in the moon did glitter.

---

charnel-dungeon: grave, tomb.

The pang, the curse, with which they died,
    Had never pass'd away:
445 I could not draw my een from theirs
    Ne turn them up to pray.

And in its time the spell was snapt,
    And I could move my een:
I look'd far-forth, but little saw
450   Of what might else be seen.

Like one, that on a lonely road
    Doth walk in fear and dread,
And having once turn'd round, walks on
    And turns no more his head:
455 Because he knows, a frightful fiend
    Doth close behind him tread.

But soon there breath'd a wind on me,
    Ne sound ne motion made:
Its path was not upon the sea
460   In ripple or in shade.

It rais'd my hair, it fann'd my cheek,
    Like a meadow-gale of spring—
It mingled strangely with my fears,
    Yet it felt like a welcoming.

465 Swiftly, swiftly flew the ship,
    Yet she sail'd softly too:
Sweetly, sweetly blew the breeze—
    On me alone it blew.

O dream of joy! is this indeed
470   The light-house top I see?
Is this the Hill? Is this the Kirk?
    Is this mine own countrée?

We drifted o'er the Harbour-bar,
    And I with sobs did pray—
475 "O let me be awake, my God!
    "Or let me sleep alway!"

The harbour-bay was clear as glass,
    So smoothly it was strewn!

---

een: eyes.

And on the bay the moon light lay,
480   And the shadow of the moon.

The moonlight bay was white all o'er,
    Till rising from the same,
Full many shapes, that shadows were,
    Like as of torches came.

485 A little distance from the prow
    Those dark-red shadows were;
But soon I saw that my own flesh
    Was red as in a glare.

I turn'd my head in fear and dread,
490   And by the holy rood,
The bodies had advanc'd, and now
    Before the mast they stood.

They lifted up their stiff right arms,
    They held them strait and tight;
495 And each right-arm burnt like a torch,
    A torch that's borne upright.
Their stony eye-balls glitter'd on
    In the red and smoky light.

I pray'd and turn'd my head away
500   Forth looking as before.
There was no breeze upon the bay,
    No wave against the shore.

The rock shone bright, the Kirk no less
    That stands above the rock:
505 The moonlight steep'd in silentness
    The steady weathercock.

And the bay was white with silent light,
    Till rising from the same
Full many shapes, that shadows were,
510   In crimson colours came.

A little distance from the prow
    Those crimson shadows were:

---

the holy rood: the cross upon which Christ died.
weathercock: weathervane.

I turn'd my eyes upon the deck—
  O Christ! what saw I there?

515 Each corse lay flat, lifeless and flat;
  And by the Holy rood
A man all light, a seraph-man,
  On every corse there stood.

This seraph-band, each wav'd his hand:
520   It was a heavenly sight:
They stood as signals to the land,
  Each one a lovely light:

This seraph-band, each wav'd his hand,
  No voice did they impart—
525 No voice; but O! the silence sank,
  Like music on my heart.

Eftsones I heard the dash of oars,
  I heard the pilot's cheer:
My head was turn'd perforce away
530   And I saw a boat appear.

Then vanish'd all the lovely lights;
  The bodies rose anew:
With silent pace, each to his place,
  Came back the ghastly crew.
535 The wind, that shade nor motion made,
  On me alone it blew.

The pilot, and the pilot's boy
  I heard them coming fast:
Dear Lord in Heaven! it was a joy,
540   The dead men could not blast.

I saw a third—I heard his voice:
  It is the Hermit good!
He singeth loud his godly hymns
  That he makes in the wood.
545 He'll shrieve my soul, he'll wash away
  The Albatross's blood.

---

corse: corpse.
seraph-man: a glowing angel.
Eftsones: again, a second time.
shrieve: hear confession, impose penance, and confer absolution.

VII

This Hermit good lives in that wood
   Which slopes down to the Sea.
How loudly his sweet voice he rears!
550 He loves to talk with Marineres
   That come from a far Contrée.

He kneels at morn and noon and eve —
   He hath a cushion plump:
It is the moss, that wholly hides
555   The rotted old Oak-stump.

The Skiff-boat ne'rd: I heard them talk,
   "Why, this is strange, I trow!
"Where are those lights so many and fair
   "That signal made but now?"

560 "Strange, by my faith!" the Hermit said —
   "And they answer'd not our cheer.
"The planks look warp'd, and see those sails
   "How thin they are and sere!
"I never saw aught like to them
565   "Unless perchance it were

"The skeletons of leaves that lag
   "My forest brook along:
"When the Ivy-tod is heavy with snow,
"And the Owlet whoops to the wolf below
570   "That eats the she-wolf's young."

"Dear Lord! it has a fiendish look —
   (The Pilot made reply)
"I am a-fear'd." — "Push on, push on!"
   Said the Hermit cheerily.

575 The Boat came closer to the Ship,
   But I ne spake ne stirr'd!
The Boat came close beneath the Ship,
   And strait a sound was heard!

Under the water it rumbled on,
580   Still louder and more dread:

---

trow: suppose.
Ivy-tod: bush of ivy.

It reach'd the Ship, it split the bay;
    The Ship went down like lead.

Stunn'd by that loud and dreadful sound,
    Which sky and ocean smote:
585 Like one that hath been seven days drown'd
    My body lay afloat:
But, swift as dreams, myself I found
    Within the Pilot's boat.

Upon the whirl, where sank the Ship,
590   The boat spun round and round:
And all was still, save that the hill
    Was telling of the sound.

I mov'd my lips: the Pilot shriek'd
    And fell down in a fit.
595 The Holy Hermit rais'd his eyes
    And pray'd where he did sit.

I took the oars: the Pilot's boy,
    Who now doth crazy go,
Laugh'd loud and long, and all the while
600   His eyes went to and fro,
"Ha! ha!" quoth he — "full plain I see,
    "The devil knows how to row."

And now all in mine own Countrée
    I stood on the firm land!
605 The Hermit stepp'd forth from the boat,
    And scarcely he could stand.

"O shrieve me, shrieve me, holy Man!
    The Hermit cross'd his brow —
"Say quick," quoth he, "I bid thee say
610   "What manner man art thou?"

Forthwith this frame of mine was wrench'd
    With a woeful agony,
Which forc'd me to begin my tale
    And then it left me free.

615 Since then at an uncertain hour,
    Now oftimes and now fewer,
That anguish comes and makes me tell
    My ghastly aventure.

I pass, like night, from land to land;
620   I have strange power of speech;
The moment that his face I see
I know the man that must hear me;
    To him my tale I teach.

What loud uproar bursts from that door!
625   The Wedding-guests are there;
But in the Garden-bower the Bride
    And Bride-maids singing are:
And hark the little Vesper-bell
    Which biddeth me to prayer.

630 O Wedding-guest! this soul hath been
    Alone on a wide wide sea:
So lonely 'twas, that God himself
    Scarce seemed there to be.

O sweeter than the Marriage-feast,
635   'Tis sweeter far to me
To walk together to the Kirk
    With a goodly company.

To walk together to the Kirk
    And all together pray,
640 While each to his great father bends,
Old men, and babes, and loving friends,
    And Youths, and Maidens gay.

Farewell, farewell! but this I tell
    To thee, thou wedding-guest!
645 He prayeth well who loveth well
    Both man and bird and beast.

He prayeth best who loveth best,
    All things both great and small:
For the dear God, who loveth us,
650   He made and loveth all.

The Marinere, whose eye is bright,
    Whose beard with age is hoar,
Is gone; and now the wedding-guest
    Turn'd from the bridegroom's door.

655 He went, like one that hath been stunn'd
    And is of sense forlorn:
A sadder and a wiser man
    He rose the morrow morn.

The Foster-Mother's Tale
A Dramatic Fragment [1]

FOSTER-MOTHER
  I never saw the man whom you describe.

MARIA
  'Tis strange! he spake of you familiarly
  As mine and Albert's common Foster-mother.

FOSTER-MOTHER
  Now blessings on the man, whoe'er he be,
5 That joined your names with mine! O my sweet lady,
  As often as I think of those dear times
  When you two little ones would stand at eve
  On each side of my chair, and make me learn
  All you had learnt in the day; and how to talk
10 In gentle phrase, then bid me sing to you —
  'Tis more like heaven to come than what *has* been.

MARIA
  O my dear Mother! this strange man has left me
  Troubled with wilder fancies, than the moon
  Breeds in the love-sick maid who gazes at it,
15 Till lost in inward vision, with wet eye
  She gazes idly! — But that entrance, Mother!

FOSTER-MOTHER
  Can no one hear? It is a perilous tale!

MARIA
  No one.

FOSTER-MOTHER
      My husband's father told it me,
  Poor old Leoni! — Angels rest his soul!
20 He was a woodman, and could fell and saw
  With lusty arm. You know that huge round beam

---

[1] By Coleridge, extracted from his tragedy *Osorio.* [ED.]

Which props the hanging wall of the old chapel?
Beneath that tree, while yet it was a tree
He found a baby wrapt in mosses, lined
25 With thistle-beards, and such small locks of wool
As hang on brambles. Well, he brought him home,
And reared him at the then Lord Velez' cost.
And so the babe grew up a pretty boy,
A pretty boy, but most unteachable —
30 And never learnt a prayer, nor told a bead,
But knew the names of birds, and mocked their notes,
And whistled, as he were a bird himself:
And all the autumn 'twas his only play
To get the seeds of wild flowers, and to plant them
35 With earth and water, on the stumps of trees.
A Friar, who gathered simples in the wood,
A grey-haired man — he loved this little boy,
The boy loved him — and, when the Friar taught him,
He soon could write with the pen: and from that time,
40 Lived chiefly at the Convent or the Castle.
So he became a very learned youth.
But Oh! poor wretch! — he read, and read, and read,
'Till his brain turned — and ere his twentieth year,
He had unlawful thoughts of many things:
45 And though he prayed, he never loved to pray
With holy men, nor in a holy place —
But yet his speech, it was so soft and sweet,
The late Lord Velez ne'er was wearied with him.
And once, as by the north side of the Chapel
50 They stood together, chained in deep discourse,
The earth heaved under them with such a groan,
That the wall tottered, and had well-nigh fallen
Right on their heads. My Lord was sorely frightened;
A fever seized him, and he made confession
55 Of all the heretical and lawless talk
Which brought this judgment: so the youth was seized
And cast into that hole. My husband's father
Sobbed like a child — it almost broke his heart:
And once as he was working in the cellar,

---

told a bead: counted a rosary bead in penitence.
simples: medicinal plants or herbs.
well-nigh: nearly.

60 He heard a voice distinctly; 'twas the youth's,
Who sung a doleful song about green fields,
How sweet it were on lake or wild savannah,
To hunt for food, and be a naked man,
And wander up and down at liberty.
65 He always doted on the youth, and now
His love grew desperate; and defying death,
He made that cunning entrance I described:
And the young man escaped.

MARIA
                          'Tis a sweet tale:
Such as would lull a listening child to sleep,
70 His rosy face besoiled with unwiped tears. —
And what became of him?

FOSTER-MOTHER
                          He went on ship-board
With those bold voyagers, who made discovery
Of golden lands. Leoni's younger brother
Went likewise, and when he returned to Spain,
75 He told Leoni, that the poor mad youth,
Soon after they arrived in that new world,
In spite of his dissuasion, seized a boat,
And all alone, set sail by silent moonlight
Up a great river, great as any sea,
80 And ne'er was heard of more: but 'tis supposed,
He lived and died among the savage men.

Lines Left upon a Seat in a Yew-Tree
Which Stands near the Lake of Esthwaite,
on a Desolate Part of the Shore,
yet Commanding a Beautiful Prospect[1]

—Nay, Traveller! rest. This lonely yew-tree stands
Far from all human dwelling: what if here
No sparkling rivulet spread the verdant herb;

---

[1] By Wordsworth. This poem was composed before most of the other poems in the volume. It was probably begun in 1795 and completed some time in 1797. Esthwaite Water is a small lake one-half mile southeast of Hawkshead, the village where Wordsworth attended school as a boy. The seat in the trunk of the tree was fashioned by the Reverend William Braithwaite (Lindop 395). [ED.]

What if these barren boughs the bee not loves;
5   Yet, if the wind breathe soft, the curling waves,
That break against the shore, shall lull thy mind
By one soft impulse saved from vacancy.

————————————Who he was
That piled these stones, and with the mossy sod
10 First covered o'er, and taught this aged tree,
Now wild, to bend its arms in circling shade,
I well remember. — He was one who own'd
No common soul. In youth, by genius nurs'd,
And big with lofty views, he to the world
15 Went forth, pure in his heart, against the taint
Of dissolute tongues, 'gainst jealousy, and hate,
And scorn, against all enemies prepared,
All but neglect: and so, his spirit damped
At once, with rash disdain he turned away,
20 And with the food of pride sustained his soul
In solitude. — Stranger! these gloomy boughs
Had charms for him; and here he loved to sit,
His only visitants a straggling sheep,
The stone-chat, or the glancing sand-piper;
25 And on these barren rocks, with juniper,
And heath, and thistle, thinly sprinkled o'er,
Fixing his downward eye, he many an hour
A morbid pleasure nourished, tracing here
An emblem of his own unfruitful life:
30 And lifting up his head, he then would gaze
On the more distant scene; how lovely 'tis
Thou seest, and he would gaze till it became
Far lovelier, and his heart could not sustain
The beauty still more beauteous. Nor, that time,
35 Would he forget those beings, to whose minds,
Warm from the labours of benevolence,
The world, and man himself, appeared a scene
Of kindred loveliness: then he would sigh
With mournful joy, to think that others felt
40 What he must never feel: and so, lost man!
On visionary views would fancy feed,
Till his eye streamed with tears. In this deep vale
He died, this seat his only monument.

If thou be one whose heart the holy forms
45 Of young imagination have kept pure,
Stranger! henceforth be warned; and know, that pride,
Howe'er disguised in its own majesty,
Is littleness; that he, who feels contempt
For any living thing, hath faculties
50 Which he has never used; that thought with him
Is in its infancy. The man, whose eye
Is ever on himself, doth look on one,
The least of nature's works, one who might move
The wise man to that scorn which wisdom holds
55 Unlawful, ever. O, be wiser thou!
Instructed that true knowledge leads to love,
True dignity abides with him alone
Who, in the silent hour of inward thought,
Can still suspect, and still revere himself,
60 In lowliness of heart.

The Nightingale
A Conversational Poem, Written in April 1798 [1]

No cloud, no relique of the sunken day
Distinguishes the West, no long thin slip
Of sullen Light, no obscure trembling hues.
Come, we will rest on this old mossy Bridge!
5 You see the glimmer of the stream beneath,
But hear no murmuring: it flows silently
O'er its soft bed of verdure. All is still,
A balmy night! and tho' the stars be dim,
Yet let us think upon the vernal showers
10 That gladden the green earth, and we shall find
A pleasure in the dimness of the stars.
And hark! the Nightingale begins its song,
"Most musical, most melancholy" [2] Bird!
A melancholy Bird? O idle thought!

---

[1] By Coleridge. "The Nightingale" was a late inclusion in the 1798 edition of *Lyrical Ballads*, substituted at the last minute for Coleridge's "Lewti, or the Circassian's Love Chant." [ED.]

[2] 'Most musical, most melancholy.' This passage in Milton possesses an excellence far superior to that of mere description: it is spoken in the character of the melancholy Man,

15 In nature there is nothing melancholy.
—But some night-wandering Man, whose heart was pierc'd
With the remembrance of a grievous wrong,
Or slow distemper or neglected love,
(And so, poor Wretch! fill'd all things with himself
20 And made all gentle sounds tell back the tale
Of his own sorrows) he and such as he
First nam'd these notes a melancholy strain;
And many a poet echoes the conceit,
Poet, who hath been building up the rhyme
25 When he had better far have stretch'd his limbs
Beside a brook in mossy forest-dell
By sun or moonlight, to the influxes
Of shapes and sounds and shifting elements
Surrendering his whole spirit, of his song
30 And of his fame forgetful! so his fame
Should share in nature's immortality,
A venerable thing! and so his song
Should make all nature lovelier, and itself
Be lov'd, like nature! —But 'twill not be so;
35 And youths and maidens most poetical
Who lose the deep'ning twilights of the spring
In ball-rooms and hot theatres, they still
Full of meek sympathy must heave their sighs
O'er Philomela's pity-pleading strains.[3]
40 My Friend, and my Friend's Sister! we have learnt
A different lore: we may not thus profane

---

and has therefore a dramatic propriety. The Author makes this remark, to rescue himself from the charge of having alluded with levity to a line in Milton: a charge than which none could be more painful to him, except perhaps that of having ridiculed his Bible." [Coleridge's note.] Coleridge refers to line 62 from John Milton's "Il Penseroso" (1645), given here with some context:

> Sweet bird that shunn'st the noise of folly,
> Most musical, most melancholy!
> Thee chantress oft the woods among,
> I woo to hear thy evensong. [. . .] (ll. 61–64)

See the nightingale poems by Charlotte Smith (336) and Coleridge (343–44). [Ed.]
[3]Philomela, or Philomel, is the classical personification of the nightingale; in Greek mythology, Philomela was raped by her brother-in-law, Tereus, who silenced her by violently removing her tongue; she was later transformed into the nightingale, whose song traditionally mimics the would-be melancholy utterance of her sorrow. [ED.]

Nature's sweet voices always full of love
And joyance! 'Tis the merry Nightingale
That crowds, and hurries, and precipitates
45 With fast thick warble his delicious notes,
As he were fearful, that an April night
Would be too short for him to utter forth
His love-chant, and disburthen his full soul
Of all its music! And I know a grove
50 Of large extent, hard by a castle huge
Which the great lord inhabits not: and so
This grove is wild with tangling underwood,
And the trim walks are broken up, and grass,
Thin grass and king-cups grow within the paths.
55 But never elsewhere in one place I knew
So many Nightingales: and far and near
In wood and thicket over the wide grove
They answer and provoke each other's songs—
With skirmish and capricious passagings,
60 And murmurs musical and swift jug jug
And one low piping sound more sweet than all—
Stirring the air with such an harmony,
That should you close your eyes, you might almost
Forget it was not day! On moonlight bushes,
65 Whose dewy leafits are but half disclos'd,
You may perchance behold them on the twigs,
Their bright, bright eyes, their eyes both bright and full,
Glistning, while many a glow-worm in the shade
Lights up her love-torch.

                    A most gentle maid
70 Who dwelleth in her hospitable home
Hard by the Castle, and at latest eve,
(Even like a Lady vow'd and dedicate
To something more than nature in the grove)
Glides thro' the pathways; she knows all their notes,
75 That gentle Maid! and oft, a moment's space,
What time the moon was lost behind a cloud,
Hath heard a pause of silence: till the Moon
Emerging, hath awaken'd earth and sky
With one sensation, and those wakeful Birds
80 Have all burst forth in choral minstrelsy,

As if one quick and sudden Gale had swept
An hundred airy harps![4] And she hath watch'd
Many a Nightingale perch giddily
On blosmy twig still swinging from the breeze,
85 And to that motion tune his wanton song,
Like tipsy Joy that reels with tossing head.
Farewell, O Warbler! till to-morrow eve,
And you, my friends! farewell, a short farewell!
We have been loitering long and pleasantly,
90 And now for our dear homes.—That strain again!
Full fain would it delay me!—My dear Babe,[5]
Who, capable of no articulate sound,
Mars all things with his imitative lisp,
How he would place his hand beside his ear,
95 His little hand, the small forefinger up,
And bid us listen! And I deem it wise
To make him Nature's playmate. He knows well
The evening star: and once when he awoke
In most distressful mood (some inward pain
100 Had made up that strange thing, an infant's dream)
I hurried with him to our orchard plot,
And he beholds the moon, and hush'd at once
Suspends his sobs, and laughs most silently,
While his fair eyes that swam with undropt tears
105 Did glitter in the yellow moon-beam! Well—
It is a father's tale. But if that Heaven
Should give me life, his childhood shall grow up
Familiar with these songs, that with the night
He may associate Joy! Once more farewell,
110 Sweet Nightingale! once more, my friends! farewell.

---

airy harps: aeolian harps.

[4] The aeolian harp or lyre is a stringed instrument designed to produce music when the wind blows upon it; see Coleridge's "Effusion XXXV" (156-58). [ED.]

[5] The "dear Babe" is Coleridge's first-born son, Hartley (1796–1849), named for philosopher David Hartley; see "Frost at Midnight" (233–35). [ED.]

The Female Vagrant [1]

By Derwent's side [2] my Father's cottage stood,
(The Woman thus her artless story told)
One field, a flock, and what the neighbouring flood
Supplied, to him were more than mines of gold.
5 Light was my sleep; my days in transport roll'd:
With thoughtless joy I stretch'd along the shore
My father's nets, or watched, when from the fold
High o'er the cliffs I led my fleecy store,
A dizzy depth below! his boat and twinkling oar.

10 My father was a good and pious man,
An honest man by honest parents bred,
And I believe that, soon as I began
To lisp, he made me kneel beside my bed,
And in his hearing there my prayers I said:
15 And afterwards, by my good father taught,
I read, and loved the books in which I read;
For books in every neighbouring house I sought,
And nothing to my mind a sweeter pleasure brought.

Can I forget what charms did once adorn
20 My garden, stored with pease, and mint, and thyme,
And rose and lily for the sabbath morn?

---

fleecy store: sheep.
pease: peas.

[1] By Wordsworth, extracted and adapted from his unpublished 1793–95 poem, *Salisbury Plain*. As a result of this comparatively early date of composition, the poetic style and political ideology of "The Female Vagrant" differ from those of most other poems in *Lyrical Ballads*. Instead of the ballad stanza, it uses the far more complex nine-line Spenserian stanza of *The Faerie Queene* and it contains numerous examples of the sort of poeticisms that Wordsworth would condemn in the Advertisement as "the inane phraseology of many modern writers" (for example, the phrases "fleecy store" in line 8 and "snowy pride" in line 27). Politically, it appears more unambiguously radical than the poems Wordsworth wrote in 1797 and 1798, at times even seeming to echo episodes from Godwin's 1794 novel, *Caleb Williams*. Its depiction of an aristocrat's selfish cruelty resembles that of the villainous Squire Tyrrel, and its largely sympathetic portrayal of a "wild brood" of gypsies recalls the band of robbers who befriend Caleb after his escape from prison. Wordsworth later revised most of these passages to tone down their radicalism. [ED.]
[2] The Derwent is a river that runs through Cockermouth, the town in which Wordsworth was born. [ED.]

The sabbath bells, and their delightful chime;
The gambols and wild freaks at shearing time;
My hen's rich nest through long grass scarce espied;
25 The cowslip-gathering at May's dewy prime;
The swans, that, when I sought the water-side,
From far to meet me came, spreading their snowy pride.

The staff I yet remember which upbore
The bending body of my active sire;
30 His seat beneath the honeyed sycamore
When the bees hummed, and chair by winter fire;
When market-morning came, the neat attire
With which, though bent on haste, myself I deck'd;
My watchful dog, whose starts of furious ire,
35 When stranger passed, so often I have check'd;
The red-breast known for years, which at my casement peck'd.

The suns of twenty summers danced along, —
Ah! little marked, how fast they rolled away:
Then rose a mansion proud our woods among,
40 And cottage after cottage owned its sway,
No joy to see a neighbouring house, or stray
Through pastures not his own, the master took;
My Father dared his greedy wish gainsay;
He loved his old hereditary nook,
45 And ill could I the thought of such sad parting brook.

But, when he had refused the proffered gold,
To cruel injuries he became a prey,
Sore traversed in whate'er he bought and sold:
His troubles grew upon him day by day,
50 Till all his substance fell into decay.
His little range of water was denied; [3]
All but the bed where his old body lay,
All, all was seized, and weeping, side by side,
We sought a home where we uninjured might abide.

---

gambols and wild freaks: dances and other fun, whimsical activities.
cowslip: yellow English primrose.
casement: window.

[3] "Several of the Lakes in the north of England are let out to different Fishermen, in parcels marked out by imaginary lines drawn from rock to rock." [Wordsworth's note.]

55 Can I forget that miserable hour,
   When from the last hill-top, my sire surveyed,
   Peering above the trees, the steeple tower,
   That on his marriage-day sweet music made?
   Till then he hoped his bones might there be laid,
60 Close by my mother in their native bowers:
   Bidding me trust in God, he stood and prayed, —
   I could not pray: — through tears that fell in showers,
   Glimmer'd our dear-loved home, alas! No longer ours!

   There was a youth whom I had loved so long,
65 That when I loved him not I cannot say.
   'Mid the green mountains many and many a song
   We two had sung, like little birds in May.
   When we began to tire of childish play
   We seemed still more and more to prize each other:
70 We talked of marriage and our marriage day;
   And I in truth did love him like a brother,
   For never could I hope to meet with such another.

   His father said, that to a distant town
   He must repair, to ply the artist's trade.
75 What tears of bitter grief till then unknown!
   What tender vows our last sad kiss delayed!
   To him we turned: — we had no other aid.
   Like one revived, upon his neck I wept,
   And her whom he had loved in joy, he said
80 He well could love in grief: his faith he kept;
   And in a quiet house once more my father slept.

   Four years each day with daily bread was blest,
   By constant toil and constant prayer supplied.
   Three lovely infants lay upon my breast;
85 And often, viewing their sweet smiles, I sighed,
   And knew not why. My happy father died
   When sad distress reduced the children's meal:
   Thrice happy! That from him the grave did hide
   The empty loom, cold hearth, and silent wheel,
90 And tears that flowed for ills which patience could not heal.

   'Twas a hard change, an evil time was come;
   We had no hope, and no relief could gain.
   But soon, with proud parade, the noisy drum

Beat round, to sweep the streets of want and pain.[4]
95 My husband's arms now only served to strain
Me and his children hungering in his view:
In such dismay my prayers and tears were vain:
To join those miserable men he flew;
And now to the sea-coast, with numbers more, we drew.[5]

100 There foul neglect for months and months we bore,
Nor yet the crowded fleet its anchor stirred.
Green fields before us and our native shore,
By fever, from polluted air incurred,
Ravage was made, for which no knell was heard.
105 Fondly we wished, and wished away, nor knew,
'Mid that long sickness, and those hopes deferr'd,
That happier days we never more must view:
The parting signal streamed, at last the land withdrew,

But from delay the summer calms were past.
110 On as we drove, the equinoctial deep
Ran mountains-high before the howling blast.[6]
We gazed with terror on the gloomy sleep
Of them that perished in the whirlwind's sweep,
Untaught that soon such anguish must ensue,
115 Our hopes such harvest of affliction reap,
That we the mercy of the waves should rue.
We reached the western world, a poor, devoted crew.

Oh! dreadful price of being to resign
All that is dear *in* being! better far
120 In Want's most lonely cave till death to pine,
Unseen, unheard, unwatched by any star;
Or in the streets and walks where proud men are,
Better our dying bodies to obtrude,
Than dog-like, wading at the heels of war,

---

equinoctial: originating near the equator.
western world: America.
devoted: doomed.

[4] The drums announce the arrival of conscription officers who would enlist poor men as soldiers for war. [ED.]
[5] The husband intends to join the British Army in America to fight against the colonists, who declared independence from England in 1776. [ED.]
[6] The ship encounters a tropical storm. [ED.]

125 Protract a curst existence, with the brood
    That lap (their very nourishment!) their brother's blood.

    The pains and plagues that on our heads came down,
    Disease and famine, agony and fear,
    In wood or wilderness, in camp or town,
130 It would thy brain unsettle even to hear.
    All perished — all, in one remorseless year,
    Husband and children! one by one, by sword
    And ravenous plague, all perished: every tear
    Dried up, despairing, desolate, on board
135 A British ship I waked, as from a trance restored.

    Peaceful as some immeasurable plain
    By the first beams of dawning light impress'd,
    In the calm sunshine slept the glittering main.
    The very ocean has its hour of rest,
140 That comes not to the human mourner's breast.
    Remote from man, and storms of mortal care,
    A heavenly silence did the waves invest;
    I looked and looked along the silent air,
    Until it seemed to bring a joy to my despair.

145 Ah! how unlike those late terrific sleeps!
    And groans, that rage of racking famine spoke,
    Where looks inhuman dwelt on festering heaps!
    The breathing pestilence that rose like smoke!
    The shriek that from the distant battle broke!
150 The mine's dire earthquake, and the pallid host
    Driven by the bomb's incessant thunder-stroke
    To loathsome vaults, where heart-sick anguish toss'd,
    Hope died, and fear itself in agony was lost!

    Yet does that burst of woe congeal my frame,
155 When the dark streets appeared to heave and gape,
    While like a sea the storming army came,
    And Fire from Hell reared his gigantic shape,
    And Murder, by the ghastly gleam, and Rape
    Seized their joint prey, the mother and the child!
160 But from these crazing thoughts my brain, escape!
    — For weeks the balmy air breathed soft and mild,
    And on the gliding vessel Heaven and Ocean smiled.

Some mighty gulph of separation past,
I seemed transported to another world: —
165 A thought resigned with pain, when from the mast
The impatient mariner the sail unfurl'd,
And whistling, called the wind that hardly curled
The silent sea. From the sweet thoughts of home,
And from all hope I was forever hurled.
170 For me — farthest from earthly port to roam
Was best, could I but shun the spot where man might come.

And oft, robb'd of my perfect mind, I thought
At last my feet a resting-place had found:
Here will I weep in peace, (so fancy wrought,)
175 Roaming the illimitable waters round;
Here watch, of every human friend disowned,
All day, my ready tomb the ocean-flood —
To break my dream the vessel reached its bound:
And homeless near a thousand homes I stood,
180 And near a thousand tables pined, and wanted food.

By grief enfeebled was I turned adrift,
Helpless as sailor cast on desart rock;
Nor morsel to my mouth that day did lift,
Nor dared my hand at any door to knock.
185 I lay, where with his drowsy mates, the cock
From the cross timber of an out-house hung;[7]
How dismal tolled, that night, the city clock!
At morn my sick heart hunger scarcely stung,
Nor to the beggar's language could I frame my tongue.

190 So passed another day, and so the third:
Then did I try, in vain, the crowd's resort,
In deep despair by frightful wishes stirr'd,
Near the sea-side I reached a ruined fort:
There, pains which nature could no more support,
195 With blindness linked, did on my vitals fall;
Dizzy my brain, with interruption short
Of hideous sense; I sunk, nor step could crawl,
And thence was borne away to neighbouring hospital.

----

hospital: charitable organization for the needy or infirm.

[7] She sleeps with a rooster and hens in the rafters of a barn. [ED.]

Recovery came with food: but still, my brain
200 Was weak, nor of the past had memory.
I heard my neighbours, in their beds, complain
Of many things which never troubled me;
Of feet still bustling round with busy glee,
Of looks where common kindness had no part,
205 Of service done with careless cruelty,
Fretting the fever round the languid heart,
And groans, which, as they said, would make a dead man start.

These things just served to stir the torpid sense,
Nor pain nor pity in my bosom raised.
210 Memory, though slow, returned with strength; and thence
Dismissed, again on open day I gazed,
At houses, men, and common light, amazed.
The lanes I sought, and as the sun retired,
Came, where beneath the trees a faggot blazed;
215 The wild brood saw me weep, my fate enquired,
And gave me food, and rest, more welcome, more desired.

My heart is touched to think that men like these,
The rude earth's tenants, were my first relief:
How kindly did they paint their vagrant ease!
220 And their long holiday that feared not grief,
For all belonged to all, and each was chief.
No plough their sinews strained; on grating road
No wain they drove, and yet, the yellow sheaf
In every vale for their delight was stowed:
225 For them, in nature's meads, the milky udder flowed.

Semblance, with straw and panniered ass, they made
Of potters wandering on from door to door:
But life of happier sort to me pourtrayed,
And other joys my fancy to allure;
230 The bag-pipe dinning on the midnight moor
In barn uplighted, and companions boon
Well met from far with revelry secure,
In depth of forest glade, when jocund June
Rolled fast along the sky his warm and genial moon.

---

faggot: a bundle of sticks.
wain: farm wagon.
panniered ass: a donkey fitted with a large basket on its back.

235 But ill it suited me, in journey dark
    O'er moor and mountain, midnight theft to hatch;
    To charm the surly house-dog's faithful bark,
    Or hang on tiptoe at the lifted latch;
    The gloomy lantern, and the dim blue match,
240 The black disguise, the warning whistle shrill,
    And ear still busy on its nightly watch,
    Were not for me, brought up in nothing ill;
    Besides, on griefs so fresh my thoughts were brooding still.

    What could I do, unaided and unblest?
245 Poor Father! gone was every friend of thine:
    And kindred of dead husband are at best
    Small help, and, after marriage such as mine,
    With little kindness would to me incline.
    Ill was I then for toil or service fit:
250 With tears whose course no effort could confine,
    By high-way side forgetful would I sit
    Whole hours, my idle arms in moping sorrow knit.

    I lived upon the mercy of the fields,
    And oft of cruelty the sky accused;
255 On hazard, or what general bounty yields,
    Now coldly given, now utterly refused.
    The fields I for my bed have often used:
    But, what afflicts my peace with keenest ruth
    Is, that I have my inner self abused,
260 Foregone the home delight of constant truth,
    And clear and open soul, so prized in fearless youth.

    Three years a wanderer, often have I view'd,
    In tears, the sun towards that country tend
    Where my poor heart lost all its fortitude:
265 And now across this moor my steps I bend—
    Oh! tell me whither—for no earthly friend
    Have I.—She ceased, and weeping turned away,
    As if because her tale was at an end
    She wept;—because she had no more to say
270 Of that perpetual weight which on her spirit lay.

---

ruth: sorrow.

Goody Blake and Harry Gill
A True Story[1]

Oh! what's the matter? what's the matter?
What is't that ails young Harry Gill?
That evermore his teeth they chatter,
Chatter, chatter, chatter still.
5 Of waistcoats Harry has no lack,
Good duffle grey, and flannel fine;
He has a blanket on his back,
And coats enough to smother nine.

In March, December, and in July,
10 'Tis all the same with Harry Gill;
The neighbours tell, and tell you truly,
His teeth they chatter, chatter still.
At night, at morning, and at noon,
'Tis all the same with Harry Gill;
15 Beneath the sun, beneath the moon,
His teeth they chatter, chatter still.

Young Harry was a lusty drover,
And who so stout of limb as he?
His cheeks were red as ruddy clover,
20 His voice was like the voice of three.
Auld Goody Blake was old and poor,

---

drover: cattle farmer.
Goody: a shortened form of "Goodwife," a polite title for a woman of the lower classes.

[1] By Wordsworth. Wordsworth derived the story for this poem from the following passage in Erasmus Darwin's *Zoönomia, or the Laws of Organic Life* (1794–96):

> A young farmer in Warwickshire, finding his hedges broke, and the sticks carried away during a frosty season, determined to watch for the thief. He lay many cold hours under a haystack, and at length an old woman, like a witch in a play, approached, and began to pull up the hedge; he waited till she had tied up her bundle of sticks, and was carrying them off, that he might convict her of the theft, and then springing from his concealment, he seized his prey with violent threats. After some altercation, in which her load was left upon the ground, she kneeled upon her bundle of sticks, and, raising her arms to Heaven, beneath the bright moon then at the full, spoke to the farmer already shivering with cold, "Heaven grant, that thou mayest never know again the blessing to be warm." He complained of cold all the next day, and wore an uppercoat, and in a few days another, and in a fortnight took to his bed, always saying that nothing made him warm; he covered himself with many blankets, and had a sieve over his face as he lay; and from this one insane idea he kept his bed above twenty years for fear of the cold air, till at length he died. [ED.]

Ill fed she was, and thinly clad;
And any man who pass'd her door,
Might see how poor a hut she had.

25 All day she spun in her poor dwelling,
And then her three hours' work at night!
Alas! 'twas hardly worth the telling,
It would not pay for candle-light.
— This woman dwelt in Dorsetshire,
30 Her hut was on a cold hill-side,
And in that country coals are dear, [2]
For they come far by wind and tide.

By the same fire to boil their pottage,
Two poor old dames, as I have known,
35 Will often live in one small cottage,
But she, poor woman, dwelt alone.
'Twas well enough when summer came,
The long, warm, lightsome summer-day,
Then at her door the *canty* dame
40 Would sit, as any linnet gay.

But when the ice our streams did fetter,
Oh! then how her old bones would shake!
You would have said, if you had met her,
'Twas a hard time for Goody Blake.
45 Her evenings then were dull and dead;
Sad case it was, as you may think,
For very cold to go to bed,
And then for cold not sleep a wink.

Oh joy for her! when e'er in winter
50 The winds at night had made a rout,
And scatter'd many a lusty splinter,

---

pottage: soup.
canty: cheerful.
linnet: small songbird.
rout: roar, bellow.

[2] Coal was expensive in Dorset because it had to be imported from Wales. Wordsworth would later replace lines 29–32 with the following quatrain:

Remote from sheltered village-green,
On a hill's northern side she dwelt,
Where from sea-blasts the hawthorns lean
And hoary dews are slow to melt. [ED.]

And many a rotten bough about.
Yet never had she, well or sick,
As every man who knew her says,
55 A pile before-hand, wood or stick,
Enough to warm her for three days.

Now, when the frost was past enduring,
And made her poor old bones to ache,
Could any thing be more alluring,
60 Than an old hedge to Goody Blake?
And now and then, it must be said,
When her old bones were cold and chill,
She left her fire, or left her bed,
To seek the hedge of Harry Gill.

65 Now Harry he had long suspected
This trespass of old Goody Blake,
And vow'd that she should be detected,
And he on her would vengeance take.
And oft from his warm fire he'd go,
70 And to the fields his road would take,
And there, at night, in frost and snow,
He watch'd to seize old Goody Blake.

And once, behind a rick of barley,
Thus looking out did Harry stand;
75 The moon was full and shining clearly,
And crisp with frost the stubble-land.
—He hears a noise—he's all awake—
Again?—on tip-toe down the hill
He softly creeps—'Tis Goody Blake,
80 She's at the hedge of Harry Gill.

Right glad was he when he beheld her:
Stick after stick did Goody pull,
He stood behind a bush of elder,
Till she had filled her apron full.
85 When with her load she turned about,
The bye-road back again to take,
He started forward with a shout,
And sprang upon poor Goody Blake.

---

rick: stack.

And fiercely by the arm he took her,
90 And by the arm he held her fast,
And fiercely by the arm he shook her,
And cried, "I've caught you then at last!"
Then Goody, who had nothing said,
Her bundle from her lap let fall;
95 And kneeling on the sticks, she pray'd
To God that is the judge of all.

She pray'd, her wither'd hand uprearing,
While Harry held her by the arm —
"God! who art never out of hearing,
100 "O may he never more be warm!"
The cold, cold moon above her head,
Thus on her knees did Goody pray,
Young Harry heard what she had said,
And icy-cold he turned away.

105 He went complaining all the morrow
That he was cold and very chill:
His face was gloom, his heart was sorrow,
Alas! that day for Harry Gill!
That day he wore a riding-coat,
110 But not a whit the warmer he:
Another was on Thursday brought,
And ere the Sabbath he had three.

'Twas all in vain, a useless matter,
And blankets were about him pinn'd;
115 Yet still his jaws and teeth they clatter,
Like a loose casement in the wind.
And Harry's flesh it fell away;
And all who see him say 'tis plain,
That, live as long as live he may,
120 He never will be warm again.

No word to any man he utters,
A-bed or up, to young or old;
But ever to himself he mutters,

---

casement: window frame.

"Poor Harry Gill is very cold."[3]
125 A-bed or up, by night or day;
His teeth they chatter, chatter still.
Now think, ye farmers all, I pray,
Of Goody Blake and Harry Gill.

Lines Written at a Small Distance from My House
and Sent by My Little Boy to the Person
to Whom They Are Addressed[1]

It is the first mild day of March:
Each minute sweeter than before,
The red-breast sings from the tall larch
That stands beside our door.

5 There is a blessing in the air,
Which seems a sense of joy to yield
To the bare trees, and mountains bare,
And grass in the green field.

My Sister![2] ('tis a wish of mine)
10 Now that our morning meal is done,
Make haste, your morning task resign;
Come forth and feel the sun.

Edward will come with you, and pray,
Put on with speed your woodland dress,
15 And bring no book, for this one day
We'll give to idleness.

No joyless forms shall regulate
Our living Calendar:
We from to-day, my friend, will date
20 The opening of the year.

---

[3] Compare Shakespeare, *King Lear:* "Poor Tom's a-cold" (3.4.147). Since Edgar is disguised as a poor beggar—practically naked—the allusion adds the irony of Harry's being reduced to a similar state. [ED.]

[1] By Wordsworth. The boy is Wordsworth's ward, Basil Montagu, Jr. [ED.]

[2] Dorothy Wordsworth (1771–1855), who had recently been reunited with her brother, in 1795, after many years apart. [ED.]

Love, now an universal birth,
From heart to heart is stealing,
From earth to man, from man to earth,
—It is the hour of feeling.

25 One moment now may give us more
Than fifty years of reason;
Our minds shall drink at every pore
The spirit of the season.

Some silent laws our hearts may make,
30 Which they shall long obey;
We for the year to come may take
Our temper from to-day.

And from the blessed power that rolls
About, below, above;
35 We'll frame the measure of our souls,
They shall be tuned to love.

Then come, my sister! come, I pray,
With speed put on your woodland dress,
And bring no book; for this one day
40 We'll give to idleness.

Simon Lee
*The Old Huntsman with an Incident
in Which He Was Concerned*[1]

In the sweet shire of Cardigan,
Not far from pleasant Ivor-hall,
An old man dwells, a little man,
I've heard he once was tall.
5 Of years he has upon his back,
No doubt, a burthen weighty;
He says he is three score and ten,
But others say he's eighty.

Cardigan: a county in Wales.

[1] By Wordsworth. Wordsworth revised this poem extensively over the years (see 442–44). [ED.]

A long blue livery-coat has he,
10 That's fair behind, and fair before;
Yet, meet him where you will, you see
At once that he is poor.
Full five and twenty years he lived
A running huntsman merry;
15 And, though he has but one eye left,
His cheek is like a cherry.

No man like him the horn could sound,
And no man was so full of glee;
To say the least, four counties round
20 Had heard of Simon Lee;
His master's dead, and no one now
Dwells in the hall of Ivor;
Men, dogs, and horses, all are dead;
He is the sole survivor.

25 His hunting feats have him bereft
Of his right eye, as you may see:
And then, what limbs those feats have left
To poor old Simon Lee!
He has no son, he has no child,
30 His wife, an aged woman,
Lives with him, near the waterfall,
Upon the village common.

And he is lean and he is sick,
His little body's half awry
35 His ancles they are swoln and thick;
His legs are thin and dry.
When he was young he little knew
Of husbandry or tillage;
And now he's forced to work, though weak,
40 —The weakest in the village.

He all the country could outrun,
Could leave both man and horse behind;
And often, ere the race was done,
He reeled and was stone-blind.

---

livery-coat: worn by servants of wealthy families.
village common: undivided land belonging to all the members of a community.
husbandry or tillage: the breeding and raising of animals or the cultivation of the land.

₄₅ And still there's something in the world
At which his heart rejoices;
For when the chiming hounds are out,
He dearly loves their voices![2]

Old Ruth works out of doors with him,
₅₀ And does what Simon cannot do;
For she, not over stout of limb,
Is stouter of the two.
And though you with your utmost skill
From labour could not wean them,
₅₅ Alas! 'tis very little, all
Which they can do between them.

Beside their moss-grown hut of clay,
Not twenty paces from the door,
A scrap of land they have, but they
₆₀ Are poorest of the poor.
This scrap of land he from the heath
Enclosed[3] when he was stronger;
But what avails the land to them,
Which they can till no longer?

₆₅ Few months of life has he in store,
As he to you will tell,
For still, the more he works, the more
His poor old ancles swell.
My gentle reader, I perceive
₇₀ How patiently you've waited,
And I'm afraid that you expect
Some tale will be related.

O reader! had you in your mind
Such stores as silent thought can bring,

---

[2] Wordsworth claims in the Fenwick note for this poem that he took this line directly from a conversation with the old huntsman at Alfoxden who served as a model for Simon Lee: "The expression when the hounds were out, 'I dearly love their voices' was word for word from his own lips" (Curtis 37). The Fenwick notes are comments about Wordsworth's poetry that he dictated to his friend Isabella Fenwick in 1843. [ED.]

[3] An ironic reference to the "Enclosure Acts" (see the headnote to "Political Backgrounds" in Part Three), which allowed landowners to fence off the very sort of common land out of which Simon has claimed his "scrap of land." The implication is that if this part of the heath had not been available to them, Simon and his wife would have been even more destitute, with no means of support other than parish relief. [ED.]

75 O gentle reader! you would find
A tale in every thing.
What more I have to say is short,
I hope you'll kindly take it;
It is no tale; but should you think,
80 Perhaps a tale you'll make it.

One summer-day I chanced to see
This old man doing all he could
About the root of an old tree,
A stump of rotten wood.
85 The mattock totter'd in his hand;
So vain was his endeavour
That at the root of the old tree
He might have worked for ever.

"You're overtasked, good Simon Lee,
90 Give me your tool" to him I said;
And at the word right gladly he
Received my proffer'd aid.
I struck, and with a single blow
The tangled root I sever'd,
95 At which the poor old man so long
And vainly had endeavour'd.

The tears into his eyes were brought,
And thanks and praises seemed to run
So fast out of his heart, I thought
100 They never would have done.
—I've heard of hearts unkind, kind deeds
With coldness still returning.
Alas! the gratitude⁴ of men
Has oftener left me mourning.

---

mattock: a tool similar to a pickax, but with one broad, flat end.

⁴Compare this representation of gratitude with discussions of gratitude in selections from Joseph Townsend, John Thelwall, and William Godwin in "Political Backgrounds" in Part Two. See also a passage from *Political Justice* that does not appear in this edition: "Observe the pauper fawning with abject vileness upon his rich benefactor, and speechless with sensations of gratitude for having received that which he ought to have claimed with erect mien, and with a consciousness that his claim was irresistible" (2.800). [ED.]

Anecdote for Fathers
Shewing How the Art of Lying
May Be Taught [1]

I have a boy of five years old,
His face is fair and fresh to see;
His limbs are cast in beauty's mould,
And dearly he loves me.

5   One morn we stroll'd on our dry walk,
Our quiet house all full in view,
And held such intermitted talk
As we are wont to do.

My thoughts on former pleasures ran;
10 I thought of Kilve's delightful shore,
My pleasant home, when spring began,
A long, long year before.

A day it was when I could bear
To think, and think, and think again;
15 With so much happiness to spare,
I could not feel a pain.

My boy was by my side, so slim
And graceful in his rustic dress!
And oftentimes I talked to him,
20 In very idleness.

The young lambs ran a pretty race;
The morning sun shone bright and warm;
"Kilve," said I, "was a pleasant place,
"And so is Liswyn farm. [2]

25 "My little boy, which like you more,"
I said and took him by the arm—

Kilve: a village on the Bristol Channel near Alfoxden.

[1] By Wordsworth. The boy in this poem is based on Wordsworth's ward, Basil Montagu, Jr. [ED.]

[2] As Wordsworth reveals in the Fenwick note, "The name of Liswin Farm was taken from a beautiful spot on the Wye" (Curtis 4). Liswyn, or Llys Wen, was where Wordsworth and Coleridge's friend John Thelwall was living at this time, so Wordsworth's choice of this location may have had personal and political resonance for him. [ED.]

"Our home by Kilve's delightful shore,
"Or here at Liswyn farm?"

"And tell me, had you rather be,"
30 I said and held him by the arm,
"At Kilve's smooth shore by the green sea,
"Or here at Liswyn farm?"

In careless mood he looked at me,
While still I held him by the arm,
35 And said, "At Kilve I'd rather be
"Than here at Liswyn farm."

"Now, little Edward, say why so;
My little Edward, tell me why;"
"I cannot tell, I do not know."
40 "Why this is strange," said I.

"For, here are woods and green-hills warm;
"There surely must some reason be
"Why you would change sweet Liswyn farm
"For Kilve by the green sea."

45 At this, my boy, so fair and slim,
Hung down his head, nor made reply;
And five times did I say to him,
"Why? Edward, tell me why?"[3]

His head he raised—there was in sight,
50 It caught his eye, he saw it plain—
Upon the house-top, glittering bright,
A broad and gilded vane.

Then did the boy his tongue unlock,
And thus to me he made reply;
55 "At Kilve there was no weather-cock,
"And that's the reason why."

Oh dearest, dearest boy! my heart
For better lore would seldom yearn,
Could I but teach the hundredth part
60 Of what from thee I learn.

---

[3] Compare with our selection from Book 2 of Jean-Jacques Rousseau's *Emilius and Sophia* (143). [ED.]

We Are Seven [1]

A simple child, dear brother Jim,
That lightly draws its breath,
And feels its life in every limb,
What should it know of death?

5   I met a little cottage girl,
She was eight years old, she said;
Her hair was thick with many a curl
That cluster'd round her head.

She had a rustic, woodland air,
10 And she was wildly clad;
Her eyes were fair, and very fair,
—Her beauty made me glad.

"Sisters and brothers, little maid,
"How many may you be?"
15 "How many? seven in all," she said,
And wondering looked at me.

"And where are they, I pray you tell?"
She answered, "Seven are we,
"And two of us at Conway dwell,
20 "And two are gone to sea.

"Two of us in the church-yard lie,
"My sister and my brother,
"And in the church-yard cottage, I
"Dwell near them with my mother."

25 "You say that two at Conway dwell,
"And two are gone to sea,
"Yet you are seven; I pray you tell
"Sweet Maid, how this may be?"

Then did the little Maid reply,
30 "Seven boys and girls are we;
"Two of us in the church-yard lie,
"Beneath the church-yard tree."

Conway: a seaport in northern Wales.

[1] By Wordsworth. In the Fenwick note, Wordsworth says that Coleridge contributed the first stanza of this poem and explains that the phrase "dear brother Jim" is a joking reference to their mutual friend, James Tobin (Curtis 3). [ED.]

"You run about, my little maid,
"Your limbs they are alive;
35 "If two are in the church-yard laid,
"Then ye are only five."

"Their graves are green, they may be seen,"
The little Maid replied,
"Twelve steps or more from my mother's door,
40 "And they are side by side.

"My stockings there I often knit,
"My 'kerchief there I hem;
"And there upon the ground I sit—
"I sit and sing to them.

45 "And often after sunset, Sir,
"When it is light and fair,
"I take my little porringer,
"And eat my supper there.

"The first that died was little Jane;
50 "In bed she moaning lay,
"Till God released her of her pain,
"And then she went away.

"So in the church-yard she was laid,
"And all the summer dry,
55 "Together round her grave we played,
"My brother John and I.

"And when the ground was white with snow,
"And I could run and slide,
"My brother John was forced to go,
60 "And he lies by her side."

"How many are you then," said I,
"If they two are in Heaven?"
The little Maiden did reply,
"O Master! we are seven."

65 "But they are dead; those two are dead!
"Their spirits are in heaven!"
'Twas throwing words away; for still

---

porringer: porridge bowl.

The little Maid would have her will,
And said, "Nay, we are seven!"

Lines Written in Early Spring[1]

I heard a thousand blended notes,
While in a grove I sate reclined,
In that sweet mood when pleasant thoughts
Bring sad thoughts to the mind.

5   To her fair works did nature link
The human soul that through me ran;
And much it griev'd my heart to think
What man has made of man.[2]

Through primrose-tufts, in that sweet bower,
10 The periwinkle trail'd its wreathes;
And 'tis my faith that every flower
Enjoys the air it breathes.

The birds around me hopp'd and play'd:
Their thoughts I cannot measure,
15 But the least motion which they made,
It seem'd a thrill of pleasure.

The budding twigs spread out their fan,
To catch the breezy air;
And I must think, do all I can,
20 That there was pleasure there.

If I these thoughts may not prevent,
If such be of my creed the plan,
Have I not reason to lament
What man has made of man?

---

[1] By Wordsworth. [ED.]

[2] An echo of Robert Burns's similar line, "Man's inhumanity to man," from his 1786 poem "Man Was Made to Mourn, A Dirge." [ED.]

The Thorn [1]

I

There is a thorn; it looks so old,
In truth you'd find it hard to say,
How it could ever have been young,
It looks so old and grey.
5 Not higher than a two-years' child,
It stands erect this aged thorn;
No leaves it has, no thorny points;
It is a mass of knotted joints,
A wretched thing forlorn.
10 It stands erect, and like a stone
With lichens it is overgrown.

II

Like rock or stone, it is o'ergrown
With lichens to the very top,
And hung with heavy tufts of moss,
15 A melancholy crop:
Up from the earth these mosses creep,[2]

---

[1] By Wordsworth. See Wordsworth's "Note to 'The Thorn'" (387–89) and William Taylor's translation of Bürger's "The Lass of Fair Wone" (261–67), a poem often cited as a source for "The Thorn." Helen Darbishire found the following lines from a Scottish ballad transcribed in one of Wordsworth's early notebooks:

Ah there she's lean'd her back to a thorn
    O and alas-a-day, O and alas-a-day
And there she has her baby born.
    Ten thousand times good-night and be wi' thee.
She has houked a grave ayont the sun,
    O and alas-a-day, O and alas-a-day
And there she has buried the sweet babe in.
    Ten thousand times good-night and be wi' thee. (Darbishire 37–38)

In the Fenwick note, Wordsworth describes his motivation for writing the poem:

Arose out of my observing, on the ridge of Quantock Hill, on a stormy day a thorn which I had often passed in calm and bright weather without noticing it. I said to myself, "Cannot I by some invention do as much to make this Thorn permanently an impressive object as the storm has made it to my eyes at this moment?" (Curtis 14). [ED.]

[2] Compare with the 21 January 1798 entry in Dorothy Wordsworth's *Alfoxden Journal*: "The tops of the beeches of a brown-red, or crimson. Those oaks, fanned by the sea breeze, thick with feathery sea-green moss, as a grove not stripped of its leaves" (1). [ED.]

And this poor thorn they clasp it round
So close, you'd say that they were bent
With plain and manifest intent,
20 To drag it to the ground;
And all had joined in one endeavour
To bury this poor thorn for ever.

III

High on a mountain's highest ridge,
Where oft the stormy winter gale
25 Cuts like a scythe, while through the clouds
It sweeps from vale to vale;
Not five yards from the mountain-path,
This thorn you on your left espy;
And to the left, three yards beyond,
30 You see a little muddy pond
Of water, never dry;
I've measured it from side to side:
'Tis three feet long, and two feet wide.[3]

IV

And close beside this aged thorn,
35 There is a fresh and lovely sight,
A beauteous heap, a hill of moss,
Just half a foot in height.
All lovely colours there you see,
All colours that were ever seen,
40 And mossy network too is there,
As if by hand of lady fair
The work had woven been,
And cups, the darlings of the eye,
So deep is their vermilion dye.

---

cups: blossoms.

[3] Lines 32 and 33 were among the most frequently criticized passages in *Lyrical Ballads*. Coleridge, in fact, cites them in *Biographia Literaria* as an example of one of the "sudden and unpleasant sinkings" in Wordsworth's poetry (52). Wordsworth would later replace these lines with the following: "Though but of compass small, and bare / To thirsty suns and parching air." [ED.]

V

45 Ah me! what lovely tints are there!
Of olive-green and scarlet bright,
In spikes, in branches, and in stars,
Green, red, and pearly white.
This heap of earth o'ergrown with moss,
50 Which close beside the thorn you see,
So fresh in all its beauteous dyes,
Is like an infant's grave in size
As like as like can be:
But never, never any where,
55 An infant's grave was half so fair.

VI

Now would you see this aged thorn,
This pond and beauteous hill of moss,
You must take care and chuse your time
The mountain when to cross.
60 For oft there sits, between the heap
That's like an infant's grave in size,
And that same pond of which I spoke,
A woman in a scarlet cloak,[4]
And to herself she cries,
65 "Oh misery! oh misery!
"Oh woe is me! oh misery!"

VII

At all times of the day and night
This wretched woman thither goes,
And she is known to every star,
70 And every wind that blows;
And there beside the thorn she sits
When the blue day-light's in the skies,
And when the whirlwind's on the hill,
Or frosty air is keen and still,
75 And to herself she cries,

---

[4]Compare Revelation 17.4, which describes the whore of Babylon as dressed in scarlet. [ED.]

"Oh misery! oh misery!
"Oh woe is me! oh misery!"

VIII

"Now wherefore thus, by day and night,
"In rain, in tempest, and in snow,
80   "Thus to the dreary mountain-top
"Does this poor woman go?
"And why sits she beside the thorn
"When the blue day-light's in the sky,
"Or when the whirlwind's on the hill,
85   "Or frosty air is keen and still,
"And wherefore does she cry?—
"Oh wherefore? wherefore? tell me why
"Does she repeat that doleful cry?"

IX

I cannot tell; I wish I could;
90   For the true reason no one knows,
But if you'd gladly view the spot,
The spot to which she goes;
The heap that's like an infant's grave,
The pond—and thorn, so old and grey;
95   Pass by her door—'tis seldom shut—
And if you see her in her hut,
Then to the spot away!—
I never heard of such as dare
Approach the spot when she is there.

X

100   "But wherefore to the mountain-top
"Can this unhappy woman go,
"Whatever star is in the skies,
"Whatever wind may blow?"
Nay rack your brain—'tis all in vain,
105   I'll tell you every thing I know;
But to the thorn, and to the pond
Which is a little step beyond,
I wish that you would go:

Perhaps when you are at the place
110 You something of her tale may trace.

XI

I'll give you the best help I can:
Before you up the mountain go,
Up to the dreary mountain-top,
I'll tell you all I know.
115 'Tis now some two and twenty years,
Since she (her name is Martha Ray)[5]
Gave with a maiden's true good will
Her company to Stephen Hill;
And she was blithe and gay,
120 And she was happy, happy still
Whene'er she thought of Stephen Hill.

XII

And they had fix'd the wedding-day,
The morning that must wed them both;
But Stephen to another maid
125 Had sworn another oath;
And with this other maid to church
Unthinking Stephen went —
Poor Martha! on that woful day
A cruel, cruel fire, they say,
130 Into her bones was sent:
It dried her body like a cinder,
And almost turn'd her brain to tinder.

XIII

They say, full six months after this,
While yet the summer leaves were green,
135 She to the mountain-top would go,
And there was often seen.
'Tis said, a child was in her womb,

---

[5] Martha Ray was the name of the grandmother of Wordsworth's ward, Basil Montagu, Jr. She was the mistress of the fourth earl of Sandwich but was murdered by a different lover in 1779. [ED.]

As now to any eye was plain;
She was with child, and she was mad,
140 Yet often she was sober sad
From her exceeding pain.
Oh me! ten thousand times I'd rather
That he had died, that cruel father!

XIV

Sad case for such a brain to hold
145 Communion with a stirring child!
Sad case, as you may think, for one
Who had a brain so wild!
Last Christmas when we talked of this,
Old Farmer Simpson did maintain,
150 That in her womb the infant wrought
About its mother's heart, and brought
Her senses back again:
And when at last her time drew near,
Her looks were calm, her senses clear.

XV

155 No more I know, I wish I did,
And I would tell it all to you;
For what became of this poor child
There's none that ever knew:
And if a child was born or no,
160 There's no one that could ever tell;
And if 'twas born alive or dead,
There's no one knows, as I have said,
But some remember well,
That Martha Ray about this time
165 Would up the mountain often climb.

XVI

And all that winter, when at night
The wind blew from the mountain-peak,
'Twas worth your while, though in the dark,
The church-yard path to seek:
170 For many a time and oft were heard
Cries coming from the mountain-head,

Some plainly living voices were,
And others, I've heard many swear,
Were voices of the dead:
175 I cannot think, whate'er they say,
They had to do with Martha Ray.

XVII

But that she goes to this old thorn,
The thorn which I've described to you,
And there sits in a scarlet cloak,
180 I will be sworn is true.
For one day with my telescope,
To view the ocean wide and bright,
When to this country first I came,
Ere I had heard of Martha's name,
185 I climbed the mountain's height:
A storm came on, and I could see
No object higher than my knee.

XVIII

'Twas mist and rain, and storm and rain,
No screen, no fence could I discover,
190 And then the wind! in faith, it was
A wind full ten times over.
I looked around, I thought I saw
A jutting crag, and off I ran,
Head-foremost, through the driving rain,
195 The shelter of the crag to gain,
And, as I am a man,
Instead of jutting crag, I found
A woman seated on the ground.

XIX

I did not speak — I saw her face,
200 Her face it was enough for me;
I turned about and heard her cry,
"O misery! O misery!"
And there she sits, until the moon
Through half the clear blue sky will go,
205 And when the little breezes make

The waters of the pond to shake,
As all the country know,
She shudders and you hear her cry,
"Oh misery! oh misery!"

XX

210 "But what's the thorn? and what's the pond?
"And what's the hill of moss to her?
"And what's the creeping breeze that comes
"The little pond to stir?"
I cannot tell; but some will say
215 She hanged her baby on the tree,
Some say she drowned it in the pond,
Which is a little step beyond,
But all and each agree,
The little babe was buried there,
220 Beneath that hill of moss so fair.

XXI

I've heard the scarlet moss is red
With drops of that poor infant's blood;
But kill a new-born infant thus!
I do not think she could.
225 Some say, if to the pond you go,
And fix on it a steady view,
The shadow of a babe you trace,
A baby and a baby's face,
And that it looks at you;
230 Whene'er you look on it, 'tis plain
The baby looks at you again.

XXII

And some had sworn an oath that she
Should be to public justice brought;
And for the little infant's bones
235 With spades they would have sought.
But then the beauteous hill of moss
Before their eyes began to stir;
And for full fifty yards around,

The grass it shook upon the ground;
240 But all do still aver
The little babe is buried there,
Beneath that hill of moss so fair.

XXIII

I cannot tell how this may be,
But plain it is, the thorn is bound
245 With heavy tufts of moss, that strive
To drag it to the ground.
And this I know, full many a time,
When she was on the mountain high,
By day, and in the silent night,
250 When all the stars shone clear and bright,
That I have heard her cry,
"Oh misery! oh misery!
"Oh woe is me! oh misery!"

The Last of the Flock[1]

In distant countries I have been,
And yet I have not often seen
A healthy man, a man full grown,
Weep in the public roads alone.
5 But such a one, on English ground,
And in the broad high-way, I met;
Along the broad high-way he came,
His cheeks with tears were wet.
Sturdy he seemed, though he was sad;
10 And in his arms a lamb he had.

He saw me, and he turned aside,
As if he wished himself to hide:
Then with his coat he made essay
To wipe those briny tears away.
15 I follow'd him, and said, "My friend

---

[1] By Wordsworth. "The Last of the Flock," one of the most overtly political poems in *Lyrical Ballads*, directly attacks the provision in the poor laws that prohibited "giving relief where any visible property remains." In his 12 February 1796 speech to Parliament, William Pitt called this regulation a "degrading condition [that] should be abolished" (*The Parliamentary History of England* 711). [ED.]

"What ails you? wherefore weep you so?"
—"Shame on me, Sir! this lusty lamb,
He makes my tears to flow.
To-day I fetched him from the rock;
20 He is the last of all my flock.

When I was young, a single man,
And after youthful follies ran,
Though little given to care and thought,
Yet, so it was, a ewe I bought;
25 And other sheep from her I raised,
As healthy sheep as you might see,
And then I married, and was rich
As I could wish to be;
Of sheep I number'd a full score,
30 And every year encreas'd my store.

Year after year my stock it grew,
And from this one, this single ewe,
Full fifty comely sheep I raised,
As sweet a flock as ever grazed!
35 Upon the mountain did they feed;
They throve, and we at home did thrive.
—This lusty lamb of all my store
Is all that is alive;
And now I care not if we die,
40 And perish all of poverty.

Ten children, Sir! had I to feed,
Hard labour in a time of need!
My pride was tamed, and in our grief,
I of the parish ask'd relief. [2]
45 They said I was a wealthy man;
My sheep upon the mountain fed,
And it was fit that thence I took
Whereof to buy us bread:"
"Do this; how can we give to you,"
50 They cried, "what to the poor is due?"

I sold a sheep as they had said,
And bought my little children bread,

---

[2] See the discussion of poor, or parish, relief in the headnote to "Political Backgrounds"
in Part Two.

And they were healthy with their food;
For me it never did me good.
55 A woeful time it was for me,
To see the end of all my gains,
The pretty flock which I had reared
With all my care and pains,
To see it melt like snow away!
60 For me it was a woeful day.

Another still! and still another!
A little lamb, and then its mother!
It was a vein that never stopp'd,
Like blood-drops from my heart they dropp'd.
65 Till thirty were not left alive
They dwindled, dwindled, one by one,
And I may say that many a time
I wished they all were gone:
They dwindled one by one away;
70 For me it was a woeful day.

To wicked deeds I was inclined,
And wicked fancies cross'd my mind,
And every man I chanc'd to see,
I thought he knew some ill of me.
75 No peace, no comfort could I find,
No ease, within doors or without,
And crazily, and wearily,
I went my work about.
Oft-times I thought to run away;
80 For me it was a woeful day.

Sir! 'twas a precious flock to me,
As dear as my own children be;
For daily with my growing store
I loved my children more and more.
85 Alas! it was an evil time;
God cursed me in my sore distress,
I prayed, yet every day I thought
I loved my children less;
And every week, and every day,
90 My flock, it seemed to melt away.

They dwindled, Sir, sad sight to see!
From ten to five, from five to three,

A lamb, a weather, and a ewe;
And then at last, from three to two;
95 And of my fifty, yesterday
I had but only one,
And here it lies upon my arm,
Alas! and I have none;
To-day I fetched it from the rock;
100 It is the last of all my flock."

The Dungeon [1]

And this place our forefathers made for man!
This is the process of our love and wisdom,
To each poor brother who offends against us —
Most innocent, perhaps — and what if guilty?
5 Is this the only cure? Merciful God!
Each pore and natural outlet shrivell'd up
By ignorance and parching poverty,
His energies roll back upon his heart,
And stagnate and corrupt; till changed to poison,
10 They break out on him, like a loathsome plague-spot;
Then we call in our pamper'd mountebanks —
And this is their best cure! uncomforted
And friendless solitude, groaning and tears,
And savage faces, at the clanking hour,
15 Seen through the steams and vapour of his dungeon,
By the lamp's dismal twilight! So he lies
Circled with evil, till his very soul
Unmoulds its essence, hopelessly deformed
By sights of ever more deformity!

20 With other ministrations thou, O nature!
Healest thy wandering and distempered child:
Thou pourest on him thy soft influences,
Thy sunny hues, fair forms, and breathing sweets,
Thy melodies of woods, and winds, and waters,
25 Till he relent, and can no more endure

---

weather: a castrated male sheep, usually spelled "wether."
mountebanks: quack doctors.

[1] Extracted from Coleridge's tragedy *Osorio*. [ED.]

To be a jarring and a dissonant thing,
Amid this general dance and minstrelsy;
But, bursting into tears, wins back his way,
His angry spirit healed and harmonized
30 By the benignant touch of love and beauty.

The Mad Mother [1]

Her eyes are wild, her head is bare,
The sun has burnt her coal-black hair,
Her eye-brows have a rusty stain,
And she came far from over the main.
5 She has a baby on her arm,
Or else she were alone;
And underneath the hay-stack warm,
And on the green-wood stone,
She talked and sung the woods among;
10 And it was in the English tongue. [2]

"Sweet babe! They say that I am mad,
But nay, my heart is far too glad;
And I am happy when I sing
Full many a sad and doleful thing:
15 Then, lovely baby, do not fear!
I pray thee have no fear of me,
But, safe as in a cradle, here
My lovely baby! thou shalt be,
To thee I know too much I owe;
20 I cannot work thee any woe.

A fire was once within my brain;
And in my head a dull, dull pain;
And fiendish faces one, two, three,
Hung at my breasts, and pulled at me.
25 But then there came a sight of joy;

---

[1] By Wordsworth. In the Fenwick note, Wordsworth recalls that the "subject was reported to me by a lady of Bristol who had seen the poor creature" (Curtis 11). [ED.]
[2] In an 1836 letter, Wordsworth commented upon the importance of her speaking English, indicating that she is either British or American: "While the distance removes her from us, the fact of her speaking our language brings us at once into close sympathy with her" (*Later Years* 3.293). [ED.]

It came at once to do me good;
I waked, and saw my little boy,
My little boy of flesh and blood;
Oh joy for me that sight to see!
30 For he was here, and only he.

Suck, little babe, oh suck again!
It cools my blood; it cools my brain;
Thy lips I feel them, baby! they
Draw from my heart the pain away.
35 Oh! press me with thy little hand;
It loosens something at my chest;
About that tight and deadly band
I feel thy little fingers press'd.
The breeze I see is in the tree;
40 It comes to cool my babe and me.

Oh! love me, love me, little boy!
Thou art thy mother's only joy;
And do not dread the waves below,
When o'er the sea-rock's edge we go;
45 The high crag cannot work me harm,
Nor leaping torrents when they howl;
The babe I carry on my arm,
He saves for me my precious soul;
Then happy lie, for blest am I;
50 Without me my sweet babe would die.

Then do not fear, my boy! for thee
Bold as a lion I will be;
And I will always be thy guide,
Through hollow snows and rivers wide.
55 I'll build an Indian bower; I know
The leaves that make the softest bed:
And if from me thou wilt not go,
But still be true 'till I am dead,
My pretty thing! then thou shalt sing,
60 As merry as the birds in spring.

Thy father cares not for my breast,
'Tis thine, sweet baby, there to rest:
'Tis all thine own! and if its hue
Be changed, that was so fair to view,
65 'Tis fair enough for thee, my dove!

My beauty, little child, is flown;
But thou wilt live with me in love,
And what if my poor cheek be brown?
'Tis well for me; thou canst not see
70 How pale and wan it else would be.

Dread not their taunts, my little life!
I am thy father's wedded wife;
And underneath the spreading tree
We two will live in honesty.
75 If his sweet boy he could forsake,
With me he never would have stay'd:
From him no harm my babe can take,
But he, poor man! is wretched made,
And every day we two will pray
80 For him that's gone and far away.

I'll teach my boy the sweetest things;
I'll teach him how the owlet sings.
My little babe! thy lips are still,
And thou hast almost suck'd thy fill.
85 —Where art thou gone my own dear child?
What wicked looks are those I see?
Alas! alas! that look so wild,
It never, never came from me:
If thou art mad, my pretty lad,
90 Then I must be for ever sad.

Oh! smile on me, my little lamb!
For I thy own dear mother am.
My love for thee has well been tried:
I've sought thy father far and wide.
95 I know the poisons of the shade,
I know the earth-nuts fit for food;
Then, pretty dear, be not afraid;
We'll find thy father in the wood.
Now laugh and be gay, to the woods away!
100 And there, my babe; we'll live for aye.

The Idiot Boy [1]

'Tis eight o'clock,—a clear March night,
The moon is up—the sky is blue,
The owlet in the moonlight air,
He shouts from nobody knows where;
5 He lengthens out his lonely shout,
Halloo! halloo! a long halloo!

—Why bustle thus about your door,
What means this bustle, Betty Foy?
Why are you in this mighty fret?
10 And why on horseback have you set
Him whom you love, your idiot boy?

Beneath the moon that shines so bright,
Till she is tired, let Betty Foy
With girt and stirrup fiddle-faddle;

---

girt: girth, the band that secures the horse's saddle.

[1] By Wordsworth. The Fenwick note reads:

> Alfoxden 1798. The last stanza [. . .] was the foundation of the whole. The words were reported to me by my dear friend, Thomas Poole; but I have since heard the same repeated of other Idiots. Let me add that this long poem was composed in the Groves of Alfoxden, almost extempore; not a word, I believe, being corrected, though one stanza was omitted. I mention this in gratitude to those happy moments, for, in truth, I never wrote anything with so much glee. (Curtis 10).

Though "The Idiot Boy" was criticized by Southey, Coleridge (who said it contained "disgusting images of ordinary morbid idiocy"), and other reviewers, it remained one of Wordsworth's favorite poems in the volume (*Biographia* 2.48). He passionately defended the poem in his 1802 letter to John Wilson. An undergraduate at Glasgow University, Wilson had written to Wordsworth to praise *Lyrical Ballads,* calling it "the book which I value next to my Bible" (336). He did, however, object to "The Idiot Boy," asserting that its depiction of Betty Foy's maternal fondness created "a certain degree of disgust and contempt" instead of pleasure and thus thwarted Wordsworth's stated intentions (338). Wordsworth responded at length:

> To this I can only say that the loathing and disgust which many people have at the sight of an Idiot, is a feeling which, though having som[e] foundation in human nature is not necessarily attached to it in any vi[rtuous?] degree, but is owing, in a great measure to a false delicacy, and, if I [may] say it without rudeness, a certain want of comprehensiveness of think[ing] and feeling. Persons in the lower classes of society have little or nothing [of] this: if an Idiot is born in a poor man's house, it must be taken car[e of] and cannot be boarded out, as it would be by gentlefolks, or sent [to a] public or private receptacle for such unfortunate beings. [Poor people] seeing frequently among their neighbors such objects, easily [forget what]ever there is of natural disgust about them, and have t[herefore a] sane state, so that without pain or suffering they [perform] their duties towards them. [ED.]

₁₅ But wherefore set upon a saddle
Him whom she loves, her idiot boy?

There's scarce a soul that's out of bed;
Good Betty! put him down again;
His lips with joy they burr at you,
₂₀ But, Betty! what has he to do
With stirrup, saddle, or with rein?

The world will say 'tis very idle,
Bethink you of the time of night;
There's not a mother, no not one,
₂₅ But when she hears what you have done,
Oh! Betty she'll be in a fright.

But Betty's bent on her intent,
For her good neighbour, Susan Gale,
Old Susan, she who dwells alone,
₃₀ Is sick, and makes a piteous moan,
As if her very life would fail.

There's not a house within a mile,
No hand to help them in distress:
Old Susan lies a bed in pain,
₃₅ And sorely puzzled are the twain,
For what she ails they cannot guess.

And Betty's husband's at the wood,
Where by the week he doth abide,
A woodman in the distant vale;
₄₀ There's none to help poor Susan Gale,
What must be done? what will betide?

And Betty from the lane has fetched
Her pony, that is mild and good,
Whether he be in joy or pain,
₄₅ Feeding at will along the lane,
Or bringing faggots from the wood.

And he is all in travelling trim,
And by the moonlight, Betty Foy
Has up upon the saddle set,

---

faggots: bundles of sticks to fuel a fire.

50 The like was never heard of yet,
Him whom she loves, her idiot boy.

And he must post without delay
Across the bridge that's in the dale,
And by the church, and o'er the down,
55 To bring a doctor from the town,
Or she will die, old Susan Gale.

There is no need of boot or spur,
There is no need of whip or wand,
For Johnny has his holly-bough,
60 And with a hurly-burly now
He shakes the green bough in his hand. [2]

And Betty o'er and o'er has told
The boy who is her best delight,
Both what to follow, what to shun,
65 What do, and what to leave undone,
How turn to left, and how to right.

And Betty's most especial charge,
Was, "Johnny! Johnny! mind that you
"Come home again, nor stop at all,
70 "Come home again, whate'er befal,
"My Johnny do, I pray you do."

To this did Johnny answer make,
Both with his head, and with his hand,
And proudly shook the bridle too,
75 And then! his words were not a few,
Which Betty well could understand.

And now that Johnny is just going,
Though Betty's in a mighty flurry,
She gently pats the pony's side,
80 On which her idiot boy must ride,
And seems no longer in a hurry.

But when the pony moved his legs,
Oh! then for the poor idiot boy!

---

hurly-burly: commotion.

[2] With this characterization of Johnny as a knight about to embark upon a heroic quest, Wordsworth adopts a mock-heroic tone reminiscent of Burns's depiction of his unlikely hero, Tam o' Shanter (285–92). [ED.]

For joy he cannot hold the bridle,
85 For joy his head and heels are idle,
He's idle all for very joy.

And while the pony moves his legs,
In Johnny's left-hand you may see,
The green bough's motionless and dead;
90 The moon that shines above his head
Is not more still and mute than he.

His heart it was so full of glee,
That till full fifty yards were gone,
He quite forgot his holly whip,
95 And all his skill in horsemanship,
Oh! happy, happy, happy John.

And Betty's standing at the door,
And Betty's face with joy o'erflows,
Proud of herself, and proud of him,
100 She sees him in his travelling trim;
How quietly her Johnny goes.

The silence of her idiot boy,
What hopes it sends to Betty's heart!
He's at the guide-post—he turns right,
105 She watches till he's out of sight,
And Betty will not then depart.

Burr, burr—now Johnny's lips they burr,
As loud as any mill, or near it,
Meek as a lamb the pony moves,
110 And Johnny makes the noise he loves,
And Betty listens, glad to hear it.

Away she hies to Susan Gale:
And Johnny's in a merry tune,
The owlets hoot, the owlets curr,
115 And Johnny's lips they burr, burr, burr,
And on he goes beneath the moon.

His steed and he right well agree,
For of this pony there's a rumour,

---

guide-post: sign post.
hies: hurries.
curr: murmur.

That should he lose his eyes and ears,
120 And should he live a thousand years,
He never will be out of humour.

But then he is a horse that thinks!
And when he thinks his pace is slack;
Now, though he knows poor Johnny well,
125 Yet for his life he cannot tell
What he has got upon his back.

So through the moonlight lanes they go,
And far into the moonlight dale,
And by the church, and o'er the down,
130 To bring a doctor from the town,
To comfort poor old Susan Gale.

And Betty, now at Susan's side,
Is in the middle of her story,
What comfort Johnny soon will bring,
135 With many a most diverting thing,
Of Johnny's wit and Johnny's glory.

And Betty's still at Susan's side:
By this time she's not quite so flurried;
Demure with porringer and plate
140 She sits, as if in Susan's fate
Her life and soul were buried.

But Betty, poor good woman! she,
You plainly in her face may read it,
Could lend out of that moment's store
145 Five years of happiness or more,
To any that might need it.

But yet I guess that now and then
With Betty all was not so well,
And to the road she turns her ears,
150 And thence full many a sound she hears,
Which she to Susan will not tell.

Poor Susan moans, poor Susan groans,
"As sure as there's a moon in heaven,"

---

porringer: porridge bowl.

Cries Betty, "he'll be back again;
155 "They'll both be here, 'tis almost ten,
"They'll both be here before eleven."

Poor Susan moans, poor Susan groans,
The clock gives warning for eleven;
'Tis on the stroke — "If Johnny's near,"
160 Quoth Betty "he will soon be here,
"As sure as there's a moon in heaven."

The clock is on the stroke of twelve,
And Johnny is not yet in sight,
The moon's in heaven, as Betty sees,
165 But Betty is not quite at ease;
And Susan has a dreadful night.

And Betty, half an hour ago,
On Johnny vile reflections cast;
"A little idle sauntering thing!"
170 With other names, an endless string,
But now that time is gone and past.

And Betty's drooping at the heart,
That happy time all past and gone,
"How can it be he is so late?
175 "The doctor he has made him wait,
"Susan! they'll both be here anon."

And Susan's growing worse and worse,
And Betty's in a sad quandary;
And then there's nobody to say
180 If she must go or she must stay:
—She's in a sad quandary.

The clock is on the stroke of one;
But neither Doctor nor his guide
Appear along the moonlight road,
185 There's neither horse nor man abroad,
And Betty's still at Susan's side.

And Susan she begins to fear
Of sad mischances not a few,
That Johnny may perhaps be drown'd,
190 Or lost perhaps, and never found;
Which they must both for ever rue.

She prefaced half a hint of this
With, "God forbid it should be true!"
At the first word that Susan said
195 Cried Betty, rising from the bed,
"Susan, I'd gladly stay with you.

"I must be gone, I must away,
"Consider, Johnny's but half-wise;
"Susan, we must take care of him,
200 "If he is hurt in life or limb" —
"Oh God forbid!" poor Susan cries.

"What can I do?" says Betty, going,
"What can I do to ease your pain?
"Good Susan tell me, and I'll stay;
205 "I fear you're in a dreadful way,
"But I shall soon be back again."

"Good Betty go, good Betty go,
"There's nothing that can ease my pain."
Then off she hies, but with a prayer
210 That God poor Susan's life would spare,
Till she comes back again.

So, through the moonlight lane she goes,
And far into the moonlight dale;
And how she ran, and how she walked,
215 And all that to herself she talked,
Would surely be a tedious tale.

In high and low, above, below,
In great and small, in round and square,
In tree and tower was Johnny seen,
220 In bush and brake, in black and green,
'Twas Johnny, Johnny, every where.

She's past the bridge that's in the dale,
And now the thought torments her sore,
Johnny perhaps his horse forsook,
225 To hunt the moon that's in the brook,
And never will be heard of more.

---

brake: a place overgrown with bushes or brambles.

And now she's high upon the down,
Alone amid a prospect wide;
There's neither Johnny nor his horse,
230 Among the fern or in the gorse;
There's neither doctor nor his guide.

"Oh saints! what is become of him?
"Perhaps he's climbed into an oak,
"Where he will stay till he is dead;
235 "Or sadly he has been misled,
"And joined the wandering gypsey-folk.

"Or him that wicked pony's carried
"To the dark cave, the goblins' hall,
"Or in the castle he's pursuing,
240 "Among the ghosts, his own undoing;
"Or playing with the waterfall."

At poor old Susan then she railed,
While to the town she posts away;
"If Susan had not been so ill,
245 "Alas! I should have had him still,
"My Johnny, till my dying day."

Poor Betty! in this sad distemper,
The doctor's self would hardly spare,
Unworthy things she talked and wild,
250 Even he, of cattle the most mild,
The pony had his share.

And now she's got into the town,
And to the doctor's door she hies;
'Tis silence all on every side;
255 The town so long, the town so wide,
Is silent as the skies.

And now she's at the doctor's door,
She lifts the knocker, rap, rap, rap,
The doctor at the casement shews,

---

down: grassy hill.
gorse: evergreen shrub.
cattle: animals.
casement: window.

260 His glimmering eyes that peep and doze;
And one hand rubs his old night-cap.

"Oh Doctor! Doctor! where's my Johnny?"
"I'm here, what is't you want with me?"
"Oh Sir! you know I'm Betty Foy,
265 "And I have lost my poor dear boy,
"You know him—him you often see;

"He's not so wise as some folks be."
"The devil take his wisdom!" said
The Doctor, looking somewhat grim,
270 "What, woman! should I know of him?"
And, grumbling, he went back to bed.

"O woe is me! O woe is me!
"Here will I die; here will I die;
"I thought to find my Johnny here,
275 "But he is neither far nor near,
"Oh! what a wretched mother I!"

She stops, she stands, she looks about,
Which way to turn she cannot tell.
Poor Betty! it would ease her pain
280 If she had heart to knock again;
—The clock strikes three—a dismal knell!

Then up along the town she hies,
No wonder if her senses fail,
This piteous news so much it shock'd her,
285 She quite forgot to send the Doctor,
To comfort poor old Susan Gale.

And now she's high upon the down,
And she can see a mile of road,
"Oh cruel! I'm almost three-score;
290 "Such night as this was ne'er before,
"There's not a single soul abroad."

She listens, but she cannot hear
The foot of horse, the voice of man;
The streams with softest sound are flowing,
295 The grass you almost hear it growing,
You hear it now if e'er you can.

The owlets through the long blue night
Are shouting to each other still:
Fond lovers, yet not quite hob nob,
300 They lengthen out the tremulous sob,
That echoes far from hill to hill.

Poor Betty now has lost all hope,
Her thoughts are bent on deadly sin;
A green-grown pond she just has pass'd,
305 And from the brink she hurries fast,
Lest she should drown herself therein.

And now she sits her down and weeps;
Such tears she never shed before;
"Oh dear, dear pony! my sweet joy!
310 "Oh carry back my idiot boy!
"And we will ne'er o'erload thee more."

A thought is come into her head;
"The pony he is mild and good,
"And we have always used him well;
315 "Perhaps he's gone along the dell,
"And carried Johnny to the wood."

Then up she springs as if on wings;
She thinks no more of deadly sin;
If Betty fifty ponds should see,
320 The last of all her thoughts would be,
To drown herself therein.

Oh reader! now that I might tell
What Johnny and his horse are doing!
What they've been doing all this time,
325 Oh could I put it into rhyme,
A most delightful tale pursuing!

Perhaps, and no unlikely thought!
He with his pony now doth roam
The cliffs and peaks so high that are,
330 To lay his hands upon a star,
And in his pocket bring it home.

---

deadly sin: suicide.

Perhaps he's turned himself about,
His face unto his horse's tail,
And still and mute, in wonder lost,
335 All like a silent horseman-ghost,
He travels on along the vale.

And now, perhaps, he's hunting sheep,
A fierce and dreadful hunter he!
Yon valley, that's so trim and green,
340 In five months' time, should he be seen,
A desert wilderness will be.

Perhaps, with head and heels on fire,
And like the very soul of evil,
He's galloping away, away,
345 And so he'll gallop on for aye,
The bane of all that dread the devil.

I to the muses have been bound,
These fourteen years, by strong indentures;[3]
Oh gentle muses! let me tell
350 But half of what to him befel,
For sure he met with strange adventures.

Oh gentle muses! is this kind?
Why will ye thus my suit repel?
Why of your further aid bereave me?
355 And can you thus unfriended leave me?
Ye muses! whom I love so well.

Who's yon, that, near the waterfall,
Which thunders down with headlong force,
Beneath the moon, yet shining fair,
360 As careless as if nothing were,
Sits upright on a feeding horse?

Unto his horse, that's feeding free,
He seems, I think, the rein to give;

---

indentures: the contract by which an apprentice was bound to his master.

[3] Since the usual term of service for an apprentice was seven years, Wordsworth implies that the speaker of this poem is by no means a quick study. What follows is a mock-epic invocation of the Muses—the Greek goddesses of artistic inspiration—and, unlike virtually every other invocation in literary history, this poet's request for inspiration is refused. [ED.]

Of moon or stars he takes no heed;
365 Of such we in romances read,
— 'Tis Johnny! Johnny! as I live.

And that's the very pony too.
Where is she, where is Betty Foy?
She hardly can sustain her fears;
370 The roaring water-fall she hears,
And cannot find her idiot boy.

Your pony's worth his weight in gold,
Then calm your terrors, Betty Foy!
She's coming from among the trees,
375 And now, all full in view, she sees
Him whom she loves, her idiot boy.

And Betty sees the pony too:
Why stand you thus Good Betty Foy?
It is no goblin, 'tis no ghost,
380 'Tis he whom you so long have lost,
He whom you love, your idiot boy.

She looks again — her arms are up —
She screams — she cannot move for joy;
She darts as with a torrent's force,
385 She has almost o'erturned the horse,
And fast she holds her idiot boy.

And Johnny burrs and laughs aloud,
Whether in cunning or in joy,
I cannot tell; but while he laughs,
390 Betty a drunken pleasure quaffs,
To hear again her idiot boy.

And now she's at the pony's tail,
And now she's at the pony's head,
On that side now, and now on this,
395 And almost stifled with her bliss,
A few sad tears does Betty shed.

She kisses o'er and o'er again,
Him whom she loves, her idiot boy,
She's happy here, she's happy there,
400 She is uneasy every where:
Her limbs are all alive with joy.

She pats the pony, where or when
She knows not, happy Betty Foy!
The little pony glad may be,
405 But he is milder far than she,
You hardly can perceive his joy.

"Oh! Johnny, never mind the Doctor;
"You've done your best, and that is all."
She took the reins, when this was said,
410 And gently turned the pony's head
From the loud water-fall.

By this the stars were almost gone,
The moon was setting on the hill,
So pale you scarcely looked at her:
415 The little birds began to stir,
Though yet their tongues were still.

The pony, Betty, and her boy,
Wind slowly through the woody dale:
And who is she, be-times abroad,
420 That hobbles up the steep rough road?
Who is it, but old Susan Gale?

Long Susan lay deep lost in thought,
And many dreadful fears beset her,
Both for her messenger and nurse;
425 And as her mind grew worse and worse,
Her body it grew better.

She turned, she toss'd herself in bed,
On all sides doubts and terrors met her;
Point after point did she discuss;
430 And while her mind was fighting thus,
Her body still grew better.

"Alas! what is become of them?
"These fears can never be endured,
"I'll to the wood." — The word scarce said,
435 Did Susan rise up from her bed,
As if by magic cured.

Away she posts up hill and down,
And to the wood at length is come,
She spies her friends, she shouts a greeting;

440 Oh me! it is a merry meeting,
  As ever was in Christendom.

  The owls have hardly sung their last,
  While our four travellers homeward wend;
  The owls have hooted all night long,
445 And with the owls began my song,
  And with the owls must end.

  For while they all were travelling home,
  Cried Betty, "Tell us Johnny, do,
  "Where all this long night you have been,
450 "What you have heard, what you have seen,
  "And Johnny, mind you tell us true."

  Now Johnny all night long had heard
  The owls in tuneful concert strive;
  No doubt too he the moon had seen;
455 For in the moonlight he had been
  From eight o'clock till five.

  And thus to Betty's question, he
  Made answer, like a traveller bold,
  (His very words I give to you,)
460 "The cocks did crow to-whoo, to-whoo,
  "And the sun did shine so cold."
  —Thus answered Johnny in his glory,
  And that was all his travel's story.

Lines Written near Richmond
upon the Thames
at Evening[1]

  How rich the wave, in front, imprest
  With evening-twilight's summer hues,
  While, facing thus the crimson west,
  The boat her silent path pursues!
5 And see how dark the backward stream!

---

[1] By Wordsworth. In the Fenwick note, Wordsworth points out that he originally conceived of the poem "during a solitary walk on the banks of the Cam" (the river that runs through Cambridge) and later changed the setting to the Thames (Curtis 36). [ED.]

A little moment past, so smiling!
And still, perhaps, with faithless gleam,
Some other loiterer beguiling.

Such views the youthful bard allure,
But, heedless of the following gloom,
He deems their colours shall endure
'Till peace go with him to the tomb.
—And let him nurse his fond deceit,
And what if he must die in sorrow!
Who would not cherish dreams so sweet,
Though grief and pain may come to-morrow?

Glide gently, thus for ever glide,
O Thames! that other bards may see,
As lovely visions by thy side
As now, fair river! come to me.
Oh glide, fair stream! for ever so;
Thy quiet soul on all bestowing,
'Till all our minds for ever flow,
As thy deep waters now are flowing.[2]

Vain thought! yet be as now thou art,
That in thy waters may be seen
The image of a poet's heart,
How bright, how solemn, how serene!
Such heart did once the poet bless,
Who, pouring here a *later* ditty,[3]
Could find no refuge from distress,
But in the milder grief of pity.

Remembrance! as we glide along,
For him suspend the dashing oar,
And pray that never child of Song

---

the poet: William Collins (1721–59).

[2]Compare John Denham, *Coopers Hill*, lines 189–92 (330). [ED.]

[3]"Collins's Ode on the death of Thomson, the last written, I believe, of the poems which were published during his life-time. This Ode is also alluded to in the next stanza." [Wordsworth's note.] The poet James Thomson (1700–48) is buried in Richmond. Collins's ode was published in 1749. [ED.]

May know his freezing sorrows more.[4]
How calm! how still! the only sound,
The dripping of the oar suspended!
—The evening darkness gathers round
40 By virtue's holiest powers attended.

Expostulation and Reply[1]

"Why William, on that old grey stone,
"Thus for the length of half a day,
"Why William, sit you thus alone,
"And dream your time away?

5 "Where are your books? that light bequeath'd
"To beings else forlorn and blind!
"Up! Up! and drink the spirit breath'd
"From dead men to their kind.

"You look round on your mother earth,
10 "As if she for no purpose bore you;
"As if you were her first-born birth,
"And none had lived before you!"

One morning thus, by Esthwaite lake,
When life was sweet I knew not why,
15 To me my good friend Matthew spake,
And thus I made reply.

"The eye it cannot chuse but see,
"We cannot bid the ear be still;
"Our bodies feel, where'er they be,
20 "Against, or with our will.

"Nor less I deem that there are powers,
"Which of themselves our minds impress,

---

[4] Compare the following lines from Collins's ode:

Remembrance oft shall haunt the shore
    When Thames in summer wreaths is drest,
And oft suspend the dashing oar
    To bid his gentle spirit rest. [ED.]

[1] By Wordsworth. [ED.]

"That we can feed this mind of ours,
"In a wise passiveness.[2]

25 "Think you, mid all this mighty sum
"Of things for ever speaking,
"That nothing of itself will come,
"But we must still be seeking?

"—Then ask not wherefore, here, alone,
30 "Conversing as I may,
"I sit upon this old grey stone,
"And dream my time away."

The Tables Turned
An Evening Scene
on the Same Subject[1]

Up! up! my friend, and clear your looks,
Why all this toil and trouble?
Up! up! my friend, and quit your books,
Or surely you'll grow double.

5 The sun above the mountain's head,
A freshening lustre mellow,
Through all the long green fields has spread,
His first sweet evening yellow.

Books! 'tis a dull and endless strife,
10 Come, hear the woodland linnet,
How sweet his music; on my life
There's more of wisdom in it.

And hark! how blithe the throstle sings!
And he is no mean preacher;
15 Come forth into the light of things,
Let Nature be your teacher.

She has a world of ready wealth,
Our minds and hearts to bless—

---

throstle: thrush.

[2] This quatrain demonstrates Wordsworth's interest in the empiricist philosophy of John Locke and the associationist psychology of David Hartley (see the headnote to "Literary and Philosophical Backgrounds" in Part Two). [ED.]
[1] By Wordsworth. [ED.]

Spontaneous wisdom breathed by health,
20 Truth breathed by chearfulness.

One impulse from a vernal wood
May teach you more of man;
Of moral evil and of good,
Than all the sages can.

25 Sweet is the lore which nature brings;
Our meddling intellect
Mishapes the beauteous forms of things;
—We murder to dissect.

Enough of science and of art;
30 Close up these barren leaves;
Come forth, and bring with you a heart
That watches and receives.

Old Man Travelling
Animal Tranquillity and Decay, a Sketch [1]

The little hedge-row birds,
That peck along the road, regard him not.
He travels on, and in his face, his step,
His gait, is one expression; every limb,
5 His look and bending figure, all bespeak
A man who does not move with pain, but moves
With thought—He is insensibly subdued
To settled quiet: he is one by whom
All effort seems forgotten, one to whom
10 Long patience has such mild composure given,
That patience now doth seem a thing, of which
He hath no need. He is by nature led
To peace so perfect, that the young behold
With envy, what the old man hardly feels.
15 —I asked him whither he was bound, and what
The object of his journey; he replied
"Sir! I am going many miles to take

---

[1] By Wordsworth. In the Fenwick note, Wordsworth says that "these verses were an over-flowing from *The Old Cumberland Beggar*" (Curtis 57). In 1800 Wordsworth retitled the poem "Animal Tranquillity and Decay, A Sketch," and in 1815 he omitted lines 15–20. [ED.]

"A last leave of my son, a mariner,
"Who from a sea-fight has been brought to Falmouth,
20 "And there is dying in an hospital."

The Complaint of a Forsaken Indian Woman [1]

When a Northern Indian, from sickness, is unable to continue his journey with his companions; he is left behind, covered over with Deer-skins, and is supplied with water, food, and fuel if the situation of the place will afford it. He is informed of the track which his companions intend to pursue, and if he is unable to follow, or overtake them, he perishes alone in the Desert; unless he should have the good fortune to fall in with some other Tribes of Indians. It is unnecessary to add that the females are equally, or still more, exposed to the same fate. See that very interesting work, Hearne's Journey from Hudson's Bay to the Northern Ocean. [2] When the Northern Lights, as the same writer informs us, vary their position in the air, they make a rustling and a crackling noise. This circumstance is alluded to in the first stanza of the following poem. [3]

Before I see another day,
Oh let my body die away!
In sleep I heard the northern gleams;
The stars they were among my dreams;
5 In sleep did I behold the skies,
I saw the crackling flashes drive;
And yet they are upon my eyes,
And yet I am alive.
Before I see another day,
10 Oh let my body die away!

My fire is dead: it knew no pain;
Yet it is dead, and I remain.
All stiff with ice the ashes lie;
And they are dead, and I will die.
15 When I was well, I wished to live,

Falmouth: a seaport in Cornwall in southwestern England.

[1] By Wordsworth. [ED.]
[2] Samuel Hearne's 1795 travel book that contains a similar account of an abandoned Indian woman. [ED.]
[3] Wordsworth's introductory note. [ED.]

For clothes, for warmth, for food, and fire;
But they to me no joy can give,
No pleasure now, and no desire.
Then here contented will I lie;
20 Alone I cannot fear to die.

Alas! you might have dragged me on
Another day, a single one!
Too soon despair o'er me prevailed;
Too soon my heartless spirit failed;
25 When you were gone my limbs were stronger,
And Oh how grievously I rue,
That, afterwards, a little longer,
My friends, I did not follow you!
For strong and without pain I lay,
30 My friends, when you were gone away.

My child! they gave thee to another,
A woman who was not thy mother.
When from my arms my babe they took,
On me how strangely did he look!
35 Through his whole body something ran,
A most strange something did I see;
— As if he strove to be a man,
That he might pull the sledge for me.
And then he stretched his arms, how wild!
40 Oh mercy! like a little child.

My little joy! my little pride!
In two days more I must have died.
Then do not weep and grieve for me;
I feel I must have died with thee.
45 Oh wind that o'er my head art flying,
The way my friends their course did bend,
I should not feel the pain of dying,
Could I with thee a message send.
Too soon, my friends, you went away;
50 For I had many things to say.

I'll follow you across the snow,
You travel heavily and slow:
In spite of all my weary pain,
I'll look upon your tents again.
55 My fire is dead, and snowy white

The water which beside it stood;
The wolf has come to me to-night,
And he has stolen away my food.
For ever left alone am I,
60 Then wherefore should I fear to die?

My journey will be shortly run,
I shall not see another sun,
I cannot lift my limbs to know
If they have any life or no.
65 My poor forsaken child! if I
For once could have thee close to me,
With happy heart I would then die,
And my last thoughts would happy be.
I feel my body die away,
70 I shall not see another day.

The Convict [1]

The glory of evening was spread through the west;
    —On the slope of a mountain I stood,
While the joy that precedes the calm season of rest
    Rang loud through the meadow and wood.

5   "And must we then part from a dwelling so fair?"
        In the pain of my spirit I said,
And with a deep sadness I turned, to repair
        To the cell where the convict is laid.

The thick-ribbed walls that o'ershadow the gate
10   Resound; and the dungeons unfold:
I pause; and at length, through the glimmering grate,
        That outcast of pity behold.

---

[1] By Wordsworth. This poem was published in the 14 December 1797 edition of the *Morning Post* under the pseudonym of Mortimer (the name of the protagonist in Wordsworth's verse drama, *The Borderers*) and may have been composed as early as 1796. Consequently, it—like *The Female Vagrant*—seems to hark back to an earlier, less experimental phase of Wordsworth's career. Its politics also appear to be more overtly radical than most of the poems in *Lyrical Ballads*. Emile Legouis calls "The Convict" a "thoroughly Godwinian poem" because it so clearly reflects "the philosopher's favourite idea for the reformation of the penal laws—i.e., that criminals should be transported to a remote location such as Australia rather than imprisoned" (309). [ED.]

His black matted head on his shoulder is bent,
    And deep is the sigh of his breath,
15 And with stedfast dejection his eyes are intent
    On the fetters that link him to death.

'Tis sorrow enough on that visage to gaze,
    That body dismiss'd from his care;
Yet my fancy has pierced to his heart, and pourtrays
20   More terrible images there.

His bones are consumed, and his life-blood is dried,
    With wishes the past to undo;
And his crime, through the pains that o'erwhelm him, descried,
    Still blackens and grows on his view.

25 When from the dark synod, or blood-reeking field,
    To his chamber the monarch is led,
All soothers of sense their soft virtue shall yield,
    And quietness pillow his head.

But if grief, self-consumed, in oblivion would doze,
30   And conscience her tortures appease,
'Mid tumult and uproar this man must repose;
    In the comfortless vault of disease.

When his fetters at night have so press'd on his limbs,
    That the weight can no longer be borne,
35 If, while a half-slumber his memory bedims,
    The wretch on his pallet should turn,

While the jail-mastiff howls at the dull clanking chain,
    From the roots of his hair there shall start
A thousand sharp punctures of cold-sweating pain,
40   And terror shall leap at his heart.

But now he half-raises his deep-sunken eye,
    And the motion unsettles a tear;
The silence of sorrow it seems to supply,
    And asks of me why I am here.

45 "Poor victim! no idle intruder has stood
    "With o'erweening complacence our state to compare,
"But one, whose first wish is the wish to be good,
    "Is come as a brother thy sorrows to share.

———————

synod: council.

"At thy name though compassion her nature resign,
50   "Though in virtue's proud mouth thy report be a stain,
"My care, if the arm of the mighty were mine,
    "Would plant thee where yet thou might'st blossom again."

Lines Written a Few Miles above Tintern Abbey
On Revisiting the Banks of the Wye
during a Tour, July 13, 1798 [1]

Five years have passed; five summers, with the length
Of five long winters! and again I hear
These waters, rolling from their mountain-springs
With a sweet inland murmur. [2] — Once again
5   Do I behold these steep and lofty cliffs, [3]
Which on a wild secluded scene impress
Thoughts of more deep seclusion; and connect
The landscape with the quiet of the sky.
The day is come when I again repose
10   Here, under this dark sycamore, and view
These plots of cottage-ground, these orchard-tufts,
Which, at this season, with their unripe fruits,
Among the woods and copses lose themselves,
Nor, with their green and simple hue, disturb
15   The wild green landscape. [4] Once again I see
These hedge-rows, hardly hedge-rows, little lines
Of sportive wood run wild; these pastoral farms
Green to the very door; [5] and wreathes of smoke
Sent up, in silence, from among the trees,

---

[1] By Wordsworth. In August 1793, Wordsworth first visited Tintern Abbey near the end of an extensive and largely solitary tour of southern England and Wales; after completing most of the manuscript for *Lyrical Ballads*, Wordsworth returned to the Wye Valley with his sister, Dorothy. The Fenwick note records Wordsworth saying, "No poem of mine was composed under circumstances more pleasant for me to remember than this" (Curtis 15). [ED.]

[2] "The river is not affected by the tides a few miles above Tintern." [Wordsworth's note.]

[3] In section 2 of *Observations on the River Wye*, Gilpin notes that "The beauty of these scenes arises chiefly from two circumstances — the *lofty banks* of the river, and its *mazy course*" (7). [ED.]

[4] As Hartley notes in *Observations on Man*, green is "the middle Colour of the Seven primary ones, and consequently the most agreeable to the Organ of Sight." [ED.]

[5] Though Wordsworth seems to draw on the language of Gilpin's *Observations* in this verse paragraph, he also appears to be consciously reacting against Gilpin's ideas. In con-

20 With some uncertain notice, as might seem,
Of vagrant dwellers in the houseless woods,
Or of some hermit's cave, where by his fire
The hermit sits alone.[6]

                    Though absent long,
These forms of beauty have not been to me,
25 As is a landscape to a blind man's eye:
But oft, in lonely rooms, and mid the din
Of towns and cities, I have owed to them,
In hours of weariness, sensations sweet,
Felt in the blood, and felt along the heart,
30 And passing even into my purer mind
With tranquil restoration:—feelings too
Of unremembered pleasure; such, perhaps,
As may have had no trivial influence
On that best portion of a good man's life;
35 His little, nameless, unremembered acts
Of kindness and of love. Nor less, I trust,
To them I may have owed another gift,
Of aspect more sublime; that blessed mood,
In which the burthen of the mystery,
40 In which the heavy and the weary weight
Of all this unintelligible world
Is lighten'd:—that serene and blessed mood,
In which the affections gently lead us on,
Until, the breath of this corporeal frame,
45 And even the motion of our human blood
Almost suspended, we are laid asleep
In body, and become a living soul:[7]
While with an eye made quiet by the power

---

trast to Gilpin's belief that roughness and variety are essential to the picturesque, Wordsworth emphasizes the uniform greenness of this landscape. Furthermore, whereas Gilpin says "Furrowed-lands, and waving corn, however charming in pastoral poetry, are ill-accommodated to painting," Wordsworth celebrates the beauty of "These plots of cottage-ground" and "these pastoral farms." [ED.]

[6] Compare this section of the poem with the following passage from section 2 of Gilpin's *Observations*: "Many of the furnaces, on the banks of the river, consume charcoal, which is manufactured on the spot; and the smoke, which is frequently seen issuing from the sides of the hills; and spreading its thin veil over a part of them, beautifully breaks their lines, and unites them with the sky" (11–12). [ED.]

[7] See Milton, *Paradise Lost*: "in his own Image hee / Created thee, in the Image of God / Express, and thou becam'st a living Soul" (8.526–28); see also Genesis 2.7. [ED.]

Of harmony, and the deep power of joy,
We see into the life of things.[8]

50   If this
Be but a vain belief, yet, oh! how oft,
In darkness, and amid the many shapes
Of joyless day-light; when the fretful stir
Unprofitable, and the fever of the world,
55 Have hung upon the beatings of my heart,
How oft, in spirit, have I turned to thee
O sylvan Wye! Thou wanderer through the woods,
How often has my spirit turned to thee!

And now, with gleams of half-extinguish'd thought,
60 With many recognitions dim and faint,
And somewhat of a sad perplexity,
The picture of the mind revives again:
While here I stand, not only with the sense
Of present pleasure, but with pleasing thoughts
65 That in this moment there is life and food
For future years. And so I dare to hope
Though changed, no doubt, from what I was, when first
I came among these hills; when like a roe
I bounded o'er the mountains, by the sides
70 Of the deep rivers, and the lonely streams,
Wherever nature led; more like a man
Flying from something that he dreads, than one
Who sought the thing he loved. For nature then
(The coarser pleasures of my boyish days,
75 And their glad animal movements all gone by,)
To me was all in all. —I cannot paint
What then I was. The sounding cataract
Haunted me like a passion: the tall rock,
The mountain, and the deep and gloomy wood,
80 Their colours and their forms, were then to me
An appetite: a feeling and a love,
That had no need of a remoter charm,
By thought supplied, or any interest

---

[8]Wordsworth's thinking in this verse paragraph seems particularly indebted to Hartley
(see the selection from *Observations on Man*, 129–32.). [ED.]

Unborrowed from the eye. —That time is past,
85 And all its aching joys are now no more,
And all its dizzy raptures. Not for this
Faint I, nor mourn nor murmur: other gifts
Have followed, for such loss, I would believe,
Abundant recompence. For I have learned
90 To look on nature, not as in the hour
Of thoughtless youth, but hearing oftentimes
The still, sad music of humanity,
Not harsh nor grating, though of ample power
To chasten and subdue. And I have felt
95 A presence that disturbs me with the joy
Of elevated thoughts; a sense sublime
Of something far more deeply interfused,
Whose dwelling is the light of setting suns,
And the round ocean, and the living air,
100 And the blue sky, and in the mind of man,
A motion and a spirit, that impels
All thinking things, all objects of all thought,
And rolls through all things. Therefore am I still
A lover of the meadows and the woods,
105 And mountains; and of all that we behold
From this green earth; of all the mighty world
Of eye and ear, both what they half create,[9]
And what perceive; well pleased to recognize
In nature and the language of the sense,
110 The anchor of my purest thoughts, the nurse,
The guide, the guardian of my heart, and soul
Of all my moral being.

                    Nor, perchance,
If I were not thus taught, should I the more
Suffer my genial spirits to decay:
115 For thou art with me, here, upon the banks
Of this fair river; thou, my dearest Friend,
My dear, dear Friend, and in thy voice I catch

---

genial: native, inborn.

[9]"This line has a close resemblance to an admirable line of Young, the exact expression of which I cannot recollect." [Wordsworth's note.] The reference is to Young's *Night Thoughts:* "And half-create the wondrous world they see" (4.427). [ED.]

The language of my former heart, and read
My former pleasures in the shooting lights
120 Of thy wild eyes. Oh! yet a little while
May I behold in thee what I was once,
My dear, dear Sister! And this prayer I make,
Knowing that Nature never did betray
The heart that loved her; 'tis her privilege,
125 Through all the years of this our life, to lead
From joy to joy: for she can so inform
The mind that is within us, so impress
With quietness and beauty, and so feed
With lofty thoughts, that neither evil tongues,[10]
130 Rash judgments, nor the sneers of selfish men,
Nor greetings where no kindness is, nor all
The dreary intercourse of daily life,
Shall e'er prevail against us, or disturb
Our chearful faith that all which we behold
135 Is full of blessings. Therefore let the moon
Shine on thee in thy solitary walk;
And let the misty mountain winds be free
To blow against thee:[11] and in after years,
When these wild ecstasies shall be matured
140 Into a sober pleasure, when thy mind
Shall be a mansion for all lovely forms,
Thy memory be as a dwelling-place
For all sweet sounds and harmonies; Oh! then,
If solitude, or fear, or pain, or grief,
145 Should be thy portion, with what healing thoughts
Of tender joy wilt thou remember me,
And these my exhortations! Nor, perchance,
If I should be, where I no more can hear
Thy voice, nor catch from thy wild eyes these gleams
150 Of past existence, wilt thou then forget
That on the banks of this delightful stream
We stood together; and that I, so long
A worshipper of Nature, hither came,

---

sister: Dorothy Wordsworth.

[10]Compare Milton, *Paradise Lost*: "On evil days though fall'n, and evil tongues" (7.25). [ED.]

[11]Compare "The Old Cumberland Beggar," lines 165–69 (318–19). [ED.]

Unwearied in that service: rather say
155 With warmer love, oh! with far deeper zeal
Of holier love. Nor wilt thou then forget,
That after many wanderings, many years
Of absence, these steep woods and lofty cliffs,
And this green pastoral landscape, were to me
160 More dear, both for themselves, and for thy sake.

END

Part Two

CONTEXTS FOR *LYRICAL BALLADS*

LITERARY AND PHILOSOPHICAL
BACKGROUNDS

Following our assertion in the Introduction—that *Lyrical Ballads* is more a reaction to Sensibility than it is to Neoclassicism—the question necessarily arises: Just what are the characteristic features of the "Age of Sensibility"? As the name itself implies, the Age of Sensibility, which begins roughly in 1740 and concludes near the end of the eighteenth century, represented a reaction against the values of the earlier eighteenth century, the so-called Age of Reason. Sensibility literally means the capacity to feel, to receive sensation and experience emotion; therefore, in contrast to earlier eighteenth-century literature that typically emphasizes moderation and restraint, works of Sensibility are usually far more passionate and impulsive, far more given to digressions and flights of fancy. To borrow Northrop Frye's terms, the aesthetic of Sensibility is characteristically one of process rather than finished product, in which a momentary effect often takes precedence over the text's overall structure (145). Or, as Jerome McGann has suggested more recently, it is a literature based upon the assumption "that no human action of any consequence is possible—including 'mental' action—that is not led and driven by feeling, affect, emotion" (*Poetics* 6).[1]

From the examples of Wordsworth's and Coleridge's early poetry that we have reprinted in this section, it is clear that these aesthetic values greatly influenced them. Many of their youthful compositions are in fact virtually indistinguishable from those of other contemporary writers. Wordsworth's first published poem, "Sonnet on Seeing Miss Helen Maria Williams Weep at a Tale of Distress," displays an overwrought emotionalism and hyperbolic diction that contrasts sharply with his later practice; Coleridge in his

---

[1] McGann points out that we tend to be suspicious of emotional excess in literature—or "sentiment"—largely because of the influence of the Modernist aesthetic of the twentieth century, which is essentially a Neoclassical one.

"effusions" consciously avoids the "*oneness* of thought" common in more highly structured poetic forms so that he can pursue more freely the course of his own shifting emotions (x). But even in *Lyrical Ballads* itself, we can still see evidence of Sensibility's influence. For instance, Wordsworth's definition of poetry in the 1800 Preface as "the spontaneous overflow of powerful feeling" seems a textbook example of Age of Sensibility aesthetics; poems such as "The Last of the Flock" and "The Mad Mother" appear to tug so insistently on the reader's heartstrings that they border on the sentimentality that characterizes much late eighteenth-century writing.

At the root of nearly all Age of Sensibility thought is the philosophy of John Locke (1632–1704). In his famous formulation, Locke denies the existence of "innate," or inborn, ideas by arguing that the mind at birth is like a *tabula rasa*, a blank tablet or slate. Over time, this tablet becomes filled with the impressions received through our senses; according to Locke, it is the combination of these sensory data (what Locke calls "sensation") and "the *Perception of the Operations of our own Minds* within us" (what he calls "reflection") that "are the two Fountains of Knowledge, from whence all the ideas we have, or can naturally have, do spring" (104–05). Thus, in contrast to the Rationalist philosophy of Descartes and Spinoza, where Sensibility is typically seen as a distraction from the truths of reason, Locke makes it central to our mental development. It is this ability to feel, this receptiveness to external stimuli, that enables us to evolve from ignorant infants to thinking, reasoning human beings.

In the work of Locke's successors, Sensibility and the emotions become even more central. The Earl of Shaftesbury, for example, emphasizes the importance of the "affections" in the development of virtue and integrity, and David Hume makes feeling rather than reason the foundation of all moral thinking: "To have a sense of virtue, is nothing but to *feel* satisfaction of a particular kind from the contemplation of a character. The very *feeling* constitutes our praise or admiration" (471). But the figure who perhaps best typifies this trend is the Scottish philosopher Adam Smith, who, in his 1759 *Theory of Moral Sentiments,* focuses on the emotion of compassion or sympathy, asserting that we naturally derive pleasure from seeing the happiness of others and sorrow or pain from seeing their misery. This theory helped create the vogue for humanitarian poetry near the end of the eighteenth century—much of which is specifically designed to elicit sympathy for the unfortunate—but it is also notable for the emphasis that Smith places on the imagination. Whereas Locke had largely dismissed the imagination as a source of error and superstition, Smith credits it with making this kind of sympathetic response possible because, as he says, "It is by the imagination only that we can form any conception of what are [another's] sensations."

Another highly influential disciple of Locke was David Hartley who, in his *Observations on Man, His Frame, His Duty, and His Expectations,* attempted to provide a physical explanation for Locke's psychological theories. To explain how Locke's *tabula rasa* becomes stored with knowledge, Hartley theorizes that vibrations—or, as he calls them, "vibratiuncles"—are transmitted through the nervous system to the soft "medullary substance" of the brain where they make impressions that are stored in the memory. Because these vibrations can be either painful or pleasurable and because the mind tends to link ideas that occur together, we naturally begin to associate pain with certain experiences and pleasure with others. Over time, these rudimentary associations form increasingly complex "chains of associations" that ultimately give rise to such sophisticated mental functions as our sense of morality and love of God. For evidence of Hartley's influence on *Lyrical Ballads,* one need only look at Wordsworth's poem "Expostulation and Reply" or his statement in the Preface that one of his "principal objects" in the volume was to trace "the primary laws of our nature: chiefly, as far as regards the manner in which we associate ideas in a state of excitement." Similarly, Coleridge—even though he would later criticize Hartley's system as too mechanistic—was at one time such a devoted disciple of Hartley that he named his first son after him.

An equally important influence on the young Wordsworth was the Swiss philosopher and novelist Jean-Jacques Rousseau. William Hazlitt, for example, considered the perspectives of these two men to be nearly identical: "The writer who most resembles [Rousseau] in our own times is the author of the *Lyrical Ballads.* We see no other difference between them, than that the one wrote in prose and the other in poetry" (92). Though the body of Rousseau's work touches on a wide range of subjects including politics, autobiography, and theology, we—because of its obvious relevance to *Lyrical Ballads*—have chosen to focus on the primitivistic element of his philosophy. Beginning with his 1750 "Discourse on the Arts and Sciences," Rousseau consistently challenged the widespread eighteenth-century belief in progress—the idea that mankind was becoming increasingly enlightened and that society was moving ever closer to an ideal state. Instead, Rousseau maintains that the more our increased knowledge moves us away from the state of nature, the more our morals degenerate. In fact, he describes the acquisition of knowledge and the establishment of civilization as a falling away from our primal innocence:

> Before art had fashioned our manners and taught our passions to speak an affected language, our mores were rustic but natural, differences in behavior heralded, at first glance, differences in character. [. . .] Today, when more subtle inquiries and a more refined taste have reduced the art of pleasing to established rules, a vile and deceitful uniformity reigns in our mores, and all minds seem to have been cast in the same mold.

Without ceasing, politeness makes demands, propriety gives orders;
without ceasing, common customs are followed, never one's own lights.
One no longer dares to seem what one really is. (4)

Describing an almost Prufrock-like condition, Rousseau anticipates the
modernist dilemma for the twentieth century, in which the individual is as-
similated by society; certainly, these concerns would be shared by the Romantics, particularly Wordsworth and Coleridge. Our selections from Rousseau are from *The Discourse on the Origin and Foundation of the Inequality
among Mankind*, in which he controversially privileges the natural instincts
of savage man over the sophistication of civilized man, and from his novel /
educational treatise, *Émile* (translated as *Emilius and Sophia*), in which he
proposes a system of education that he believes will help overcome the pernicious and corrupting influence of the contemporary society.

In the selections of Age of Sensibility verse, we focus on those trends that
most directly affected Wordsworth and Coleridge at the time they were
composing *Lyrical Ballads*. Like Mark Akenside's *The Pleasures of the Imagination* (1744) and William Collins's "Ode on the Poetical Character"
(1746), the first poem in this section, Joseph Warton's "Ode I. To Fancy,"
obviously demonstrates the increasing emphasis placed on the imagination, or fancy, in the later eighteenth century. But more than this, the poem
also serves as a kind of poetic manifesto for its age. With its concluding
prayer that Fancy will spur some "chosen swain" to "rise above the rhyming
throng" of contemporary poets and restore England to its former literary
greatness, Warton clearly prescribes a cure for the age's poetic ills. As opposed to the highly polished and refined poetry of Pope and his Augustan
followers, this poet will write verse of passion and inspiration. He will
"O'erwhelm our souls with joy and pain" and will "With native beauties
win applause, / Beyond cold critics' studied laws."

Although the young Wordsworth and Coleridge may have assented to
many of these aims, Warton's ode also exhibits several features to which they
would have objected — most notably its extensive use of personification. To
readers in the 1740s, there would have been nothing objectionable about
this practice. Personification — or, as it was called at the time, *prosopopeia* —
was extremely fashionable throughout the second half of the eighteenth
century; thousands of odes were written to personifications of such abstract
qualities as Fear, Pity, and Melancholy. Moreover, in the case of Warton's
ode, the trope would have been seen as particularly appropriate since most
readers and critics of the time considered this ability to invest an abstract
quality with human characteristics to be a tremendous imaginative feat.
For Wordsworth, however, personification was merely an example of the
sort of artificial poetic diction that he condemns throughout the Preface to

Lyrical Ballads: "The Reader will find that personifications of abstract ideas rarely occur in these volumes; and are utterly rejected as an ordinary device to elevate the style, and raise it above prose." Thus, far from being a feat of imaginative daring and innovation, personification had become a threadbare device to which poets reflexively turned when they wanted to raise the level of their discourse a notch.

The poetry by the so-called Della Cruscans demonstrates even more vividly the sort of artificiality that Wordsworth objected to in Age of Sensibility verse. Led by Robert Merry (whose pen name, Della Crusca,[2] later became a somewhat pejorative rubric for this entire group of poets), the Della Cruscans wrote in a highly ornate style that sought to capture the kind of emotional intensity so prized during this time. Many of these poems center on the playful love affair between Della Crusca and Anna Matilda, the pseudonym of Hannah Cowley (1743–1809), an older married woman whose interest in Merry was strictly literary. While this poetry did enjoy great popularity when it was published in a 1790 volume called *The British Album,* Della Cruscan verse was also widely ridiculed — as in the following excerpt from William Gifford's 1791 satirical poem, *The Baviad:*

> Lo, Della Crusca! In his closet pent,
> He toils to give the crude conception vent.
> Abortive thoughts that right and wrong confound,
> Truth sacrificed to letters, sense to sound,
> False glare, incongruous images, combine;
> And noise, and nonsense clatter through the line. (39–44)

The Della Cruscan style thus came to typify all that was pretentious, artificial, and ponderously extravagant in late eighteenth-century poetry.

To round out this brief anthology of Age of Sensibility verse, we have included a number of poems by some of the period's most accomplished writers. As its title suggests, Helen Maria Williams's "To Sensibility" is very much a representative poem of its time. Responding to Frances Greville's 1756 poem, "A Prayer for Indifference," Williams argues that, even if indifference could shield her from life's sorrows, the sacrifice would be too great. It would deprive her of "the sacred power to weep" — the source "of every finer bliss." One of the most popular volumes of poetry in the late eighteenth century, Charlotte Smith's brilliant *Elegiac Sonnets* entranced readers with its eloquent and impassioned cameos of sorrow and bitterness. It would be a mistake, however, to read these poems as simply outpourings of Smith's

---

[2]Ironically, Merry took this pen name from the Della Crusca Academy in Florence, which was dedicated to the purification of the Italian language.

personal grief and to ignore how highly allusive and carefully crafted these poems truly are. The opening sonnet, for example, subtly refers both to the "fantastic garlands" of the dead Ophelia to create a powerful image of the female poet—at once inspired and flirting with madness—and to the poetic laurel worn by her great precursor, Petrarch, whose sonnets prefigure Sensibility, achieving for him poetic fame in their interior explorations of his love for Laura and his grief over her death. Similarly, Smith's "Sonnet XLIV. Written in the Church Yard at Middleton in Sussex" unmistakably calls to mind "Elegy Written in a Country Churchyard," only to transform Thomas Gray's solemn meditation on the lives of the rural poor into an apocalyptic vision of the dead being unearthed from their graves.

We also have provided two selections from "The Task" by William Cowper, a poet who illustrates several different facets of Age of Sensibility verse. On the one hand—as we can see from the famous passage from Book III in which Cowper compares his life-long struggles with madness to the plight of a "stricken deer"—much of his poetry is filled with pathos and sentiment. Therefore, it is hardly surprising that Jane Austen should have chosen him in *Sense and Sensibility* as the favorite poet of Marianne, the passionate and high-strung sister to the more practical Elinor.[3] On the other hand, Cowper was also the poet whom Coleridge praised as "the first who combined natural thoughts with natural diction; the first who reconciled the heart with the head" (*Biographia* 1.25), and his extremely fluent and flexible style of blank verse—at once colloquial and formal, playful and serious—strongly influenced the poetic development of both Coleridge and Wordsworth. This more thoughtful and meditative dimension of Cowper's poetry is evident in his description of a winter evening from Book IV, which, with its depiction of "sooty films" playing upon the bars of a fireplace grate, clearly anticipates Coleridge's "Frost at Midnight" (233–35). Moreover, its discussion of those "less distinguish'd than ourselves" exemplifies the kind of poetry about the lower classes that achieved great popularity near the end of the eighteenth century and that we shall explore more fully in the Rustic and Humanitarian Poetry section.

This survey of Age of Sensibility writing concludes with excerpts from Joanna Baillie's "Introductory Discourse" to her 1798 *Series of Plays*. With her emphasis on the importance of the "sympathetick curiosity," Baillie vividly demonstrates the influence of Adam Smith's moral philosophy on late eighteenth-century literature, but—more important for our purposes— her general aesthetic stance prefigures much of Wordsworth's argument in

---

[3] Austen began writing the book in 1797, just as Wordsworth and Coleridge were composing the poems for *Lyrical Ballads*. The title allegorizes the two women as poles of reason and emotion.

the 1800 Preface to *Lyrical Ballads*. Her assertion that "those works which strongly characterize human nature in the middling and lower classes of society [. . .] will ever be the most popular" closely resembles Wordsworth's decision to focus on "low and rustic life," and her insistence upon a more natural kind of dramatic dialogue resembles his call for a poetry written in "the real language" of ordinary people.

ODE I

TO FANCY

Joseph Warton [1]

O Parent of each lovely Muse,
Thy spirit o'er my soul diffuse,
O'er all my artless songs preside,
My footsteps to thy temple guide,
5 To offer at thy turf-built shrine,
In golden cups no costly wine,
No murder'd fatling of the flock,
But flowers and honey from the rock.
O Nymph, with loosely-flowing hair,
10 With buskin'd leg, and bosom bare,
Thy waist with myrtle-girdle bound,
Thy brows with Indian feathers crown'd,
Waving in thy snowy hand
An all-commanding magic wand,
15 Of pow'r to bid fresh gardens blow
'Midst chearless Lapland's barren snow,
Whose rapid wings thy flight convey
Thro' air, and over earth and sea,
While the vast, various landscape lies
20 Conspicuous to thy piercing eyes;

From *Odes on Various Subjects*. London: Dodsley, 1746.

Fancy: imagination.
buskin'd: wearing a buskin, a high, thick-soled boot.
Lapland: a region in northern Scandinavia.

[1] Warton (1722–1800), poet and critic, is often seen as a "pre-Romantic" because of the influence of his poem *The Enthusiast, or the Lover of Nature* (1744) —which, like "Ode to Fancy," emphasizes the correspondence between nature and the imagination —and of his critical insights in *An Essay on the Writings and Genius of Pope* (1756; 1782), in which he distinguishes between true poets and more commonplace men of wit. [ED.]

O lover of the desert, hail!
Say, in what deep and pathless vale,
Or on what hoary mountain's side,
'Midst fall of waters, you reside,
25 'Midst broken rocks, a rugged scene,
With green and grassy dales between,
'Midst forests dark of aged oak,
Ne'er echoing with the woodman's stroke,
Where never human art appear'd,
30 Nor ev'n one straw-rooft cot was rear'd,
Where Nature seems to sit alone,
Majestic on a craggy throne;
Tell me the path, sweet wand'rer, tell,
To thy unknown sequester'd cell,
35 Where woodbines cluster round the door,
Where shells and moss o'erlay the floor,
And on whose top an hawthorn blows,
Amid whose thickly-woven boughs,
Some nightingale still builds her nest,
40 Each evening warbling thee to rest;
Then lay me by the haunted stream,
Wrapt in some wild, poetic dream,
In converse while methinks I rove
With Spenser through a fairy grove;
45 Till suddenly awoke, I hear
Strange whisper'd music in my ear,
And my glad soul in bliss is drown'd,
By the sweetly-soothing sound!
Me, Goddess, by the right-hand lead,
50 Sometimes thro' the yellow mead,
Where Joy and white-rob'd Peace resort,
And Venus keeps her festive court,
Where Mirth and Youth each evening meet,
And lightly trip with nimble feet,
55 Nodding their lilly-crowned heads,
Where Laughter rose-lipp'd Hebe leads;

---

cot: cottage.
Spenser: Edmund Spenser (c. 1552–99), author of *The Faerie Queene* (1590; 1596).
Hebe: Greek goddess of youth and spring, daughter of Zeus and Hera and wife of Heracles (Hercules).

Where Echo walks steep hills among,
List'ning to the shepherd's song:
Or sometimes in thy fiery car
60   Transport me to the rage of war;
There whirl me o'er the hills of slain,
Where Tumult and Destruction reign;
Where mad with pain, the wounded steed
Tramples the dying and the dead;
65   Where giant Terror stalks around,
With sullen joy surveys the ground,
And pointing to th' ensanguin'd field
Shakes his dreadful Gorgon-shield!
Then guide me from this horrid scene
70   To high-archt walks and alleys green,
Where lovely Laura walks, to shun
The fervors of the mid-day sun;
The pangs of absence, O remove,
For thou canst place me near my love,
75   Can'st fold in visionary bliss,
And let me think I steal a kiss,
While her ruby lips dispense
Luscious nectar's quintessence!
When young-ey'd Spring profusely throws
80   From her green lap the pink and rose,
When the soft turtle of the dale,
To Summer tells her tender tale,
When Autumn cooling caverns seeks,
And stains with wine his jolly cheeks,
85   When Winter, like poor pilgrim old,
Shakes his silver beard with cold,

Echo: in Greek mythology, a mountain nymph who languished for the love of Narcissus until she became only a disembodied voice. According to another version, the forest god Pan, angry that she did not love him, compelled shepherds to butcher her until only her voice remained.
car: Fancy's chariot.
ensanguin'd: bloody.
Gorgon-shield: The face of the Gorgon Medusa was so horrific that it turned to stone anyone who gazed upon it. After Perseus cut off the Gorgon's head, he gave it to Athena, who placed it in the center of her shield.
Laura: The idealized beloved of Petrarch's sonnets.
turtle: turtle dove.

At every season let my ear
Thy solemn whispers, Fancy, hear.
O warm, enthusiastic maid,
90 Without thy powerful, vital aid,
That breathes an energy divine,
That gives a soul to every line,
Ne'er may I strive with lips profane
To utter an unhallow'd strain,
95 Nor dare to touch the sacred string,
Save when with smiles thou bid'st me sing.
O hear our prayer, O hither come
From thy lamented Shakespear's tomb,[2]
On which thou lov'st to sit at eve,
100 Musing o'er thy darling's grave;
O queen of numbers, once again
Animate some chosen swain,
Who fill'd with unexhausted fire,
May boldly smite the sounding lyre,
105 Who with some new, unequall'd song,
May rise above the rhyming throng,
O'er all our list'ning passions reign,
O'erwhelm our souls with joy and pain,
With terror shake, with pity move,
110 Rouze with revenge, or melt with love.
O deign t'attend his evening walk,
With him in groves and grottos talk;
Teach him to scorn with frigid art
Feebly to touch th' unraptur'd heart;
115 Like lightning,[3] let his mighty verse
The bosom's inmost foldings pierce;
With native beauties win applause,
Beyond cold critic's studied laws;
O let each Muse's fame increase,
120 O bid Britannia rival Greece!

---

queen of numbers: muse of poetry, specifically meter.
swain: youth.
Britannia: ancient Roman name for the island of Great Britain.

[2] Shakespeare's tomb is inside Holy Trinity Church at Stratford-upon-Avon. [ED.]
[3] Lightning had suggested the sublime since the first century A.D. when Longinus famously defined the sublime as "a well-timed stroke" that "scatters everything before it like a thunderbolt, and in a flash reveals the full power of the speaker" (100). [ED.]

FROM *OBSERVATIONS ON MAN*

His Frame, His Duty, and His Expectations

David Hartley[1]

FROM CHAPTER IV, SECTION I

Prop. 94

To examine how far the just-mentioned Pleasures and Pains of the Imagination are agreeable to the Doctrine of Association.

Of the Pleasures Arising from the Beauty of the Natural World

The pleasures arising from the Contemplation of the Beauties of the natural World seem to admit to the following Analysis. The pleasant Tastes and Smells, and the fine Colours of Fruits and Flowers, the Melody of Birds, and the grateful Warmth or Coolness of the Air, in the proper Seasons, transfer Miniatures of these Pleasures upon rural Scenes, which start up instantaneously so mixed with each other, and with such as will be immediately enumerated, as to be separately indiscernible.

If there be a Precipice, a Cataract, a Mountain of Snow, &c. in one Part of the Scene, the nascent Ideas of Fear and Horror magnify and enliven all the other Ideas, and by degrees pass into Pleasures, by suggesting the Security from Pain.

In like manner the Grandeur of some Scenes, and the Novelty of others, by exciting Surprize and Wonder, *i.e.* by making a great Difference in the preceding and subsequent States of Mind, so as to border upon, or even enter the Limits of Pain, may greatly enhance the Pleasure.[2]

Uniformity and Variety in Conjunction are also principal Sources of the Pleasures of Beauty, being made so partly by their Association with the Beauties of Nature; partly by that with the Works of Art; and with the many Conveniences which we receive from the Uniformity and Variety of the Works of Art, and from the Head of Convenience, upon the Works of Nature.

Poetry and Painting are much employed in setting forth the Beauties of the natural World, at the same time that they afford us a high Degree of

---

Bath: Leake and Frederick; London: Hatch, 1749.

[1] Hartley (1705–57) was a physician and philosopher; see pages 120–21. [ED.]

[2] The kinds of natural scenes that Hartley describes in this and the preceding paragraph illustrate what Edmund Burke calls "the sublime" in his 1757 treatise, *A Philosophical Enquiry into the Origins of our Ideas of the Sublime and Beautiful.* [ED.]

Pleasure from many other Sources. Hence the Beauties of Nature delight Poets and Painters, and such as are addicted to the Study of their Works, more than others. Part of this Effect is indeed owing to the greater Attention of such Persons to the other Sources; but this comes to the same thing, as far as the general Theory of the factitious, associated Nature of these Pleasures is concerned.[3]

The many Sports and Pastimes, which are peculiar to the Country, and whose Ideas and Pleasures are revived by the View of rural Scenes, in an evanescent State, and so mixed together as to be separately indiscernible, do farther augment the Pleasures suggested by the Beauties of Nature.

To these we may add, the Opposition between the Offensiveness, Dangers, and Corruption of populous Cities, and the Health, Tranquillity, and Innocence, which the actual View, or the mental Contemplation of rural Scenes introduces; also the Pleasures of Sociality and Mirth, which are often found in the greatest Perfection in Country Retirements, the amorous Pleasures, which have many Connexions with rural Scenes, and those which the Opinions and Encomiums of others beget in us, in this, as in other Cases, by means of the Contagiousness observable in mental Dispositions, as well as bodily ones.[4]

Those Persons who have already formed high Ideas of the Power, Knowledge, and Goodness of the Author of Nature, with suitable Affections, generally feel the exalted Pleasures of Devotion upon every View and Contemplation of his Works, either in an explicit and distinct Manner, or in a more secret and implicit one. Hence, part of the general indeterminate Pleasures, here considered, is deducible from the Pleasures of Theopathy.[5]

We must not omit in this Place to remind the reader of a Remark made above; *viz.* That Green, which is the middle Colour of the Seven primary ones, and consequently the most agreeable to the Organ of Sight, is also the general Colour of the Vegetable Kingdom, *i.e.* of external Nature.

These may be considered as some of the principal Sources of the Beauties of Nature to Mankind in general. Inquisitive and philosophical Persons have some others, arising from their peculiar Knowledge and Study of Natural History, Astronomy, and Philosophy, in general. For the Profusion of Beauties, Uses, Fitnesses, Elegance in minute Things, and Magnificence in

---

factitious: artificial or man-made.
Theopathy: religious emotion evoked by the contemplation of God.

[3]Hartley is suggesting that the pleasure afforded by poetry and painting derives from their association with the beauty of Nature and is therefore mental—or factitious. [ED.]
[4]Compare "Tintern Abbey," lines 26–36. [ED.]
[5]Compare "Tintern Abbey," lines 36–49. [ED.]

great ones, exceed all Bounds of Conception, Surprize, and Astonishment; new Scenes, and those of unbounded Extent, separately considered, ever presenting themselves to View, the more any one studies and contemplates the Works of God.

And, upon the Whole, the Reader may see, that there are sufficient Sources for all those Pleasures of Imagination, which the Beauties of Nature excite in different Persons; and that the Differences which are found in different Persons in this respect, are sufficiently analogous to the Differences of their Situations in Life, and of the consequent Associations formed in them.

An attentive Person may also, in viewing or contemplating the Beauties of Nature, lay hold, as it were, of the Remainders and Miniatures of many of the particular Pleasures here enumerated, while they recur in a separate State, and before they coalesce with the general indeterminate Aggregate, and thus verify the History now proposed.

It is a Confirmation of this History, that an attentive Person may also observe great Differences in the Kind and Degree of Relish which he has for the Beauties of Nature in Different Periods of his Life; especially as the Kind and Degree may be found to agree in the main with this History.

To the same Purpose we may remark, that these Pleasures do not cloy very soon, but are of a lasting Nature, if compared with the sensible ones; since this follows naturally from the great Variety of their sources, and the evanescent Nature of their constituent Parts.

When a beautiful Scene is first presented, there is generally great Pleasure from Surprize, from being struck with Objects and Circumstances which we did not expect. This presently declines; but is abundantly compensated for afterwards by the gradual alternate Exaltation of the several constituent Parts of the Complex Pleasures, which also do probably enhance one another. And thus we may take several Reviews of the same Scene, before the Pleasure, which it affords comes to its *Maximum*. After this Pleasure must decline if we review it often: But if at considerable Intervals, so as that many foreign states of Mind intervene, also so as that new Sources of the Pleasures of this kind be broken up, the Pleasure may recur for many Successions of nearly the same Magnitude.[6]

The same Observations hold in respect of the Pleasures from the Beauties of Nature in general, and indeed from all the other Sources, Works of Art, liberal Arts, Sciences, &c. These all strike and surprise the young mind at first, but require a considerable Time before they come to their *Maximum;* after which some or other will always be at its *Maximum* for a considerable Time. However, the Pleasures of Imagination in general, as well

---

[6]Compare "Tintern Abbey," lines 66–88. [ED.]

as each particular Set and Individual, must decline at last from the Nature of our Frame. In what manner they ought to decline, so as to be consistent with our *summum Bonum,* by yielding, in due time, to more exalted and pure Pleasure, whose Composition they enter, I will endeavour to shew hereafter.

FROM *THE THEORY OF MORAL SENTIMENTS*

Adam Smith[1]

PART I
OF THE PROPRIETY OF ACTION

Section I

Of Sympathy

How selfish soever man may be supposed, there are evidently some principles in his nature, which interest him in the fortune of others, and render their happiness necessary to him, though he derives nothing from it except the pleasure of seeing it. Of this kind is pity or compassion, the emotion which we feel for the misery of others, when we either see it, or are made to conceive it in a very lively manner. That we often derive sorrow from the sorrow of others is too obvious to require any instances to prove it; for this sentiment, like all the other original passions of human nature, is by no means confined to the virtuous and humane, though they perhaps may feel it with the most exquisite sensibility. The greatest ruffian, the most hardened violator of the laws of society, is not altogether without it.

As we have no immediate experience of what other men feel, we can form no idea of the manner in which they are affected, but by conceiving what we ourselves should feel in the like situation. Though our brother is upon the rack, as long as we ourselves are at our ease, our senses will never inform us of what he suffers. They never did and never can carry us beyond our own persons, and it is by the imagination only that we can form any conception of what are his sensations. Neither can that faculty help us to this any other way, than by representing to us what would be our own if we

---

summum Bonum: the highest good.

London: Millar; Edinburgh: Kincaid and Bell, 1759.

[1] Smith (1723–90), a Scottish philosopher and economist, is best known today for his landmark 1776 treatise, *An Inquiry into the Nature and Causes of the Wealth of Nations.* [ED.]

were in his case. It is the impressions of our own senses only, not those of his, which our imaginations copy. By the imagination we place ourselves in his situation, we conceive ourselves enduring all the same torments, we enter as it were into his body and become in some measure him, and thence form some idea of his sensations, and even feel something which, though weaker in degree, is not altogether unlike them. His agonies, when they are thus brought home to ourselves, when we have thus adopted and made them our own, begin at last to affect us, and we then tremble and shudder at the thought of what he feels. For as to be in pain or distress of any kind excites the most excessive sorrow, so to conceive or to imagine that we are in it, excites some degree of the same emotion, in proportion to the vivacity or dulness of the conception.

That this is the source of our fellow-feeling for the misery of others, that it is by changing places in fancy with the sufferer, that we come either to conceive or to be affected by what he feels, may be demonstrated by many obvious observations, if it should not be thought sufficiently evident of itself. When we see a stroke aimed and just ready to fall upon the leg or arm of another person, we naturally shrink and draw back our own leg or our own arm; and when it does fall, we feel it in some measure, and are hurt by it as well as the sufferer. The mob, when they are gazing at a dancer on the slack rope, naturally writhe and twist and balance their own bodies, as they see him do, and as they feel that they themselves must do if in his situation. Persons of delicate fibres and a weak constitution of body complain that, in looking on the sores and ulcers which are exposed by beggars in the streets, they are apt to feel an itching or uneasy sensation in the correspondent part of their own bodies. The horror which they conceive at the misery of those wretches affects that particular part in themselves more than any other; because that horror arises from conceiving what they themselves would suffer, if they really were the wretches whom they are looking upon, and if that particular part in themselves was actually affected in the same miserable manner. The very force of this conception is sufficient, in their feeble frames, to produce that itching or uneasy sensation complained of. Men of the most robust make observe that in looking upon sore eyes they often feel a very sensible soreness in their own, which proceeds from the same reason; that organ being in the strongest man more delicate, than any other part of the body is in the weakest.

Neither is it those circumstances only, which create pain or sorrow, that call forth our fellow-feeling. Whatever is the passion which arises from any object in the person principally concerned, an analogous emotion springs up, at the thought of his situation, in the breast of every attentive spectator. Our joy for the deliverance of those heroes of tragedy or romance who interest us is as sincere as our grief for their distress, and our fellow-feeling with their misery is not more real than that with their happiness. We enter into their gratitude towards those faithful friends who did not desert them in their difficulties; and we heartily go along with their resentment against those perfidious traitors who injured, abandoned, or deceived them. In every passion of which the mind of man is susceptible, the emotions of the by-stander always correspond to what, by bringing the case home to himself, he imagines, should be the sentiments of the sufferer.

Pity and compassion are words appropriated to signify our fellow-feeling with the sorrow of others. Sympathy, though its meaning was, perhaps, originally the same, may now, however, without much impropriety, be made use of to denote our fellow-feeling with any passion whatever.

Upon some occasions sympathy may seem to arise merely from the view of a certain emotion in another person. The passions, upon some occasions, may seem to be transfused from one man to another, instantaneously and antecedent to any knowledge of what excited them in the person principally concerned. Grief and joy, for example, strongly expressed in the look and gestures of any one, at once affect the spectator with some degree of a like painful or agreeable emotion. A smiling face is, to every body that sees it, a chearful object; as a sorrowful countenance, on the other hand, is a melancholy one.

This, however, does not hold universally, or with regard to every passion. There are some passions of which the expressions excite no sort of sympathy, but before we are acquainted with what gave occasion to them, serve rather to disgust and provoke us against them. The furious behaviour of an angry man is more likely to exasperate us against himself than against his enemies. As we are unacquainted with his provocation, we cannot bring his case home to ourselves, nor conceive any thing like the passions which it excites. But we plainly see what is the situation of those with whom he is angry, and to what violence they may be exposed from so enraged an adversary. We readily, therefore, sympathize with their fear or resentment, and are immediately disposed to take part against the man from whom they appear to be in so much danger.

If the very appearances of grief and joy inspire us with some degree of the like emotions, it is because they suggest to us the general idea of some good or bad fortune that has befallen the person in whom we observe them: and in these passions this is sufficient to have some little influence upon us. The effects of grief and joy terminate in the person who feels those emotions, of which the expressions do not, like those of resentment, suggest to us the idea of any other person for whom we are concerned, and whose interests are opposite to his. The general idea of good or bad fortune, therefore, creates some concern for the person who has met with it, but the general idea of provocation excites no sympathy with the anger of the man who has received it. Nature, it seems, teaches us to be more averse to enter into this passion, and, till informed of its cause, to be disposed rather to take part against it.

Even our sympathy with the grief or joy of another, before we are informed of the cause of either, is always extremely imperfect. General lamentations, which express nothing but the anguish of the sufferer, create rather a curiosity to inquire into his situation, along with some disposition to sympathize with him, than any actual sympathy that is very sensible. The first question which we ask is, What has befallen you? 'Till this be answered, tho' we are uneasy both from the vague idea of his misfortune, and still more from torturing ourselves with conjectures about what it may be, yet our fellow-feeling is not very considerable.

Sympathy, therefore, does not arise so much from the view of the passion, as from that of the situation which excites it. We sometimes feel for another a passion of which he himself seems to be altogether incapable; because when we put ourselves in his case, that passion arises in our breast from the imagination, though it does not in his from the reality. We blush for the impudence and rudeness of another, though he himself appears to have no sense of the impropriety of his own behaviour; because we cannot help feeling with what confusion we ourselves should be covered, had we behaved in so absurd a manner.

Of all the calamities to which the condition of mortality exposes mankind, the loss of reason appears, to those who have the least spark of humanity, by far the most dreadful, and they behold that last stage of human wretchedness with deeper commiseration than any other. But the poor wretch, who is in it, laughs and sings perhaps, and is altogether insensible of his own misery. The anguish which humanity feels, therefore, at the sight of such an object, cannot be the reflection of any sentiment of the sufferer. The compassion of the spectator must arise altogether from the consideration of what he himself would feel if he was reduced to the same unhappy situation, and, what perhaps is impossible, was at the same time able to regard it with his present reason and judgment.

What are the pangs of a mother, when she hears the moanings of her infant that during the agony of disease cannot express what it feels? In her idea of what it suffers, she joins, to its real helplessness, her own consciousness of that helplessness, and her own terrors for the unknown consequences of its disorder; and out of all these, forms, for her own sorrow, the most complete image of misery and distress. The infant, however, feels only the uneasiness of the present instant, which can never be great. With regard to the future, it is perfectly secure, and in its thoughtlessness and want of foresight possesses an antidote against fear and anxiety, the great tormentors of the human breast, from which reason and philosophy will in vain attempt to defend it, when it grows up to a man.

We sympathize even with the dead, and overlooking what is of real importance in their situation, that awful futurity which awaits them, we are chiefly affected by those circumstances which strike our senses, but can have no influence upon their happiness. It is miserable, we think, to be deprived of the light of the sun; to be shut out from life and conversation; to be laid in the cold grave a prey to corruption and the reptiles of the earth; to be no more thought of in this world, but to be obliterated in a little time from the affections and almost from the memory of their dearest friends and relations. Surely, we imagine, we can never feel too much for those who have suffered so dreadful a calamity. The tribute of our fellow-feeling seems doubly due to them now when they are in danger of being forgot by every body: and, by the vain honours which we pay to their memory, we endeavour, for our own misery, artificially to keep alive our melancholy remembrance of their misfortune. That our sympathy can afford them no consolation seems to be an addition to their calamity; and to think that all we can do is unavailing, and that, what alleviates all other distress, the regret, the love and the lamentation of their friends, can yield no comfort to them, serves only to exasperate our sense of their misery. The happiness of the dead, however, most assuredly, is affected by none of these circumstances; nor is it the thought of these things which can ever disturb the profound security of their repose. The idea of that dreary and endless melancholy, which the fancy naturally ascribes to their condition, arises altogether from our joining to the change which has been produced upon them, our own consciousness of that change, from our putting ourselves in their situation, and from our lodging, if I may be allowed to say so, our own living souls in their inanimated bodies, and thence conceiving what would be our emotions in this case. It is this very illusion of the imagination which renders the foresight of our own dissolution so terrible to us, and the idea of those circumstances, which undoubtedly can give us no pain when we are dead, makes us miserable while we are alive. And from thence arises one of the most important principles in human nature, the dread of death, the great poison to the happiness, but the great restraint upon the injustice of mankind, which, while it afflicts and mortifies the individual, guards and protects the society.

FROM *A DISCOURSE UPON THE ORIGIN*
AND FOUNDATION OF THE INEQUALITY
AMONG MANKIND

Jean-Jacques Rousseau[1]

QUESTION PROPOSED
BY THE ACADEMY OF DIJON

What is the Origin of the Inequality among Mankind; and whether
such Inequality is authorized by the Law of Nature?

'Tis of Man I am to speak; and the very Question, in answer to which I am
to speak of him, sufficiently informs me that I am going to speak to Men;
for to those alone, who are not afraid of honouring Truth, it belongs to propose Discussions of this Kind. I shall therefore maintain with Confidence
the Cause of Mankind before the Sages, who invite me to stand up in its defence; and I shall think myself happy, if I can but behave in a manner not
unworthy of my subject and of my judges.

I conceive two Species of Inequality among Men; one which I call Natural, or Physical Inequality, because it is established by Nature, and consists
in the difference of Age, Health, bodily Strength, and the Qualities of the
Mind, or of the Soul; the other which may be termed Moral, or Political Inequality, because it depends on a Kind of Convention, and is established,
or at least authorized by the common Consent of Mankind. This Species of
Inequality consists in the different Privileges, which some Men enjoy, to the
Prejudice of others, such as that of being richer, more honoured, more
powerful, and even that of exacting obedience from them.

It were absurd to ask, what is the Cause of Natural Inequality, seeing the
bare Definition of Natural Inequality answers the Question: it would be
more absurd still to enquire, if there might not be some essential Connection between the two Species of Inequality, as it would be asking, in other
Words, if those who command are necessarily better Men than those who
obey; and if Strength of Body or of Mind, Wisdom or Virtue are always to
be found in Individuals, in the same Proportion with Power, or Riches: a

---

English translation. London: Dodsley, 1761.

[1] Rousseau (1712–78) was a French-Swiss philosopher whose protests against society and
its artificial restraints influenced the French Revolution and whose emphasis on education from nature profoundly influenced Wordsworth. Rousseau's *Discours sur l'origine et
les fondements de l'inégalité parmi les hommes* was published in France in 1754; the English translation was published anonymously. [ED.]

Question, fit perhaps to be discussed by Slaves in the hearing of their Masters, but unbecoming free and reasonable Beings in quest of Truth.

What therefore is precisely the Subject of this Discourse? It is to point out, in the Progress of Things, that Moment, when, Right taking place of Violence, Nature became subject to Law; to display that Chain of surprising Events, in consequence of which the strong submitted to serve the weak, and the People to purchase imaginary Ease, at the Expence of real Happiness.

The Philosophers, who have examined the Foundations of Society, have, every one of them, perceived the Necessity of tracing it back to a state of Nature, but not one of them has ever arrived there. Some of them have not scrupled to attribute to Man in that State the Ideas of Justice and Injustice, without troubling their Heads to prove, that he really must have had such Ideas, or even that such Ideas were useful to him: others have spoken of the natural Right of every Man to keep what belongs to him, without letting us know what they meant by the Word *belong;* others, without further Ceremony ascribing to the strongest an Authority over the weakest, have immediately struck out Government, without thinking of the Time requisite for Men to form any Notion of the Things signified by the Words Authority and Government. All of them, in fine, constantly harping Wants, Avidity, Oppression, Desires and Pride, have transferred to the state of Nature Ideas picked up in the bosom of Society. In speaking of Savages they described Citizens. Nay, few of our own Writers seem to have so much as doubted, that a State of Nature did once actually exist; tho' it plainly appears by Sacred History, that even the first Man, immediately furnished as he was by God himself with both Instructions and Precepts, never lived in that State, and that, if we give to the Books of Moses that Credit which every Christian Philosopher ought to give to them, we must deny that, even before the Deluge, such a State ever existed among Men, unless they fell into it by some extraordinary Event: a Paradox very difficult to maintain, and altogether impossible to prove.

Let us begin therefore, by laying aside Facts, for they do not affect the Question. The Researches, in which we may engage on this Occasion, are not to be taken for Historical Truths, but merely as hypothetical and conditional Reasonings, fitter to illustrate the Nature of Things, than to show their true Origin, like those Systems, which our Naturalists daily make of the Formation of the World. Religion commands us to believe, that Men, having been drawn by God himself out of a State of Nature, are unequal, because it is his Pleasure they should be so; but Religion does not forbid us to draw Conjectures solely from the Nature of Man, considered in itself, and from that of the Beings which surround him, concerning the Fate of Mankind, had they been left to themselves. This is then the Question I am to answer, the Question I propose to examine in the present Discourse. As

Mankind in general have an Interest in my subject, I shall endeavour to use a Language suitable to all Nations; or rather, forgetting the Circumstances of Time and Place in order to think of nothing but the Men I speak to, I shall suppose myself in the Lyceum of Athens, repeating the Lessons of my Masters before the Platos and the Xenocrateses of that famous Seat of Philosophy as my Judges, and in presence of the whole Human Species as my Audience.

O Man, whatever Country you may belong to, whatever your Opinions may be, attend to my Words; you shall hear your History such as I think I have read it, not in Books composed by those like you, for they are liars, but in the Book of Nature which never lies. All that I shall repeat after her, must be true, without any Intermixture of Falsehood, but where I may happen, without intending it, to introduce my own Conceits. The Times I am going to speak of, are very remote. How much you are changed from what you once was! 'Tis in a manner the Life of your Species that I am going to write, from the Qualities which you have received, and which your Education and your Habits could deprave, but could not destroy. There is, I am sensible, an Age at which every Individual of you would choose to stop; and you will look out for the Age at which, had you your wish, your Species had stopt. Uneasy at your present Condition for Reasons which threaten your unhappy Posterity with still greater Uneasyness, you will perhaps wish it were in your Power to go back; and this Sentiment ought to be considered, as the Panegyrick of your first Parents, the Condemnation of your Contemporaries, and a Source of Terror to all those, who may have the Misfortune of succeeding you.

Lyceum: the grove where Aristotle taught philosophy.
Xenocrateses: Xenocrates (d. 314 B.C.), Greek philosopher, was head of the Greek Academy after Plato, his teacher.

FROM *EMILIUS AND SOPHIA*

or A New System of Education [1]

Jean-Jacques Rousseau

FROM BOOK I

All things are good as their Creator made them, but every thing degenerates in the hands of man. By human art is our native soul compelled to
nourish exotic plants, and one tree to bear the fruits of another. Improving man makes a general confusion of elements, climates, and seasons: he
mutilates his dogs, his horses, and his slaves: he defaces, he confounds every
thing, as if he delighted in nothing but monsters and deformity. He is not
content with any thing in its natural state, not even with his own species.
His very offspring must be trained up for him, like a horse in the menage,
and be taught to grow, after his own fancy, like a tree in his garden.

Without this, indeed, in the present state of things, matters would be still
worse than they are, and mankind be civilized by halves. Should a man, in a
state of society, be given up, from the cradle, to his own notions and conduct,
he would certainly turn out the most prepostrous of human beings. The
influence of prejudice, authority, necessity, example, and of all those social
institutions in which we are immerged, would stifle in him the emotions of
nature, and substitute nothing in their place. His humanity would resemble
a shrub, growing by accident in the highway, which would soon be destroyed
by the casual injuries it must receive from the frequent passenger. [. . .] [2]

Plants are formed by culture, and men by education. If a man should
come into the world in full growth and vigour, his bulk and strength would
be useless, till he should have learnt how to exert them: they would be even
prejudicial to him, as they would prevent others from thinking it needful

---

English translation. Vol. 1. London: Becket, 1763.

menage: riding school.

[1] Rousseau's treatise, *Émile, ou l'education* (1762), is cast as a philosophical romance in
which the hero is raised away from society. Rousseau introduces Sophie (or Sophia) in
Book V to demonstrate his view of the proper education for women. [ED.]

[2] In the passage omitted here and in its lengthy accompanying footnote, Rousseau points
out that his primary audience is "the tender and provident mother" because the earliest
educational influence on the child is the mother; he justifies this view on the grounds
that men are not provided with breast milk, noting also that the influence of the father
is corrupting and detrimental to the child: "The ambition, avarice, insolence, and mistaken foresight of fathers, their negligence and cruel insensibility are an hundred times
more destructive to children than the blind fondness of mothers" (3). [ED.]

to lend him any assistance;[3] and thus, left to himself, he would perish before he had discovered the objects of his wants. We lament the state of infancy, without reflecting that the human race must have been extinct, had not man been first a child.[4]

We are born weak, we have need of help; we are born destitute of every thing, we stand in need of assistance; we are born stupid, we have need of understanding. All that we are not possessed of at our birth, and which we require when grown up, is bestowed upon us by education.

This education we receive from nature, from men, or from circumstances. The constitutional exertion of our organs and faculties is the education of nature: the uses we are taught to make of that exertion, constitute the education given us by men; and in the acquisitions made by our own experience, on the objects that surround us, consists our education from circumstances.

We are formed, therefore, by three kinds of masters. The pupil, in whom the effects of their different lessons are contradictory, is badly educated, and can never be consistent with himself. He, in whom they are perfectly consonant, and always tend to the same point, hath only attained the end of a complete education. His life and actions demonstrate this, and that he alone is well brought up.

Of these three different kinds of education, that of nature depends not on ourselves; and but in a certain degree that of circumstances: the third, which belongs to men, is that only we have in our power: and even of this we are masters only in imagination; for who can flatter himself he will be able entirely to govern the discourse and actions of those who are about a child?

No sooner, then, doth education become an art, or profession, than it is almost impossible it should succeed, as the concurrent circumstances necessary to its success are not to be depended on. All that can be done, with our utmost solicitude, is to approach as near as possible the end we aim at, attributing it to good fortune if it be attained.

---

those who are about a child: those who are responsible for the care of a child.

[3] "For, being in external appearance like themselves, ignorant of speech as well as destitute of those ideas it might express, he would be incapable to make them understand the need in which he stood of their assistance; nor would any thing in his appearance suggest it to the spectator." [Rousseau's note.]

[4] In his preface, Rousseau clarifies this point: "We are not sufficiently acquainted with a state of infancy: the farther we proceed on our present mistaken ideas, the farther we wander from the point. Even the most sagacious instructors apply themselves to those things which man is required to know, without considering what it is children are capacitated to learn. They are always expecting the *man* in the *child,* without reflecting what he is before he can be a man" (xiii–xiv, italics in original). [Ed.]

If it be asked, what is this end? it may be answered, that of nature, which has been already proved. For, since the concurrence of three kinds of education is necessary to its perfection, it is by that one, which is entirely independent of us, we must regulate the two others. But perhaps this word, Nature, may appear vague and equivocal; let us therefore endeavour to give it a precise and determinate meaning.

Nature, it has been said, is only habit. But to what purpose is this said? Are there not habits, which are contracted only upon compulsion, and which can never suppress the tendency of nature? Such is, for example, the habitual growth of plants, restrained from pursuing their vertical direction. Take off the restraint, and it is true, they preserve the inclination they have been compelled to take: but, you will find, the rise of the sap has not on that account changed its primitive direction; if the plant continues to vegetate, its future growth being still upwards.

It is the same with the inclinations and dispositions of mankind. While we remain in exactly the same situation in which they were acquired, we may retain even the most unnatural habits; but as soon as circumstances change, the force of habit ceases, and that of nature exerts itself. Education itself is certainly nothing but habit: but are there not persons in whom the impressions they received in education are effaced? Are there not others again, that retain them? Whence arises this difference? If it be pretended that by nature is only meant habits conformable to nature, the position itself is unmeaning and absurd.

We are born capable of sensibility, and from our birth are variously affected by the different objects that surround us. We no sooner acquire, if I may so express myself, a consciousness of our sensations, than we are disposed to avoid or pursue, the objects producing them, in proportion as they are at first sight agreeable or displeasing: We next learn to approve or dislike them, according to the convenient or inconvenient relation that subsists between ourselves and such objects; and lastly, according to the judgment we form of their consistency with those ideas, which reason gives us of happiness or perfection. These dispositions extend and confirm themselves, in proportion as we become more susceptible and enlightened: but, subject to the restraint of custom, they are more or less diversified by our opinions. Before they have taken this tincture of habit, they are what I call the dispositions of our nature.

It is to these original dispositions, therefore, we should on every occasion recur: this might also be effected, if our three kinds of education were merely different: but what can be done, when they are directly opposite, and totally contradictory? when, instead of educating a man for himself, he must be educated for others? Their concurrent action is here destroyed; reduced to the dilemma of acting in opposition to nature, or to the institutions of society, we must chuse either to form the man or the citizen; for to do both at once is impossible.

FROM BOOK II

Nature requires children to be children before they are men. By endeavouring to pervert this order, we produce forward fruits that have neither maturity nor taste, and will not fail soon to wither and corrupt. Hence it is we have so many young professors and old children. Childhood hath its manner of seeing, perceiving, and thinking, peculiar to itself; nor is there any thing more absurd than our being anxious to substitute our own in its stead. I would as soon require an infant to be five foot high, as a boy to have that judgment at ten years of age. In fact, of what use would reason be to him at that age? Reason is given us as a check upon our power; a child has no need of such restraint.

SONNET I

Charlotte Smith[1]

The partial Muse has, from my earliest hours,
   Smil'd on the rugged path I'm doom'd to tread,
And still with sportive hand has snatch'd wild flowers,
   To weave fantastic garlands[2] for my head:
5 But far, far happier is the lot of those
   Who never learn'd her dear delusive art,
Which, while it decks the head with many a rose,
   Reserves the thorn—to fester in the heart.
For still she bids soft Pity's melting eye
10 Stream o'er the ills she knows not to remove,

From *Elegiac Sonnets and Other Essays*. 2nd ed. London: Dodsley, 1784.

forward: early in the season.

[1] Smith (1749–1806), poet and novelist, revived the sonnet form, much maligned at the time, with the popularity of her *Elegiac Sonnets,* which went through nine editions by 1800. [ED.]

[2] See Gertrude's description, in *Hamlet,* of the mad Ophelia's drowning and possible suicide:

> There is a willow grows askaunt the brook,
> That shows his hoary leaves in the glassy stream,
> Therewith fantastic garlands did she make
> Of crow-flowers, nettles, daisies, and long purples
> That liberal shepherds give a grosser name,
> But our cull-cold maids do dead men's fingers call them. (5.1.166–71) [ED.]

Points every pang, and deepens every sigh
   Of mourning friendship, or unhappy love.
Ah! then, how dear the Muse's favours cost,
If those paint sorrow best who feel it most![3]

SONNET II

WRITTEN AT THE CLOSE OF SPRING

Charlotte Smith

The garlands fade that Spring so lately wove,
   Each simple flower which she had nursed in dew,
Anemonies,[1] that spangled every grove,
   The primrose wan, and hare-bell mildly blue.
5 No more shall violets linger in the dell,
   Or purple orchis variegate the plain,
Till spring again shall call forth every bell,
   And dress with humid hands her wreaths again. —
      Ah! poor Humanity! so frail, so fair,
10   Are the fond visions of thy early day,
      Till tyrant Passion, and corrosive Care,
         Bid all thy fairy colours fade away!
Another May new buds and flowers shall bring;
Ah! why has happiness no second spring?

SONNET IV

TO THE MOON

Charlotte Smith

Queen of the silver bow, by thy pale beam,
   Alone and pensive, I delight to stray,
And watch thy shadow trembling in the stream,
   Or mark the floating clouds that cross thy way.
5 And, while I gaze, thy mild and placid light

---

[3]Compare Alexander Pope, *Eloisa to Abelard* (1717), lines 365–66. [ED.]

From *Elegiac Sonnets and Other Essays*. 2nd ed. London: Dodsley, 1784.

orchis: orchids.

[1]"Anemony Nemeroso, the wood anemony." [Smith's note.]

From *Elegiac Sonnets and Other Essays*. 2nd ed. London: Dodsley, 1784.

Sheds a soft calm upon my troubled breast;
And oft I think, fair planet of the night,
   That in thy orb the wretched may have rest:
The sufferers of the earth perhaps may go,
10   Released by death, to thy benignant sphere,
And the sad children of despair and woe
   Forget, in thee, their cup of sorrow here.
Oh! that I soon may reach thy world serene,
Poor wearied pilgrim—in this toiling scene!

FROM *THE TASK*

A Poem in Six Books
William Cowper[1]

FROM BOOK III

I was a stricken deer that left the herd
Long since; with many an arrow deep infixt
110 My panting side was charged when I withdrew
To seek a tranquil death in distant shades.
There was I found by one who had himself
Been hurt by th' archers. In his side he bore
And in his hands and feet the cruel fears.
115 With gentle force soliciting the darts
He drew them forth, and heal'd and bade me live.
Since then, with few associates, in remote
And silent woods I wander, far from those
My former partners of the peopled scene,
120 With few associates, and not wishing more.
Here much I ruminate, as much I may,
With other views of men and manners now
Than once, and others of a life to come.
I see that all are wand'rers, gone astray
125 Each in his own delusions; they are lost
In chace of fancied happiness, still wooed
And never won. Dream after dream ensues,

London: Johnson, 1785.

[1] Throughout most of his adult life, Cowper (1731–1800) suffered from chronic depression, a condition that in 1763 led him to attempt suicide on two separate occasions. In part, he wrote *The Task* in order to counteract this depression. [ED.]

And still they dream that they shall still succeed,
And still are disappointed; rings the world
130 With the vain stir. I sum up half mankind,
And add two-thirds of the remainder half,
And find the total of their hopes and fears
Dreams, empty dreams. The million flit as gay
As if created only like the fly
135 That spreads his motley wings in th' eye of noon
To sport their season and be seen no more.
The rest are sober dreamers, grave and wise,
And pregnant with discov'ries new and rare.

FROM BOOK IV

Just when our drawing-rooms begin to blaze
With lights by clear reflection multiplied
From many a mirrour, in which he of Gath
270 Goliath, might have seen his giant bulk
Whole without stooping, tow'ring crest and all,
My pleasures too begin. But me perhaps
The glowing hearth may satisfy awhile
With faint illumination that uplifts
275 The shadow to the ceiling, there by fits
Dancing uncouthly to the quiv'ring flame.
Not undelightful is an hour to me
So spent in parlour twilight; such a gloom
Suits well the thoughtful or unthinking mind,
280 The mind contemplative, with some new theme
Pregnant, or indisposed alike to all.
Laugh ye, who boast your more mercurial pow'rs
That never feel a stupor, know no pause
Nor need one. I am conscious, and confess
285 Fearless, a soul that does not always think.
Me oft has fancy ludicrous and wild
Sooth'd with a waking dream of houses, tow'rs,
Trees, churches, and strange visages express'd
In the red cinders, while with poring eye

---

motley: many-colored.
Goliath: giant Philistine warrior from the city of Gath, whom David kills with a sling-shot (I Samuel 17.1–51).

290 I gazed, myself creating what I saw.
    Nor less amused have I quiescent watch'd
    The sooty films that play upon the bars
    Pendulous, and foreboding in the view
    Of superstition prophesying still
295 Though still deceived, some stranger's near approach.[2]
    'Tis thus the understanding takes repose
    In indolent vacuity of thought,
    And sleeps and is refresh'd. Meanwhile the face
    Conceals the mood lethargic with a mask
300 Of deep deliberation, as the man
    Were task'd to his full strength, absorb'd and lost.
    Thus oft reclin'd at ease, I lose an hour
    At evening, till at length the freezing blast
    That sweeps the bolted shutter, summons home
305 The recollected powers, and snapping short
    The glassy threads with which the fancy weaves
    Her brittle toys, restores me to myself.
    How calm is my recess, and how the frost
    Raging abroad, and the rough wind, endear
310 The silence and the warmth enjoy'd within.
    I saw the woods and fields at close of day
    A variegated show; the meadows green
    Though faded, and the lands where lately waved
    The golden harvest, of a mellow brown,
315 Upturn'd so lately by the forceful share.
    I saw far off the weedy fallows smile
    With verdure not unprofitable, grazed
    By flocks fast feeding and selecting each
    His fav'rite herb; while all the leafless groves
320 That skirt th' horizon wore a sable hue,
    Scarce noticed in the kindred dusk of eve.
    To-morrow brings a change, a total change!

---

quiescent: still, inactive.
share: plowshare, the cutting part of a plow.
fallows: plowed land that has not been planted.

[2] These "sooty films" that appear on fireplace grates were commonly called "strangers" and, according to folklore, thought to foretell the appearance of some unexpected visitor. This passage clearly influenced Coleridge's use of the "stranger" legend in "Frost at Midnight" (233–34). [ED.]

Which even now, though silently perform'd
And slowly, and by most unfelt, the face
325 Of universal nature undergoes.
Fast falls a fleecy show'r. The downy flakes
Descending and with never-ceasing lapse
Softly alighting upon all below,
Assimilate all objects. Earth receives
330 Gladly the thick'ning mantle, and the green
And tender blade that fear'd the chilling blast,
Escapes unhurt beneath so warm a veil.

In such a world, so thorny, and where none
Finds happiness unblighted, or if found,
335 Without some thistly sorrow at its side,
It seems the part of wisdom, and no sin
Against the law of love, to measure lots
With less distinguish'd than ourselves, that thus
We may with patience bear our mod'rate ills,
340 And sympathize with others, suffering more.
Ill fares the trav'ller now, and he that stalks
In pond'rous boots beside his reeking team.
The wain goes heavily, impeded sore
By congregated loads adhering close
345 To the clogg'd wheels; and in its sluggish pace
Noiseless, appears a moving hill of snow.
The toiling steeds expand the nostril wide,
While ev'ry breath by respiration strong
Forced downward, is consolidated soon
350 Upon their jutting chests. He, form'd to bear
The pelting brunt of the tempestuous night,
With half-shut eyes and pucker'd cheeks, and teeth
Presented bare against the storm, plods on.
One hand secures his hat, save when with both
355 He brandishes his pliant length of whip,
Resounding oft, and never heard in vain.
Oh happy! and in my account, denied
That sensibility of pain with which
Refinement is endued, thrice happy thou.

---

reeking: breathing heavily.
wain: farmer's wagon.

360 Thy frame robust and hardy, feels indeed
   The piercing cold, but feels it unimpair'd.[3]

TO SENSIBILITY

Helen Maria Williams[1]

In *Sensibility*'s lov'd praise
   I tune my trembling reed;
And seek to deck her shrine with bays,
   On which my heart must bleed!

5 No cold exemption from her pain
   I ever wish'd to know;
Cheer'd with her transport, I sustain
   Without complaint her woe.

Above whate'er content can give,
10   Above the charm of ease,
The restless hopes, and fears that live
   With her, have power to please.

Where but for her, were Friendship's power
   To heal the wounded heart,
15 To shorten sorrow's ling'ring hour,
   And bid its gloom depart?

'Tis she that lights the melting eye
   With looks and anguish dear;
She knows the price of ev'ry sigh,
20   The value of a tear.

She prompts the tender marks of love
   Which words can scarce express;
The heart alone their force can prove,
   And feel how much they bless.

From *Poems*. Vol. 1. London: Cadell, 1786.

[3] Compare Cowper's sympathetic description of this poor traveler with that in Wordsworth's "Old Man Travelling" (105). [ED.]

[1] Williams (1762–1827), a successful poet and novelist, became associated with the moderate Girondists in Paris, where she lived from 1790 until her death. During the French Revolution, her *Letters from France* (1790–96), published in London, became a chief source of information on the events occurring across the Channel. [ED.]

25 Of every finer bliss the source!
    'Tis she on love bestows
The softer grace, the boundless force
    Confiding passion knows;

When to another, the fond breast
30   Each thought for ever gives;
When on another, leans for rest,
    And in another lives!

Quick, as the trembling metal flies,
    When heat or cold impels,
35 Her anxious heart to joy can rise,
    Or sink where anguish dwells!

Yet tho' her soul must griefs sustain
    Which she alone, can know;
And feel that keener sense of pain
40   Which sharpens every woe;

Tho' she the mourner's grief to calm,
    Still shares each pang they feel,
And, like the tree distilling balm,
    Bleeds, others wounds to heal;

45 While she, whose bosom fondly true,
    Has never wish'd to range;
One alter'd look will trembling view,
    And scarce can bear the change;

Tho' she, if death the bands should tear,
50   She vainly thought secure;
Thro' life must languish in despair
    That never hopes a cure;

Tho' wounded by some vulgar mind,
    Unconscious of the deed,
55 Who never seeks those wounds to bind
    But wonders why they bleed; —

She oft will heave a secret sigh,
    Will shed a lonely tear,

---

trembling metal: mercury in a thermometer.

O'er feelings nature wrought so high,
60   And gave on terms so dear;

Yet who would hard Indifference choose,
    Whose breast no tears can steep?[2]
Who, for her apathy, would lose
    The sacred power to weep?

65 Tho' in a thousand objects, pain,
    And pleasure tremble nigh,
Those objects strive to reach, in vain,
    The circle of her eye.

Cold, as the fabled god appears
70   To the poor suppliant's grief,[3]
Who bathes the marbled form in tears,
    And vainly hopes relief.

Ah Greville! why the gifts refuse
    To souls like thine allied?
75 No more thy nature seem to lose
    No more thy softness hide.

No more invoke the playful sprite
    To chill, with magic spell,
The tender feelings of delight,
80   And anguish sung so well;

That envied ease thy heart would prove
    Were sure too dearly bought
With friendship, sympathy, and love,
    And every finer thought.

---

[2] Williams here refers to Frances Greville's poem "A Prayer for Indifference" (1756), which asks for indifference as a relief from the intense pangs afforded by refined sensibility. See McGann's *Poetics of Sensibility* (50–54). [ED.]

[3] The "poor suppliant" is Niobe, the daughter of Tantalus, who bore seven sons and seven daughters to her husband, Amphion. Because of this good fortune, she boasted that she was more blest with children than Leto, the mother of Apollo and Artemis. This of course angered the goddess, who ordered her son and daughter to kill all of Niobe's children. In her grief, Niobe prayed for mercy to Zeus, who turned her into a stone from which tears continued to flow. [ED.]

SONNET ON SEEING MISS HELEN MARIA WILLIAMS
WEEP AT A TALE OF DISTRESS

William Wordsworth[1]

She wept.—Life's purple tide began to flow
In languid streams through every thrilling vein;
Dim were my swimming eyes—my pulse beat slow,
And my full heart was swell'd to dear delicious pain.
5   Life left my loaded heart, and closing eye;
A sigh recall'd the wanderer to my breast;
Dear was the pause of life, and dear the sigh
That call'd the wanderer home, and home to rest.
That tear proclaims——in thee each virtue dwells,
10 And bright will shine in misery's midnight hour;
As the soft star of dewy evening tells
What radiant fires were drown'd by day's malignant pow'r,
That only wait the darkness of the night
To chear the wand'ring wretch with hospitable light.

SONNET XLIV
WRITTEN IN THE CHURCH YARD
AT MIDDLETON IN SUSSEX

Charlotte Smith

Press'd by the Moon, mute arbitress of tides,
    While the loud equinox its power combines,
    The sea no more its swelling surge confines,
But o'er the shrinking land sublimely rides.
5   The wild blast, rising from the Western cave,
    Drives the huge billows from their heaving bed;

European Magazine 12 (March 1787).

[1] Wordsworth's first published poem, this sonnet was signed "Axiologus," which in Greek literally means "Wordsworth." Wordsworth is responding to a passage from Williams's poem *Peru* (1784), imagining the poet's response; Wordsworth would not actually meet Williams until 1820, during a visit to Paris. [ED.]

From *Elegiac Sonnets*. 5th ed. London: Cadell, 1789.

Tears from their grassy tombs the village dead,[1]
And breaks the silent sabbath of the grave!
With shells and sea-weed mingled, on the shore
10   Lo! their bones whiten in the frequent wave;
     But vain to them the winds and waters rave;
They hear the warring elements no more:
While I am doom'd—by life's long storm opprest,
To gaze with envy, on their gloomy rest.

TO ANNA MATILDA

Della Crusca [Robert Merry]

    And have I strove in vain to move
Thy Heart, fair Phantom of my Love?
And cou'dst thou think 'twas my design,
Calmly to list thy Notes Divine,
5   That I responsive Lays might send,
To gain a cold Platonic Friend?
Far other hopes thy Verse inspir'd,
And all my Breast with Passion fir'd.
For Fancy to my mind had given
10   Thy form, as of the forms of Heaven——
Had bath'd thy lips with vermil dew;
Had touch'd thy cheek with Morning's hue!
And down thy neck had sweetly roll'd
Luxuriant locks of mazy gold.[1]
15   Yes, I had hopes, at last to press,
And lure thee to the chaste caress;
Catch from thy breath the quiv'ring sigh,

---

[1] "Middleton is a village on the margin of the sea in Sussex, containing only two or three houses. There were formerly several acres of ground between its small church and the sea; which now, by its continual encroachments, approaches within a few feet of this half ruined and humble edifice. The wall, which once surrounded the church yard, is entirely swept away, many of the graves broken up, and the remains of bodies interred washed into the sea: whence human bones are found among the sand and shingles on the shore." [Smith's note.]

The British Album. 3rd ed. Vol. 1. London: Bell, 1790.

vermil: vermillion, a bright red or scarlet.

[1] Lines 13–14 ("And down [. . .] mazy gold") resemble the description of Eve in *Paradise Lost* 4.304–07. Milton, however, specifically uses the adjective *mazy* to characterize the folds of the "Serpent sleeping" in 9.161. [ED.]

And meet the *murder of thine eye.*[2]
Ah! when I deem'd such joys at hand,
20 Remorseless comes the stern command,
Nor calls my wand'ring footsteps home,
But far, and farther bids me roam;
And then thy Vestal Notes dispense
The meed of Cold Indifference![3]
25 Curs'd Pow'r! that to myself unknown,
Still turns the heart I love, to stone!
Dwells with the Fair whom most I prize,
And scorns my tears, and mocks my sighs.

Yes, Anna! I will hasten forth
30 To the bleak regions of the North,
Where Erickson, immortal Lord![4]
Pour'd on the Dane his vengeful sword;
Or where wide o'er the barb'rous plain,
Fierce Rurick[5] held his ancient reign.
35 Then once more will I trace the Rhine,
And mark the Rhone's swift billows shine;
Once more on Virgil's tomb[6] I'll muse,
And Laura's[7] gemm'd with evening dews;
Once more Rome's *Via Sacra* tread,
40 And ponder on the mighty dead.
More Eastward then direct my way,
To thirsty Egypt's desarts stray,
Fix in wonder, to behold
The Pyramids renown'd of old;
45 Fallen near one of which, I ween,
The Hieroglyphic Sphinx is seen!

Vestal: chaste, pure.
Via Sacra: sacred way.
ween: think.

[2] Compare Alexander Pope, *The Rape of the Lock* (1714) 5.145. [ED.]
[3] In a series of poetic exchanges, Della Crusca scolds Anna Matilda for her "Ode to Indifference," an imitation of Frances Greville's poem of the same title, and for her affected abhorrence of sensibility. [ED.]
[4] A reference to Leif Eriksson (fl. 1000), Norwegian sailor, believed to be the first to discover North America. [ED.]
[5] Rurik (d. 879), Scandinavian prince, progenitor of the Russian monarchy. [ED.]
[6] Virgil is buried in Naples. [ED.]
[7] Petrarch's beloved Laura was believed to be Laure de Noves of Avignon (1308–48), buried in Vaucluse, Petrarch's home, in southeast France. [ED.]

The Lion Virgin Sphinx[8] is seen!
What time the rich Nile overflows.
Then will I sail th' Egean tide,
50 Or seek Scamander's tuneful side;[9]
Wander the sacred groves among,
Where Homer wak'd th' immortal Song;
Traverse the Nemaean Wood,
Mark the spot where Sparta stood;
55 Or at humbled Athens see
Its still remaining Majesty! ——
Yet to *Indiff'rence* e'er a foe,
May Beauty other joys bestow;
Her rapt'rous Science I'll pursue,
60 The Science Newton never knew.[10]

Now blows the wind with melancholy force,
And o'er the Baltic points my weary course;
Loud shout the Mariners, the white sails swell——
Anna Matilda! fare thee, fare thee well!
65 Farewel whoe'er thou art, and may'st thou find
Health and repose, and lasting peace of mind;
Still pour the various Verse with fancy clear,
To thrill the pulse, and charm th' attentive ear;
Nor may relentless Care thy days destroy,
70 But ev'ry hope be ripen'd into joy!

And O! farewel to distant Britain's shore,
Which I perhaps am doom'd to see no more;
Where Valour, Wisdom, Taste, and Virtue dwell,
Dear Land of Liberty, alas! farewel! ——
75 Yet oft, e'en there, by wild Ambition tost,
The Soul's best season settles in a frost.
Yet even there, desponding, late I knew,

Nemaean: in classical mythology, an epithet for Zeus, who had a temple in Nemea, a valley in southeast Greece.

[8] "The overflowing of the Nile always happens while the Sun is in Leo and Virgo." [Merry's note.]
[9] Scamander (or Xanthos) is the ancient name for the Menderes, a river in northwest Turkey that flows into the Aegean Sea and is mentioned in stories of the Trojan War. [ED.]
[10] In his *Philosophiae naturalis principia mathematica* (1687), Sir Isaac Newton (1642–1727) presents an empirical system of deducing scientific laws from observing the physical world. [ED.]

That Friendship, foreign-form'd, is rarely true.
For they, whom most I lov'd, whose kindness sav'd
80 My shatter'd Bark, when erst the tempest rav'd:
At Home, e'en with the common herd could fly,
Gaze on the wounded Deer, and pass him by!
Nor yet can Pride subdue my pangs severe,
But Scorn itself evap'rates in a Tear.

85   Thou too, delusive Maid! whose winning charms
Seduc'd me first from slow Wealth's beckning arms;
Sweet Poetry! my earliest, falsest Friend,
Here shall my frantic adoration end.
Take back the simple Flute thy treach'ry gave,
90 Take back, and plunge it in Oblivion's wave,
So shall its sad Notes hence no malice raise —
The Bard unknown — forgotten be the Lays. —
But should, with Anna's Verse, his hapless Rhime,
In future meet th'impartial eye of Time,
95 Say, that thy wretched victim long endur'd,
Pains which are seldom left, and never cur'd!
Say 'midst the lassitude of hopes o'erthrown,
Matilda's strain could comfort him alone.
Yet was the veil mysterious ne'er remov'd,
100 From *him th' admiring* and from *her the lov'd,*
And no kind intercourse the Song repaid,
But each to each remain'd — a *Shadow and a Shade.*

EFFUSION XXXV

COMPOSED AUGUST 20TH, 1795,

AT CLEVEDON, SOMERSETSHIRE

Samuel Taylor Coleridge

My pensive Sara![1] thy soft cheek reclin'd
Thus on mine arm, most soothing sweet it is

Bark: boat.

From *Poems on Various Subjects, by S. T. Coleridge, Late of Jesus College, Cambridge.* London: Robinsons; Bristol: Cottle, 1796. (A revised version of this poem appears as "The Eolian Harp" in Coleridge's 1828 *Poetical Works.*)

[1] Sara Fricker (1770–1845), to whom Coleridge became engaged the month he composed this poem. [ED.]

To sit beside our cot, our cot o'er grown
With white-flower'd Jasmin, and the broad-leav'd Myrtle,
5 (Meet emblems they of Innocence and Love!)
And watch the clouds, that late were rich with light,
Slow-sad'ning round, and mark the star of eve
Serenely brilliant (such should Wisdom be)
Shine opposite! How exquisite the scents
10 Snatch'd from yon bean-field! and the world *so* hush'd!
The stilly murmur of the distant Sea
Tells us of Silence. And that simplest Lute
Plac'd length-ways in the clasping casement, hark!
How by the desultory breeze caress'd,
15 Like some coy Maid half-yielding to her Lover,
It pours such sweet upbraidings, as must needs
Tempt to repeat the wrong! And now its strings
Boldlier swept, the long sequacious notes
Over delicious surges sink and rise,
20 Such a soft floating witchery of sound
As twilight Elfins make, when they at eve
Voyage on gentle gales from Faery Land,
Where Melodies round honey-dropping flowers
Footless and wild, like birds of Paradise,[2]
25 Nor pause nor perch, hov'ring on untam'd wing.[3]
And thus, my Love! as on the midway slope
Of yonder hill I stretch my limbs at noon
Whilst thro' my half-clos'd eyelids I behold
The sunbeams dance, like diamonds, on the main,

---

cot: cottage.
Lute: aeolian harp, a stringed instrument placed in a window and tuned so that, when the wind blows through it, it plays music.
sequacious: successive.

[2] Birds of Paradise were reputed to have no feet and to spend all of their time in the air. [ED.]
[3] For the 1828 version, Coleridge here added the following lines:

O! the one Life within us and abroad,
Which meets all motion and becomes its soul,
A light in sound, a sound-like power in light,
Rhythm in all thought, and joyance every where —
Methinks, it should have been impossible
Not to love all things in a world so fill'd;
Where the breeze warbles, and the mute still air
Is Music slumbering on her instrument. (*Poetical Works* 101) [ED.]

30 And tranquil muse upon tranquillity;
    Full many a thought uncall'd and undetain'd,
    And many idle flitting phantasies,
    Traverse my indolent and passive brain
    As wild and various, as the random gales
35 That swell and flutter on this subject Lute!
    And what if all of animated nature
    Be but organic Harps diversly fram'd,
    That tremble into thought, as o'er them sweeps,
    Plastic and vast, one intellectual Breeze,
40 At once the Soul of each, and God of all?
    But thy more serious eye a mild reproof
    Darts, O beloved Woman! nor such thoughts
    Dim and unhallow'd dost thou not reject,
    And biddest me walk humbly with my God.

45 Meek daughter in the Family of Christ,
    Well hast thou said and holily disprais'd
    These shapings of the unregenerate mind,
    Bubbles that glitter as they rise and break
    On vain Philosophy's aye-babbling spring.
50 For never guiltless may I speak of Him
    Th' Incomprehensible! save when with awe
    I praise him, and with Faith that inly⁴ *feels*;
    Who with his saving mercies healed me,
    A sinful and most miserable man
55 Wilder'd and dark, and gave me to possess
    Peace, and this Cot, and Thee, heart-honor'd Maid!

Plastic: having the power to shape or mold.

⁴"L'athée n'est point à mes yeux un faux esprit; je puis vivre avec lui aussi bien et mieux qu'avec le dévot, car il raisonne davantage, mais il lui manque un sens, et mon ame ne se fond point entièrement avec la sienne: il est froid au spectacle le plus ravissant, et il cherche un syllogisme lorsque je rends une action de grace. 'Appel a l'impartiale postérié, par la Citoyenne Roland,' troisieme partie, p. 67." ["The atheist, to my eyes, is no false spirit; I can live with him as well as and better than I can with the devotee, for he has greater reason; but he lacks sensibility, and my soul does not harmonize with his at all: he is cold to the most ravishing spectacle, and he searches for a syllogism where I offer a prayer. *Appeal to Impartial Posterity*, third part, p. 67." Coleridge's note.]
　　Coleridge quotes from Manon Roland de La Platière (1754–93), a Girondin intellectual accused of having Royalist sympathies and guillotined during the Reign of Terror. Joseph Johnson, who published Coleridge's *Fears in Solitude,* published her *Appeal* in 1795. [Ed.]

SONNET LXX
ON BEING CAUTIONED AGAINST WALKING
ON AN HEADLAND OVERLOOKING THE SEA
BECAUSE IT WAS FREQUENTED BY A LUNATIC
Charlotte Smith

Is there a solitary wretch who hies
    To the tall cliff, with starting pace or slow,
And, measuring, views with wild and hollow eyes
    Its distance from the waves that chide below;
5 Who, as the sea-born gale with frequent sighs
    Chills his cold bed upon the mountain turf,
With hoarse, half-utter'd lamentation, lies
    Murmuring responses to the dashing surf?
In moody sadness, on the giddy brink,
10 I see him more with envy than with fear;
He has no nice felicities that shrink
    From giant horrors; wildly wandering here,
He seems (uncursed with reason) not to know
The depth or the duration of his woe.

FROM *A SERIES OF PLAYS*
Joanna Baillie[1]

FROM THE INTRODUCTORY DISCOURSE

From that strong sympathy which most creatures, but the human above all, feel for others of their kind, nothing has become so much an object of man's curiosity as man himself. We are all conscious of this within ourselves, and so constantly do we meet with it in others, that like every circumstance of continually repeated occurrence, it thereby escapes observation. Every person, who is not deficient in intellect, is more or less occupied in tracing,

---

From *Elegiac Sonnets and Other Poems*. Vol. 2. London: Cadell, 1797.

A Series of Plays: In Which It Is Attempted to Delineate the Stronger Passions of the Mind. Each Passion Being the Subject of a Tragedy and a Comedy. London: Cadell, 1798.

[1]Baillie (1762–1851), at the time, was considered by many the greatest playwright in the English language since Shakespeare; her most successful play, *De Montfort*, published in the 1798 volume, was produced in 1800. See her ballad "The Storm-Beat Maid" (248–53). [ED.]

amongst the individuals he converses with, the varieties of understanding and temper which constitute the characters of men; and receives great pleasure from every stroke of nature that points out to him those varieties. This is, much more than we are aware of, the occupation of children, and of grown people also, whose penetration is but lightly esteemed; and that conversation which degenerates with them into trivial and mischievous tattling, takes its rise not unfrequently from the same source that supplies the rich vein of the satirist and the wit. That eagerness so universally shewn for the conversation of the latter, plainly enough indicates how many people have been occupied in the same way with themselves. Let any one, in a large company, do or say what is strongly expressive of his peculiar character, or of some passion or humour of the moment, and it will be detected by almost every person present. How often may we see a very stupid countenance animated with a smile, when the learned and the wise have betrayed some native feature of their own minds! and how often will this be the case when they have supposed it to be concealed under a very sufficient disguise! From this constant employment of their minds, most people, I believe, without being conscious of it, have stored up in idea the greater part of those strong marked varieties of human character, which may be said to divide it into classes; and in one of those classes they involuntarily place every new person they become acquainted with.

I will readily allow that the dress and the manners of men, rather than their characters and disposition are the subjects of our common conversation, and seem chiefly to occupy the multitude. But let it be remembered that it is much easier to express our observations upon these. It is easier to communicate to another how a man wears his wig and cane, what kind of house he inhabits, and what kind of table he keeps, that from what slight traits in his words and actions we have been led to conceive certain impressions of his character: traits that will often escape the memory, when the opinions that were founded upon them remain. Besides, in communicating our ideas of the characters of others, we are often called upon to support them with more experience of reasoning than we can well afford, but our observations on the dress and appearance of men, seldom involve us in such difficulties. For these, and other reasons too tedious to mention, the generality of people appear to us more trifling than they are: and I may venture to say that, but for this sympathetick curiosity towards others of our kind, which is so strongly implanted within us, the attention we pay to the dress and the manners of men would dwindle into an employment as insipid, as examining the varieties of plants and minerals, is to one who understands not natural history.

In our ordinary intercourse with society, this sympathetick propensity of our minds is exercised upon men, under the common occurrences of life, in which we have often observed them. Here vanity and weakness put themselves forward to view, more conspicuously than the virtues: here men encounter those smaller trials, from which they are not apt to come off victorious; and here, consequently, that which is marked with the whimsical and ludicrous will strike us more forcibly, and make the strongest impression on our memory. To this sympathetick propensity of our minds, so exercised, the genuine and pure comick of every composition, whether drama, fable, story, or satire is addressed.

If man is an object of so much attention to man, engaged in the ordinary occurrences of life, how much more does he excite his curiosity and interest when placed in extraordinary situations of difficulty and distress? It cannot be any pleasure we receive from the sufferings of a fellow-creature which attracts such multitudes of people to a publick execution, though it is the horrour we conceive for such a spectacle that keeps so many more away. To see a human being bearing himself up under such circumstances, or struggling with the terrible apprehensions which such a situation impresses, must be the powerful incentive, which makes us press forward to behold what we shrink from, and wait with trembling expectation for what we dread.[2] For though few at such a spectacle can get near enough to distinguish the expression of face, or the minuter parts of a criminal's behaviour, yet from a considerable distance will they eagerly mark whether he steps firmly; whether the motions of his body denote agitation or calmness; and if the wind does but ruffle his garment, they will, even from that change upon the outline of his distant figure, read some expression connected with his dreadful situation. Though there is a greater proportion of people in whom this strong curiosity will be overcome by other dispositions and motives; though there are many more who will stay away from such a sight than will go to it; yet there are very few who will not be eager to converse with a person who has beheld it; and to learn, very minutely, every circumstance connected with it, except the very act itself of inflicting death. To lift up the roof of his dungeon, like *Diable boiteux*, and look upon a criminal the night before he suffers, in his still hours of privacy, when all that disguise, which respect for the opinion of others, the strong motive by which even the lowest

---

Diable boiteux: a toy similar to a jack-in-the-box.

[2] "In confirmation of this opinion I may venture to say, that of the very great numbers who go to see a publick execution, there are but very few who would not run away from, and avoid it, if they happened to meet with it unexpectedly. We find people stopping to look at a procession, or any other uncommon sight, they may have fallen in with accidentally, but almost never an execution. No one goes there who has not made up his mind for the occasion; which would not be the case, if any natural level of cruelty were the cause of such assemblies." [Baillie's note.]

and wickedest of men still continue to be moved, would present an object to the mind of every person, not withheld from it by great timidity of character, more powerfully attractive than almost any other. [...]

Amongst the many trials to which the human mind is subjected, that of holding intercourse, real or imaginary, with the world of spirits: of finding itself alone with a being terrifick and awful, whose nature and power are unknown, has been justly considered as one of the most severe. The workings of nature in this situation, we all know, have ever been the object of our most eager enquiry. No man wishes to see the Ghost himself, which would certainly procure him the best information on the subject, but every man wishes to see one who believes that he sees it, in all the agitation and wildness of that species of terror. To gratify this curiosity how many people have dressed up hideous apparitions to frighten the timid and superstitious! and have done it at the risk of destroying their happiness or understanding for ever. For the instances of intellect being destroyed by this kind of trial are more numerous, perhaps, in proportion to the few who have undergone it than by any other.

How sensible are we of this strong propensity within us, when we behold any person under the pressure of great and uncommon calamity! Delicacy and respect for the afflicted will, indeed, make us turn ourselves aside from observing him, and cast down our eyes in his presence; but the first glance we direct to him will involuntarily be one of the keenest observation, how hastily soever it may be checked; and often will a returning look of enquiry mix itself by stealth with our sympathy and reserve.

But it is not in situations of difficulty and distress alone, that man becomes the object of this sympathetick curiosity; he is no less so when the evil he contends with arises in his own breast, and no outward circumstance connected with him either awakens our attention or our pity. What human creature is there, who can behold a being like himself under which the violent agitation of those passions which all have, in some degree, experienced, without feeling himself most powerfully excited by the sight? I say, all have experienced; for the bravest man on earth knows what fear is as well as the coward; and will not refuse to be interested for one under the dominion of this passion, provided there be nothing in the circumstances attending it to create contempt. Anger is a passion that attracts less sympathy than any other, yet the unpleasing and distorted features of an angry man will be more eagerly gazed upon, by those who are no wise concerned with his fury of the objects of it, than the most amiable placid countenance in the world. Every eye is directed to him; every voice hushed to silence in his presence; even children will leave off their gambols as he passes, and gaze after him more eagerly than the gaudiest equipage.[3] The wild tossings of despair; the gnashing of hatred and revenge; the yearnings of affection, and the softened mien of love; all that language of the agitated soul, which every age and nation understands, is never addressed to the dull nor inattentive.

It is not merely under the violent agitations of passion, that man so rouses and interests us; even the smallest indications of an unquiet mind, the restless eye, the muttering lip, the half- checked exclamation, and the hasty start, will set our attention as anxiously upon the watch, as the first distant flashes of a gathering storm. When some great explosion of passion bursts forth, and some consequent catastrophe happens, if we are at all acquainted with the unhappy perpetrator, how minutely will we endeavor to remember every circumstance of his past behaviour! and with what avidity will we seize upon every recollected word or gesture, that is in the smallest degree indicative of the supposed state of his mind, at the time when they took place. If we are not acquainted with him, how eagerly will we listen to similar recollections from another! Let us understand, from observation or report, that any person harbours in his breast, concealed from the world's eye, some powerful rankling passion of what kind soever it may be, we will observe every word, every motion, every look, even the distant gait of such a man, with a constancy and attention bestowed upon no other. Nay, should we meet him unexpectedly on our way, a feeling will pass across our minds as though we found ourselves in the neighbourhood of some secret and fearful thing. If invisible, would we not follow him into his lonely haunts, into his closet, into the midnight silence of his chamber? There is, perhaps, no employment which the human mind will with so much avidity pursue, as the discovery of concealed passion, as the tracing the varieties and progress of a perturbed soul.

It is to this sympathetick curiosity of our nature, exercised upon mankind in great and trying occasions, and under the influence of the stronger passions, when the grand, the generous, the terrible attract our attention far more than the base and depraved, that the high and powerfully tragick, or every composition, is addressed.[4]

This propensity is universal. Children begin to shew it very early; it enters into many of their amusements, and that part of them too, for which they shew the keenest relish. It tempts them many times, as well as the mature in years, to be guilty of tricks, vexations, and cruelty; yet God Almighty has implanted it within us, as well as all our other propensities and passions, for wise and good purposes. It is our best and most powerful instructor. From it we are taught the proprieties and decencies of ordinary life, and are prepared for distressing and difficult situations. In examining others we

---

[3] Compare with Adam Smith's discussion of anger, pages 134–35.
[4] Baillie echoes Aristotle's *On the Art of Poetry*, in which he asserts that tragedy affects the audience through a sympathetic catharsis of fear or pity. [Ed.]

know ourselves. With limbs untorn, with head unsmitten, with senses un-impaired by despair, we know what we ourselves might have been on the rack, on the scaffold, and in the most afflicting circumstances of distress. Unless when accompanied with passions of the dark and malevolent kind, we cannot well exercise this disposition without becoming more just, more merciful, more compassionate; and as the dark and malevolent passions are not the predominant inmates of the human breast, it hath produced more deeds—O many more! of kindness than of cruelty. It holds up for our ex-ample a standard of excellence, which, without its assistance, our inward consciousness of what is right and becoming might never have dictated. It teaches us, also, to respect ourselves, and our kind; for it is a poor mind, indeed, that from this employment of its faculties, learns not to dwell upon the noble view of human nature rather than the mean. [. . .]

In proportion as moral writers of every class have exercised within them-selves this sympathetick propensity of our nature, and have attended to it in others, their works have been interesting and instructive. They have struck the imagination more forcibly, convinced the understanding more clearly, and more lastingly impressed the memory. If unseasoned with any reference to this, the fairy bowers of the poet, with all his gay images of delight, will be admired and forgotten; the important relations of the historian, and even the reasonings of the philosopher will make a less permanent impression. [. . .]

Our desire to know what men are in the closet as well as the field, by the blazing hearth, and at the social board, as well as in the council and the throne, is very imperfectly gratified by real history; romance writers, there-fore, stepped boldly forth to supply the deficiency; and tale writers, and novel writers, of many descriptions, followed after. If they have not been very skillful in their delineations of nature; if they have represented men and women speaking and acting as men and women never did speak or act; if they have caricatured both our virtues and our vices; if they have given us such pure and unmixed, or such heterogeneous combinations of character as real life never presented, let it not be imputed to the dulness of man in discerning what is genuinely natural in himself. There are many inclina-tions belonging to us, besides this great master-propensity of which I am treating. Our love of the grand, the beautiful, the novel, and above all of the marvellous, is very strong; and if we are richly fed with what we have a good relish for, we may be weaned to forget our native and favourite aliment. Yet we can never so far forget it, but that we will cling to, and acknowledge it again, whenever it is presented before us. In a work abounding with the marvellous and unnatural, if the author had any how stumbled upon an unsophisticated genuine stroke of nature, we will immediately perceive and be delighted with it, though we are foolish enough to admire at the same time, all the nonsense with which it is surrounded. After all the wonderful

incidents, dark mysteries, and secrets revealed, which eventful novel so lib-
erally presents to us; after the beautiful fairy ground, and even the grand
and sublime scenes of nature with which descriptive novel so often en-
chants us; those works which most strongly characterize human nature in
the middling and lower classes of society, where it is to be discovered by
stronger and more unequivocal marks, will ever be the most popular. For
though great pains have been taken in our higher sentimental novels to interest us in the delicacies, embarrassments, and artificial distresses of the
more refined part of society, they have never been able to cope in the publick opinion with these. The one is a dressed and beautiful pleasure-ground,
in which we are enchanted for a while, amongst the delicate and unknown
plants of artificial cultivation; the other is a rough forest of our native land;
the oak, the elm, the hazle, and the bramble are there; and amidst the endless varieties of its paths we can wander for ever. Into whatever scenes the
novelist may conduct us, what objects soever he may present to our view,
still is our attention most sensibly awake to every touch faithful to nature;
still are we upon the watch for every thing that speaks to us of ourselves.

The fair field of what is properly called poetry, is enriched with so many
beauties, that in it we are often tempted to forget what we really are, and
what kind of being we belong to. Who in the enchanted regions of simile,
metaphor, allegory and description, can remember the plain order of
things in this every-day world? From heroes whose majestick forms rise like
a lofty tower, whose eyes are lightening, whose arms are irresistible, whose
course is like the storms of heaven, bold and exalted sentiments we will
readily receive; and will not examine them very accurately by that rule of
nature which our own breast prescribes to us. A shepherd whose sheep, with
fleeces of the purest snow, browze the flowery herbage of the most beautiful vallies; whose flute is ever melodious, and whose shepherdess is ever
crowned with roses; whose every care is love, will not be called very strictly
to account for the loftiness and refinement of his thoughts. The fair Nymph,
who sighs out her sorrows to the conscious and compassionate wilds;
whose eyes gleam like the bright drops of heaven; whose loose tresses stream
to the breeze, may say what she pleases with impunity. I will venture, however, to say that, amidst all this decoration and ornament, all this loftiness
and refinement, let one simple trait of the human heart, one expression of
passion genuine and true to nature, be introduced, and it will stand forth
alone in the boldness of reality, whilst the false and unnatural around it,
fades away upon every side, like the rising exhalations of the morning. With
admiration, and often with enthusiasm we proceed on our way through the
grand and the beautiful images, raised to our imagination by the lofty Epic
muse; but what even here are those things that strike upon the heart; that
we feel and remember? Neither the descriptions of war, the sound of the

trumpet, the clanging of arms, the combat of heroes, nor the death of the mighty, will interest our minds like the fall of the feeble stranger, who simply expresses the anguish of his soul, at the thoughts of that far-distant home which he must never return to again, and closes his eyes amongst the ignoble and forgotten; like the timid stripling goaded by the shame of reproach, who urges his trembling steps to the fight, and falls like a tender flower before the first blast of winter. How often will some simple picture of this kind be all that remains upon our minds of the terrifick and magnificent battle, whose description we have read with admiration! How comes it that we relish so much the episodes of an heroick poem? It cannot merely be that we are pleased with a resting-place, where we enjoy the variety of contrast; for were the poem of the simple and familiar kind, and an episode after the heroick style introduced into it, ninety readers out of an hundred would pass over it altogether. Is it not that we meet such a story, so situated, with a kind of sympathetick good will, as in passing through a country of castles and of palaces, we should pop unawares upon some humble cottage, resembling the dwellings of our own native land, and gaze upon it with affection. The highest pleasures we receive from poetry, as well as from the real objects which surround us in the world, are derived from the sympathetick interest we all take in beings like ourselves; and I will even venture to say, that were the grandest scenes which can enter into the imagination of man, presented to our view, and all reference to man completely shut out from our thoughts, the objects that composed it would convey to our minds little better than dry ideas of magnitude, colour, and form; and the remembrance of them would rest upon our minds like the measurement and distances of the planets. [. . .]

POLITICAL BACKGROUNDS

To William Hazlitt, Wordsworth's poetry was the perfect embodiment of its historical moment. In *The Spirit of the Age*, he writes:

> It is one of the innovations of the time. It partakes of, and is carried along with, the revolutionary movement of our age: the political changes of the day were the model on which he formed and conducted his poetical experiments. His Muse (it cannot be denied, and without this we cannot explain its character at all) is a levelling one. It proceeds on a principle of equality, and strives to reduce all things to the same standard. It is distinguished by a proud humility. It relies upon its own resources, and disdains external show and relief. It takes the commonest events and objects, as a test to prove that nature is always interesting from its inherent truth and beauty, without any of the ornaments of dress or pomp of circumstances to set it off. Hence the unaccountable mixture of seeming simplicity and real abstruseness of the *Lyrical Ballads*. (*Lectures* 253)

Although several recent critics have disputed Hazlitt's claim and argued that by 1798 Wordsworth and Coleridge were becoming increasingly less interested in politics, his basic point is difficult to deny: *Lyrical Ballads* responds not only to the poetic theory and practice of its time but also to the ideas and events of the French Revolution.[1] After all, Wordsworth's stated goal of adapting "the language of conversation of the middle and lower classes [. . .] for the purposes of poetic pleasure" is on one level a democratic gesture, an attempt to do for poetry what the Revolution had done for politics.

Therefore, because we believe that it is virtually impossible to understand what Wordsworth and Coleridge are doing in *Lyrical Ballads* without

---

[1] See, for example, Jerome McGann's remark in *The Romantic Ideology: A Critical Investigation* that "between 1793 and 1798 Wordsworth lost the world merely to gain his immortal soul" (88).

knowing something about late-eighteenth-century politics, we have included a sampling of English political writing from the 1790s. We have not, however, attempted to distill in a few pages the entire debate over the French Revolution. That — as Marilyn Butler's fine anthology, *Burke, Paine, Godwin, and the Revolution Controversy,* demonstrates — is a subject so rich and complex that it can only be covered in a book fully devoted to that topic. Instead, we briefly summarize the major positions in this debate and then focus on a related issue at the heart of *Lyrical Ballads:* the place of the poor in British society.

In the immediate aftermath of the storming of the Bastille — the Parisian prison that came to symbolize the oppression of the "Old Order" — the French Revolution served as a kind of political Rorschach test for English observers. To the more liberal and reform-minded, it represented the logical culmination of the movement toward greater political freedom and economic opportunity that began with the English Revolution of 1688 (the so-called Glorious Revolution) and continued with the recently completed American Revolution. For instance, in his 1789 speech commemorating the one hundredth anniversary of the Glorious Revolution, the Reverend Richard Price hails the French Revolution as the dawning of a new age that will deliver Europe from centuries of tyranny:

> Be encouraged, all ye friends of freedom and writers in its defence! The times are auspicious. Your labours have not been in vain. Behold kingdoms, admonished by you, starting from sleep, breaking their fetters, and claiming justice from their oppressors! Behold, the light you have struck out, after setting America free, reflected to France and there kindled into a blaze that lays despotism in ashes and warms and illuminates Europe! Tremble all ye oppressors of the world! Take warning all ye supporters of slavish governments and slavish hierarchies! Call no more (absurdly and wickedly) reformation, innovation. You cannot now hold the world in darkness. Struggle no longer against increasing light and liberality. Restore to mankind their rights, and consent to the correction of abuses, before they and you are destroyed together. (195–96)

Thus, as Price's apocalyptic rhetoric implies, the French Revolution seemed to many English observers to anticipate Armageddon and the new millennium of peace promised in Revelation.

To the more cautious and conservative, however, the Revolution looked far less auspicious. The most prominent spokesperson for this position was Edmund Burke, who began his career as a Whig reformer but whose name ultimately became synonymous with British conservatism. Far from seeing the Revolution as a continuation of the quite laudable earlier revolutions, he viewed it as an event without precedent or justification:

All circumstances taken together, the French Revolution is the most astonishing that has hitherto happened in the world. The most wonderful things are brought about in many instances by means the most absurd and ridiculous; in the most ridiculous modes; and apparently, by the most contemptible instruments. Every thing seems out of nature in this strange chaos of levity and ferocity, and of all sorts of crimes jumbled together with all sorts of follies. (*Reflections* 92)

Moreover, Burke feared that what was happening in France would have consequences far beyond its own borders and would ultimately threaten the very fabric of European culture:

Nothing is more certain, than that our manners, our civilization, and all the good things which are connected with manners, and with civilization, have, in this European world of ours, depended for ages upon two principles; and were indeed the result of both combined; I mean the spirit of a gentleman, and the spirit of religion. The nobility and the clergy, the one by profession, the other by patronage, kept learning in existence, even in the midst of arms and confusions, and whilst governments were rather in their causes than formed. Learning paid back what it received to nobility and to priesthood; and paid with usury, by enlarging their ideas, and by furnishing their minds. Happy if they had all continued to know their indissoluble union, and their proper place. Happy if learning, not debauched by ambition, had been satisfied to continue the instructor, and not aspired to be the master! Along with its natural protectors and guardians, learning will be cast into the mire, and trodden under the hoofs of a swinish multitude. (*Reflections* 173)

Burke's response is conservative in its assertion of the authority of class status, established through bloodlines, and of the primacy of religion, established through tradition.

As is obvious from the mere title of a radical magazine such as Thomas Spence's *Pig's Meat, or Lessons for the Swinish Multitudes,* this sort of hyperbolic prose made Burke an easy target for ridicule from the left; and, at first, it was easy for his critics to dismiss his position as sentimental and old-fashioned. Mary Wollstonecraft, in the first published rebuttal to Burke's *Reflections,* derisively refers to his "reverence for the rust of antiquity" and his "gothic notions of beauty." Thomas Paine, in his extraordinarily popular and influential *The Rights of Man,* compares Burke to Don Quixote:

In the rhapsody of his imagination, he has discovered a world of windmills, and his sorrows are, that there are no Quixotes to attack them. But if the age of the aristocracy, like that of chivalry, should fall, (and they had originally some connection), Mr. Burke, the trumpeter of the order, may continue his parody to the end, and finish with exclaiming, *"Othello's occupation's gone!"* (50)[2]

With these allusions to Cervantes and Shakespeare, Paine sardonically undermines Burke's credibility, depicting him as a ludicrous figure dominated by his raging emotions and overheated imagination.

But beginning with the September Massacres in 1792 — the execution of 1,200 to 1,400 of the king's supporters — a series of events took place in France that made Burke's "horrid paintings" look almost prophetic. By October 1793 Louis XVI and Marie Antoinette had been executed; France had invaded its eastern neighbors and had declared war on England; the people of Paris (not of France) had given control of the government to the radical Jacobins; and the Reign of Terror was in full swing, leading to the guillotining of thousands of "counterrevolutionaries" including many former leaders of the Revolution. As a result, support for the French Revolution even among its most ardent English sympathizers began to dwindle with each passing year. For example, before the September Massacres, Whig leader Charles Fox called the Revolution "the greatest event [. . .] that ever happened in the world"; afterward, he was unqualified in his denunciation: "There is not, in my opinion, a shadow of an excuse for this horrid massacre, not even the possibility of extenuating it in the smallest degree" (qtd. in Trevelyan 411).

To those young English men and women who had been inspired by the initial phase of the French Revolution, this violent turn of events was utterly dispiriting. Having believed that the Revolution was a millennial event that would abolish despotism and liberate humanity, they now had to witness the French Republic seemingly lapse into chaos and bloodshed and betray its initial principles. Still, dismayed as they were at the course of the Revolution, liberals could by no means support the conservative English government's attempts to return France to monarchical rule or its repressive efforts to stifle sedition and political reform at home. Therefore, when William Godwin's *Enquiry Concerning the Principles of Political Justice* appeared in 1793, it seemed to many a revelation. Unlike Paine's *The Rights of Man,* which openly called for "a complete and universal revolution," Godwin's book methodically expounded an egalitarian and humanitarian vision of society that explicitly rejected revolutionary violence. Instead, he outlined a progressive view of history, predicting that the human race would gradually become more and more enlightened until it one day approached moral "perfection." For Godwin then, far from furthering humanity's advancement, revolutions were likely to disrupt or even retard this

---

[2] *Othello* 3.3.357.

forward progress because—as the events in France had so clearly demon-strated—such abrupt transformations inevitably and impetuously push so-ciety ahead of "the still and quiet progress of reason" (Godwin 1.204). As he put it in the 1798 edition of *Political Justice,* "They propose to give us some-thing for which we are not prepared, and which we cannot effectually use. They suspend the wholesome advancement of science, and confound the process of nature and reason" (274).[3]

But, as the 1790s wore on, readers—including many one-time disciples of Godwin—increasingly questioned the basic tenets of his philosophy. Thomas Malthus's *An Essay on the Principle of Population* (1798), for ex-ample, grows out of his skepticism of Godwin's belief in the "perfectibility of man" and dismisses *Political Justice* as a piece of "enchanting" but thor-oughly impractical utopianism. Others, such as Coleridge and Words-worth, reacted against the hyperrationality of Godwin's philosophy—his so-called moral arithmetic. After lavishly praising Godwin in his 1794 son-net, Coleridge by 1795 denounces Godwinism as "that proud Philosophy, which affects to inculcate Philanthropy while it denounces every home-born feeling, by which it is produced and nurtured."[4] Similarly, Words-worth was at first so taken with *Political Justice* that he began making plans to publish a political journal called the *Philanthropist* in order to promote Godwinian ideas, but by 1796 he was already distancing himself from God-win. In a letter to his friend and one-time fellow Godwinite, William Mat-thews, he condemns the preface to the second edition as "a piece of bar-barous writing" (*Early Years* 170). Looking back on this period in his autobiographical poem, *The Prelude,* he describes the devastating effect that this type of rationalistic philosophy had upon his state of mind:

> Thus, I fared,
> Dragging all passions, notions, shapes of faith,
> Like culprits to the bar; suspiciously
> Calling the mind to establish in plain day
> Her titles and her honours; now believing,
> Now disbelieving, endlessly perplexed
> With impulse, motive, right and wrong, the ground
> Of moral obligation—what the rule
> And what the sanction—till, demanding proof,
> And seeking it in every thing, I lost
> All feeling of conviction, and, in fine,

---

[3] Our selections from *Political Justice* come from the 1793 edition, published just as the Jacobin government was taking shape; the later editions were revised to reflect Godwin's sensitivity to subsequent events.

[4] See *Conciones ad Populum* (218).

Sick, wearied out with contrarieties,
Yielded up moral questions in despair.[5] (1805, 10.889–901)

Finding moral philosophy something of a will-o-the-wisp, Wordsworth describes how the confluence of violence in France with the increasing economic crisis at home precipitated for him an emotional crisis.

Another passage from *The Prelude* vividly illustrates how thoroughly intertwined the revolutionary cause and the issue of poverty were in the minds of many during this time. Pointing to "a hunger-bitten girl / Who crept along fitting her languid self / Unto a heifer's motion," an officer in the French Revolutionary Army, Michel Beaupuy, says simply: "'Tis against that / Which we are fighting" (9.511–13, 519–20). Wordsworth's response is equally revealing:

> I with him believed
> Devoutly that a spirit was abroad
> Which could not be withstood, that poverty,
> At least like this, would in a little time
> Be found no more. (9.520–24)

This same note of concern resounds throughout the English revolutionary debate—from Wollstonecraft's outrage at what she calls Burke's "contempt for the poor," to Paine's witty characterization of Burke's seeming aristocratic bias: "He pities the plumage, but forgets the dying bird," to Godwin's repeated emphasis on "philanthropy"—the moral imperative to benefit those who have less than yourself: "The true object that should be kept in view, is to extirpate all ideas of condescension and superiority, to oblige every man to feel, that the kindness he exerts is what he is bound to perform, and the assistance he asks what he has a right to claim" (1793, 2.801).

By the mid-1790s a series of bad harvests, high food prices, and bread riots in Coventry, Nottingham, and Sussex caused the plight of the poor to figure even more prominently in the English consciousness.[6] Although poor laws had been in force since the time of Queen Elizabeth, these policies were becoming increasingly outmoded. Designed for an almost entirely agrarian society, the existing poor laws relegated the responsibility for caring for the poor to individual parishes (the local ecclesiastical districts into which the country was divided), with each parish being required to provide work for its unemployed, technical education for its poor children, and relief for its "lame, impotent, old, blind, and such other among them

---

[5] Though Wordsworth does not mention Godwin by name here, both Stephen Gill (114) and Nicholas Roe (196) are confident that this passage refers to Godwin.
[6] The most comprehensive discussion of the English Poor Laws in the late eighteenth and early nineteenth centuries is J. R. Poynter's *Society and Pauperism*.

being poor and not able to work." Unfortunately, because of the system's frequent mismanagement, these admirable goals were rarely achieved. Overseers of poor relief were largely untrained and unpaid for their services, resulting in widespread corruption and inflated costs to the general public. This corruption also led to abuses in the workhouses (euphemistically termed "houses of industry"), in which parishes confined those who could not support themselves. Although some of these institutions were well run and even profitable, they were detested by the poor themselves. As Frederick Morton Eden described the situation, "Many distressed families prefer the chance of starving among friends and neighbours in their own native village to the mortifying alternative of being well fed, well lodged, and well clothed in a Poor-house, the motley receptacle of idiots and vagrants" (150). Other commentators painted an even bleaker picture:

> The want of room and the bad management of that which they possess, occasion similar inconveniences; the cloathes, or rather the covering of the inhabitants; the improprieties arising from the two sexes of all ages, and dispositions, long kept together; the ignorance and filth the children are brought up in [. . .] give propriety to the opinion and expression that a parish workhouse is a parish bugbear, to frighten distress from applying for relief. (Ruggles 285)

Given its parochial structure, the traditional system of poor relief was hard pressed to accommodate the massive social changes occurring in the second half of the eighteenth century. The beginning of the Industrial Revolution brought about not only a growing migration to the city but also the decline of many cottage, or domestic, industries—such as handloom weaving—by which many rural inhabitants had traditionally supported themselves. Nearly as dramatic were the effects of enclosure: the series of parliamentary acts that enabled landowners to combine smaller tenant farms into much larger units and to fence off tracts of unused common land, which had traditionally been open to anyone who chose to cultivate it. As Raymond Cowherd explains, this practice did allow for a more efficient means of food production, but it also deprived the rural poor of a traditional source of food and income:

> This improvement in agriculture deprived many laborers of the use of land. Some lost their garden plots; others lacked access to wasteland for fuel and game. Rural laborers, therefore, became dependent on daily wages for their subsistence; and increasingly there was a lack of employment during winter months. (xi)

To address these ever more pressing problems, numerous reforms were proposed and enacted in the second half of the eighteenth century. In 1782 Thomas Gilbert succeeded in getting legislation passed that authorized individual parishes to join together in order to manage their poor more efficiently and effectively. As a result, smaller parishes could now share a common workhouse, thus saving each parish the expense of constructing a separate building; and its requirement of an elected board of commissioners to supervise the parish overseers also helped curb their formerly almost unchecked power.

Still, many abuses and inequities persisted, and, with the bad harvests and grain shortages of the mid-1790s, the emphasis in the poor law debate shifted to increasing laborers' wages. Several communities adopted policies (commonly referred to as the "Speenhamland system") that required parishes to adjust the wages of rural workers in accordance with the price of food. The most ambitious proposal in this direction, however, was Samuel Whitbread's 1796 bill to set a minimum wage for farm laborers in order, as he put it, "to enable the husbandman, who dedicated his days to incessant toil, to feed, to clothe, and to lodge his family with some degree of comfort" (*Parliamentary History* 703). Although Whig leader Charles Fox gave this bill only lukewarm support, preferring voluntary rather than compulsory measures to raise wages, Whitbread's proposal did reflect the characteristic Whig attitude to the poor. As opposed to the more paternalistic attitudes of the conservative Tory party that emphasized the need for charitable donations from the rich, Fox and other leading Whigs stressed the independence of the working poor:

> It is, indeed, a melancholy and alarming fact, that the great majority of the people of England—an enormous and dreadful majority—are no longer in a situation in which they can boast that they live by the produce of their labour; and that it does regularly happen, during the pressure of every inclement season, that the industrious poor are obliged to depend for subsistence on the supplies afforded by the charity of the rich. I agree in opinion with those who think that the price of labour ought to be advanced, and the great majority of the people of England, freed from a precarious and degrading dependence. (*Parliamentary History* 24)

But the conservative Tories thought otherwise, and the result was a debate that foreshadowed the American argument today over aid to the poor, including welfare reform.

Largely due to the efforts of William Pitt—the British prime minister from 1783 to 1801—Whitbread's bill was ultimately rejected; in December 1796 Pitt put forward his own proposal for Poor Law reform. Beginning with the premise that the existing laws "had contributed to fetter the circulation of labour, and to substitute a system of abuses, in room of the evils they were meant to redress," Pitt argued that it was necessary to overhaul the system substantially (*Parliamentary History* 707). Among his proposals were that relief, whenever possible, should be given in the form of employment, workhouses for adults and "Schools of Industry" for children should be encouraged, and an annual report should be made to Parliament in order to oversee how poor relief was being conducted. Due to the divisive nature of the issue and the complicated nature of his proposals, Pitt's bill also failed; consequently—as the vogue for Humanitarian poetry throughout the 1790s attests—the problems of rural and urban poor continued to be at the forefront of British politics as the eighteenth century came to a close.

In the selections for this subsection, we provide a variety of perspectives on this issue. The excerpt from Hannah More's *Thoughts on the Importance of the Manners of the Great to General Society* illustrates the influence of Evangelical Christianity on the public debate over the poor. Although generally very conservative in her politics (a staunch Tory throughout her life and later an outspoken critic of the French Revolution), More was deeply concerned about the status of the lower classes and dedicated to improving their moral characters and living conditions. In this relatively early tract, she asserts that the upper classes, because of their eminent place in society, have a responsibility to provide both charity and positive role models for the poor. The selections from both Joseph Townsend and Edmund Burke also stress the importance of private charity, but their views represent what is often called the "natural law" approach toward poor relief—a school of thought that culminates with Thomas Malthus's *Essay on the Principle of Population* (1798). Arguing that poverty was the inevitable result of fundamental capitalistic principles, these thinkers considered most attempts at poor relief to be either utopian or counterproductive; Townsend, for example, baldly states, "To promote industry and economy, it is necessary that the relief given to the poor be limited and precarious" (35). Writing nearly a decade later during a time of food shortages, economic recession, and popular unrest, Burke provides a sweeping denunciation of the various proposals to offer additional poor relief or to raise workers' wages. In line with his unapologetically *laissez-faire* approach, he asserts that, even in hard times, "to provide for us in our necessities is not in the power of government." Jeremy Bentham's 1797 "Outline of a Work Entitled 'Pauper Management Improved'" in many ways represents the antithesis of the natural law position since, rather than advocating the abolition of the Poor Laws, Bentham insists on the need for public assistance for the poor. He therefore proposes a wildly ambitious plan to construct a series of massive and highly supervised workhouses in which all those unable to support themselves would be confined, thereby doing away with the need for private charity (which he saw as necessarily capricious and unequally dispensed) and eliminating all "outdoor relief"—the relief given to supplement the income of the working poor. Still, despite Bentham's genuine desire to address the problems of the poor, his clinical and seemingly unfeeling approach may well have prompted Wordsworth to write "The Old Cumberland Beggar" as a rebuttal to his ideas.[7] Finally, we have provided a series of left-wing reactions to the problem of the poor: Mary Wollstonecraft's *A Vindication of the Rights of Men,* George Dyer's *The Complaints of the Poor People of England,* and John Thelwall's *Peripatetic.* In sharp contrast to Bentham's belief that the sight of the poor causes "feelings of disgust," these authors emphasize the humanity and dignity of the working classes. Unlike the natural law theorists who see poverty as inevitable and even necessary, they argue that it is often the result of oppressive institutions in British society designed to keep the poor "in their place."

FROM *A DISSERTATION ON THE POOR LAWS*
Joseph Townsend[1]

SECTION VII

It seems to be a law of nature, that the poor should be to a certain degree improvident, that there may always be some to fulfill the most servile, the most sordid, and the most ignoble offices in the community. The stock of human happiness is thereby much increased, whilst the more delicate are not only relieved from drudgery, and freed from those occasional employments which would make them miserable, but are left at liberty, without interruption, to pursue those callings which are suited to their various dispositions, and most useful to the state. As for the lowest of the poor, by custom they are reconciled to the meanest occupations, to the most laborious works, and to the most hazardous pursuits; whilst the hope of their reward makes them chearful in the midst of all their dangers and their toils. The fleets and armies of a state would soon be in want of soldiers and of sailors, if sobriety and diligence universally prevailed: for what is it but distress and poverty which can prevail upon the lower classes of the people to encounter all the horrors which await them on the tempestuous ocean, or in the field

---

London: Dilly, 1786. Originally published anonymously and signed simply, "By a Well Wisher to Mankind."

improvident: lacking in foresight.

[7]See Mark Koch, "Utilitarian and Reactionary Arguments for Almsgiving in Wordsworth's 'The Old Cumberland Beggar'" (20–24).

[1]Townsend (1739–1816) was a practicing physician, a widely respected geologist, and a Methodist minister, who served as the chaplain to the Duke of Atholl and the rector of Pewsey. [ED.]

of battle? Men who are easy in their circumstances are not among the foremost to engage in a seafaring or military life. There must be a degree of pressure, and that which is attended with the least violence will be the best. When hunger is either felt or feared, the desire of obtaining bread will quietly dispose the mind to undergo the greatest hardships, and will sweeten the severest labours. The peasant with a sickle in his hand is happier than the prince upon his throne.

Now a fixed, a certain, and constant provision for the poor weakens this spring; it increases their improvidence, but does not promote their chearful compliance with those demands, which the community is obliged to make on the most indigent of its members; it tends to destroy the harmony and beauty, the symmetry and order of that system, which God and nature have established in the world. The improvident among the poor have been advancing in their claims: they now begin to understand that they have a legal right to all. When this, which hitherto has been only felt, shall be clearly seen, and universally acknowledged, nothing will remain but to cast lots, who among the active and the virtuous shall perform the vilest offices for the indolent and vicious.

FROM SECTION XIV [2]

To relieve the poor by voluntary donations is not only most wise, politic, and just; is not only most agreeable both to reason and to revelation; but it is most effectual in preventing misery, and most excellent in itself, as cherishing, instead of rancour, malice, and contention, the opposite and most amiable affections of the human breast, pity, compassion, and benevolence in the rich, love, reverence, and gratitude in the poor. Nothing in nature can be more disgusting than a parish pay-table, attendant upon which, in the same objects of misery, are too often found combined, snuff, gin, rags, vermin, insolence, and abusive language; nor in nature can any thing be more beautiful than the mild complacency of benevolence, hastening to the humble cottage to relieve the wants of industry and virtue, to feed the hungry, to cloath the naked, and to sooth the sorrows of the widow with her tender orphans; nothing can be more pleasing, unless it be their sparkling eyes, their bursting tears, and their uplifted hands, the artless expressions of unfeigned gratitude for unexpected favours.[3] Such scenes will frequently

---

[2] In this concluding section of his tract, Townsend outlines his own plan for addressing the problems of the poor. His solution is essentially to reduce the amount of public assistance (by nine-tenths in space of nine years) and leave the support of the poor to a combination of their own efforts and the voluntary charity of the rich. [ED.]

[3] See "Simon Lee," lines 97–104. [ED.]

occur whenever men shall have power to dispose of their own property. When the poor are obliged to cultivate the friendship of the rich, the rich will never want inclination to relieve the distresses of the poor.

FROM *THOUGHTS ON THE IMPORTANCE OF THE MANNERS OF THE GREAT TO GENERAL SOCIETY*
Hannah More[1]

Nothing more benumbs the exertions of ardent youthful virtue, than the cruel sneer which worldly prudence bestows on active goodness; and the cool derision it expresses at the defeat of a benevolent scheme, of which malice, rather than penetration, had foreseen the failure. Alas! there is little need of any such discouragements. The world is a climate which too naturally chills a glowing generosity, and contracts an expanded heart. The zeal of the most sanguine is but too apt to cool, and the activity of the most diligent, to slacken of itself: and the disappointments which Benevolence encounters in the failure of her best concerted projects, and the frequent depravity of the most chosen objects of her bounty, would soon dry up the amplest streams of charity, were they not fed by the living fountain of religious principle.

I cannot dismiss this part of my subject without animadverting on the too prompt alacrity, even of worthy people to, disseminate, in public and general conversation, instances of their unsuccessful attempts to do good. I never hear a charity story begun to be related in mixed company, that I do not tremble for the catastrophe, lest it should exhibit some mortifying disappointment, which may deter the inexperienced from running any generous hazards, and excite harsh suspicions, at an age, when it is less dishonourable to meet with a few casual hurts, and transient injuries, than to

---

Philadelphia: Thomas Dobson, 1788.

sanguine: optimistic.
animadverting: speaking against.

[1] More (1745–1833) was an English playwright, poet, and eminent member of the Blue-stocking Circle, a group of learned women who hosted receptions for literary men and women. Beginning with the premise that "those, who filling the higher ranks in life, are naturally regarded as patterns, by which the manner of the rest of the world are to be fashioned," More designed this tract as a kind of conduct book for the aristocracy, instructing them in how they should behave, given their eminent place in society. This section, which focuses on the importance of charity, demonstrates both More's strongly Evangelical faith and her somewhat tempered view of sensibility as a "humane and exquisitely tender sentiment" that God implants within us as "a stimulus to remove the distresses of others," but which must be strengthened by Christian principle if it is to be anything more than an occasional or transient pang of sympathy. [ED.]

go cased in the cumbersome and impenetrable armor of distrust. The liberal should be particularly cautious how they furnish the avaricious with creditable pretences for saving their money, as all the instances of the mortifications of the humane are added to the armoury of the covetous man's arguments, and produced, as defensive weapons, upon every fresh attack on his heart or his purse.

But I am willing to hope that that uncharitableness which we so often meet with in persons of advanced years, is not always the effect of a heart naturally hard. Misanthropy is very often nothing but abused sensibility. Long habits of the world, and a melancholy conviction how little good he has been able to do in it, harden many a tender-hearted person. The milk of human kindness becomes soured by repeated acts of ingratitude. This commonly induces an indifference to the well-being of others, and a hopelessness of adding to the stock of human virtue and human happiness. This uncomfortable disease is very fond of spreading its own contagion; which is a cruelty to the health of young and uninfected virtue. —For this distemper, generated by a too sanguine disposition, and grown chronical from repeated disappointments, there is but one remedy, or rather one prevention: and this is a genuine principle of piety. He who is once convinced that he is to assist his fellow creatures, because it is the will of God, and one of the conditions of obtaining his favour, will soon get above all uneasiness when the consequence does not answer his expectation. He will soon become only anxious to do his duty, humbly committing events to higher hands. Disappointments will then only serve to refine his motives and purify his virtue. His charity will then become a sacrifice less unworthy of the altar on which it is offered. His affections will be more spiritualized, and his devotions more intense. Nothing short of such a courageous piety can preserve a heart hackneyed in the world from relaxed diligence, or criminal despair.

People in general are not aware of the mischief of judging of the rightness of any action by its prosperity, or the excellence of any institution by the abuse of it. We must never proportion our exertions to our success, but to our duty. If every laudable undertaking were to be dropped because it failed in some cases, or was abused in others, there would not be left an Alms-House, a Charity School, or an Hospital in the land. And if every right practice were to be discontinued because it had been found not to be successful in every instance, this false reasoning, pushed to the extreme, might at last be brought as an argument for shutting up our churches, and burning our bibles.

---

liberal: generous.
chronical: chronic; habitual.
Alms-house: poorhouse.
Hospital: charitable institution for the needy or infirm.

But if, on the other hand, there is a proud and arrogant discretion which ridicules, as Utopian and romantic, every generous project of the active and the liberal; so there is on the other, a sort of popular bounty which arrogates to itself the exclusive name of *feeling,* and rejects with disdain the influence of an higher principle. I am far from intending to depreciate this humane and exquisitely tender sentiment, which the beneficent Author of our nature gave us, as a stimulus to remove the distresses of others, in order to get rid of our own uneasiness. I would only observe, that where not strengthened by superior motives, it is a casual and precarious instrument of good, and ceases to operate, except in the immediate presence, and within the audible cry of misery. This sort of feeling forgets that any calamity exists which is out of its own sight; and though it would empty its purse for such an occasional object as rouses transient sensibility, yet it seldom makes any stated provision for miseries, which are not the less real because they do not obtrude upon the sight, and awaken the tenderness of immediate sympathy. This is a mechanical charity, which requires springs and wheels to set it a going; whereas real Christian charity does not wait to be acted upon by impressions and impulses.

FROM *A VINDICATION OF THE RIGHTS OF MEN*
Mary Wollstonecraft [1]

A LETTER TO THE RIGHT HONOURABLE EDUMUND BURKE

Sir,

[. . .] Almost every vice that has degraded our nature might be justified by shewing that it had been productive of *some* benefit to society: for it would be as difficult to point out positive evil as unallayed good, in this im-

---

A Vindication of the Rights of Men, in a Letter to the Right Honourable Edmund Burke; Occasioned by His Reflections on the Revolution in France. London: Johnson, 1790.

[1] Wollstonecraft (1759–97) was a political liberal and feminist philosopher. She married William Godwin (187–94) in 1797 and died in 1798 after giving birth to Mary Godwin, later Mary Shelley, the author of *Frankenstein.*

Despite his previous support for American independence, Edmund Burke (1729–97) argues in his *Reflections* (1790) for reform rather than revolution, rejecting the "rights of man" as dangerous to society and defending inherited status and property as part of the established order. The phrase "the rights of men/man" suggests democratic or republican sympathies. Wollstonecraft's tract was the first published response to Burke's *Reflections.* [ED.]

perfect state. What indeed would become of morals, if they had no other test than prescription? The manners of men may change without end; but, wherever reason receives the least cultivation—wherever men rise above brutes, morality must rest on the same base. And the more man discovers of the nature of his mind and body, the more clearly he is convinced, that to act according to the dictates of reason is to conform to the will of God. The test of honour may be arbitrary and fallacious, and, retiring into subterfuge, elude close enquiry; but true morality shuns not the day, nor shrinks from the ordeal of investigation. Most of the happy revolutions that have taken place in the world have happened when weak princes held the reins they could not manage; but are they, on that account, to be canonized as saints or demi-gods, and pushed forward to notice on the throne of ignorance? Pleasure wants a zest, if experience cannot compare it with pain; but who courts pain to heighten his pleasures? A transient view of society will further illustrate arguments that appear so obvious. I am almost ashamed to produce illustrations. How many children have been taught economy, and many other virtues, by the extravagant thoughtlessness of their parents; yet a good education is allowed to be an inestimable blessing. The tenderest mothers are often the most unhappy wives; but can the good that accrues from the private distress that produces a sober dignity of mind justify the inflictor? Right or wrong may be estimated according to the point of sight, and other adventitious circumstances; but, to discover its real nature, the enquiry must go deeper than the surface, and beyond the local consequences that confound good and evil together. But the rich and weak, a numerous train, will certainly applaud your system, and loudly celebrate your pious reverence for authority and establishments—they find it pleasanter to enjoy than to think; to justify oppression than correct abuses.— *The rights of men* is a grating sound that sets their teeth on edge; the impertinent enquiry of philosophic meddling innovation. If the poor are in distress, they will make some *benevolent* exertions to assist them; they will confer obligations, but not do justice. Benevolence is a very amiable specious quality; yet the aversion which men feel to accept a right as a favour, should rather be extolled as a vestige of native dignity, than stigmatized as the odious offspring of ingratitude. The poor consider the rich as their lawful prey; but we ought not too severely to animadvert on their ingratitude. When they receive an alms they are commonly grateful at the moment; but old habits quickly return, and cunning has ever been a substitute for force.

That both physical and moral evil were not only foreseen, but entered into the scheme of Providence, when this world was contemplated in the Divine mind, who can doubt, without robbing Omnipotence of a most exalted

---

animadvert: speak unfavorably.

attribute?[2] But the business of life of a good man should be to separate light from darkness; to diffuse happiness, whilst he submits to unavoidable misery. And a conviction that there is much unavoidable wretchedness, appointed by the grand Disposer of all events, should not slacken his exertions: the extent of what is possible can only be discerned by God. The justice of God may be vindicated[3] by a belief in a future state; but, only by believing that evil is educing good for the individual, and not for an imaginary whole. The happiness of the whole must arise from the happiness of the constituent parts, or the essence of justice is sacrificed to a supposed grand argument. And that may be good for the whole of a creature's existence, that disturbs the comfort of a small portion. The evil which an individual suffers for the good of the community is partial, it must be allowed, if the account is settled by death. — But the partial evil which it suffers, during one stage of existence, to render another stage more perfect, is strictly just.[4] The Father of all only can regulate the education of his children. To suppose that, during the whole or part of its existence, the happiness of any individual is sacrificed to promote the welfare of ten, or ten thousand, other beings — is impious. But to suppose that the happiness, or animal enjoyment, of one portion of existence is sacrificed to improve and ennoble the being itself, and render it capable of more perfect happiness, is not to reflect on either the goodness or wisdom of God.

It may be confidently asserted that no man chooses evil, because it is evil; he only mistakes it for happiness, the good he seeks. And the desire of rectifying these mistakes, is the noble ambition of an enlightened understanding, the impulse of feelings that Philosophy invigorates. To endeavour to make unhappy men resigned to their fate, is the tender endeavour of short-sighted benevolence, of transient yearnings of humanity; but to labour to increase human happiness by extirpating error is a masculine godlike affection. This remark may be carried still further. Men who possess uncommon sensibility, whose quick emotions shew how closely the eye and heart are connected, soon forget the most forcible sensations. Not being reflected on, nor tarrying long in the brain, the next sensations, of course, obliterated them. Memory, however, treasures up these proofs of native goodness; and the being who is not spurred on to any virtuous act, still thinks itself of consequence, and boasts of its feelings. Why? Because the sight of distress, or an affecting narrative, made its blood flow with more velocity, and the heart, literally speaking, beat with sympathetic emotion.

---

[2] Compare Alexander Pope, *An Essay on Man* 1.141–64. [ED.]
[3] Compare Milton, *Paradise Lost* 1.26 and Pope 1.16. [ED.]
[4] Compare Pope 1.281–94. [ED.]

We ought to beware of confounding mechanical instinctive sensations with emotions that reason deepens, and justly terms the feelings of humanity. This word discriminates the active exertions of virtue from the vague declamation of sensibility.

[. . .] But, among all your [Burke's] plausible arguments, and witty illustrations, your contempt for the poor always appears conspicuous, and rouses my indignation. The following paragraph in particular struck me, as breathing the most tyrannic spirit, and displaying the most factitious feelings. "Good order is the foundation of all good things. To be enabled to acquire it, the people, without being servile, must be tractable and obedient. The magistrate must have his reverence, the laws their authority. The body of the people must not find the principles of natural subordination by art rooted out of their minds. They *must* respect that property of which they *cannot* partake. *They must labour to obtain what by labour can be obtained; and when they find, as they commonly do, the success disproportioned to the endeavor, they must be taught their consolation in the final proportions of eternal justice.* Of this consolation, whoever deprives them, deadens their industry, and strikes at the root of all acquisition as of all conservation. He that does this, is the cruel oppressor, the merciless enemy, of the poor and wretched; at the same time that, by his wicked speculations, he exposes the fruits of successful industry, and the accumulations of fortune, (ah! there's the rub) to the plunder of the negligent, the disappointed, and the unprosperous."[5]

This is contemptible hard-hearted sophistry, in the specious form of humility, and submission to the will of Heaven. — It is, Sir, *possible* to render the poor happier in this world, without depriving them of the consolation which you gratuitously grant them in the next. They have a right to more comfort than they at present enjoy; and more comfort might be afforded them, without encroaching on the pleasures of the rich: not now waiting to enquire whether the rich have any right to exclusive pleasures. What do I say? — encroaching! No; if an intercourse were established between them, it would impart the only true pleasure that can be snatched in this land of shadows, this hard school of moral discipline.

I know, indeed, that there is often something disgusting in the distresses of poverty, at which the imagination revolts, and starts back to exercise itself in the more attractive Arcadia of fiction. The rich man builds a house, art and taste give it the highest finish. His gardens are planted, and the trees

---

Arcadia: region in Greece typically depicted in pastoral poetry as a rural paradise.

[5] The quotation is from Burke's *Reflections on the Revolution in France* (372); the parenthetical insertion is Wollstonecraft's, from *Hamlet* 3.1.65. [ED.]

grow to recreate the fancy of the planter, though the temperature of the climate may rather force him to avoid the dangerous damps they exhale, than seek the umbrageous retreat. Every thing on the estate is cherished but man; —yet, to contribute to the happiness of man, is the most sublime of all enjoyments. But if, instead of sweeping pleasure-grounds, obelisks, temples, and elegant cottages, as *objects* for the eye, the heart was allowed to beat true to nature, decent farms would be scattered over the estate, and plenty smile around. Instead of the poor being subject to the griping hand of an avaricious steward, they would be watched over with fatherly solicitude, by the man whose duty and pleasure it was to guard their happiness, and shield from rapacity the beings who exalted him, by the sweat of their brow, above his fellows.

I could almost imagine I see a man thus gathering blessings as he mounted the hill of life; or consolation, in those days when the spirits lag, and the tired heart finds no pleasure in them. It is not by squandering alms that the poor can be relieved, or improved—it is the fostering sun of kindness, the wisdom that finds them employments calculated to give them habits of virtue, that meliorates their condition. Love is only the fruit of love; condescension and authority may produce the obedience you applaud; but he has lost his heart of flesh who can see a fellow-creature humbled before him, and trembling at the frown of a being, whose heart is supplied by the same vital current, and whose pride ought to be checked by a consciousness of having the same infirmities.

What salutary dews might not be shed to refresh this thirsty land, if men were more *enlightened!* Smiles and premiums might encourage cleanliness, industry, and emulation. —A garden more inviting than Eden would then meet the eye, and springs of joy murmur on every side. The clergyman would superintend his own flock, the shepherd would then love the sheep he daily tended; the school might rear its decent head, and the buzzing tribe, let loose to play, impart a portion of their vivacious spirits to the heart that longed to open their minds, and lead them to taste the pleasures of men. Domestic pleasure, the civilizing relations of husband, brother, and father, would soften labour, and render life contented.

Returning once from a despotic country to a part of England well cultivated, but not very picturesque—with what delight did I not observe the poor man's garden!—The homely palings and twining woodbine, with all the rustic contrivances of simple, unlettered taste, was a sight which relieved the eye that had wandered indignant from the stately palace to the

---

umbrageous: shady.
despotic country: Portugal, which Wollstonecraft visited in 1785.

pestiferous hovel, and turned from the awful contrast into itself to mourn the fate of man, and curse the arts of civilization!

Why cannot large estates be divided into small farms? These dwellings would indeed grace our land. Why are huge forests still allowed to stretch out with idle pomp and all the indolence of Eastern grandeur? Why do the brown wastes meet the traveller's view, when men want to work? But commons cannot be enclosed without *acts of parliament* to increase the property of the rich![6] Why might not the industrious peasant be allowed to steal a farm from the heath? This sight I have seen; — the cow that supported the children grazed near the hut, and the cheerful poultry were fed by the chubby babes, who breathed a bracing air, far from the diseases and the vices of cities. Domination blasts all these prospects; virtue can only flourish amongst equals, and the man who submits to a fellow-creature, because it promotes his worldly interest, and he who relieves only because it is his duty to lay up a treasure in heaven, are much on a par, for both are radically degraded by the habits of their life.

In this great city, that proudly rears its head, and boasts of its population and commerce, how much misery lurks in pestilential corners, whilst idle mendicants assail, on every side, the man who hates to encourage impostors, or repress, with angry frown, the plaints of the poor! How many mechanics, by a flux of trade or fashion, lose their employment; whom misfortunes, not to be warded off, lead to the idleness that vitiates their character and renders them afterwards averse to honest labour! Where is the eye that marks these evils, more gigantic than any of the infringements of property, which you piously deprecate? Are these remediless evils? And is the human heart satisfied with turning the poor over to *another* world, to receive the blessings this could afford? If society was regulated on a more enlarged plan; if man was contented to be the friend of man, and did not seek to bury the sympathies of humanity in the servile appellation of master; if, turning his eyes from ideal regions of taste and elegance, he laboured to give the earth he inhabited all the beauty it is capable of receiving, and was ever on the watch to shed abroad all the happiness which human nature can enjoy; — he who, respecting the rights of men, wishes to convince or persuade society that this is true happiness and dignity, is not the cruel *oppressor* of the

---

pestiferous: full of disease.
great city: London.

[6] For more on enclosure, see the headnote to this section. Wollstonecraft's primary point here is that land was being used inefficiently and for the wrong purposes. Although "huge forests" graced the estates of aristocrats, the poor were often prevented from using common land to support themselves. Compare "The Female Vagrant," lines 37–54. [ED.]

poor, nor a short-sighted philosopher—He fears God and loves his fellow-creatures.—Behold the whole duty of man!—the citizen who acts differ-ently is a sophisticated being.

Surveying civilized life, and seeing, with undazzled eye, the polished vices of the rich, their insincerity, want of natural affections, with all the specious train that luxury introduces, I have turned impatiently to the poor, to look for man undebauched by riches or power—but, alas! what did I see? a being scarcely above the brutes, over which it tyrannized; a broken spirit, worn-out body, and all those gross vices which the example of the rich, rudely copied, could produce. Envy built a wall of separation, that made the poor hate, whilst they bent to their superiors; who, on their part, stepped aside to avoid the loathsome sight of human misery.

What were the outrages of a day[7] to these continual miseries? Let those sorrows hide their diminished head before the tremendous mountain of woe that thus defaces our globe! Man preys on man; and you mourn for the idle tapestry that decorated a gothic pile, and the dronish bell that sum-moned the fat priest to prayer. You mourn for the empty pageant of a name, when slavery flaps her wing, and the sick heart retires to die in lonely wilds, far from the abodes of man. Did the pangs you felt for insulted nobility, the anguish that rent your heart when the gorgeous robes were torn off the idol human weakness had set up, deserve to be compared with the long-drawn sigh of melancholy reflection, when misery and vice thus seem to haunt our steps, and swim on the top of every cheering prospect? Why is our fancy to be appalled by terrific perspectives of a hell beyond the grave?—Hell stalks abroad;—the lash resounds on the slave's naked sides; and the sick wretch, who can no longer earn the sour bread of unremitting labour, steals to a ditch to bid the world a long good night—or, neglected in some ostenta-tious hospital, breathes its last amidst the laugh of mercenary attendants.

Such misery demands more than tears—I pause to recollect myself; and smother the contempt I feel rising for your rhetorical flourishes and infan-tine sensibility.

---

[7] "The 6th of October." [Wollstonecraft's note.] On 6 October 1789, 20,000 members of the National Guard stormed the Palace of Versailles, killed some of the royal attendants, and forced Louis XVI and Marie Antoinette to walk the twelve miles back to Paris to be "lodged in one of the old palaces of Paris now converted into a Bastile [sic] for kings" (*Reflections* 165). To Burke, this blatantly disrespectful treatment of the royal family was an absolute outrage. [ED.]

FROM *AN ENQUIRY CONCERNING THE PRINCIPLES OF POLITICAL JUSTICE*
William Godwin[1]

BOOK II, CHAPTER II
OF JUSTICE

Connection of Politics and Morals—Extent and Meaning of Justice— Subject of Justice: Mankind—Its Distribution Measured by the Capacity of Its Subject—By His Usefulness—Family Affection Considered— Gratitude Considered—Objections: From Ignorance—From Utility—An Exception Stated—Degrees of Justice—Application— Idea of Political Justice

From what has been said it appears, that the subject of the present enquiry is strictly speaking a department of the science of morals. Morality is the source from which its fundamental axioms must be drawn, and they will be made somewhat clearer in the present instance, if we assume the term justice as a general appellation for all moral duty.

That this appellation is sufficiently expressive of the subject will appear, if we consider for a moment mercy, gratitude, temperance, or any of those duties which in looser speaking are contradistinguished from justice. Why should I pardon this criminal, remunerate this favour, abstain from this indulgence? If it partake of the nature of morality, it must be either right or wrong, just or unjust. It must tend to the benefit of the individual, either without intrenching upon, or with actual advantage to the mass of individuals. Either way it benefits the whole, because individuals are parts of the whole. Therefore to do it is just, and to forbear it is unjust. If justice have any meaning, it is just that I should contribute every thing in my power to the benefit of the whole.

Considerable light will probably be thrown upon our investigation, if, quitting for the present the political view, we examine justice merely as it

---

An Enquiry Concerning the Principles of Political Justice, and Its Influence on General Virtue and Happiness. London: Robinson, 1793.

[1] Godwin (1756–1836), a moral philosopher, was an anarchist in the most literal sense. He believed that, were humans to behave virtuously and rationally, governments and laws would become obsolete (*anarchy* means "without law"); his philosophy was essentially progressive and optimistic, anticipating the perfection of humanity. He married Mary Wollstonecraft (see 180–86) in 1797. [ED.]

exists among individuals. Justice is a rule of conduct originating in the connection of one percipient being with another. A comprehensive maxim which has been laid down upon the subject is, "that we should love our neighbour as ourselves." But this maxim, though possessing considerable merit as a popular principle, is not modelled with the strictness of philosophical accuracy.

In a loose and general view I and my neighbour are both of us men; and of consequence entitled to equal attention. But in reality it is probable that one of us is a being of more worth and importance than the other. A man is of more worth than a beast; because, being possessed of higher faculties, he is capable of a more refined and genuine happiness. In the same manner the illustrious archbishop of Cambray[2] was of more worth than his chambermaid, and there are few of us that would hesitate to pronounce, if his palace were in flames, and the life of only one of them could be preserved, which of the two ought to be preferred.

But there is another ground of preference, beside the private consideration of one of them being farther removed from the state of a mere animal. We are not connected with one or two percipient beings, but with a society, a nation, and in some sense with the whole family of mankind. Of consequence that life ought to be preferred which will be most conducive to the general good. In saving the life of Fenelon, suppose at the moment he was conceiving the project of his immortal Telemachus,[3] I should be promoting the benefit of thousands, who have been cured by the perusal of it of some error, vice and consequent unhappiness. Nay, my benefit would extend farther than this, for every individual, thus cured has become a better member of society, and has contributed in his turn to the happiness, the information and improvement of others.

Suppose I had been myself the chambermaid, I ought to have chosen to die, rather than that Fenelon should have died. The life of Fenelon was really preferable to that of the chambermaid. But understanding is the fac-

---

percipient: perceiving.

[2] François de Salignac de la Mothe Fénelon (1651–1715), Archbishop of Cambrai and author of the epic *Télémaque* (1699), the liberal and reformist subtext of which offended Louis XIV and later made it a favorite of the French philosophers, who generally distrusted the authority of the Church and the king and who partially inspired the French Revolution. Fénelon intended the work to educate future kings, advising greater concern for the public good and curbing aristocratic excess; a member of the Académie Française, he himself was famous for tutoring the dauphin, the duc de Bourgogne, grandson of Louis XIV. [ED.]

[3] Fénelon's *Télémaque* is based on the character of Telemachus, the son of Odysseus in Homer's *Odyssey*. [ED.]

ulty that perceives the truth of this and similar propositions; and justice is the principle that regulates my conduct accordingly. It would have been just in the chambermaid to have preferred the archbishop to herself. To have done otherwise would have been a breach of justice.

Supposing the chambermaid had been my wife, my mother, or my benefactor. This would not alter the truth of the proposition. The life of Fenelon would still be more valuable than that of the chambermaid; and justice, pure, unadulterated justice, would still have preferred that which was most valuable. Justice would have taught me to save the life of Fenelon at the expense of the other. What magic is there in the pronoun "my," to overturn the decisions of everlasting truth? My wife or my mother may be a fool or a prostitute, malicious, lying or dishonest. If they be, of what consequence is it that they are mine?

"But my mother endured for me the pains of childbearing, and nourished me in the helplessness of infancy." When she first subjected herself to the necessity of these cares, she was probably influenced by no particular motives of benevolence to her future offspring. Every voluntary benefit however entitles the bestower to some kindness and retribution. But why so? Because a voluntary benefit is an evidence of benevolent intention, that is, of virtue. It is the disposition of the mind, not the external action, that entitles to respect. But the merit of this disposition is equal, whether the benefit were conferred upon me or upon another. I and another man cannot both be right in preferring our own individual benefactor, for no man can be at the same time both better and worse than his neighbour. My benefactor ought to be esteemed, not because he bestowed a benefit upon me, but because he bestowed it upon a human being. His desert will be in exact proportion to the degree in which that human being was worthy of the distinction conferred. Thus every view of the subject brings us back to the consideration of my neighbour's moral worth and his importance to the general weal, as the only standard to determine the treatment to which he is entitled. Gratitude therefore, a principle which has so often been the theme of the moralist and the poet, is no part either of justice or virtue. By gratitude I understand a sentiment, which would lead me to prefer one man to another, from some other consideration than that of his superior usefulness of worth: that is, which would make something true to me (for example this preferableness), which cannot be true to another man, and is not true in itself.[4]

It may be objected, "that my relation, my companion, or my benefactor, will of course in many instances obtain an uncommon portion of my

---

[4] "This argument respecting gratitude is stated with great clearness in an Essay on the Nature of True Virtue, by the Rev. Jonathan Edwards." [Godwin's note.] Edwards (1703–58) was an American preacher and predestinarian philosopher. [ED.]

regard: for, not being universally capable of discriminating the comparative worth of different men, I shall inevitably judge most favourably of him, of whose virtues I have received the most unquestionable proofs; and thus shall be compelled to prefer the man of moral worth whom I know, to another who may possess, unknown to me, an essential superiority."

This compulsion however is founded only in the present imperfection of human nature. It may serve as an apology for my error, but can never turn error into truth. It will always remain contrary to the strict and universal decisions of justice. The difficulty of conceiving this, is owing merely to our confounding the disposition from which an action is chosen, with the action itself. The disposition, that would prefer virtue to vice, and a greater degree of virtue to a less, is undoubtedly a subject of approbation; the erroneous exercise of this disposition by which a wrong object is selected, if unavoidable, is to be deplored, but can by no colouring and under no denomination be converted into right.

It may in the second place be objected, "that a mutual commerce of benefits tends to increase the mass of benevolent action, and that to increase the mass of benevolent action is to contribute to the general good." Indeed! Is the general good promoted by falsehood, by treating a man of one degree of worth, as if he had ten times that worth? or as if he were in any degree different from what he really is? Would not the most beneficial consequences result from a different plan; from my constantly and carefully enquiring into the deserts of all those with whom I am connected, and from their being sure, after a certain allowance for the fallibility of human judgment, of being treated by me exactly as they deserved? Who can tell what would be the effects of such a plan of conduct universally adopted?

There seems to be more truth in the argument, derived chiefly from the unequal distribution of property, in favour of my providing in ordinary cases for my wife and children, my brothers and relations, before I provide for strangers. As long as providing for individuals belongs to individuals, it seems as if there must be a certain distribution of the class needing superintendence and supply among the class affording it, that each man may have his claim and resource. But this argument, if admitted at all, is to be admitted with great caution. It belongs only to ordinary cases; and cases of a higher order or a more urgent necessity will perpetually occur, in competition with which these will be altogether impotent. We must be severely scrupulous in measuring the quantity of supply; and, with respect to money in particular, must remember how little is yet understood of the true mode of employing it for the public benefit.

Having considered the persons with whom justice is conversant, let us next enquire into the degree in which we are obliged to consult the good of others. And here I say, that it is just that I should do all the good in my power. Does a person in distress apply to me for relief? It is my duty to grant it, and I commit a breach of duty in refusing. If this principle be not of universal application, it is because, in conferring a benefit upon an individual, I may in some instances inflict an injury of superior magnitude upon myself or society. Now the same justice, that binds me to any individual of my fellow men, binds me to the whole. If, while I confer a benefit upon one man, it appear, in striking an equitable balance, that I am injuring the whole, my action ceases to be right and becomes absolutely wrong. But how much am I bound to do for the general weal, that is, for the benefit of the individuals of whom the whole is composed? Every thing in my power. What to the neglect of the means of my own existence? No; for I am myself a part of the whole. Beside, it will rarely happen that the project of doing for others every thing in my power, will demand for its execution the preservation of my own existence; or in other words, it will rarely happen that I can do more good in twenty years than in one. If the extraordinary case should occur in which I can promote the general good by my death, more than by my life, justice requires that I should be content to die. In all other cases, it is just that I should be careful to maintain my body and mind in the utmost vigour, and in the best condition for service.

I will suppose for example that it is right for one man to possess a greater portion of property than another, either as the fruit of his industry, or the inheritance of his ancestors. Justice obliges him to regard this property as a trust, and calls upon him maturely to consider in what manner it may be employed for the increase of liberty, knowledge and virtue. He has no right to dispose of a shilling of it at the will of his caprice. So far from being entitled to well earned applause for having employed some scanty pittance in the service of philanthropy, he is in the eye of justice a delinquent if he withhold any portion from that service. Nothing can be more incontrovertible. Could that portion have been better or more worthily employed? That it could is implied in the very terms of the proposition. Then it was just it should have been so employed. —In the same manner as my property, I hold my person as a trust in behalf of mankind. I am bound to employ my talents, my understanding, my strength and my time for the production of the greatest quantity of general good. Such are the declarations of justice, so great is the extent of my duty.

But justice is reciprocal. If it be just that I should confer a benefit, it is just that another man should receive it, and, if I withhold from him that to which he is entitled, he may justly complain. My neighbour is in want of ten pounds that I can spare. There is no law of political institution to reach this case, and to transfer this property from me to him. But in the eye of simple justice, unless it can be shewn that the money can be more beneficently employed, his claim is as complete, as if he had my bond in his possession, or had supplied me with goods to the amount.[5]

To this it has sometimes been answered, "that there is more than one person, that stands in need of the money I have to spare, and of consequence I must be at liberty to bestow it as I please." I answer, if only one person offer himself to my knowledge or search, to me there is but one. Those others that I cannot find belong to other rich men to assist (rich men, I say, for every man is rich, who has more than his just occasions demand), and not to me. If more than one person offer, I am obliged to balance their fitness, and conduct myself accordingly. It is scarcely possible to happen that two men shall be of exactly equal fitness, or that I should be equally certain of the fitness of the one as of the other.

It is therefore impossible for me to confer upon any man a favour, I can only do him a right. Whatever deviates from the law of justice, even I will suppose in the too much done in favour of some individual or some part of the general whole, is so much subtracted from the general stock, so much of absolute injustice.

The inference most clearly afforded by the preceding reasonings, is the competence of justice as a principle of deduction in all cases of moral enquiry. The reasonings themselves are rather of the nature of illustration and example, and any error that may be imputed to them in particulars, will not invalidate the general conclusion, the propriety of applying moral justice as a criterion in the investigation of political truth.

Society is nothing more than an aggregation of individuals. Its claims and duties must be the aggregate of their claims and duties, the one no more precarious and arbitrary than the other. What has the society a right to require from me? The question is already answered: everything that it is my duty to do. Anything more? Certainly not. Can they change eternal truth, or subvert the nature of men and their actions? Can they make it my duty to commit intemperance, to maltreat or assassinate my neighbour?— Again. What is it that the society is bound to do for its members? Every thing that can contribute to their welfare. But the nature of their welfare is defined by the nature of mind. That will most contribute to it, which enlarges the understanding, supplies incitements to virtue, fills us with a generous consciousness of our independence, and carefully removes whatever can impede our exertions.

---

[5] "A spirited outline of these principles is sketched in Swift's Sermon on Mutual Subjection." [Godwin's note.]

Should it be affirmed, "that it is not in the power of political system to secure to us these advantages," the conclusion I am drawing will still be incontrovertible. It is bound to contribute every thing it is able to these purposes, and no man was ever yet found hardy enough to affirm that it could do nothing. Suppose its influence in the utmost degree limited, there must be one method approaching nearer than any other to the desired object, and that method ought to be universally adopted. There is one thing that political institutions can assuredly do, they can avoid positively counteracting the true interests of their subjects. But all capricious rules and arbitrary distinctions do positively counteract them. There is scarcely any modification of society but has in it some degree of moral tendency. So far as it produces neither mischief nor benefit, it is good for nothing. So far as it tends to the improvement of the community, it ought to be universally adopted.

FROM BOOK III, CHAPTER VII
OF FORMS OF GOVERNMENT

Truth is in reality single and uniform. There must in the nature of things be one best form of government, which all intellects, sufficiently roused from the slumber of savage ignorance, will be irresistibly incited to approve. If an equal participation of the benefits of nature be good in itself, it must be good for you and me and all mankind. Despotism may be of use to keep human beings in ignorance, but can never conduce to render them wise or virtuous or happy. If the general tendency of despotism be injurious, every portion and fragment of it must be a noxious ingredient. Truth cannot be so variable, as to change its nature by crossing an arm of the sea, a petty brook or an ideal line, and become falsehood. On the contrary it is at all times and in all places the same.

The subject of legislation is every where the same, man. The points in which human beings resemble are infinitely more considerable than those in which they differ. We have the same senses, the same inlets of pain and pleasure, the same faculty to reason, to judge and to infer. The same causes that make me happy will make you happy. We may differ in our opinions upon this subject at first, but this difference is only in prejudice, and is by no means invincible. An event may often conduce most to the benefit of a human being, which his erroneous judgment perhaps regarded with least complacency. A wise superintendent of affairs would pursue with steady attention the real advantage of those over whom he presided, careless of the temporary disapprobation he incurred, and which would last no longer than the partial and misguided apprehension from which it flowed. [. . .]

Man is in a state of perpetual progress. He must grow either better or worse, either correct his habits or confirm them. The government proposed must either increase our passions and prejudices by fanning the flame, or, by gradually discouraging tend to extirpate them. In reality, it is sufficiently difficult to imagine a government that shall have the latter tendency. By its very nature political institution has a tendency to suspend the elasticity, and put an end to the advancement of mind. Every scheme for embodying imperfection must be injurious. That which is to-day a considerable melioration, will at some future period, if preserved unaltered, appear a defect and disease in the body politic. It is earnestly to be desired that each man was wise enough to govern himself, without the intervention of any compulsory restraint; and, since government even in its best state is an evil, the object principally to be aimed at is, that we should have as little of it as the general peace of human society will permit.

FROM *THE COMPLAINTS OF THE POOR PEOPLE OF ENGLAND*
George Dyer [1]

The subject, which I am about to examine, appears to me of importance; but, as it relates immediately to the poor, I must first beg leave to observe, I have many reasons for being interested in their happiness. It has been my fortune to have had as much connection with the poor people of England, as with the rich; and, indeed, I have sometimes even preferred having my lot with the former, for reasons which I do not think it necessary now to mention. Yet, without entering into particulars, I will, with the late John Hales, declare, "That in all my pursuits truth has been my only care------------- for this I have forsaken all hopes, all friends, all desires, which bias me, and hinder me from driving right at what I aimed. For this I have spent my youth, my means, all that I have."

If, through my connection with the poor, I feel a friendship for them, I must, on other accounts, feel compassion. My intimacy with them has led me to an acquaintance with their sufferings. I have seen the rich man pay with reluctance, what has been earned with hard labour; and insult, when he ought to have relieved. I have seen the poor man, after the toil of the day,

---

London: Ridgway, 1793.

[1] Dyer (1755–1841), a schoolmaster and tutor, became part of a circle of Unitarians that included Joseph Priestley, William Frend, and, later, Samuel Taylor Coleridge and Charles Lamb. Unitarian doctrine asserts a belief in one God, as opposed to the conventional Christian doctrine of the Trinity. [ED.]

return at night to behold nothing but want and wretchedness in a numerous family. The poor widow, whose only crime has been, that she has lived too long, hath had her weekly allowance shortened.[2] I have been in many poor houses. I have heard men plead for keeping slaves in the West-Indies, and treating them like beasts, by asking, Are they not as well off as many poor people in England? I have been witness to the miseries, and, in many instances, the oppressions of men confined in gaol: there are cases, wherein the poor cannot get justice done them, because they cannot afford to pay for it; and poor boys and girls, sometimes suffer death for crimes, when the laws, by which they suffer are more criminal than they.

But if I love and pity the poor, I also respect them. I am not disposed to deal in general censure, nor to express myself in terms of personal dislike. My friendships will prevent this; nor would it, indeed, be just. Great wealth and extreme poverty are evils in governments, and the effects of public injustice. But the orders of rich and the poor produce mutual advantages. Distinctions, (I speak not here of titles or rank, this would be trifling) distinctions which are attached to office, should be connected with duties, and are the badges of good citizens: these have public utility: and though riches are often, I had liked to have said generally, the product of public plunder (of a species of plunder, not always perceived by honest men) they are sometimes justly obtained, and innocently enjoyed. At the same time, were I to say, that the rich are the most valuable part of the community, I should not be true to my convictions. The prosperity of nations depends on the poor. They dig the ore out of the mine, and the stone out of the quarry. They build our houses, work our vessels, and fight our battles: yet, while the rich enjoy almost all the benefit, the poor undergo all the labour. The rich have little to do, but to give orders, or to sign their names, and sometimes not even that. As to the poor, what they eat, and what they wear, their firing, candle, window-light, and small beer are taxed, not always for good, but very frequently for evil purposes. Many are even living in the greatest profligacy, and the poor are toiling to pay for it. In short, they are the support of the English government, and, on a fair estimate, would be found to

---

gaol: jail.
firing: fuel.

[2] "I was some years ago employed, in company with another person, by a lady of great fortune and benevolence, to visit a very aged woman in the neighbourhood of New-market. This extraordinary person (for such she was) assured me she was about 130 years of age. On expressing my surprise that she should be in so wretched a condition as I found her in, she assured me, that her parish allowance had been shortened, because she lived so long, as to be a burden to the parish. This was the remark of one of the overseers." [Dyer's note.]

be the most valuable part of the community. But what do they meet in return? They are oppressed and insulted by government.[3]

Governments are, in general, much on their guard against the poor. Princes, and courtiers, priests, men of learning, those too who only think themselves so, and poets, the flatterers of the great, talk of the *profane* and *faithless* vulgar, and every upstart is talking of a mob. I own it is prudent for certain gentlemen in England to insinuate, that the poor cannot understand the affairs of government. I say it is prudent, but it is false. The *common* people (so we call the poor) in America and France, understand the nature of government, Why? In those countries government is formed by the people, and made to serve their interest. This was also the case of some of the States of ancient Greece, particularly of Athens and Argos. Strange too as it may appear, this was the character of almost all the German nations, long before they became overwhelmed by a cruel despotism; their governments being free, their armies a national militia, and each member considering himself a constituent part of the whole, and even of the Spanish states, particularly those called Gothic, making some allowances for feudal customs, which left many in a state of servitude. The English government is formed by the rich and great, and to them it is favorable, but to the poor it is highly injurious. Is it then surprising that our great men should say, the poor cannot understand government? The rich take care they shall not understand it. Indeed many of our gentry and learned men are, in this respect, no better off, than the vulgar and ignorant. No men understand the secrets of government but those who plan them. These men are enriching themselves and their families, and leave the *common* people to toil and beggary; telling them, they have enough to do to mind their business. Should they not add, they are perfectly at leisure to enjoy the fruits of their industry? When a man is deep and mysterious, so that you cannot get at his meaning, even on those subjects wherein your interest is at stake, it requires little penetration to discover he is a knave. It has been smartly observed of the Romish clergy, they contrived to make men believe, the *laity* could not understand religion, but that they could: and while the laity were held in amazement, the priests ran away with their land.

Romish: Roman Catholic.

[3] Compare this estimation of the relative value to society of the rich and the poor with Joseph Townsend's (176–77). [ED.]

THE OLD PEASANT

John Thelwall[1]

"Detested villains! — Proud parochial tyrants! — And are these violators of all that endears society the objects who are to monopolize your generosity, while the oppressed mechanic groans in our streets unpitied, and the aged and infirm, whose strength has been exhausted in the labours most important to the community, feel the oppressions of want and sorrow accumulated to the infirmities of years, and apply for relief in vain![2] — How different, my Wentworth![3] — oh, how different were the appearance, the sentiments, and the fate of the honest unfortunate peasant, whom (bending with age, and propping his feeble steps upon his hoe) we met upon Ewel common, on a late excursion. — Do you not see him again in fancy — Does not the tear start again into your eye, as he lifts his hat, in humble obeisance, from his hairless forehead, as we approach him. Unmerited complacency! Why was that obeisance paid to us. For aught you knew, poor victim! we might have been in the number of your oppressors; and that distinction of appearance which claimed your reverence, might have entitled us to your execration. But the bruised reed turns not upon its destroyer, but bends beneath the foot that tramples it; else what *proud Gentility!* in this insolence of thy oppression, what must be thy instant fate? — Poor old man! at such a time of life to be doomed to wander from place to place for employment, and be doomed to wander in vain! to be repulsed from every door, on account of those infirmities which former toils and former sorrows had brought upon thee; and to have thy appeals for charity retorted by the

---

From *The Peripatetic, or Sketches of the Heart, of Nature and Society; in a Series of Politico-Sentimental Journals, in Verse and Prose, of the Eccentric Excursions of Sylvanus Theophrastus; Supposed to Be Written by Himself.* Vol. 3. London: Eaton, 1793.

[1] Thelwall (1764–1834) was a poet, essayist, political radical, and member of the London Corresponding Society, which supported the French Revolution, opposed the war with France, and urged parliamentary reform in Great Britain, including extending the vote to all adult males. His activities incurred the interest of government spies, and he was arrested, charged with treason, and imprisoned for six months in 1794 but was acquitted. [ED.]

[2] The previous chapter, "The Informer," tells the story of a working-class man who accepted money from the local authorities (the "Proud parochial tyrants" referred to here) in exchange for information about a fellow laborer who had uttered sentiments "dangerous to the government, and hostile to the constitution of our country." [ED.]

[3] Wentworth — and the later mentioned Ambulator and Philanthropa — are friends of the narrator, Sylvanus Theophrastus. [ED.]

unfeeling malevolence of that upstart opulence, which in thy better days had crouched to thee for obligations!"

"Your lamentation is interesting;" said Ambulator; "but you forget that here are two of us unacquainted with the story it alludes to." — "It is short and simple; but it is not, therefore, the less pathetic. My wife," said he, with a mixed expression of anguish and resignation, "is out of her distresses. Heaven has taken her from her sorrows. I have but *one* to care for—but that is *one too much.* Times go very hard; particularly with us, who are grown old and slow. I have wandered from place to place, and though I am willing to work for less wages, nobody will employ a feeble old man, now there are so many young ones out of other works, who are glad to go into the fields. I have applied to the parish here—for I was an inhabitant, about five and twenty years ago, and lived in a better way.[4] I had a little farm, and few cows, and two or three sheep of my own; till my landlord turned me out, that he might make three or four joining farms into one.[5] So, as I could not afford to take a large farm, I was obliged to sell my stock, and go into another country. The churchwarden as is now, who is grown so proud, and lives so grand, was a poor man then, and owed me seven pounds.—But as it is so long since, I find I can't demand it; and when I asked him for relief, and told him the times were very hard, he told me he had nothing for me; and that, if times were hard, I must live hard; and so shut the door in my face; I would have asked him else, what we were to do when times are so hard that we cannot live at all? Every thing is very dear—there is no work to be had—and I am too old to go a soldiering: beside, why should we poor folks go and help the rich to fight against the poor." — Perhaps, with some, this concluding sentiment may destroy all the compassion excited by his tale; but O! that I had a voice like thunder, to shout the solemn truth in the ears of all the poor in Europe; that the kings and nobles of the earth might be reduced to the sole option of fighting their own battle, or restoring peace.

---

dear: expensive.

[4] A reference to the Act of Settlements that prohibited the poor from receiving relief from any parish other than that in which they were born or had legal residence. [ED.]

[5] For more on the practice of enclosure, see the headnote to this subsection. [ED.]

THE BENEVOLENCE

John Thelwall

"Your anecdote of the generous church-warden," said Ambulator, "brings to my mind an incident, so much to the honour of a benevolent old lady of your acquaintance, that I cannot resist the temptation of relating it. Besides, in a country where such immense sums of money are levied upon *one part* of the oppressed community, under pretense of relieving the distresses of *another* (for it is not the *rich,* but the *poor,* who support the poor of this country) and at a time when poor fellows are wheedled into the naval service by such pompous pretenses of provisions for their wives and families,[6] it is important to shew what kind of relief is afforded to the wants of those who seem most entitled to our compassion.

"Philanthropa was walking, some little time ago, through one of the principal streets of London, turning to the right and to the left for the most proper objects to exercise her compassion (and God knows, in the present state of society, there are few places where we need search in vain), when the downcast look, the melancholy silence, and modest obeisance of a poor neat-looking pregnant woman, with a child in her arms, and another hanging on her hand, attracted her attention. Want and emaciation were written in her countenance; and the whole groop was so interesting, that Philanthropa, who is little in the habit of resisting these impressions, immediately stopped, and enquired into the story of their distress. The poor woman briefly informed her, that her husband was a weaver, but that, as he had been to sea in the former part of his life, he had been pressed at the breaking out of the war, and had left her no other means to support her two infants, and provide for the season of pain and perplexity that was approaching, but the labour of her own hands; 'and, alas!' said she, 'what can I do, in my present situation, with my two babes to take care of into the bargain? I endeavoured to get a little washing to do at home: but there are so many poor women who wish to get a bit of bread this way, that there is but a little bit for each of us. In this distress I applied to the overseers of the parish; but they only gave me a *shilling,* and bade me call again in a fortnight, and I should have *another.*' Such was the tale of the poor creature whom these *British Slave*

From *The Peripatetic, or Sketches of the Heart, of Nature and Society; in a Series of Politico-Sentimental Journals, in Verse and Prose, of the Eccentric Excursions of Sylvanus Theophrastus; Supposed to Be Written by Himself.* Vol. 3. London: Eaton, 1793.

[6] A reference to the practice of *impressment,* by which recruiting officers would use either force or enticing offers of financial reward to lure men into enlisting in the navy. [ED.]

merchants, these *wholesale dealers in their brethren's blood,* had left to rot in the cold embraces of Want and Misery, that the stay and comfort of her life, the father and protector of her infants, might lavish his limbs and life for them in a struggle,[7] in which (to say the least of it) neither he nor his family, had the slightest interest or concern: and, alas! how many thousands are there at this time languishing for the same cause in situations of equal misery. The story was too circumstantial to be doubted; and Philanthropa, putting a half crown into her hand, hurried away to avoid that profusion of gratitude, which, how pleasing soever it may be to the mere spectator, is always painful to the ear of the truly generous benefactor.[8]

"I identify the sum, to shew at how small an expense we may sometimes be enabled to rescue, not an individual only, but a whole family, from distress: for as Philanthropa was some little time coming out from a tradesman's shop, in another part of the town, she was greeted by the grateful ejaculation of a woman, whose hands were loaded with a quantity of earthenware — 'God bless you, madam,' said she, 'for you have been the making of me and my poor family! — you saved us from starving.' — 'Indeed, poor woman,' was the reply, 'I fancy you are mistaken: for I do not recollect you.' — 'Alas! madam,' replied the woman, 'do you not remember giving me a half crown in Cornhill.' — The benefactress looked again in her face, and recollected her. Nor was she suffered to remain long in ignorance about the manner in which so small a sum had produced so extensive an effect. The poor creature had gone immediately with her little capital, and laid it out in pitchers, and other utensils of that kind; and as she had been fortunate in selling them again quickly at a small profit, she had contrived by excellent oeconomy, to keep her stock in a constant way of increase, till she had become a kind of little shopkeeper, and had the happiness of seeing her prospect brightening, in some degree, before her."

I have given these stories simple and unadorned; as incidents that serve to display [how] the situation of the country, and the tendency of existing institutions, ought to be delivered; and I leave it to the lovers of war, — of bloodshed, and aristocracy (crying out, as they constantly are, about the grandeur and happiness of the country) to draw from them what inferences they think fit.

It will naturally be supposed, that these anecdotes would lead us immediately into a consideration of the condition of the labouring poor in this

---

[7]The war against France, which to many English supporters of the French Revolution seemed a totally unjustifiable campaign. [ED.]

[8]Compare "Simon Lee," lines 97–104. [ED.]

country; nor to those who are at all informed upon this important topic (upon which, after all the empty boasts of placemen and senators about wealth and grandeur, power and political importance, depends, in reality, the happiness or the misery, the exaltation or depression of the state, and the utility or viciousness of every government) will it appear at all surprising that we should find the subject so copious, and the abuses and oppressions so numerous, that our journey was completed before our enquiry; and that the beautiful and picturesque of Nature was forgotten in the affecting tale of the miseries and depression of the great majority of Nature's most perfect and (but for the scourges of tyranny and aristocracy) Nature's most favoured offspring.

FROM *THOUGHTS AND DETAILS ON SCARCITY*
Edmund Burke[1]

Of all things, an indiscreet tampering with the trade of provisions is the most dangerous, and it is always worst in the time when men are most disposed to it:—that is, in the time of scarcity. Because there is nothing on which the passions of men are so violent, and their judgment so weak, and on which there exists such a multitude of ill-founded popular prejudices.

The great use of Government is as a restraint; and there is no restraint which it ought to put upon others, and upon itself too, rather than on the fury of speculating under circumstances of irritation. The number of idle tales spread about by the industry of faction, and by the zeal of foolish good-intention, and greedily devoured by the malignant credulity of mankind, tends infinitely to aggravate prejudices, which, in themselves, are more than sufficiently strong. In that state of affairs, and of the publick with relation to them, the first thing that Government owes to us, the people, is *information;* the next is timely coercion:—the one to guide our judgment; the other to regulate our tempers.

Thoughts and Details on Scarcity, Originally Presented to the Right Hon. William Pitt, in the Month of November, 1795. London: Rivington, 1800.

placemen: appointed government officials.

[1]Burke (1729–97), statesman, aesthetician, political philosopher, and farmer, gave the speech upon which this essay is based in Parliament in response to the shockingly poor wheat and barley harvest of 1795, which followed a shortage the previous year and raised fears of famine. The dearth also exacerbated the economic crisis resulting from the costly ongoing war with France. *Thoughts and Details on Scarcity* was published posthumously, edited from a series of letters on rural economics Burke wrote to his friend Arthur Young (1741–1820), editor of the *Annals of Agriculture*. Another shortage in 1799 precipitated the publication of Burke's views on the subject. [ED.]

To provide for us in our necessities is not in the power of Government. It would be a vain presumption in statesmen to think they can do it. The people maintain them, and not they the people. It is in the power of Government to prevent much evil; it can do very little positive good in this, or perhaps in any thing else. It is not only so of the state and statesman, but of all the classes and descriptions of the Rich—they are the pensioners of the poor, and are maintained by their superfluity. They are under an absolute, hereditary, and indefeatible dependence on those who labour, and are miscalled the Poor.

The labouring people are only poor, because they are numerous. Numbers in their nature imply poverty. In a fair distribution among a vast multitude, none can have much. That class of dependent pensioners called the rich is so extremely small that, if all their throats were cut, and a distribution made of all they consume in a year, it would not give a bit of bread and cheese for one night's supper to those who labour, and who in reality feed both the pensioners and themselves.

But the throats of the rich ought not to be cut, nor their magazines plundered; because, in their persons they are trustees for those who labour, and their hoards are the banking-houses of these latter. Whether they mean it or not, they do, in effect, execute their trust—some with more, some with less fidelity and judgment. But on the whole, the duty is performed, and every thing returns, deducting some very trifling commission and discount, to the place from whence it arose. When the poor rise to destroy the rich, they act as wisely for their own purposes as when they burn mills, and throw corn into the river, to make bread cheap.

When I say, that we of the people ought to be informed, inclusively I say, we ought not to be flattered: flattery is the reverse of instruction. The *poor* in that case would be rendered as improvident as the rich, which would not be at all good for them.

Nothing can be so base and so wicked as the political canting language, "The Labouring *Poor.*" Let compassion be shewn in action, the more the better, according to every man's ability, but let there be no lamentation of their condition. It is no relief to their miserable circumstances; it is only an insult to their miserable understandings. It arises from a total want of charity, or a total want of thought. Want of one kind was never relieved by want of any other kind. Patience, labour, sobriety, frugality, and religion should be recommended to them; all the rest is downright *fraud.* It is horrible to call them "The *once happy* labourer."

Whether what may be called moral or philosophical happiness of the laborious classes is increased or not, I cannot say. The feat of that species of

---

magazines: storehouses.

happiness is in the mind; and there are few data to ascertain the comparative state of the mind at any two periods. Philosophical happiness is to want little. Civil or vulgar happiness is to want much, and to enjoy much.

If the happiness of the animal man (which certainly goes somewhere towards the happiness of the rational man) be the object of our estimate, then I assert, without the least hesitation, that the condition of those who labour (in all descriptions of labour, and in all gradations of labour, from the highest to the lowest inclusively) is on the whole extremely meliorated, if more and better food is any standard of melioration. They work more, it is certain; but they have the advantage of their augmented labour; yet whether that increase of labour be on the whole a *good* or an *evil* is a consideration that would lead us a great way and is not for my present purpose. But as to the fact of the melioration of their diet, I shall enter into the detail of proof whenever I am called upon: in the mean time, the known difficulty of contenting them with any thing but bread made of the finest flour, and meat of the first quality, is proof sufficient.

I further assert, that even under all the hardships of the last year, the labouring people did, either out of their direct gains, or from charity, (which it seems is now an insult to them) in fact, fare better than they did, in seasons of common plenty, 50 or 60 years ago; or even at the period of my English observation, which is about 44 years. I even assert, that full as many in that class, as ever were known to do it before, continued to save money; and this I can prove, so far as my own information and experience extend.

It is not true that the rate of wages has not encreased with the nominal price of provisions. I allow it has not fluctuated with that price, nor ought it; and the Squires of Norfolk had dined, when they gave it as their opinion, that it might or ought to rise and fall with the market of provisions.[2] The rate of wages in truth has no *direct* relation to that price. Labour is a commodity like every other, and rises or falls according to the demand. This is in the nature of things; however, the nature of things has provided for their necessaries. Wages have been twice raised in my time, and they bear a full proportion, or even a greater than formerly, to the medium of provision during the last bad cycle of twenty years. They bear a full proportion to the result of their labour. If we were wildly to attempt to force them beyond it, the stone which we had forced up the hill would only fall back upon them in a diminished demand, or, what indeed is the far lesser evil, an aggravated price of all the provisions, which are the result of their manual toil.

---

[2] Burke refers to the efforts during this time of some magistrates (called "squires") to link wages to the price of food. He may be implying that, having eaten their principal meal of the day, they felt comfortable enough to express a view that Burke believes may hurt their prosperity in the long run. [ED.]

[. . .] But what if the rate of hire to the labourer comes far short of his necessary subsistence, and the calamity of the time is so great as to threaten actual famine? Is the poor labourer to be abandoned to the flinty heart and griping hand of base self-interest, supported by the sword of law, especially when there is reason to suppose that the very avarice of farmers themselves has concurred with the errors of Government to bring famine on the land?

In that case, my opinion is this. Whenever it happens that a man can claim nothing according to the rules of commerce, and the principles of justice, he passes out of that department, and comes within the jurisdiction of mercy. In that province the magistrate has nothing at all to do: his interference is a violation of the property which it is his office to protect. Without all doubt, charity to the poor is a direct and obligatory duty upon all Christians, next in order after the payment of debts, full as strong, and by nature made infinitely more delightful to us. Puffendorf,[3] and other casuists do not, I think denominate it quite properly, when they call it a duty of imperfect obligation. But the manner, mode, time, choice of objects, and proportion are left to private discretion; and perhaps, for that very reason it is performed with the greater satisfaction, because the discharge of it has more the appearance of freedom; recommending us besides very specially to the divine favour, as the exercise of a virtue most suitable to a being sensible of its own infirmity.

The cry of the people in cities and towns, though unfortunately (from a fear of their multitude and combination) the most regarded, ought, in *fact,* to be the *least* attended to upon this subject: for citizens are in a state of utter ignorance of the means by which they are to be fed, and they contribute little or nothing, except in an infinitely circuitous manner, to their own maintenance. They are truly "*Fruges consumere nati.*"[4] They are to be heard with great respect and attention upon matters within their province, that is, on trades and manufactures; but on any thing that relates to agriculture, they are to be listened to with the same *reverence* which we pay to the dogmas of other ignorant and presumptuous men.

---

casuists: those who engage in overly subtle or even deceitful reasoning.

[3] Samuel Puffendorf (1632–94), German legal theorist and historian. [ED.]

[4] The phrase literally means "born to eat the fruit of the earth." Burke is quoting Horace's first book of Epistles (2.27), in which he uses the phrase to make an unflattering comparison with the suitors of Penelope in the *Odyssey* who consume Odysseus's stores of cattle while he is away. A long-standing economic condition in Europe was that the wealthy ate meat, which was expensive, while the poor ate produce. [ED.]

FROM *OUTLINE OF A WORK ENTITLED* "*PAUPER MANAGEMENT IMPROVED*"

Jeremy Bentham[1]

Chapter II. Mendicity extirpated——Section 1. *Compulsion indispensable*— The Industry-house[2] system (the Company being invested with the necessary powers) a certain means, and, in this country, at least, the only possible means, of extirpating mendicity. In this country, under the existing poor laws, every man has a right to be maintained, in the character of a pauper, at the public charge: under which right he is in fact, with a very few exceptions, (amounting not to one perhaps in fifty,) maintained in idleness. But in this same country the condition of the common beggar is more eligible, in his own estimation at least, than that of a pauper, maintained in idleness; for, if it were not, he would become a pauper, having it in his option so do to at any time. It would be absurd, therefore, to expect that by any management—at least, by any good management—the Industry-house provision could be rendered generally acceptable to beggars: that is, that a system which affords bare maintenance—maintenance in the most frugal and least luxurious shape—nor that otherwise than on the condition of working, as far as ability extends, to the full amount of it, should be preferred to a mode of life exempt from working—to the condition of him who is not at present the lowest of those who are maintained in idleness. If, in any country out of England, plans for the extirpation of mendicity without compulsion, (*i.e.* without bodily compulsion,) have met with a temporary success, no inference can be drawn from the success of such a plan in those countries, to the success of a similar plan in England; since, in those countries, beggars being liable to starve, and many, doubtless, being starved, the question will have been, whether to accept of the proffered provision, or starve:—whereas *here* the question would be, whether to accept of it, or to be maintained in idleness. If, not withstanding the adoption of the proposed system in other respects, begging were to be tolerated, the nuisance

---

From *Annals of Agriculture, and Other Useful Arts* 30 (1798). The *Annals of Agriculture* was edited by Arthur Young (1741–1820), a friend of Edmund Burke (see the preceding selection from *Thoughts and Details on Scarcity*).

mendicity: the practice of begging.

[1] Bentham (1748–1832), a political theorist, is best known as the founder of utilitarianism, the belief that a government's usefulness is its primary objective; its utility, then, is evaluated based on the extent to which its laws and institutions promote the greatest amount of happiness for the greatest number of its people. [ED.]

[2] For industry-houses or workhouses, see the headnote to this section. [ED.]

would be much greater than at the present: since, of those who are now maintained in idleness in the character of paupers, multitudes, rather than be set to work, would become beggars.

Section 2. *Compulsion justifiable.*—Mischiefs produced by the practice of begging—1. In the instance of passengers in general, considered as exposed to the importunity of beggars—to some, the pain of sympathy:—no pain, no alms-giving;—begging is a species of extortion to which the tender-hearted, and they only, are exposed. 2. Disgust; which may exist where there is no sympathy:—the sympathy experiences a sort of relief by giving; the disgust finds no relief.—From the disgust excited by the presence of a filthy beggar, none but the equally filthy stand exempted. The multitude of the persons subject to this pain of sympathy, or to this disgust, considered, there can be little doubt but that the sum of these pains taken together is greater than the difference to the beggar in point of comfort between begging and working. 3. Discouragement to industry. Every penny spent is the reward of industry: every penny given, a bounty upon idleness.—The luxuries seen in many instances to be enjoyed by beggars, are a sort of insult to the hard-working child of industry: by holding him out as a dupe, who toils and torments himself to earn a maintenance inferior to what is to be earned by canting and grimace. 4. Facility afforded to real crimes.—Mendicity, by the removal of shame, removes one of the chief safe-guards to honesty: and to tolerate beggars, would be to tolerate habitual depredators; for those who are now *unavowed-employment* hands, would then, if under that name subjected to compulsive industry, declare themselves beggars. 5. Unfavourable influence on happiness, even in the instance of the begging tribe itself, taking the whole together.—There are many, it is true, who, for a time at least, would, unquestionably, be no inconsiderable sufferers by the proposed change. But the greater part would be gainers in point of happiness, at least in the long run: since—(it being a property of this as of other unlaborious professions to be overstocked)—for one prosperous and happy beggar, there are probably many unprosperous and miserable ones; wretches who, notwithstanding, keep lingering in their wretchedness; sometimes for want of power, sometimes for want of resolution, to emerge from it. The discomfort would cease at any rate with the existing stock of prosperous beggars: the benefits would be everlasting: and the disturbance of the prosperity of the prosperous ones appears to be a sacrifice necessary to the attainment of the benefit.

Section 3. *Plan for the Apprehension of Beggars.*—Power to anyone to apprehend a beggar, begging in any public place, and conduct him either to

---

canting: speaking in the whiny or sing-song manner that was thought to be characteristic of beggars.

a constable or to the next Industry-house.[3] — Obligation on constables and magistrates, with power of commanding assistance. — Reward 10s. or 20s. advanced by the Governor, and charged to the beggar's account. The whole to the constable, if he apprehends on view: if on simple information, the informer to have a quarter: in on information, accompanied with apprehension, half. — Necessity in this case of admitting the informer as good evidence. Power of commitment to the governor, or else to the chaplain; the latter being without pecuniary interest in the management. — Intervention of a magistrate (unless the chaplain should be nominated to the magistracy) would produce complication and delay, and might render the execution of the law less steady.[4] Time of detention, till the beggar's self-liberation account is balanced, — (See further on.) — *Items* for which the beggar is to be debited. — 1. Reward for apprehension, as above. 2. Expense of conveyance.[5] 3. Diet, while in the house. 4. Use of clothing and bedding, while in ditto. 5. Medicine, or any other articles of separate expense. 6. Individual's share of the joint expense of the house for the time. 7. Ordinary profit upon so much of the Company's capital as is employed in the defraying of that expense. 8. Expense of life-assurance in this instance: *i.e.* equivalent for the chance of his dying before his account is balanced.

Section 5. *Provision after Discharge.* — Beggar's *offer of service,* for any employment of his choice, to be previously inserted in the Employment Gazette. No discharge, however, without a responsible bondsman, (a housekeeper paying taxes,) undertaking for the giving him a specific employment, not to be withdrawn till after (suppose a week's) notice to the house: giving notice also to the house of the beggar's departure, on whatever day it happens, or the next. The beggar to enter into a corresponding engagement on his part — not to depart from such service without (suppose a week's) notice to the employer; and, upon departure, to return that same day to the Industry-house, unless provided with another employer, on the same terms; — and so *toties quoties.*[6] This *probation period* to continue (say) a year: and at the end of it, the beggar to be entitled to his certificate of *full emancipation.* — Failure

---

[3] "This power exists already in the case of felons, and seems in little danger of being abused; since, in exhibiting the beggar, a man exhibits himself at the same time." [Bentham's note.]

[4] "In the Shrewsbury house of industry, a similar power is vested in the Board of Directors." [Bentham's note.]

[5] "As in the case of a beggar unable, or pretending to be unable, to walk; or in the case of his being refractory, and extra assistance hired. This will render it to the beggar's interest not to give unnecessary trouble." [Bentham's note.]

[6] *Toties quoties,* literally "as often, so often," means in this case that each time the beggar leaves his employment, he will be immediately returned to the workhouse. [ED.]

of such notice or return, to be considered as an *escape,* and advertised as such in the *Employment Gazette,* with a reward quadruple the original one. In case of a relapse into the begging trade, the original reward doubled; in case of a second relapse, quadrupled: and so on, doubling it each time. — The self-liberation account not to be balanced by money, but by labour (otherwise rich beggars might, in despite of the provision, continue their trade) or, if balanced by money, only in part. By coming in as a volunteer, a beggar will save himself from the expense of being pressed, and from the clog of the *probation period.* The provision will tend so far to execute itself.

Section 6. *Evasions obviated.* — Classes that must be considered as beggars, or the provisions would be nugatory. 1. Offerers of pretended services to passengers. — Examples: Street and road sweepers — Layers of boards over kennels — Link-bearers — the two last are apt to be in confederacy with pick-pockets. 2. Pretended hawkers. — Hawking to be deemed a *pretence,* if the quantity remaining exposed to sale be too small to afford a profit equal to a day's subsistence. *Licences* might serve to distinguish the real from the pretended. Acceptance of alms, in a road, street, or other public place, with or without previous petition, sufficient *evidence* of begging: — dumb show may be as expressive as words.

Section 7. *Almsgivers unpunishable.* — 1. Penalties on *givers* of alms would be *needless;* since if nobody durst take, nobody could give. 2. *Unpopular:* being penalties on the exercise of what, in respect of the disposition and motive, at least, could not be denied to be a virtue. 3. *Obstructive* of the *end* in view: since, in the case of begging by dumb show, it would take off the only *evidence.* — Punishment is out of the question on both sides: even in the case of the beggar, what is proposed to be done is no more a punishment, than sending a boy to school is a punishment. No pain inflicted on purpose, for the purpose of operating on others by the prospect of it: and the duration of the discipline is made to depend upon the exertions of the party subject to it: — in the instance of the *lazy* hand, as in the instance of any industrious *self-liberation* hand.

Section 8. *Existing Remedies incompetent.* —— Remedy. 1. Punishment under the Vagrant Act, &c. (17 Geo. 2. ch. 5.)[7] The effect of this provision is rather to *obstruct* the design than promote it. — Whipping does not give employment. Imprisonment in a common jail, so far from giving employment, excludes a man from it: besides corrupting him, by aggregating him with bad characters of all sorts, out of the reach of all tutelary aggregation and

---

nugatory: insignificant or trivial.

[7]This (as well as the reference to 5 Eliz. ch. 4 in the next paragraph) is a citation to the various acts of Parliament, under the reigns of the respective monarchs, that have established English law. [ED.]

inspection. — The prisons called *houses of correction* are not universal; and where they exist they afford little or nothing of *correction* but the name. They either afford him no employment at all, or an employment which will be no resource after discharge: an employment not to be had elsewhere, because not affording a maintenance to the workman, together with an adequate profit to a master-employer.[8] 2. The law is *inexecutable.* — The mere want of jail-room would itself be a physical bar to the execution of it. The spare room in all the existing jails and houses of correction put together would scarcely *lodge,* much less *set to work,* the *beggars* alone, without reckoning the *unavowed-employment hands,* and other classes aimed at by the act. Were it even capable of being executed, the necessary parties would not generally concur with the degree of willingness requisite for the execution of it: — *magistrates* not, were it only in consideration of the useless expense to the public: *constables* not, through compassion, and fear of odium: private *informers* not, the reward being so small, and, on account of the known disinclination of the other parties, the trouble of the business being so much more certain than the success. Hence it is, that (excepting the punishment here and there of an individual who happens to be particularly obnoxious) things go on as if there were no such law: and the limits that are set to the number of this tribe, are set — not by the operation of the laws, but by the quantum of encouragement afforded, within a given space, to this mode of life. — If the law had any effect, otherwise than in the way of casual and useless punishment, it could only be that of driving a man out of the street into the poorhouse: that is, quartering him upon the *unwilling,* instead of the *willing.*

Remedy 2d. — *Private Bondage;* — by an old statute still existing, but scarcely known. — (5 Eliz. ch. 4.) — In the case of *males,* under a *self-appointed* master, from any age not under twelve, up to sixty. — This remedy, such as it is, includes beggars no otherwise than as it includes everybody, certain denominations only excepted. 2. *Females* do not lie quite so completely at the mercy of a self-appointed master: servitude expires when beauty begins

---

[8] "List of *requisites,* the *concurrence* of which is necessary to the carrying on a branch of manufacturing industry without loss. 1. Building suitable — in point of space — materials — dimensions — and divisions. — 2. Land sufficient. — 3. Appropriate stock of all kinds, in hand or at command, in sufficient quantity and value. — 4. Scale of the establishment, in point of number of hands, etc., large enough to afford adequate recompense for a suitably-qualified manager's time. — 5. Mode or terms of management, mercantile — the manager having a sufficient pecuniary interest in the success. — 6. Stock of hands so circumstanced, as to be depended upon for a continuance. — 7. Appropriate instruction administered. — 8. The managing hands, by education and habits, qualified for the charge. — 9. A system of bookkeeping appropriate, adequate, and regular.

"The existence of the united requisites, in here and there an instance, would avail nothing, unless it were universal; since the preparing for the beggar, in one district, a place of reception which was not to his taste, would but drive him into another." [Bentham's note.]

to fade: — at forty years of age: — and the magistrate has a control upon the choice.[9] The very existence of a law like this, is sufficient proof of the inefficiency of it; since the execution of it would never be endured. 3. With all its harshness towards the untended servant, it holds out no adequate advantage to the intended master: — for it affords him no adequate means of securing either the service or the person of the bondsman. While willing servants are to be had upon such easy terms, no man will encumber himself with an unwilling one, without the power either of confining him to prevent escape, or apprehending him afterwards.

Parallel between the Proposed Remedy and the Two Existing Ones

EXISTING REMEDY 1ST	PROPOSED REMEDY
1. Whipping.	1. No whipping, or other punishment.
2. Scene of confinement, a close prison.	2. Scene of confinement, a spacious country farm.
3. Duration not abridgable by a man's own exertions.	3. Duration abridgable by a man's own exertions.
4. No means of industry.	4. Means and habit of industry uninterrupted.
5. No means of future livelihood.	5. Future livelihood secured.

EXISTING REMEDY 2D	PROPOSED REMEDY
1. Term of servitude, any number of *years* up to forty-eight, according to a man's age.	1. Term, a very few *weeks* or *days:* more or fewer, according to a man's own exertions.
2. Master, self-appointed — anybody, be his character ever so bad, and temper ever so intolerable.	2. Master, a man of character and education, appointed by a great public company.
3. Scene, a private house — unconspicuous — uninspectable.	3. Scene, a public establishment, of the most conspicuous kind. — Management transparent, — inspection uninterrupted and universal.

---

[9] "*Appius*, therefore, under this law could not have possessed himself of *Virginia*, without taking the part that he took at Rome." [Bentham's note.] Bentham refers to the story, recounted by Roman historian Livy (59 B.C.–A.D. 17), and later by Chaucer in "The Physician's Tale," from *The Canterbury Tales*, of Appius Claudius, one of the twelve magistrates of Rome, who claimed the beautiful plebeian Virginia as his slave. [ED.]

FEARS IN SOLITUDE
AND OTHER POLITICAL
WRITINGS BY COLERIDGE

Unlike the highly circumspect Wordsworth, who refrained from publishing any of his more overt political statements, Coleridge throughout the 1790s voiced his support for the French Revolution frequently and conspicuously. His volumes of poetry from this time abound with sonnets addressed to politicians such as Pitt and Burke and prophetic diatribes such as the 1796 "Religious Musings" in which he depicts the French Revolution as the sign of a coming apocalypse:

> The hour is nigh:
> And lo! the Great, the Rich, the Mighty Men,
> The Kings and the Chief Captains of the World,
> With all that fixed on high like stars of Heaven
> Shot baleful influence, shall be cast to earth,
> Vile and down-trodden, as the untimely fruit
> Shook from the fig-tree by a sudden storm. (*Poetical Works* 120–21)

He also was extremely active as a journalist during this time, contributing a host of articles and editorials to liberal publications such as the *Morning Post* and in 1796 issuing his own short-lived weekly newspaper, the *Watchman,* in order "THAT ALL MAY KNOW THE TRUTH AND THAT THE TRUTH MAY MAKE US FREE." Perhaps his most dramatic contribution to the Revolution controversy, however, was his 1795 series of lectures in Bristol that caused such a controversy that Coleridge feared that he had become a marked man:

> Mobs and Mayors, Blockheads and Brickbats, Placards and Press Gangs have leagued in horrible Conspiracy against me—The Democrats are as sturdy in the support of me–but their number is comparatively small— / Two or three uncouth and unbrained Automata have threatened my Life. (*Letters* 1.152)

We begin our survey of Coleridge's political thinking with two selections that relate to "Pantisocracy," the plan devised by Coleridge and Robert Southey in which "twelve gentlemen of good education and liberal principles" and twelve like-minded women would immigrate to Pennsylvania and found a new society on the banks of the Susquehanna River.[1] The Pantisocrats would abolish private property and class distinctions, and all would work together for the common good of the community. In this way, Coleridge, Southey, and the others hoped to realize the egalitarian ideals of the French Revolution while avoiding its increasingly obvious excesses. And though the plan quickly collapsed when Southey backed out of it in order to pursue a law degree, it is clear from the sonnet contained in Coleridge's 1794 letter to Southey just how much hope and energy he had invested in the project. The highly sentimental and widely lampooned "Address to a Young Jack-Ass, and Its *Tether'd* Mother" also grows out of Coleridge's pantisocratic ideals as he uses this address to a mistreated beast of burden in order to criticize the social hierarchy and to express his vision of a utopian society.

The next two selections reveal Coleridge's growing ambivalence toward both the Revolution and the beliefs of his fellow English radicals. In the excerpt from *Conciones ad Populum,* the published text of his Bristol lectures, he sharply criticizes all but one class "among the professed Friends of Liberty" (what he calls "thinking and disinterested Patriots") and clearly distinguishes his radical Christianity from the atheistic views of William Godwin. In "Remonstrance to the French Legislators," one of his essays from the *Watchman,* we can see even more clearly how divided his loyalties have become. On the one hand, he refers to the French as "The Guardians of Liberty" and recalls how his heart had once "proudly expatriated itself" to revel in the "victories of Frenchmen." On the other hand, he sternly warns about the dangers of France's current course and predicts that it will lead to anarchy and the continued suppression of liberty.

With France's invasion of the democratic cantons of Switzerland in 1798, Coleridge finally repudiated the French Revolution once and for all; and, in his letter of 10 March 1798 to his brother George, he laments his former association with the radical movement: "A man's character follows him long after he has ceased to deserve it—but I have snapped my squeaking baby-trumpet of Sedition & the fragments lie scattered in the lumber-room of Penitence. I wish to be a good man & a Christian—but I am no Whig, no Reformist, no Republican." It would be a mistake, however, to see this as the beginning of Coleridge's political conservatism or his retreat from pol-

---

[1] "Pantisocracy," a term that Coleridge himself coined, literally means "rule by all."

itics into the world of the imagination. In fact, as his "other" 1798 volume of poems, *Fears in Solitude, Written in France, during the Alarm of an Invasion,* vividly demonstrates, Coleridge continued to comment on political issues and to assert his claim to the prophetic mantle.[2] By this point, he had come to regret that—even after publicly criticizing the Terror as well as many aspects of English Jacobinism—he was still generally associated with the most radical strain of British politics. Therefore, one of his principal objectives in *Fears in Solitude* is to change his public image from that of an obstinate critic of government policy to that of a devoted British patriot. By setting the volume's title poem "during the alarm of an invasion," Coleridge immediately establishes his recognition of the danger that France now poses, and, after a lengthy analysis of what has brought on the current "evil days," he concludes with an almost St. Crispin's Day–like call to his British "brethren" to repel the French (whom he now calls "an impious foe" and a "light yet cruel race"). Moreover, he consistently uses the poem as an opportunity to testify to his love of his "mother Isle," claiming that "There lives nor form nor feeling in my soul / Unborrow'd from my country."

In "France: An Ode," Coleridge relies on a similar argument in order to justify his former support of the French Revolution. To frame his account of the events leading to his final repudiation of the Revolution, he describes in both the opening and closing stanzas his lifelong love of the "spirit of divinest liberty" that exists only in the natural world. His support of the Revolution, then, becomes simply a "profitless" attempt to find this kind of natural liberty "in forms of human power," a mistaken but understandable outgrowth of the principles he learned from his childhood encounters with the English countryside. The final poem in the volume, "Frost at Midnight," appears at first glance to have nothing to do with politics; but, as Paul Magnuson convincingly demonstrates, the poem—when read in conjunction with the other poems in the volume—takes on decidedly political overtones (67–94). In sharp contrast to "France: An Ode," "Frost at Midnight" carefully elides the period of his revolutionary enthusiasm; it begins in 1798 after he has already become disillusioned with France and then looks back to his schooldays in London—a time well before he became embroiled in the political controversies of the 1790s. Given his highly politicized representation of nature in the two preceding poems, Coleridge's vow in the final section of the poem to educate his son amid England's "lakes and shores /

---

[2] Coleridge's outspokenness is particularly surprising given the fact that this volume was published only three years after the passage in 1795 of the notorious Seditious Meetings and Treasonable Practices Acts, which greatly increased the government's ability to crack down on what it deemed to be seditious speech and writing.

And mountain crags" demonstrates not only that he is not the sort of dangerous "seditionist" he was reputed to be but also that he has dedicated himself to instilling this kind of natural patriotism in future generations. Thus, having in the first two poems worked through the guilt and disappointment aroused by his former support of the French Revolution, he essentially writes this troubled era out of existence in the third and looks ahead to a time when it will no longer haunt his thoughts or divide him from his native land.

FROM LETTER TO ROBERT SOUTHEY

Sept—18th—[1794]   10 o clock Thursday Morning[1]

No more my Visionary Soul shall dwell
On Joys that were! No more endure to weigh
The Shame and Anguish of the evil Day,
Wisely forgetful! O'er the Ocean swell
Sublime of Hope I seek the cottag'd Dell,
Where Virtue calm with careless step may stray,
And dancing to the moonlight Roundelay
The Wizard Passions weave an holy Spell.
Eyes that have ach'd with Sorrow! ye shall weep
Tears of doubt-mingled Joy, like theirs who start
From Precipices of distemper'd Sleep,
On which the fierce-eyed Fiends their Revels k[eep,]
And see the rising Sun, & feel it dart
New Rays of Pleasance trembling to the Heart.

ADDRESS TO A YOUNG JACK-ASS
AND ITS *TETHER'D* MOTHER

In Familiar Verse[1]

Poor Little Foal, of an oppressed race!
I love the languid patience of thy face;

From *Collected Letters of Samuel Taylor Coleridge*. Ed. Earl Leslie Griggs. Vol. 1. Oxford: Clarendon, 1956.

[1] The poem follows an exuberant letter in which Coleridge discusses the plans for Pantisocracy. [ED.]

Morning Chronicle (30 December 1794).

[1] "Familiar verse" means less formal poetry, making this poem a precursor to Coleridge's "conversation poems" such as "The Nightingale" and "Frost at Midnight." [ED.]

And oft, with friendly hand, I give thee bread—
And clap thy ragged coat, and scratch thy head!
5   But what thy dulled spirit hath dismay'd,
That never thou dost sport upon the glade;
And (most unlike the nature of things young)
That still to earth thy moping head is hung?
Do thy prophetic fears anticipate,
10 Meek Child of Misery! thy future fate;
The starving meal, and all the thousand aches.
Which "patient Merit of th' Unworthy takes?"[2]
Or is thy sad heart thrill'd with filial pain,
To see thy wretched Mother's lengthen'd Chain?
15 And, truly, very piteous is *her* lot—
Chain'd to a Log upon a narrow spot,
Where the close-eaten grass is scarcely seen,
While sweet around her waves the tempting Green?
Poor Ass! Thy Master should have learnt to shew
20 Pity—best taught by fellowship of woe:
For much I fear me, that *he* lives, like *thee,*
Half-famish'd in a Land of Luxury!

How *askingly* its steps towards me bend!—
It seems to say, "And have I, then, *one* Friend?"
25 Innocent Foal! thou poor, despis'd Forlorn!
I hail thee *Brother,* 'spite of the Fool's scorn;
And fain I'd take thee with me, in the dell
Of Peace and mild Equality to dwell;
Where Toil shall call the Charmer, Health, his Bride,
30 And Laughter tickle Plenty's ribless side!
How thou would'st toss thy heels, in gamesome play—
And frisk about, as Lamb or Kitten gay!
Yea; and more musically sweet to me
Thy dissonant harsh Bray of Joy would be
35 Than warbled Melodies, that soothe to rest
The tumult of some Scoundrel Monarch's breast!

---

[2]*Hamlet* 3.1.73. [ED.]

FROM *CONCIONES AD POPULUM*

or Addresses to the People[1]

Yes! there are those who have loved Freedom with wise ardour, and prop-agated its principles with unshaken courage! For it was ordained at the foundation of the world, that there should always remain Pure Ones and uncorrupt, who should shine like Lights in Darkness, reconciling us to our own nature.

That general Illumination should precede Revolution, is a truth as ob-vious, as that the Vessel should be cleansed before we fill it with a pure Liquor. But the mode of diffusing it is not discoverable with equal facility. We certainly should never attempt to make Proselytes by appeals to the *selfish* feelings—and consequently, should plead *for* the Oppressed, not *to* them. The Author of an essay on political Justice[2] considers private Socie-ties as the sphere of real utility—that (each one illuminating those imme-diately beneath him,) Truth by a gradual descent may at last reach the low-est order. But this is rather plausible than just or practicable. Society as at present constituted does not resemble a chain that ascends in a continuity of Links.—There are three ranks possessing an intercourse with each other: these are well comprized in the superscription of a Perfumer's advertise-ment, which I lately saw—"the Nobility, Gentry, and People of Dress." But alas! between the Parlour and the Kitchen, the Tap and the Coffee-Room—there is a gulph that may not be passed. He would appear to me to have adopted the best as well as the most benevolent mode of diffusing Truth, who uniting the zeal of the Methodist with the views of the Philosopher, should be *personally* among the Poor, and teach them their *Duties* in order that he may render them susceptible to their *Rights*.

Bristol: 1795.

tap: taproom.

[1]The pamphlet reprinted Coleridge's political lectures given in Bristol in February 1795. In it, Coleridge addresses the consequences of the French Revolution and the subsequent war between England and France, memorably pointing out that "Revolutions are sud-den to the unthinking only" (13). This excerpt follows Coleridge's delineation of three classes of hypocritical "Friends of Liberty": first, the "*dough-baked* Patriots," whose po-litical decisions are lazily determined by gossip and not by "thorough investigation"; sec-ond, those apostates who are too easily swayed by demagoguery, "the inflammatory harangues of some mad-headed Enthusiast"; third, subversives who are motivated pri-marily by their own self-interest (14–19). Our selection addresses "that small but glori-ous band, whom we may truly distinguish by the name of thinking and disinterested Pa-triots" (20). [ED.]

[2]The reference is to Godwin. See pages 187–93. [ED.]

Yet by what means can the lower Classes be made to learn their Duties, and urged to practice them? The human Race may perhaps possess the capability of all excellence; and Truth, I doubt not, is omnipotent to a mind already disciplined for its reception; but assuredly the over-worked Labourer, skulking into an Ale-house, is not likely to exemplify the one, or prove the other. In that barbarous tumult of inimical Interests, which the present state of Society exhibits, *Religion* appears to offer the only means universally *efficient*. The perfectness of future Men[3] is indeed a benevolent tenet, and may operate on a few Visionaries, whose studious habits supply them with employment, and seclude them from temptation. But a distant prospect, which we are never to reach, will seldom quicken our footsteps, however lovely it may appear; and a Blessing, which not ourselves but *posterity* are destined to enjoy, will scarcely influence the actions of *any*—still less of the ignorant, the prejudiced, and the selfish.

"Go, preach the Gospel to Poor."[4] By its Simplicity it will meet their comprehension, by its Benevolence soften their affections, by its Precepts it will direct their conduct, by the vastness of its Motives ensure their obedience. The situation of the Poor is perilous: they are indeed both

> from within and from without
> *Unarm'd* to all Temptations.[5]

Prudential reasonings will in general be powerless with them. For the incitements of this world are weak in proportion as we are wretched —

> The World is not *my* Friend, nor the World's Law.
> The World has got no Law to make *me* rich.[6]

They too, who live *from Hand to Mouth,* will most frequently become improvident. Possessing no *stock* of happiness they eagerly seize the gratifications of the moment, and snatch the froth from the wave as it passes by them. Nor is the desolate state of their families a restraining motive, unsoftened as they are by education, and benumbed into selfishness by the torpedo touch of extreme Want. Domestic affections depend on association. We love an object if, as often as we see or recollect it, an agreeable sensation arises in

---

improvident: lacking in foresight.

[3] Throughout this section, Coleridge uses phraseology highly reminiscent of Godwin's philosophy: e.g., "the omnipotence of Truth" and "perfectness of future Men." [ED.]
[4] Compare Mark 16.15 and Luke 4.18. [ED.]
[5] Milton, *Paradise Lost:* "other Powers as great / Fell not, but stand unshak'n, from within / Or from without, to all temptations arm'd" (4.63–65). [ED.]
[6] Shakespeare, *Romeo and Juliet:* "The world is not thy friend, nor the world's law, / The world affords no law to make thee rich" (5.1.72–73). [ED.]

our minds. But alas! how should *he* glow with the charities of Father and Husband, who gaining scarcely more, than his own necessities demand, must have been accustomed to regard his wife and children, not as the Soothers of finished labour, but as Rivals for the insufficient meal! In a man so circumstanced the Tyranny of the *Present* can be overpowered only by the tenfold mightiness of the *Future.* Religion will cheer his gloom with her promises, and by habituating his mind to anticipate an infinitely great Revolution hereafter, may prepare it even for the sudden reception of a less degree of amelioration in this World.

But if we hope to instruct others, we should familiarize our own minds to some fixed and determinate principles of action. The World is a vast labyrinth, in which almost every one is running a different way, and almost every one manifesting hatred to those who do not run the same way. A few indeed stand motionless, and not seeking to lead themselves or others out of the maze laugh at the failures of their brethren. Yet with little reason: for more grossly than the most bewildered wanderer does *he* err,[7] who never aims to go right. It is more honourable to the Head, as well as to the Heart, to be misled by our eagerness in the pursuit of Truth, than to be safe from blundering by contempt of it. The happiness of Mankind is the *end* of Virtue, and Truth is the Knowledge of the *means;* which he will never seriously attempt to discover, who has not habitually interested himself in the welfare of others. The searcher after Truth must love and be beloved; for general Benevolence is a necessary motive to constancy of pursuit; and this general Benevolence is begotten and rendered permanent by social and domestic affections. Let us beware of that proud Philosophy, which affects to inculcate Philanthropy while it denounces every home-born feeling, by which it is produced and nurtured.[8] The paternal and filial duties discipline the Heart and prepare it for the love of all Mankind. The intensity of private attachments encourages, not prevents, universal Benevolence. The nearer we approach to the Sun, the more intense its heat: yet what corner of the system does he not cheer and vivify?

The Man who would find Truth, must likewise seek it with an humble and simple Heart, otherwise he will be precipitant and overlook it; or he will be prejudiced, and refuse to see it. *To emancipate itself from the Tyranny of Association,* is the most arduous effort of the mind, particularly in Reli-

---

precipitant: hasty, impetuous.
oppugner: opponent, antagonist.

[7]Coleridge here puns on the Latin word *errare*, which means "to wander." [Ed.]
[8]Here again, Coleridge's primary target is Godwinism. [Ed.]

gious and Political disquisitions. The asserter of the system has associated with it the preservation of Order, and public Virtue; the oppugner Imposture, and Wars, and Rapine. Hence, when they dispute, each trembles at the *consequences* of the other's opinions instead of attending to his train of arguments. Of this however we may be certain, whether we be Christians or Infidels, Aristocrats or Republicans, that our minds are in a state unsusceptible of Knowledge, when we feel an eagerness to detect the Falsehood of an Adversary's reasonings, not a sincere wish to discover if there be Truth in them; — when we examine an argument in order that we may answer it, instead of answering because we have examined it.

REMONSTRANCE TO THE FRENCH LEGISLATORS [1]

Guardians of the Liberty of Europe! the Individual, who has devoted his Joys and his Sorrows to the Interests of the whole, partakes of the importance of the object which he has accustomed himself to contemplate. He addresses you therefore with that dignity with which his subject interests him: for he speaks in the name of Human Kind. When America emancipated herself from the oppressive capriciousness of her old and doting Foster-Mother, we beheld an instructive speculation on the probable *Loss and Gain* of unprotected and untributary Independence; and considered the Congress as a respectable body of Tradesmen, deeply versed in the ledgers of Commerce, who well understood their own worldly concerns, and adventurously improved them. France presented a more interesting spectacle. Her great men with a profound philosophy investigated the interests common to all intellectual beings, and legislated for the World. The lovers of Mankind were every where fired and exalted by their example: each heart proudly expatriated itself, and we heard with transport of the victories of Frenchmen, as the victories of Human Nature. But the effects of Despotism could not be instantly removed with the cause: and the Vices, and the Ignorance, and the Terrors of the multitude conspired to subject them to the tyranny of a bloody and fanatic faction.[2] The fortune of France prevailed; and a Government has been established, which without counteracting the

---

Watchman (27 April 1796).

[1] Coleridge produced ten issues of the *Watchman*, his political and literary journal, in 1796; much of its political writing was opposed to Prime Minister William Pitt's war policies. [ED.]

[2] Coleridge refers to the radical Jacobins and the Reign of Terror carried out during their administration of the government. [ED.]

progressiveness, gratifies the more importunate frailties, of our present nature. To give stability to such a Constitution, it is needful only that its effects should be experienced.[3] Peace therefore is necessary.

At this season, when all the creative powers of nature are in action, and all things animated and inanimate inspire the human heart with joy and kindliness, at this season, your executive Department have transmitted a paper, which, they knew would be the signal for recommencing the horrors of War. Legislators of France! if you had been nursed amid the insolent splendour of hereditary prosperity, ignorant of misery and unsympathizing with the miserable, I should not dare to repeat to you the commonplace pleadings of humanity. — But *you* are from among your countrymen.

> But *you* were nurs'd upon the self-same hills,
> Fed the same stocks by fountains, shades, or rills:[4]

You ought to tremble and weep beneath the stern necessity, that should command you to issue the mandate for the death even of *one* man — alas! what if for the death of perhaps half-a-Million? Permit me then to examine whether or no this necessity existed. — The Directory assign as their motives for rejecting his Britannic Majesty's overtures, first, their doubts respecting the sincerity of the English Court, and secondly, "the constitutional act, which does not permit it to consent to any alienation of that which according to existing laws, constitutes the Territory of the Republic." — The Directory doubts the sincerity of the English Court, because Mr. Wickham who transmitted the overture, was not himself authorized to negotiate. [5]— If a disposition favourable to Peace had been discovered in the French Government, a man of greater name and dignity than the Minister to the Swiss Cantons, would have been appointed to treat with the August Legislature of France; but it ought not to have been expected, that the English Court should send a special messenger of high rank on an uncertain errand. To enquire concerning the intentions of the French Government, Mr. Wickham was well qualified by his being on the spot with the French Ambassador.

They doubt it likewise because a congress was proposed, "*of which the*

---

[3] The French National Convention, prior to disbanding in October 1795 and led by the moderate Girondins, established a new constitution and a new legislature that elected a five-man executive branch, the Directory. In March the Directory had rejected proposed peace talks with England. [ED.]

[4] Coleridge adapts lines 23–24 from Milton's *Lycidas* (1638): "For we were nurst upon the self-same hill, / Fed the same flock, by fountain, shade, and rill." [ED.]

[5] William Wickham (1761–1840), an English agent operating out of Switzerland, was dispatched by Pitt to initiate peace talks with the Directory in March 1796; the French government knew Wickham previously to have employed French émigrés as spies (Sutherland 300–04.) [ED.]

necessary result would be to render all negociation endless." The English Court on the other hand wished *"for the establishment of a congress, which has been so often and so happily the means of restoring Peace to Europe."* A mere assertion opposed to a mere assertion, and therefore both without force. But the Directory *did* communicate the general grounds of a pacification: they inform the contending Powers, that France is determined to retain her most important conquests: That an act of the Constitution forbids their restoration. — How are other Nations dependent on your internal regulations? What if in a paroxysm of victory ye had passed an act for the junction of England to France? But the inhabitants of the Netherlands themselves wish this union: and it would be unworthy a generous Republic to yield them up to their former Despotism.[6] We should not use those arguments, of which our adversaries may equally avail themselves. To the same motives expressed in the same words the horrors of La Vendee are to be attributed.[7] That no nation has the right of interfering with the internal affairs of another Country is a general law: and general laws must not be dispensed with in compliment to the supposed justice of a particular case.

The detention of the Netherlands cannot therefore be defended on the ground of *Justice:* its *Policy* alone remains to be considered! O France! have thy Legislators already degenerated into such abject court-craft, as to know any distinction between Justice and Policy? — But wherein does this Policy consist? Your Commissioners have informed you that these Provinces, reserving an ample supply for themselves, produce Corn enough to supply a third of France. Surely the toil and the treasures, which must be wasted in another campaign, might enable France not to need this supply. Or even if this were impracticable (which it would be insolent unthankfulness to nature to affirm), yet how easily might the free Commerce between France and the Netherlands be made one of the articles of Peace! And is there such magic in the *name* of internal commerce, as to make it the fit object of another series of crimes and miseries? Again, some among you have asserted, that in order to your security against the future ambitious attempts of your

---

[6] In October 1795 France annexed Belgium, making the region a part of the Republic; at the same time, France established Holland as the "independent" Batavian Republic. The Directory refused to part with the territories they had conquered. The question is what would become of these territories in order to secure peace: whether or not France will keep Belgium and whether or not France will give Holland back to Austria. Coleridge's phrase "their former Despotism" refers to the previous control of the Netherlands by Austria and the Dutch princes of Orange. [ED.]

[7] Led by a variety of French notables with English backing, La Vendee was a peasant insurrection against the French republican government in the western region of the Vendée, during the suppression of which thousands of people were killed on both sides. England's attempt to support the rebellion was poorly organized and ineffectual. [ED.]

enemies, it is necessary that you should retain the Netherlands. Your enemies assert with at least equal plausibility, that in order to their security against your ambition, it is necessary that you should not enlarge your territories. But, Legislators of France! if your system be true, a few years only of Peace would so increase your population and multiply your resources, as to place you beyond all danger of attack. The Tyrants of Europe will be ineffectually employed in preventing the irresistible influence of your example on your own subjects. — Let only your magnificent promises be performed, and we shall have no reason to doubt the Almightiness of Truth. That which in Theory has been ridiculed, must necessarily excite imitation, if realized: for why has it been ridiculed except that the despairing children of this world think it too excellent to be practicable? "Let us (says Condorcet[8]) be cautious not to despair of the human race. Let us dare to foresee in the ages that will succeed us, a knowledge and a happiness of which *we* can only form a vague and undetermined idea. Let us count on the *perfectibility* with which nature has endowed us; and on the strength of the human genius, from which long experience give us a right to expect prodigies." These are the revolutionary measures which Wisdom prescribes — not the intrigues of your Emissaries, not the terror of your arms.

If however you persevere in your intentions, will your soldiers fight with the same enthusiasm for the Ambition as they have done for the Liberty of their Country? Will they not by degrees amid the stern discipline of arms and the horrors of War, forget the proud duties of *Citizens,* and become callous to the softer claims of domestic life? May not some future Dumourier[9] find a more pliant Army? May not the distresses of the poor drive them to Anarchy? May not the rising generation, who have only *heard* of the evils of Despotism but have *felt* the horrors of a revolutionary Republic, imbibe sentiments favourable to Royalty? Will not the multitude of discontented men make *such* regulations necessary for the preservation of your Freedom, as in themselves destroy Freedom? Have not some of your supposed Patriots already deemed it expedient to limit the liberty of the Press? Legislators of France! in the name of Posterity we adjure you to consider, that misused success is soon followed by adversity, and that the adversity of France may lead, in its train of consequences, the slavery of all Europe!

Citizens: a politically charged term (as opposed to "royal subjects") with republican and revolutionary connotations.

[8] Marie Jean Antoine de Caritat, Marquis de Condorcet (1743–94), French philosopher. Coleridge quotes from Condorcet's posthumous *Outlines of an Historical View of the Progress of the Human Mind* (1795). [ED.]

[9] Charles-François Dumouriez (1739–1823), French general who led campaigns in the Netherlands and who defected to Austria in April 1793. [ED.]

FEARS IN SOLITUDE

Written April 1798
During the Alarm of an Invasion[1]

A green and silent spot amid the hills!
small and silent dell! — O'er stiller place
No singing sky-lark ever pois'd himself!
The hills are heathy, save that swelling slope,
5 Which hath a gay and gorgeous covering on,
All golden with the never-bloomless furze,
Which now blooms most profusely; but the dell,
Bath'd by the mist, is fresh and delicate,
As vernal corn field, or the unripe flax,
10 When thro' its half-transparent stalks, at eve,
The level sunshine glimmers with green light.
O 'tis a quiet spirit-healing nook,
Which all, methinks, would love; but chiefly he,
The humble man, who in his youthful years
15 Knew just so much of folly as had made
His early manhood more securely wise:[2]
Here he might lie on fern or wither'd heath,
While from the singing lark (that sings unseen
The minstrelsy that solitude loves best),
20 And from the sun, and from the breezy air,
Sweet influences trembled o'er his frame;[3]
And he with many feelings, many thoughts,
Made up a meditative joy, and found
Religious meanings in the forms of nature!
25 And so, his senses gradually wrapp'd
In a half sleep, he dreams of better worlds,

From *Fears in Solitude, Written in 1798, during the Alarm of an Invasion, to Which Are Added "France, an Ode" and "Frost at Midnight."* London: Johnson, 1798.

furze: an evergreen shrub.

[1] In February 1797, the French landed an invasionary force of 1,200 troops at Fishguard in Wales, with orders to burn Bristol and other English port cities. Although these troops were easily captured by the local militia, the incident greatly alarmed residents along the southern coast of England and led to frequent rumors of subsequent invasions. [ED.]
[2] Compare "The Rime of the Ancyent Marinere," lines 657–58. [ED.]
[3] Compare "Effusion XXXV," lines 37–38. [ED.]

And dreaming hears thee still, O singing lark!
That singest like an angel in the clouds.

    My God! it is a melancholy thing
30 For such a man, who would full fain preserve
His soul in calmness, yet perforce must feel
For all his human brethren—O my God,
It is indeed a melancholy thing,
And weighs upon the heart, that he must think
35 What uproar and what strife may now be stirring
This way or that way o'er these silent hills—
Invasion, and the thunder and the shout,
And all the crash of onset; fear and rage,
And undetermined conflict—even now,
40 Ev'n now, perchance, and in his native Isle,
Carnage and screams beneath this blessed sun!
We have offended, O my countrymen!
We have offended very grievously,
And have been tyrannous. From east to west
45 A groan of accusation pierces heaven!
The wretched plead against us, multitudes
Countless and vehement, the sons of God,
Our brethren! like a cloud that travels on,
Steam'd up from Cairo's swamps of pestilence,
50 Ev'n so, my countrymen! have we gone forth
And borne to distant tribes slavery and pangs,[4]
And, deadlier far, our vices, whose deep taint
With slow perdition murders the whole man,
His body and his soul! Meanwhile, at home,
55 We have been drinking with a riotous thirst
Pollutions from the brimming cup of wealth,[5]
A selfish, lewd, effeminated race,
Contemptuous of all honourable rule,
Yet bartering freedom, and the poor man's life,
60 For gold, as at a market! The sweet words
Of christian promise, words that even yet

---

[4]Throughout this verse paragraph, Coleridge laments England's continued participation in the African slave trade. [ED.]
[5]Here Coleridge is speaking metaphorically about the deleterious effects of luxury on the nation's moral character; however, his image of drinking "Pollutions from the brimming cup of wealth" probably also contains a reference to the boycott of West Indian sugar by British abolitionists to protest the slave trade. [ED.]

Might stem destruction, were they wisely preach'd,
Are mutter'd o'er by men, whose tones proclaim,
How flat and wearisome they feel their trade.
65 Rank scoffers some, but most too indolent,
To deem them falsehoods, or to *know* their truth.
O blasphemous! the book of life is made
A superstitious instrument, on which
We gabble o'er the oaths we mean to break;
70 For all must swear—all, and in every place,
College and wharf, council and justice-court;
All, all must swear, the briber and the brib'd,
Merchant and lawyer, senator and priest,
The rich, the poor, the old man and the young,
75 All, all make up one scheme of perjury,
That faith doth reel; the very name of God
Sounds like a juggler's charm; and bold with joy,
Forth from his dark and lonely hiding-place,
(Portentious sight!) the owlet, Atheism,
80 Sailing on obscene wings athwart the noon,
Drops his blue-fringed lids, and holds them close,
And, hooting at the glorious sun in heaven,
Cries out, "Where is it?" [6]
                                    Thankless too for peace,
(Peace long preserv'd by fleets and perilous seas)
85 Secure from actual warfare, we have lov'd
To swell the war-whoop, passionate for war!
Alas! for ages ignorant of all
Its ghastlier workings (famine or blue plague,
Battle, or siege, or flight thro' wintry snows)
90 We, this whole people, have been clamorous
For war and bloodshed, animating sports,
The which we pay for, as a thing to talk of,
Spectators and not combatants! no guess
Anticipative of a wrong unfelt,
95 No speculation on contingency,
However dim and vague, too vague and dim
To yield a justifying cause: and forth

---

blue plague: diseases arising from the corruption of dead bodies.

[6] See Coleridge's condemnation of the atheism of his fellow "Friends of Liberty" in *Conciones ad Populum* (216–19). [ED.]

(Stuff'd out with big preamble, holy names,
And adjurations of the God in Heaven,)
100 We send our mandates for the certain death
Of thousands and ten thousands! Boys and girls,
And women that would groan to see a child
Pull off an insect's leg, all read of war,
The best amusement for our morning meal!
105 The poor wretch, who has learnt his only prayers
From curses, who knows scarcely words enough
To ask a blessing of his heavenly Father,
Becomes a fluent phraseman, absolute
And technical in victories and defeats,
110 And all our dainty terms for fratricide,
Terms which we trundle smoothly o'er our tongues
Like mere abstractions, empty sounds to which
We join no feeling and attach no form,
As if the soldier died without a wound;
115 As if the fibres of this godlike frame
Were gor'd without a pang: as if the wretch,
Who fell in battle, doing bloody deeds,
Pass'd off to heaven, *translated* and not kill'd;
As tho' he had no wife to pine for him,
120 No God to judge him! —Therefore evil days
Are coming on us, O my countrymen!
And what if all-avenging Providence,
Strong and retributive, should make us know
The meaning of our words, force us to feel
125 The desolation and the agony
Of our fierce doings? —
                                        Spare us yet a while,
Father and God! O spare us yet a while!
O let not English women drag their flight
Fainting beneath the burden of their babes,
130 Of the sweet infants, that but yesterday
Laugh'd at the breast! Sons, brothers, husbands, all
Who ever gaz'd with fondness on the forms,
Which grew up with you round the same fire side,
And all who ever heard the sabbath bells
135 Without the infidel's scorn, make yourselves pure!
Stand forth! be men! repel an impious foe,
Impious and false, a light yet cruel race,

Who laugh away all virtue, mingling mirth
With deeds of murder; and still promising
140 Freedom, themselves too sensual to be free,
Poison life's amities, and cheat the heart
Of Faith and quiet Hope, and all that soothes
And all that lifts the spirit! Stand we forth;
Render them back upon th' insulted ocean,
145 And let them toss as idly on its waves,
As the vile sea-weeds, which some mountain blast
Swept from our shores! And O! may we return
Not with a drunken triumph, but with fear,
Repenting of the wrongs, with which we stung
So fierce a foe to frenzy!
150   I have told,
O Britons! O my brethren! I have told
Most bitter truth, but without bitterness.
Nor deem my zeal or factious or mistim'd;
For never can true courage dwell with them,
155 Who, playing tricks with conscience, dare not look
At their own vices. We have been too long
Dupes of a deep delusion! Some, belike,
Groaning with restless enmity, expect
All change from change of constituted power:
160 As if a government had been a robe,
On which our vice and wretchedness were tagg'd
Like fancy-points and fringes, with the robe
Pull'd off at pleasure. Fondly these attach
A radical causation to a few
165 Poor drudges of chastising Providence,
Who borrow all their hues and qualities
From our own folly and rank wickedness,
Which gave them birth, and nurse them. Others, meanwhile,
Dote with a mad idolatry; and all,
170 Who will not fall before their images,
And yield them worship, they are enemies
Even of their country! —Such have I been deem'd.
But, O dear Britain! O my mother Isle!
Needs must thou prove a name most dear and holy
175 To me, a son, a brother, and a friend,
A husband, and a father! who revere
All bonds of natural love, and find them all

Within the limits of thy rocky shores.
O native Britain! O my mother Isle!
180 How should'st thou prove aught else but dear and holy
To me, who from thy lakes and mountain-hills,
Thy clouds, thy quiet dales, thy rocks, and seas,
Have drunk in all my intellectual life,
All sweet sensations, all ennobling thoughts,
185 All adoration of God in nature,
All lovely and all honourable things,
Whatever makes this mortal spirit feel
The joy and greatness of its future being?
There lives nor form nor feeling in my soul
190 Unborrow'd from my country! O divine
And beauteous island, thou hast been my sole
And most magnificent temple, in the which
I walk with awe, and sing my stately songs,
Loving the God that made me! —
                                        May my fears,
195 My filial fears, be vain! and may the vaunts
And menace of the vengeful enemy
Pass like the gust, that roar'd and died away
In the distant tree, which heard, and only heard;
In this low dell bow'd not the delicate grass.
200 But now the gentle dew-fall sends abroad
The fruitlike perfume of the golden furze:
The light has left the summit of the hill,
Tho' still a sunny gleam lies beautiful
On the long-ivied beacon. — Now, farewell,
205 Farewell, awhile, O soft and silent spot!
On the green sheep-track, up the heathy hill,
Homeward I wind my way; and lo! recall'd
From bodings, that have well nigh wearied me,
I find myself upon the brow, and pause
210 Startled! And after lonely sojourning
In such a quiet and surrounded scene,
This burst of prospect, here the shadowy main,
Dim-tinted, there the mighty majesty
Of that huge amphitheatre of rich
215 And elmy fields, seems like society,
Conversing with the mind, and giving it
A livelier impulse, and a dance of thought;

And now, beloved Stowey! I behold
Thy church-tower, and (methinks) the four huge elms
220 Clust'ring, which mark the mansion of my friend;
And close behind them, hidden from my view,
Is my own lowly cottage, where my babe
And my babe's mother dwell in peace! With light
And quicken'd footsteps thitherward I tend,
225 Rememb'ring thee, O green and silent dell!
And grateful, that by nature's quietness
And solitary musings all my heart
Is soften'd, and made worthy to indulge
Love, and the thoughts that yearn for human kind.

Nether Stowey, April 20th, 1798

FRANCE

An Ode[1]

I

Ye Clouds, that far above me float and pause,
Whose pathless march no mortal may control!
Ye ocean-waves, that, wheresoe'er ye roll,
Yield homage only to eternal laws!
5 Ye woods, that listen to the night-bird's singing,
Midway the smooth and perilous steep reclin'd;
Save when your own imperious branches swinging
Have made a solemn music of the wind!
Where, like a man belov'd of God,
10 Thro' glooms, which never woodman trod,

From *Fears in Solitude, Written in 1798, during the Alarm of an Invasion, to Which Are Added "France, an Ode" and "Frost at Midnight."* London: Johnson, 1798.

Stowey: the village of Nether Stowey, where Coleridge lived from 1797 to 1798 with his wife, Sara, and his son, Hartley.
the mansion of my friend: Alfoxden, where Wordsworth lived with his sister, Dorothy, from 1797–98.

[1] An earlier version of this poem titled "The Recantation, an Ode" appeared in the 16 April 1798 edition of the *Morning Post*. [ED.]

How oft, pursuing fancies holy,
My moonlight way o'er flowering weeds I wound,
Inspir'd beyond the guess of folly,
By each rude shape, and wild unconquerable sound!
15 O, ye loud waves, and O, ye forests high!
And O, ye clouds, that far above me soar'd!
Thou rising sun! thou blue rejoicing sky!
Yea, every thing that is and will be free,
Bear witness for me wheresoe'er ye be,
20 With what deep worship I have still ador'd
The spirit of divinest liberty.

II

When France in wrath her giant limbs uprear'd,
And with that oath, which smote air, earth, and sea,
Stamp'd her strong foot and said, she would be free,
25 Bear witness for me, how I hop'd and fear'd!
With what a joy my lofty gratulation
Unaw'd I sung amid a slavish band:
And when to whelm the disenchanted nation,
Like fiends embattled by a wizard's wand,
30 The monarchs march'd in evil day,
And Britain join'd the dire array;[2]
Though dear her shores, and circling ocean,
Though many friendships, many youthful loves
Had swoln the patriot emotion,
35 And flung a magic light o'er all her hills and groves;
Yet still my voice unalter'd sang defeat
To all that brav'd the tyrant-quelling lance,
And shame too long delay'd, and vain retreat!
For ne'er, O Liberty! with partial aim
40 I dimm'd thy light, or damp'd thy holy flame;
But blest the paeans of deliver'd France,
And hung my head, and wept at Britain's name.

---

still: always.

[2] In 1792 Austria and Prussia invaded France in the hopes of restoring it to monarchical
rule. In February 1793, after France had repelled the Austrian and Prussia armies at the
Battle of Valmy and had in turn invaded the Rhineland and the Netherlands, England
declared war on the French Republic. [ED.]

III

"And what (I said) tho' blasphemy's loud scream
"With that sweet music of deliv'rance strove;
45 "Tho' all the fierce and drunken passions wove
"A dance more wild than e'er was maniac's dream;
"Ye storms, that round the dawning east assembled,
"The sun was rising, tho' ye hid his light!"
And when to sooth my soul, that hop'd and trembled,
50 The dissonance ceas'd, and all seem'd calm and bright;
When France, her front deep-scarr'd and gory,
Conceal'd with clust'ring wreaths of glory;
When insupportably advancing,
Her arm made mock'ry of the warrior's ramp,
55 While, timid looks of fury glancing,
Domestic treason, crush'd beneath her fatal stamp,
Writh'd, like a wounded dragon in his gore;
Then I reproach'd my fears that would not flee,
"And soon (I said) shall wisdom teach her lore
60 "In the low huts of them that toil and groan!
"And conqu'ring by her happiness alone,
"Shall France compel the nations to be free,
"Till love and joy look round, and call the earth their own!"[3]

IV

Forgive me, Freedom! O forgive these dreams!
65 I hear thy voice, I hear thy loud lament,
From bleak Helvetia's[4] icy caverns sent—
I hear thy groans upon her blood-stain'd streams!
Heroes, that for your peaceful country perish'd,

Helvetia's: Switzerland's.

[3] In this stanza, Coleridge describes his continued support of revolutionary France throughout the early and mid-1790s—despite the violence of the Reign of Terror and France's invasion of its eastern neighbors. [ED.]

[4] In February 1798 France invaded Switzerland, a country that was both neutral and democratic. To Coleridge and many other "Friends of Liberty," this invasion represented a complete betrayal of the Revolution's original aims since it was now clear that France was no longer trying to "compel the nations to be free" but simply engaging in imperialistic aggression. [ED.]

And ye, that fleeing spot the mountain snows
70 With bleeding wounds;[5] forgive me, that I cherish'd
One thought, that ever bless'd your cruel foes!
To scatter rage and trait'rous guilt
Where Peace her jealous home had built;
A patriot race to disinherit
75 Of all that made their stormy wilds so dear
And with inexpiable spirit
To taint the bloodless freedom of the mountaineer. —
O France! that mockest heav'n, adult'rous, blind,
And patriot only in pernicious toils!
80 Are these thy boasts, champion of human kind:
To mix with kings in the low lust of sway,
Yell in the hunt, and share the murd'rous prey;
T' insult the shrine of liberty with spoils
From freemen torn; to tempt and to betray!

V

85 The sensual and the dark rebel in vain,
Slaves by their own compulsion! In mad game
They burst their manacles, and wear the name
Of freedom graven on a heavier chain!
O Liberty! with profitless endeavour
90 Have I pursued thee many a weary hour:
But thou nor swell'st the victor's strain, nor ever
Didst breathe thy soul in forms of human pow'r.
Alike from all, howe'er they praise thee,
(Nor pray'r, nor boastful name delays thee)
95 Alike from priesthood's harpy minions,
And factious blasphemy's obscener slaves,[6]
Thou speedest on thy subtle pinions,
To live amid the winds, and move upon the waves!
And then I felt thee on that sea-cliff's verge,
100 Whose pines, scarce travell'd by the breeze above,

---

sway: dominion, power.

[5] Compare the imagery of this stanza to that of Milton's sonnet "On the Late Massacre in Piedmont." [ED.]

[6] Coleridge is referring to those "Friends of Liberty" who expressed antireligious or atheistic sentiments. [ED.]

Had made one murmur with the distant surge!
Yes! while I stood and gaz'd, my temples bare,
And shot my being thro' earth, sea, and air,
Possessing all things with intensest love,
105 O Liberty! my spirit felt thee there.

February 1798

FROST AT MIDNIGHT

The Frost performs its secret ministry,
Unhelp'd by any wind. The owlet's cry
Came loud—and hark, again! loud as before.
The inmates of my cottage, all at rest,
5   Have left me to that solitude, which suits
Abstruser musings: save that at my side
My cradled infant slumbers peacefully.
'Tis calm indeed! so calm, that it disturbs
And vexes meditation with its strange
10 And extreme silentness. Sea, hill, and wood,
This populous village! Sea, and hill, and wood,
With all the numberless goings-on of life,
Inaudible as dreams! The thin blue flame
Lies on my low-burnt fire, and quivers not:
15 Only that film,[1] which flutter'd on the grate,
Still flutters there, the sole unquiet thing,
Methinks, its motion in this hush of nature
Gives it dim sympathies with me, who live,
Making it a companionable form,
20 With which I can hold commune. Idle thought!
But still the living spirit in our frame,
That loves not to behold a lifeless thing,
Transfuses into all its own delights

From *Fears in Solitude, Written in 1798, during the Alarm of an Invasion, to Which Are Added "France, an Ode" and "Frost at Midnight."* London: Johnson, 1798.

cradled infant: Coleridge's son, Hartley.

[1] "*Only that film.* In all parts of the kingdom these films are called *strangers,* and supposed to portend the arrival of some absent friend." [Coleridge's note.] See Cowper's discussion of "strangers" in our selection from 4.292–95 of *The Task* (147). [ED.]

Its own volition, sometimes with deep faith,
25 And sometimes with fantastic playfulness.
Ah me! amus'd by no such curious toys
Of the self-watching subtilizing mind,
How often in my early school-boy days,
With most believing superstitious wish
30 Presageful have I gaz'd upon the bars,
To watch the *stranger* there! and oft belike,
With unclos'd lids, already had I dreamt
Of my sweet birth-place, and the old church-tower,
Whose bells, the poor man's only music, rang
35 From morn to evening, all the hot fair-day,
So sweetly, that they stirr'd and haunted me
With a wild pleasure, falling on mine ear
Most like articulate sounds of things to come!
So gaz'd I, till the soothing things, I dreamt,
40 Lull'd me to sleep, and sleep prolonged my dreams!
And so I brooded all the following morn,
Aw'd by the stern preceptor's[2] face, mine eye
Fix'd with mock study on my swimming book:
Save if the door half open'd, and I snatch'd
45 A hasty glance, and still my heart leapt up,
For still I hop'd to see the *stranger's* face,
Townsman, or aunt, or sister more belov'd,
My play-mate when we both were cloth'd alike!

Dear babe, that sleepest cradled by my side,
50 Whose gentle breathings, heard in this deep calm,
Fill up the interspersed vacancies
And momentary pauses of the thought!
My babe so beautiful! it fills my heart
With tender gladness, thus to look at thee,
55 And think, that thou shalt learn far other lore,
And in far other scenes! For I was rear'd
In the great city, pent mid cloisters dim,[3]

---

my sweet birth-place: Ottery St. Mary in Devon.
sister more belov'd: Coleridge's sister, Ann, or, as she was called by the family, Nancy.

[2]This "stern preceptor" (teacher) is usually identified as the Rev. James Bowyer of Christ's Hospital, the London grammar school that Coleridge attended following the death of his father. [ED.]
[3]Milton, *Paradise Lost* 9.445: "As one who long in populous City pent." [ED.]

And saw nought lovely but the sky and stars.
But *thou*, my babe! shalt wander like a breeze,
60 By lakes and sandy shores, beneath the crags
Of ancient mountain, and beneath the clouds,
Which image in their bulk both lakes and shores
And mountain crags: so shalt thou see and hear
The lovely shapes and sounds intelligible
65 Of that eternal language, which thy God
Utters, who from eternity doth teach
Himself in all, and all things in himself.
Great universal Teacher! he shall mould
Thy spirit, and by giving make it ask.

70 Therefore all seasons shall be sweet to thee,
Whether the summer clothe the general earth
With greenness, or the redbreast sit and sing
Betwixt the tufts of snow on the bare branch
Of mossy apple-tree, while all the thatch
75 Smokes in the sun-thaw: whether the eave-drops fall
Heard only in the trances of the blast,
Or whether the secret ministry of cold
Shall hang them up in silent icicles,
Quietly shining to the quiet moon,
80 Like those, my babe! which, ere to-morrow's warmth
Have capp'd their sharp keen points with pendulous drops,
Will catch thine eye, and with their novelty
Suspend thy little soul; then make thee shout,
And stretch and flutter from thy mother's arms
85 As thou would'st fly for very eagerness.[4]

February 1798

---

redbreast: European robin which, unlike the North American robin, is a winter bird and thus not a sign of spring.
pendulous: hanging.

[4] Lines 80–85 were deleted in later editions of this poem. [ED.]

THE BALLAD REVIVAL

As we have suggested in the Introduction, the title *Lyrical Bal-lads* is something of an oxymoron in its suggestion of a hy-brid—one might even say bastardized—form. Lyrics and ballads are practically the opposite of each other. The late eighteenth century, however, was indeed a time when poets attempted to yoke seemingly disparate forms to create something new. In 1784, for instance, Charlotte Smith published her *Elegiac Sonnets,* suggesting in the book's title a deviation from the rhyme scheme of the Italian sonnet that, at that time, was deemed the only "legitimate" kind of sonnet; also in 1784 another innovative poet, Anna Seward, published *Louisa,* which she called "a poetical novel in four epistles," casting popular epistolary prose fiction in heroic couplets. Since few reviewers even remarked on the title of *Lyrical Ballads* when it appeared in 1798, we may assume that readers had become accustomed to the playful impropriety of such potentially gimmicky titles.

So, what is a "lyrical ballad"? The phrase has proven to be a delightfully amorphous and mischievous term.[1] Most contemporary readers of *Lyrical Ballads,* however, would have understood at least the basic ground rules of the game: A *lyric,* a term derived from ancient Greek poetry for a poem sung to the accompaniment of a lyre, tends to be a short poem—such as the sonnet, which was popular at the time—with a single speaker who develops a subjective insight, mood, or emotion. *Ballads* were ubiquitous in the eighteenth century as popular, entertaining narrative poems that carried with them a cultural link to Anglo-Saxon and medieval poetry of ancient Britain. Given the interest Wordsworth's poems in particular take in ordinary life and conversational language, and given the way Coleridge's "Ancyent Marinere" deliberately employs archaic English, the somewhat subversive juxtaposition of the classical (high culture) and the folk (popular culture) must not have been lost on the two authors.

---

[1] For more on this question, see Robert Mayo 506–14, John Jordan 172–86, Stephen Parrish 80–187, Paul Sheats 184–85, and Stuart Curran, *Poetic Form* 182.

To readers in 1798, though, the lyric was probably a more abstract generic distinction than the ballad, or at least a general, loosely employed one. Wordsworth's Preface to *Lyrical Ballads* provides something of a clue to the "lyrical" implication of the title; he writes,

> one other circumstance which distinguishes these Poems from the popular Poetry of the day; it is this, that the feeling therein developed gives importance to the action and situation, and not the action and situation to the feeling.

Without reading too much into this remark, we might suppose at the very least that Wordsworth intends to subordinate plot to lyrical introspection, as we have suggested he does with "Simon Lee" (see Introduction). And he clearly means to distinguish these "lyrical" ballads, a title he retained through subsequent editions of the book, from commonplace, more consumable "ballads" whose *raison d'être* is simply the telling of stories. In his review of the volume, Robert Southey's apparent consternation over what he considered the flimsy, negligible plot of "The Idiot Boy," for instance, gives us a sense of the contemporary expectations for a ballad that Wordsworth thwarts.[2]

The designation that these are "lyrical" ballads, moreover, as Wordsworth would explain in the 1802 Preface, indicates a metrical improvement upon conventional ballads. "The metre of the old Ballads is very artless," Wordsworth writes, but he finds that, in a few instances, the meter works to increase the aesthetic enjoyment of the narrative. For Wordsworth, meter tempers the extreme sensibility a fantastic tale or powerful image might induce through the assertion of regularity, implicitly the regularity of stressed and unstressed syllables. In describing the meter of the old, Anglo-Saxon poets as "artless," no doubt Wordsworth recognizes the ancient tendency in English meter to quantify only stressed syllables, whereas continental poetry traditionally counts the total number of syllables per line. The English line, since Chaucer, counts both stressed and unstressed syllables, which is why iambic pentameter is always a ten-syllable line. Thus, modern English versification is more regular in its rhythm; this regularity, according to Wordsworth, is essential to poetic pleasure:

> the co-presence of something regular, something to which the mind has been accustomed in various moods and in a less excited state, cannot but have great efficacy in tempering and restraining the passion by an intertexture of ordinary feeling, and of feeling not strictly and necessarily connected with the passion.

---

[2] See the headnote to "Contemporary Reviews" in Part Three.

Wordsworth, moreover, believes the assertion of meter to be an essential quality of his "lyrical" ballads that makes them superior to their predecessors. In the Preface, he particularly distinguishes "Goody Blake and Harry Gill" as having "a more impressive metre than is usual in Ballads." Clearly, he finds meter also essential in poems, such as "Goody Blake," that offer particular challenges to the imagination. Meter, to use Coleridge's famous definition of "poetic faith," aids considerably in the suspension of one's disbelief; or, in other words, the regularity of meter, like that of rhyme, makes an idea seem more true.

Although Wordsworth may not have had as sophisticated an understanding of Anglo-Saxon prosody as, say, Ezra Pound would later, he recognized a distinction between his use of meter in the ballad, making it "lyrical," and that of popular — and "artless" — ballads derived or imitated from the old English balladeers. *Lyrical Ballads* came toward the end of the eighteenth-century ballad revival sparked by the publication in 1765 of *Reliques of Ancient English Poetry*, a collection of various kinds of poetry from various periods of history, some quite ancient. Thomas Percy drew upon a seventeenth-century manuscript (now called "The Percy Folio") of old English ballads, adding his own revisions and more recent works by such authors as John Dryden, William Shenstone, Richard Lovelace, and others. Although antiquarians such as Joseph Ritson (1752–1803) attacked Percy for some rather creative and misleading editorial practices, Percy expanded the *Reliques* to four editions by 1794, and they remained popular throughout the nineteenth century. The *Reliques* participated in a vogue for primitivism in the second half of the eighteenth century that was at least partially motivated by the thinking of Jean-Jacques Rousseau and that included a new emphasis on rustic life, an interest in exotic travelogues, a penchant for "wild" landscapes, and a general curiosity in anything "savage" or uncultivated. The rage for primitive poetry produced even archaic forgeries such as Thomas Chatterton's Felix Farley and Thomas Rowleie poems and James Macpherson's *The Poems of Ossian*. Interestingly, Joanna Baillie, the writer who would anticipate some of the ideas in Wordsworth's Preface in her "Introductory Discourse" (159–66), published in 1790 a volume of poems, including several ballads, that explicitly set out to describe "rustic manners." Her "Storm-Beat Maid" (248–53), for instance, claims to have been written "after the style of our old English ballads." Percy's *Reliques*, moreover, did much to instill in the general reading public a sense of national pride in England's own literary tradition that inspired similar attempts at cultural archaeology by such Scottish writers as Robert Burns and Walter Scott.

Given the tastes of readers during the Age of Sensibility, the popularity of these ballads makes sense because they are raw and deal with emotions in direct and unadorned manner and frequently draw upon the supernatural. The vogue for Gothic literature in the second half of the century begins with Percy's ballads and the corresponding rise of Sensibility; moreover, the supernatural quality of these poems coincides with the contemporary appreciation of the sublime, which Edmund Burke, in his *Enquiry into the Origins of Our Ideas of the Sublime and Beautiful* (1757), explicitly associates with the experience of terror.

The popularity of the *Reliques* provided Wordsworth with an understanding of the ancient ballad tradition (even though he did not own a copy of the book until 1800). What Wordsworth calls "artless" in the old ballads, Percy presents as something distinctly English. In 1815 Wordsworth wrote of the influence of Percy's *Reliques* on him in relation to the *Lyrical Ballads:* "I do not think there is an able writer in verse of the present day who would not be proud to acknowledge his debt to the Reliques; I know that it is so with my friends; and, for myself, I am happy in this occasion to make a public avowal of my own" (*Prose Works* 3.78). Wordsworth also believed that the book "absolutely redeemed" English versification.[3] Percy's introductory essay shows that he understands the improvement of English versification since the ancient balladeers: "The old Minstrel-ballads are in the northern dialect, abound with antique words and phrases, are extremely incorrect, and run into the utmost license of metre; they have also a romantic wildness, and are in the true spirit of chivalry" (xxii). Despite their being metrically uncouth, Percy considers the ancient ballads—more primitive because the northern regions, he points out, were civilized later—to be superior to the later balladeers, "who wrote narrative songs meerly for the press" (xxii). Having written at length on how the ancient balladeers continued the tradition of singing to the harp, Percy contrasts their method to the more recent breed of balladeer whose poems appear instead on paper, the broadside, intended to be sung to any number of well-known tunes: these, he writes,

> are written in exacter measure [meter], have a low or subordinate correctness, sometimes bordering on the insipid, yet often well adapted to the pathetic; these are generally in the southern dialect, exhibit a more modern phraseology, and are commonly descriptive of more modern manners. (xxii–xxiii)

Percy recognized an improvement, over time, in style if not in substance in that these later poems were, strictly speaking, more "lyrical" in being more metrically regular. In other words, their being written down necessitated the achievement of musical effects through meter. But, as Robert

---

[3] See Mary Jacobus's chapter on the ballad revival (209–32).

Mayo has pointed out, the popular ballads filling the pages of magazines and newspapers by the end of the century showed that their authors had little conception of the meaning of "lyrical" or, for that matter, "ballad" (507). Wordsworth's "lyrical" ballads would aim to correct this defect.

Percy's *Reliques* made the ballad form popular again. But even Percy himself apologized for their imperfections, hoping that their "pleasing simplicity, and many artless graces" may "compensate for the want of higher beauties" and that "if they do not dazzle the imagination" they may be "frequently found to interest the heart" (x). It would take the innovations of a German poet influenced by the *Reliques,* Gottfried August Bürger, to realize the imaginative potential of the form. Many of the *Reliques* develop Gothic settings and macabre themes, such as the famous Scottish ballad "Sweet William's Ghost," in which young Margaret is carried away by the ghost of her lover. Bürger exploited fully the hair-raising potential of the ancient ballads, reinventing the Scottish ballad as his own German poem "Lenore." These self-consciously imitative literary ballads, or "art ballads" — thus differentiated from the folk ballads composed by the common people of the past — became ubiquitous in various literary periodicals of the time, particularly the *Monthly Magazine,* in which Wordsworth and Coleridge originally planned to publish "The Ancyent Marinere."[4]

The success of Bürger's ballads, translated by William Taylor of Norwich, then, had no small influence on *Lyrical Ballads.* Recognizing the deliberate artfulness of his poetry in 1796, Taylor praised Bürger for his "manly sentiment and force of style"; Taylor's description of Bürger's style anticipates the way in which Wordsworth would describe his own style in the Advertisement to *Lyrical Ballads:*

> His extraordinary powers of language are founded on a rejection of the conventional phraseology of regular poetry, in favour of popular forms of expression, caught by the listening artist from the voice of agitated nature. [. . .] The hurrying vigour of his impetuous diction is unrivalled; yet, it is so natural, even in its sublimity, that his poetry is singularly fitted to become national popular song. (118)

But Bürger's ballads, lyrical though they may be, are different from Wordsworth's primarily because they are not about everyday life or humble and rustic people; they are in keeping with the German Gothic tradition of supernaturalism, full of ghosts and demons and whatever else goes bump in the night. Wordsworth enjoyed Bürger but found this kind of poetry con-

---

[4] As Jacobus notes, Sir Walter Scott, in his 1830 "Essay on Imitations of the Ancient Ballad," recognized the "art ballad" as a particular brand of poetry (212).

sumable but not nutritious: "Bürger," he wrote to Coleridge, "is the poet of the animal spirits. I love his *'Tra ra la'* dearly; but less of the horn and more of the lute—and far, far more of the pencil" (*Early Years* 235). Wordsworth wants more craft and less bombast, referring, in the Preface to *Lyrical Ballads*, to the craze for the Gothic as a "degrading thirst after outrageous stimulation" that he aims to "counteract." Because of its "manners," meaning its craftsmanship, Wordworth much preferred Burns's "Tam o' Shanter" to anything Bürger wrote (*Early Years* 255).[5]

The fantastic element of this poetry typically appealed more to Coleridge, who, in 1798, disagreed sharply with Wordsworth's disparagement of "Lenore" (*Letters* 1.565–66). Coleridge's masterpieces "The Rime of the Ancyent Marinere" and "Christabel" clearly color Percy's primitivism with Bürger's supernaturalism; a reviewer for the *Analytical Review* unfavorably made the comparison, writing that "The Ancyent Marinere" "has more of the extravagance of a mad german poet, than of the simplicity of our ancient ballad writers." This influence no doubt partially accounts for Wordsworth's increasing ambivalence toward "The Ancyent Marinere," his demotion of it to the end of the first volume of the 1800 *Lyrical Ballads*, and his decision to drop "Christabel" altogether from the book's second edition. Greatly disappointed, Coleridge realized that "Christabel" contrasted sharply with Wordsworth's poetic agenda, which by 1800 had determined the contents of the 1800 edition. "Christabel," he could see,

> was in direct opposition to the very purpose for which the *Lyrical Ballads* were published, viz. an experiment to see how far those passions, which alone give any value to extraordinary incidents, were capable of interesting, in and for themselves, in the incidents of common life. (*Letters* 1.631)

Coleridge knew that Wordsworth wanted only slight touches of the sublime and fantastic to shade the mundane and ordinary—his most innovative contribution to the ballad revival, the elision or parody of the supernatural inherent in the tradition. Wordsworth wanted Percy's form but wanted it regularized through meter and stanza and stripped of the unsavory associations with the Gothic it had picked up through Bürger's (and Taylor's) revisioning. Coleridge, in contrast, wanted to revel in the irregularity and nightmarish fantasy of the ancient ballads. Where Wordsworth recognized

---

[5] See "Rustic and Humanitarian Poetry." But, as both Parrish (88–90) and Jacobus (219–20) point out, Bürger did influence Wordsworth's lyrical ballads, particularly "The Idiot Boy" and "The Thorn." By 1800 Wordsworth may have felt encouraged to express his contempt for the Gothic ballad by Samuel Whyte's vitriolic 1799 critique of "Lenore," of which he says famously, "It out-herods Herod" (Jacobus 224).

poetic pleasure in regulating the excesses of the form, Coleridge recognized in the ballad demonic metaphorical implications for exploring the unconscious mind and the psychological anguish of guilt—as Fanny Holcroft puts it in our selection, "Conscience [Is] the Worst of Tortures." "The Wandering Jew," for instance, from Percy's *Reliques,* provides an archetype for Coleridge's mariner, his sin, and his dubious redemption. Percy's "Barbara Allen's Cruelty," Taylor's translations of Bürger's "Lenora" and "The Lass of Fair Wone," and M. G. Lewis's "Alonzo the Brave and Fair Imogine" develop the psychosexual implications of the ballad that would prove so essential in interpreting "Christabel" through the suggested atmosphere of sexual or spiritual perversity that galvanizes the narratives of each.

THE WANDERING JEW [1]

Anonymous

When as in faire Jerusalem
   Our Saviour Christ did live,
And for the sins of all the worlde
   His own deare life did give:
5 The wicked Jewes with scoffes and scornes
   Did dailye him molest,
That never till he left his life,
   Our Saviour could not rest.

When they had crown'd his head with thornes,
10   And scourg'd him to disgrace,
In scornfull sort they led him forthe
   Unto his dying place;
Where thousand thousands in the streete
   Beheld him passe along,
15 Yet not one gentle heart was there,
   That pityed this his wrong.

From *Reliques of Ancient English Poetry: Consisting of Old Heroic Ballads, Songs, and Other Pieces of Our Earlier Poets, (Chiefly of the Lyric Kind) Together with Some Few of Later Date.* Ed. Thomas Percy. 2nd ed. Vol. 2. London: Dodsley, 1767.

[1] There are many variations of this legend, but virtually all follow the basic details of this version—how a man, named Ahasuerus in many accounts, is doomed to wander the earth because of his abuse of Christ while he is carrying his cross to Calvary. Percy (1729–1811), an antiquarian scholar and translator, became bishop of Dromore in 1782. The first edition of Percy's *Reliques* appeared in 1765; the second edition included more poems. [ED.]

But old and young reviled him,
    As in the streete he wente,
And nought he found but churlich tauntes,
20   By every ones consente:
His own deare crosse he bore himselfe,
    A burthen far too great,
Which made him in the street to fainte,
    With blood and water sweat.

25 Being weary thus, he sought for rest,
    To ease his burthened soule,
Upon a stone: the which a wretch
    Did churlishly controule;
And sayd, Awaye, thou king of Jewes,
30   Thou shalt not rest thee here;
Pass on; the execution place
    Thou seest nowe draweth neare.

And thereupon he thrust him thence;
    At which our Saviour sayd,
35 I sure will rest, but thou shalt walke,
    And have no journey stayed.
With that this cursed shoemaker,
    For offering Christ this wrong,
Left wife and children, house and all,
40   And went from thence along.

Where after he had seene the bloude
    Of Jesus Christ thus shed,
And to the crosse his bodye nail'd,
    Awaye with speed he fled
45 Without returning backe againe
    Unto his dwelling place,
And wandred up and downe the worlde,
    A runnagate most base.

No resting could he finde at all,
50   No ease, nor hearts content;
No house, nor home, nor biding place:
    But wandring forth he went

---

churlich: rude, boorish.
runnagate: fugitive, outcast.

From towne to towne in foreigne landes,[2]
   With grieved conscience still,
55 Repenting for the heinous guilt
   Of his fore-passed ill.

Thus after some fewe ages past
   In wandring up and downe;
He much again desired to see
60   Jerusalems renowne,
But finding it all quite destroyed,
   He wandred thence with woe,
Our Saviours wordes, which he had spoke,
   To verefie and showe.

65 "I'll rest, sayd hee, but thou shalt walke,"
   So doth this wandering Jew
From place to place, but cannot rest
   For seeing countries newe;
Declaring still the power of him,
70   Whereas he comes or goes,
And of all things done in the east,
   Since Christ his death, he showes.

The world he hath still compast round
   And seene those nations strange,
75 The hearing of the name of Christ,
   Their idol gods doe change:
To whom he hath told wondrous thinges
   Of time forepast, and gone,
And to the princes of the worlde
80   Declares his cause to moane:

Desiring still to be dissolv'd,
   And yield his mortal breath;
But, if the Lord hath thus decreed,
   He shall not yet see death.
85 For neither lookes he old nor young,
   But as he did those times,
When Christ did suffer on the crosse
   For mortall sinners crimes.

---

[2]Compare "The Rime of the Ancyent Marinere," line 619: "I pass, like night, from land to land." [ED.]

He hath past through many a foreigne place,
90 Arabia, Egypt, Africa,
Grecia, Syria, and great Thrace,
    And throughout all Hungaria:
Where Paul and Peter preached Christ,
    Those blest apostles deare;
95 There he hath told our Saviours wordes,
    In countries far, and neare.

And lately in Bohemia,
    With many a German towne;
And now in Flanders, as 'tis thought,
100 He wandreth up and downe:
Where learned men with him conferre
    Of those his lingering dayes,
And wonder much to heare him tell
    His journeyes, and his wayes.

105 If people give this Jew an almes,
    The most that he will take
Is not above a groat a time;
    Which he, for Jesus' sake,
Will kindlye give unto the poore,
110 And therefore make no spare,
Affirming still that Jesus Christ
    Of him hath dailye care.

He ne'er was seene to laugh nor smile,
    But weepe and make great moane;
115 Lamenting still his miseries,
    And dayes forepast and gone:
If he heare any one blaspheme,
    Or take God's name in vaine,
He telles them that they crucifie
120 Their Saviour Christe againe.

If you had seene his death, saith he,
    As these mine eyes hath done,
Ten thousand thousand times would yee
    His torments think upon:
125 And suffer for his sake all paine
    Of torments, and all woes.

These are his wordes and eke his life
    Whereas he comes or goes.

BARBARA ALLEN'S CRUELTY

Anonymous

*Given, with some corrections, from an old printed copy in the editor's
possession, intitled "Barbara Allen's cruelty or the young man's tragedy."*

In Scarlet towne, where I was borne,
    There was a faire maid dwellin,
Made every youth crye, wel-awaye!
    Her name was Barbara Allen.

5   All in the merrye month of May,
    When greene buds they were swellin,
Yong Jemmye Grove on his death-bed lay,
    For love of Barbara Allen.

He sent his man unto her then,
10   To the town, where shee was dwellin;
You must come to my master deare,
    Giff your name be Barbara Allen.

For death is printed on his face,
    And ore his hart is stealin:
15   Then haste away to comfort him,
    O lovelye Barbara Allen.

Though death be printed on his face,
    And ore his harte is stealin,
Yet little better shall he bee,
20   For bonny Barbara Allen.

So slowly, slowly, she came up,
    And slowly she came nye him;

---

eke: also.

From *Reliques of Ancient English Poetry: Consisting of Old Heroic Ballads,
Songs, and Other Pieces of Our Earlier Poets, (Chiefly of the Lyric Kind) Together with Some Few of Later Date.* Ed. Thomas Percy. 2nd ed. Vol. 2. London: Dodsley, 1767.

Giff: if.

And all she sayd, when there she came,
    Yong man, I think y'are dying.

25 He turnd his face unto her strait,
    With deadlye sorrow sighing;
O lovely maid, come pity mee,
    Ime on my death-bed lying.

If on your death-bed you doe lye,
30   What needs the tale you are tellin:
I cannot keep you from your death;
    Farewell, sayd Barbara Allen.

He turnd his face unto the wall,
    As deadlye pangs he fell in:
35 Adieu! adieu! adieu to you all,
    Adieu to Barbara Allen.

As she was walking ore the fields,
    She heard the bell a knellin;
And every stroke did seem to saye,
40   Unworthy Barbara Allen.

She turnd her bodye round about,
    And spied the corps a coming:
Laye downe, laye downe the corps, she sayd,
    That I may look upon him.

45 With scornful eye she looked downe,
    Her cheeke with laughter swellin;
That all her friends cryd out amaine,
    Unworthye Barbara Allen.

When he was dead, and laid in grave,
50   Her harte was struck with sorrowe,
O mother, mother, make my bed,
    For I shall dye to morrowe.

Hard harted creature him to slight,
    Who loved me so dearlye:
55 O that I had beene more kind to him,
    When he was live and neare me!

———————

amaine: suddenly, with great emphasis.

She, on her death-bed as she laye,
   Beg'd to be buried by him;
And sore repented of the daye,
60   That she did ere denye him.

Farewell, she sayd, ye virgins all,
   And shun the fault I fell in:
Henceforth take warning by the fall
   Of cruel Barbara Allen.

THE STORM-BEAT MAID

Joanna Baillie [1]

Somewhat after the style of our old English ballads

All shrouded in the winter snow,
   The maiden held her way;
Nor chilly winds that roughly blow,
   Nor dark could her stay.

5   O'er hill and dale, through bush and briar,
   She on her journey kept;
Save often when she 'gan to tire,
   She stop'd awhile and wept.

Wild creatures left their caverns drear,
10   To raise their nightly yell;
But little doth the bosom fear,
   Where inward troubles dwell.

No watch-light from the distant spire,
   To cheer the gloom of deep,
15   Nor twinkling star, nor cottage fire
   Did thro' the darkness peep.

Yet heedless still she held her way,
   Nor fear'd she crag nor dell;
Like ghost that thro' the gloom to stray,
20   Wakes with the midnight bell.

From *Poems; Wherein It Is Attempted to Describe Certain Views of Nature and of Rustic Manners*. London: Johnson, 1790.

[1] See the selection from *A Series of Plays* (159–66). [ED.]

Now night thro' her dark watches ran,
  Which lock the peaceful mind;
And thro' the neighboring hamlets 'gan
  To wake the yawning hind.

25 Yet bark of dog, nor village cock,
  That spoke in the morning near;
Nor gray-light trembling on the rock,
  Her 'nighted mind could cheer.

The whirling flail, and clacking mill
30 Wake with the early day;
And careless children, loud and shrill,
  With new-made snow-balls play.

And as she pass'd each cottage door,
  They did their gambols cease;
35 And old men shook their locks so hoar,
  And wish'd her spirit peace.

For sometimes slow, and sometimes fast,
  She held her wav'ring pace;
Like early spring's inconstant blast,
40 That ruffles evening's face.

At length with weary feet she came,
  Where in a shelt'ring wood,
Whose master bore no humble name,
  A stately castle stood.

45 The open gate, and smoking fires,
  Which cloud the air so thin;
And shrill bell twinkling from the spires,
  Bespoke a feast within.

With busy looks, and hasty tread,
50 The servants cross the hall;
And many a page, in buskins red,
  Await the master's call.

Fair streaming bows of bridal white
  On ev'ry shoulder play'd;

---

hind: farmhand.
gambols: play.
buskins: boots.

₅₅ And clean, in lily kerchief dight,
    Trip'd every houshold maid.

She ask'd for neither lord nor dame,
    Nor who the mansion own'd;
But straight into the hall she came
₆₀   And sat her on the ground.

The busy crew all crouded nigh,
    And round the stranger star'd;
But still she roll'd her wand'ring eye,
    Nor for their questions car'd.

₆₅ "What dost thou want, thou storm-beat' maid,
    "That thou these portals past?
"Ill suiteth here thy looks dismay'd
    "Thou art no bidden guest."

"O chide not!" said a gentle page,
₇₀   And wip'd his tear-wet cheek,
"Who would not shun the winter's rage?
    "The wind is cold and bleak.

"Her robe is stiff with drizly snow,
    "And rent her mantle grey;
₇₅ "None ever bade the wretched go
    "Upon his wedding-day."

Then to his lord he hied him straight,
    Where round on silken seat
Sat many a courteous dame and knight,
₈₀   And made obeisance meet.

"There is a stranger in your hall,
    "Who wears no common mien;
"Hard were the heart, as flinty wall,
    "That would not take her in.

₈₅ "A fairer dame in hall or bower
    "Mine eyes did ne'er behold;
"Tho' shelter'd in no father's tower,
    "And turn'd out in the cold.

---

dight: adorned.
hied him straight: hastened directly.

"Her face is like an early morn,
90   "Dimm'd with the nightly dew;
"Her skin is like the sheeted torn,
    "Her eyes are wat'ry blue.

"And tall and slender is her form,
    "Like willow o'er the brook;
95 "But in her brow there broods a storm,
    "And restless is her look.

"And well her troubled motions shew
    "The tempest in her mind;
"Like the unshelter'd sapling bough
100   "Vex'd with the wintry wind.

"Her head droops on her ungirt breast,
    "And scatter'd is her hair;
"Yet lady brac'd in courtly vest
    "Was never half so fair."

105 Reverse, and cold the turning blood
    The bridegrooms's cheek forsook:
He shook and stagger'd as he stood,
    And falter'd as he spoke.

"So soft and fair I know a maid,
110   "There is but only she;
"A wretched man her love betray'd,
    "And wretched let him be."

Deep frowning, turn'd the bride's dark eye,
    For bridal morn unmeet;
115 With trembling steps her lord did hie
    The stranger fair to greet.

Tho' loose in scatter'd weeds array'd
    And ruffled with the storm;
Like lambkin from its fellows stray'd,
120   He knew her graceful form.

But when he spy'd her sunken eye,
    And features sharp and wan,

---

torn: tarn, a mountain lake.
unmeet: ill suited.

He heav'd a deep and heavy sigh,
    And down the big tears ran.

125 "Why droops thy head, thou lovely maid,
    "Upon thy hand of snow?
"Is it because thy love betray'd,
    "That thou art brought so low?"

Quick from her eye the keen glance came
130   Who question'd her to see:
And oft she mutter'd o'er his name,
    And wist not it was he.

Full hard against his writhing brows
    His clenched hands he prest;
135 Full high his lab'ring bosom rose,
    And rent its silken vest.

"O cursed be the golden price,
    "That did my baseness prove!
"And cursed be my friends advice,
140   "That wil'd me from thy love!

"And cursed be the woman's art,
    "That lur'd me to her snare!
"And cursed be the faithless heart
    "That left thee to despair!

145 "Yet now I'll hold thee by my side,
    "Tho' worthless I have been,
"Nor friends, nor wealth, nor dizen'd bride,
    "Shall ever stand between.

"When thou art weary and depress'd,
150   "I'll lull thee to thy sleep;
"And when dark fancies vex thy breast,
    "I'll sit by thee and weep.

"I'll tend thee like a restless child
    "Where'er thy rovings be;
155 "Nor gesture keen, nor eye-ball wild,
    "Shall turn my love from thee.

---

wist: knew.
dizen'd: gaudily dressed.

"Night shall not hang cold o'er thy head,
   "And I securely lie;
"And drizly clouds upon thee shed,
160   "And I in covert dry.

"I'll share the cold blast on the heath,
   "I'll share thy wants and pain:
"Nor friend nor foe, nor life nor death,
   "Shall ever make us twain."

LENORA

A Ballad

Gottfried August Bürger[1]

At break of day, with frightful dreams
   Lenora struggled sore:
My William, art thou slaine, say'd she,
   Or dost thou love no more?

5 He went abroade with Richard's host,
   The Paynim foes to quell;
But he no word to her had writt,
   An he were sick or well.

With sowne of trump and beat of drum,
10   His fellow soldyers come;

Monthly Magazine (March 1796).

Richard's host: the crusade to the Holy Land in 1190 led by King Richard I.
Paynim: pagan.
An: if.
sowne: sound.

[1] Bürger (1747–94), a German poet, based his version on the Scottish ballad "Sweet William's Ghost," which appeared in Percy's *Reliques*. This poem and the following were both translated by William Taylor (1765–1836) from the German "Lenore," first published in 1774. Taylor's "Lenora" appeared in the *Monthly Magazine* prefaced with: "The following translation (made some years since) of a celebrated piece, of which other versions have appeared, and are now on the point of appearing, possesses so much peculiar and intrinsic merit, that we are truly happy in being permitted to present it to our Readers." One notable version, not included here, is Sir Walter Scott's "William and Helen," which was inspired by Taylor's translation and published later the same year. [ED.]

Their helmes bydeckt with oaken boughs,
   They seeke their long'd-for home.

And ev'ry roade, and ev'ry lane
   Was full of old and young,
15 To gaze at the rejoicing band,
   To hail with gladsome toung.

"Thank God!" their wives and children saide,
   "Welcome!" the brides did saye:
But greete or kiss Lenora gave
20   To none upon that daye.

She askte of all the passing traine,
   For him she wisht to see:
But none of all the passing traine
   Could tell if lived hee.

25 And when the soldyers all were bye,
   She tore her raven haire,
And cast herself upon the growne
   In furious despaire.

Her mother ran and lyfte her up,
30   And clasped in her arme,
   "My child, my child, what dost thou ail?
   God shield thy life from harm!"

"O mother, mother! William's gone!
   What's all besyde to me?
35 There is no mercye, sure, above!
   All, all were spar'd but hee!"

"Kneel downe, thy paternoster saye,
   'Twill calm thy troubled spright:
The Lord is wyse, the Lord is good;
40   What hee hath done is right."

"O mother, mother! say not so;
   Most cruel is my fate:
I prayde, and prayde; but watte avayl'd?
   'Tis now, alas! too late."

---

bydeckt: bedecked, adorned.
paternoster: the Lord's Prayer.
spright: spirit.

45 "Our Heavenly Father, if we praye,
    Will help a suff'ring childe:
Go take the holy sacrament;
    So shall thy grief grow milde."

"O mother, what I feel within,
50   No sacrament can staye;
No sacrament can teche the dead
    To bear the sight of daye."

"May be, among the heathen folk
    Thy William false doth prove,
55 And puts away his faith and troth,
    And takes another love.

"Then wherefore sorrow for his loss?
    Thy moans are all in vain:
And when his soul and body parte,
60   His falsehode brings him paine."

"O mother, mother! gone is gone:
    My hope is all forlorne;
The grave mie onlye safeguarde is —
    O, had I ne'er been borne!

65 Go out, go out, my lampe of life;
    In grislie darkness die:
There is no mercye, sure, above!
    For ever let me die."

"Almighty God! O do not judge
70   My poor unhappy childe;
She knows not what her lips pronounce,
    Her anguish makes her wilde.

"My girl, forget thine earthly woe,
    And think on God and bliss;
75 For so, at least, shall not thy soule
    Its heavenly bridegroom miss."

"O mother, mother! what is blisse,
    And what the fiendis celle?
With him 'tis heaven any where,
80   Without my William, helle.

---

fiendis: fiend's.

"Go out, go out, my lamp of life;
   In endless darkness die:
Without him I must loathe the earth,
   Without him scorne the skye."

85 And so despaire did rave and rage
   Athwarte her boiling veins;
Against the Providence of God
   She hurlde her impious strains.

She bet her breaste, and wrung her hands,
90   And rollde her tearlesse eye,
From rise of morne, till the pale stars
   Again did freeke the skye.

When harke! abroade she hearde the trampe
   Of nimble-hoofed steed;
95 She hearde a knighte with clank alighte,
   And climb the staire in speede.

And soon she herde a tinkling hande,
   That twirled at the pin;
And thro' her door, that open'd not,
100   These words were breathed in.

"What ho! what ho! thy dore undoe;
   Art watching or asleepe?
My love, dost yet remember mee,
   And dost thou laugh or weep?"

105 "Ah! William here so late at night!
   Oh! I have watchte and wak'd:
Whence dost thou come? For thy return
   My herte has sorely ak'd."

"At midnight only we may ride;
110   I come o'er land and sea:
I mounted late, but soone I go;
   Aryse, and come with me."

"O William, enter first my bowre,
   And give me one embrace:

---

freeke: fleck or streak.
twirled at the pin: rattled at the door latch.

115 The blasts athwarte the hawthorne hiss;
    Awayte a little space."

"Tho' blasts athwarte the hawthorn hiss,
    I may not harboure here;
My spurre is sharpe, my courser pawes,
120   My houre of flighte is nere.

"All as thou lyest upon thy couch,
    Aryse, and mount behinde;
To-night we'le ride a thousand miles,
    The bridal bed to finde."

125 "How, ride to-night a thousand miles?
    Thy love thou dost bemocke:
Eleven is the stroke that still
    Rings on within the clocke."

"Looke up; the moone is bright, and we
130   Outstride the earthlie men:
I'll take thee to the bridal bed,
    And night shall end but then."

"And where is, then, thy house and home;
    And where thy bridal bed?"
135 "'Tis narrow, silent, chilly, dark;
    Far hence I rest my head."

"And is there any room for mee,
    Wherein that I may creepe?"
There's room enough for thee and me,
140   Wherein that wee may sleepe.

All as thou ly'st upon thy couch,
    Aryse, no longer stop;
The wedding guests thy coming waite,
    The chamber dore is ope."

145 All in her sarke, as there she lay,
    Upon his horse she sprung;
And with her lilly hands so pale
    About her William clung.

---

courser: horse.
sarke: slip or chemise.

And hurry-skurry forth they goe,
150   Unheeding wet or drye;
And horse and rider snort and blowe,
        And sparkling pebbles flye.

How swift the flood, the mead, the wood,
        Aright, aleft, are gone!
155 The bridges thunder as they pass,
        But earthlie sowne is none.

Tramp, tramp, across the land they speed;
        Splash, splash, across the see:
"Hurrah! the dead can ride apace;
160   Dost feare to ride with mee?

"The moone is bryghte, and blue the nyghte;
        Dost quake the blast to stem?
Dost shudder, mayde, to seeke the dead?"
        "No, no, but what of them?

165 "How glumlie sownes yon dirgye song!
        Night-ravens flappe the wing.
What knell doth slowlie toll ding dong?
        The psalmes of death who sing?

"It creeps: the swarthie funeral traine,
170   The corse is onn the beere;
Like croke of todes from lonely moores,
        The chaunte doth meet the eere."

"Go, bear her corse when midnight's past,
        With song, and tear, and wayle;
175 I've gott my wife, I take her home,
        My howre of wedlocke hayl.

"Lead forth, O clarke, the chaunting quire,
        To swell our nuptial song:
Come, preaste, and reade the blessing soone;
180   For bed, for bed we long."

They heede his calle, and husht the sowne;
        The biere was seene no more;

---

corse: corpse.

And followde him ore feeld and flood
    Yet faster than before.

185 Halloo! halloo! away they goe,
    Unheeding wet or drye;
And horse and rider snort and blowe,
    And sparkling pebbles flye.

How swifte the hill, how swifte the dale,
190   Aright, aleft, are gone!
By hedge and tree, by thorpe and towne,
    They gallop, gallop on.

Tramp, tramp, across the land they speede;
    Splash, splash, across the see;
195 "Hurrah! the dead can ride apace;
    Dost fear to ride with mee?

Look up, look up, an airy crewe
    In roundel daunces reele:
The moone is bryghte, and blue the nyghte,
200   Mayst dimlie see them wheele.

Come to, come to, ye gostlie crew,
    Come to, and follow mee,
And daunce for us the wedding daunce,
    When we in bed shall be."

205 And brush, brush, brush, the gostlie crew
    Come wheeling ore their heads,
All rustling like the wither'd leaves
    That wyde the wirlwind spreads.

Halloo! halloo! away they goe,
210   Unheeding wet or drye;
And horse and rider snort and blowe,
    And sparkling pebbles flye.

And all that in the moonshyne lay,
    Behynde them fled afar;
215 And backward scudded overhead
    The skye and every star.

_____

thorpe: village.

Tramp, tramp, across the lande they speede;
  Splash, splash, across the see:
"Hurrah! the dead can ride apace;
220 Dost fear to ride with me?

"I weene the cock prepares to crowe;
  The sand will soon be runne:
I snuffe the earlye morning aire;
  Downe, downe! our work is done.

225 "The dead, the dead can ryde apace;
  Oure wed-bed here is fit:
Our race is ridde, oure journey ore,
  Oure endlesse union knit."

And lo! an yren-grated gate
230 Soon biggens to their viewe:
He crackte his whyppe; the clangynge boltes,
  The doores asunder flewe.

They pass, and 'twas on graves they trode;
  "'Tis hither we are bounde:"
235 And many a tombstone gostlie white
  Lay inn the moonshyne round.

And when hee from his steede alytte,
  His armour, black as cinder,
Did moulder, moulder all awaye,
240 As were it made of tinder.

His head became a naked skull;
  Nor haire nor eyne had hee:
His body grew a skeleton,
  Whilome so blythe of blee.

245 And att his drye and boney heele
  No spur was left to be;
And inn his witherde hande you might
  The scythe and houre-glasse see.

---

weene: think.
yren-grated: iron grated.
Whilome: once.
blee: complexion.

And lo! his steede did thin to smoke,
250   And charnel fires outbreathe;
And pal'd, and bleach'd, then vanish'd quite
   The mayde from underneathe.

And hollow howlings hung in aire,
   And shrekes from vaults arose.
255 Then knew the mayde she mighte no more
   Her living eyes unclose.

But onwarde to the judgement seat,
   Thro' myste and moonlighte dreare,
The gostlie crewe their flyghte persewe,
260   And hollowe inn her eare: —

"Be patient, tho' thyne herte should breke,
   Arrayne not Heven's decree;
Thou nowe art of thie bodie refte,
   Thie soule forgiven bee!"

THE LASS OF FAIR WONE [1]

Gottfried August Bürger

Beside the parson's bower of yew
   Why strays a troubled spright,
That peaks and pines, and dimly shines
   Thro' curtains of the night?

5 Why steals along the pond of toads
   A gliding fire so blue,
That lights a spot where grows no grass,
   Where falls no rain nor dew? —

The parson's daughter once was good,
10   And gentle as the dove,

Monthly Magazine (Apr. 1796).

[1] Taylor's translation of Bürger's "Des Pfarrers Tochter von Taubenhain" — literally, "The Parson's Daughter of Taubenhain." Taylor's translation is rather free and somewhat ambiguous because it is not clear what the archaic word *wone* means. The most likely possibilities are (1) "the lass of fair habitation" (i.e., who comes from a pretty place) or (2) "the lass of fair hope or expectation." Given the tragic nature of the tale, either meaning would be fairly ironic, but the latter seems especially so since it would allude to the lass's hopes of marrying an aristocrat — the very thing that leads to her destruction. Scholars generally agree that this poem influenced Wordsworth's "The Thorn." [ED.]

And young and fair —— and many came
    To win the damsel's love.

High o'er the hamlet, from the hill,
    Beyond the winding stream,
15 The windows of a stately house
    In sheen of evening gleam.

There dwelt, in riot, rout, and roar,
    A lord so frank and free,
That oft, with inward joy of heart,
20   The maid beheld his glee—

Whether he met the dawning day,
    In hunting trim so fine,
Or tapers, sparkling from his hall,
    Beshone the midnight wine.

25 He sent the maid his picture, girt
    With diamond, pearl, and gold;
And silken paper, sweet with musk,
    This gentle message told:

"Let go thy sweethearts, one and all;
30   Shalt thou be basely woo'd,
That worthy art to gain the heart
    Of youths of noble blood?

The tale I would to thee bewray,
    In secret must be said:
35 At midnight hour I'll seek thy bower;
    Fair lass, be not afraid.

And when the amorous nightingale
    Sings sweetly to his mate,
I'll pipe my quail-call from the field:
40   Be kind, nor make me wait."

In cap and mantle clad he came,
    At night, with lonely tread;
Unseen, and silent as a mist,
    And hush'd the dogs with bread.

---

bewray: reveal.

45 And when the amorous nightingale
      Sung sweetly to his mate,
   She heard his quail-call in the field,
      And, ah! ne'er made him wait.

   The words he whisper'd were so soft,
50   They won her ear and heart:
   How soon will she, who loves, believe!
      How deep a lover's art!

   No lure, no soothing guise, he spar'd,
      To banish virtuous shame;
55 He call'd on holy God above,
      As witness to his flame.

   He clasp'd her to his breast, and swore
      To be for ever true:
   "O yield thee to my wishful arms,
60   Thy choice thou shalt not rue."

   And while she strove, he drew her on,
      And led her to the bower
   So still, so dim—and round about
      Sweet smelt the beans in flower.

65 There beat her heart, and heav'd her breast,
      And pleaded every sense;
   And there the glowing breath of lust
      Did blast her innocence.

   But when the fragrant beans began
70   Their sallow blooms to shed,
   Her sparkling eyes their lustre lost;
      Her cheek, its roses fled:

   And when she saw the pods increase,
      The ruddier cherries strain,
75 She felt her silken robe grow tight,
      Her waist new weight sustain.

   And when the mowers went afield,
      The yellow corn to ted,

---

ted: spread out to dry.

She felt her burden stir within,
80   And shook with tender dread.

And, when the winds of autumn hist
      Along the stubble field;
Then could the damsel's piteous plight
      No longer be conceal'd.

85 Her sire, a harsh and angry man,
      With furious voice revil'd:
"Hence from my sight! I'll none of thee —
      I harbour not thy child."

And fast, amid her fluttering hair,
90   With clenched fist he gripes,
And seiz'd a leathern thong, and lash'd
      Her sides with sounding stripes.

Her lily skin, so soft and white,
      He ribb'd with bloody weales;
95 And thrust her out, tho' black the night,
      Tho' sleet and storm assails.

Up the harsh rock, on flinty paths,
      The maiden had to roam;
On tottering feet she grop'd her way,
100   And sought her lover's home.

"A mother thou has made of me,
      Before thou mad'st a wife:
For this, upon my tender breast,
      These livid stripes are rife:

105 Behold." — And then, with bitter sobs,
      She sank upon the floor ——
"Make good the evil thou has wrought;
      My injur'd name restore."

"Poor soul; I'll have thee hous'd and nurs'd;
110   Thy terrors I lament.
Stay here; we'll have some further talk —
      The old one shall repent —"

---

stripes: strokes of a whip.
weales: welts.

"I have no time to rest and wait;
   That saves not my good name:
115 If thou with honest soul hast sworn,
   O leave me not to shame;

But at the holy altar be
   Our union sanctify'd;
Before the people and the priest
120   Receive me for thy bride."

"Unequal matches must not blot
   The honours of my line:
Art thou of wealth or rank for me,
   To harbour thee as mine?

125 What's fit and fair I'll do for thee;
   Shalt yet retain my love —
Shalt wed my huntsman — and we'll then
   Our former transports prove."

"Thy wicked soul, hard-hearted man,
130   May pangs in hell await!
Sure, if not suited for thy bride,
   I was not for thy mate.

Go, seek a spouse of nobler blood,
   Nor God's just judgments dread —
135 So shall, ere long, some base-born wretch
   Defile thy marriage-bed. —

Then, traitor, feel how wretched they
   In hopeless shame immerst;
Then smite thy forehead on the wall,
140   While horrid curses burst.

Roll thy dry eyes in wild despair —
   Unsooth'd thy grinning woe:
Thro' thy pale temples fire the ball,
   And sink to fiends below."

145 Collected then, she started up,
   And, thro' the hissing sleet,
Thro' thorn and brier, thro' flood and mire,
   She fled with bleeding feet.

"Where now," she cried, "my gracious God!
150 What refuge have I left?"
And reach'd the garden of her home,
 Of hope in man bereft.

On hand and foot she feebly crawl'd
 Beneath the bower unblest;
155 Where withering leaves and gathering snow,
 Prepar'd her only rest.

There rending pains and darting throes
 Assail'd her shuddering frame;
And from her womb a lovely boy,
160 With wail and weeping came.

Forth from her hair a silver pin
 With hasty hand she drew,
And prest against its tender heart,
 And the sweet babe she slew.

165 Erst when the act of blood was done,
 Her soul its guilt abhorr'd:
"My Jesus! what has been my deed?
 Have mercy on me, Lord!"

With bloody nails, beside the pond,
170 Its shallow grave she tore:
"There rest in God; there shame and want
 Thou canst not suffer more:

Me vengeance waits. My poor, poor child,
 Thy wound shall bleed afresh,
175 When ravens from the gallows tear
 Thy mother's mould'ring flesh." —

Hard by the bower her gibbet stands:
 Her skull is still to show;
It seems to eye the barren grave,
180 Three spans in length below —

That is the spot where grows no grass;
 Where falls no rain nor dew:

Erst: before.
gibbet: gallows.

Whence steals along the pond of toads
    A hovering fire so blue.

185 And nightly, when the ravens come,
    Her ghost is seen to glide;
Pursues and tries to quench the flame,
    And pines the pool beside.

ALONZO THE BRAVE AND FAIR IMOGINE
M. G. Lewis[1]

A warrior so bold, and a Virgin so bright
    Conversed, as they sat on the green;
They gazed on each other with tender delight;
Alonzo the Brave was the name of the Knight,
5   The maid's was the Fair Imogine.

"And, oh!" said the youth, "since to-morrow I go
    To fight in a far distant land,
Your tears for my absence soon leaving to flow,
Some other will court you, and you will bestow
10   On a wealthier suitor your hand."

"Oh! hush these suspicions," Fair Imogine said,
    "Offensive to Love and to me!
For, if you be living, or if you be dead,
I swear by the Virgin, that none in your stead
15   Shall Husband of Imogine be.

"If e'er I, by lust or by wealth led aside,
    Forget my Alonzo the Brave,
God grant, that to punish my falsehood and pride
Your ghost at the marriage may sit by my side,
20 May tax me with perjury, claim me as bride,
    And bear me away to the grave!"

From *The Monk: A Romance.* Vol. 3. London: Bell, 1796.

[1] Lewis (1775–1818), a novelist, earned the sobriquet "Monk" Lewis. "Alonzo the Brave and Fair Imogine" is one of several interpolated poems that appear in Lewis's Gothic novel *The Monk;* at one point the heroine, Antonia, who is "susceptible of terrors," discovers "a volume of old Spanish ballads," thus explaining the setting of the poem during the Christian Crusades; in a gloomy mood, she reads the poem, which, understandably, does little to dispel her melancholy. [ED.]

To Palestine hastened the Hero so bold;
　　His Love, she lamented him sore:
But scarce had a twelvemonth elapsed, when behold,
25　A Baron all covered with jewels and gold
　　Arrived at Fair Imogine's door.

His treasure, his presents, his spacious domain
　　Soon made her untrue to her vows:
He dazzled her eyes; he bewildered her brain;
30　He caught her affections so light and so vain,
　　And carried her home as his spouse.

And now had the marriage been blest by the priest;
　　The revelry now was begun:
The tables they groaned with the weight of the feast;
35　Nor yet had the laughter and merriment ceased,
　　When the Bell of the Castle told—"One!"

Then first with amazement Fair Imogine found
　　That a stranger was placed by her side:
His air was terrific; he uttered no sound;
40　He spoke not, he moved not, he looked not around,
　　But earnestly gazed on the bride.

His vizor was closed, and gigantic his height;
　　His armour was sable to view:
All pleasure and laughter were hushed at his sight;
45　The dogs as they eyed him drew back in affright;
　　The lights in the chamber burned blue!

His presence all bosoms appeared to dismay;
　　The guests sat in silence and fear.
At length spoke the bride, while she trembled; "I pray,
50　Sir Knight, that your helmet aside you would lay,
　　And deign to partake of our chear."

The lady is silent: the stranger complies.
　　His vizor he slowly unclosed:
Oh! God! what a sight met Fair Imogine's eyes!
55　What words can express her dismay and surprise,
　　When a skeleton's head was exposed.

All present then uttered a terrified shout;
　　All turned with disgust from the scene.

The worms they crept in, and the worms they crept out,
60 And sported his eyes and his temples about,
    While the spectre addressed Imogine.

"Behold me, thou false one! behold me!" he cried;
    "Remember Alonzo the Brave!
God grants, that to punish thy falsehood and pride
65 My ghost at thy marriage should sit by thy side,
Should tax thee with perjury, claim thee as bride
    And bear thee away to the grave!"

Thus saying, his arms round the lady he wound,
    While loudly she shrieked in dismay;
70 Then sank with his prey through the wide-yawning ground:
Nor ever again was Fair Imogine found,
    Or the spectre who bore her away.

Not long lived the Baron; and none since that time
    To inhabit the castle presume;
75 For chronicles tell that, by order sublime,
There Imogine suffers the pain of her crime,
    And mourns her deplorable doom.

At midnight four times in each year does her spright,
    When mortals in slumber are bound,
80 Arrayed in her bridal apparel of white,
Appear in the hall with the Skeleton-Knight,
    And shriek as he whirls her around.

While they drink out of skulls newly torn from the grave,
    Dancing round them the Spectres are seen:
85 Their liquor is blood, and this horrible stave
They howl: — "To the health of Alonzo the Brave,
    And his consort, the False Imogine!"

---

spright: spirit.
stave: verse of a song.

CONSCIENCE THE WORST OF TORTURES

Fanny Holcroft[1]

'Twas night; mysterious silence reign'd;
    Sleep wav'd his magic wand;
E'en prowling wolves, to mischief train'd,
    Repos'd, a harmless band.

5 High surging waves, and tempests bleak,
    Were hush'd, awhile to rest;
Fierce Aetna ceas'd in flames to break,
    Nor once disgorg'd her breast:

When, stretch'd on straw, the murd'rer lay,
10   Terrific to behold!
His tott'ring frame spoke sad dismay,
    His eye convulsed roll'd!

His chains he shook with frantic grief;
    Thrice smote his tortur'd breast:
15 Till fainting nature brought relief,
    And lull'd his limbs to rest.

But fearful visions rack'd his brain;
    His transient slumbers broke:
Before him stood Montalto slain!
20   He started, groan'd, and woke.

Yet woke, alas, to mad'ning woe:
    The ghastly form pursued;
With bosom pierc'd, step sad and slow,
    His shroud with blood bedew'd!

25 Its woe-fraught brow and haggard cheek
    Uprais'd the fiend despair:
A wild and soul-distracted shriek
    Dissolv'd it into air!

———————

Monthly Magazine (Apr. 1798).

Aetna: volcano in Sicily.

[1] Holcroft (1780–1844)—the daughter of the radical activist Thomas Holcroft—wrote poetry, drama, and novels. [ED.]

"Stay, stay," he cried, "thou damning shade!
30   Revenge shall soon be thine.
No more my tardy death upbraid:
        Eternal death is mine!

I'm call'd! The vengeful sword they raise!
        Racks, whips, and fury wait?
35 The pious brands of torture blaze,
        Ferocious man to fate!

Yet sword and flames I'll dauntless brave:
        No groan shall racks extort;
If blood they thirst, blood let them have:
40   Revenge too dearly bought!"

Thus rav'd the wretch, with anguish torn,
        Pursu'd by fell despair,
Till soon the sanguinary morn
        Bad him for death prepare.

45 With well-intention'd vengeance fraught,
        The fearful cohort meet:
Their mind to holy terror wrought;
        Their brow with ire replete.

Yet unappall'd their victim stood,
50   Death's threat'ning pangs defied;
"Montalto, lo! here's blood for blood!
        Behold, and quaff," he cried.

Then dauntless met each fearful stroke,
        No pangs could force one groan;
55 His threatening eye defiance spoke,
        Till sense and life were flown.

---

sanguinary: bloody.

RUSTIC AND HUMANITARIAN
POETRY

Like Wordsworth's own poetry in *Lyrical Ballads,* most eighteenth-century representations of "low and rustic life" fall into two basic categories. Some, like "Expostulation and Reply," "The Tables Turned," and "Lines Written at a Small Distance from My House," idealize rural or lower-class existence, whereas others, like "Simon Lee," "The Female Vagrant," or "Goody Blake and Harry Gill," vividly dramatize the hardships of poverty. Still, within these basic divisions, there is a tremendous amount of diversity and variation. Many of the more idyllic depictions hark back to the ancient pastoral tradition, and, though they do not usually depict actual shepherds, they serve the same basic function: to provide their readers with a bucolic escape from the anxieties and frustrations of urban life. Poems such as "The Happy Cottage" (284) clearly exemplify this mode; for most late eighteenth-century readers, however, it was Oliver Goldsmith's *The Deserted Village* that most memorably celebrated the simple joys of the country. Written to protest the effects of enclosure and England's growing commercialism, the poem serves as a passionate elegy to what Goldsmith feared was soon to be a "paradise lost":[1]

Sweet Auburn! loveliest village of the plain,
Where health and plenty cheered the labouring swain,
Where smiling spring its earliest visit paid,
And parting summer's lingering blooms delayed,
Dear lovely bowers of innocence and ease,
Seats of my youth, when every sport could please,
How often have I loitered o'er thy green,
Where humble happiness endeared each scene;
How often have I paused on every charm,
The sheltered cot, the cultivated farm,
The never failing brook, the busy mill,

---

[1] See the explanation of enclosure in the headnote to "Political Backgrounds" (173).

The decent church that topt the neighbouring hill,
The hawthorn bush, with seats beneath the shade,
For talking age and whispering lovers made. (1–12)

Thus, at a time when the British population was becoming increasingly urban, Goldsmith envisions this rural utopia in which young and old, man and nature coexist in peace and harmony.

This idealized vision of rustic life also appeared in what was called *peasant poetry*—that is, poems written by real-life laborers such as Stephen Duck, the Thresher poet; Ann Yearsley, the Bristol milkmaid; and, of course, Robert Burns, the "Heaven-taught ploughman," who in such poems as "The Cotter's Saturday Evening" privileged the humble values of the lower class over the refinement and sophistication of their social "betters":

From Scenes like these, old Scotia's grandeur springs,
    That makes her lov'd at home, rever'd abroad:
Princes and lords are but the breath of kings,
    "An honest man's the noble work of God:"
And *certes,* in fair Virtue's heavenly road,
    The *Cottage* leaves the *Palace* far behind:
What is a lordling's pomp? a cumbrous load,
    Disguising oft the *wretch* of human kind,
Studied in arts of Hell, in wickedness refin'd! (164–71)

In contrast to commentators like Joseph Townsend who accused the poor of improvidence and profligacy, Burns here presents the common people, not the decadent aristocracy, as the moral guardians of the nation.

Other peasant poems, however (e.g., Stephen Duck's "The Thresher's Labour" or Burns's "To a Mouse"), reveal that these working-class bards were also keenly aware of the harsher side of rural and lower-class existence; and, as the eighteenth century came to a close, this more realistic, less idealized depiction of "low and rustic life" became increasingly common. A particularly striking example is George Crabbe's antipastoral poem, *The Village,* which seeks to paint "a real picture of the poor" by describing in detail the corruption that exists within the sort of community that Goldsmith had celebrated. In this way, Crabbe exposes the falsity of most poetic depictions of rural life, suggesting that these poems only trivialize the very real problems faced by the poor. As Crabbe himself puts it, these people need bread, not "the barren flattery of a rhyme."

Related to Crabbe's poetry is what was often called *humanitarian poetry*—poems usually written by middle- or upper-class poets in order to elicit sympathy for the poor and disadvantaged. But once again, this general category covers a wide range of possible approaches and ideological stands. Much humanitarian poetry came from writers with leftist leanings, who, inspired by the ideals of the French Revolution, sought to bring about social and political reform. The poetry of the young Robert Southey is very much in this vein — as is Charlotte Smith's "The Dead Beggar," in which she not only laments the death of this one poor man but also uses his example to indict the existing system of poor relief.

While this more reformist strain of humanitarian verse typically appeared in the *Monthly Magazine* and other liberal publications, more conservative journals such as the *Gentleman's Magazine* also published less inflammatory versions of this type of poem.[2] "The Beggar's Petition," for instance, contains the same sort of appeal for sympathy that we see in Southey and Smith, but it suggests none of their broader social implications. There is no implied criticism of the privileged classes as in Southey's "The Widow," no call for reform as in Smith's "The Dead Beggar" — just a simple appeal for a single act of charity to relieve a single unfortunate individual. Still other poems, such as Hannah More's contributions to *Cheap Repository for Moral and Religious Tracts,* were targeted directly at lower-class readers in order to provide them with an edifying alternative to the usual broadside ballad:

> When it is considered what vast multitudes there are whose reading is in a great measure confined to these corrupt performances [. . .] it must be obvious that it is become a point of no small consequence to correct so great an evil, which is not likely to be done effectually without condescending to supply tracts equally cheap, and adapted in a like manner to the common people. (qtd. Jacobus 237)

As a result, in poems such as "Patient Joe," More includes nothing that is even vaguely subversive. Rather, Joe accepts everything no matter how unfair it may seem because — as More boasts — he had "a mind so submissive" that it "prepared him for all."

One other important variety of humanitarian verse is what we might call the "forsaken-woman" poem. As the presence of "The Thorn," "The Mad Mother," "The Female Vagrant," and "The Complaint of a Forsaken Indian Woman" in the 1798 *Lyrical Ballads* vividly attests, this type of poem greatly interested the young Wordsworth. With their sentimental and often sensational tales of young women driven to madness or death, these poems were ideally suited to Age of Sensibility tastes; but, like other humanitarian poems, they also addressed very real social problems. As Mary Wollstonecraft points out in *A Vindication of the Rights of Woman* (1792), unmarried or widowed women during this time frequently found themselves utterly

---

[2] For more on the characteristics of magazine poetry in the 1790s, see Mayo 487–522 and Glen 33–56.

destitute or dependent upon the charity of others, and many forsaken-woman poems explore the ramifications of this situation. In most cases — as in Southey's "Hannah: A Plaintive Tale" — they adopt a compassionate approach toward the "fallen" woman's plight. "The Story of Sinful Sally," however, places the responsibility for the title character's misfortunes squarely on her own greed and lasciviousness. Thus, instead of a plea for tolerance or reform, the poem provides a dire warning to young women against trying to rise above their station.

FROM *THE VILLAGE*

A Poem
in Two Books

 George Crabbe[1]

BOOK I

The village life, and every care that reigns
O'er youthful peasants and declining swains;
What labor yields, and what, that labour past,
Age, in its hour of languor, finds at last;
5 What forms the real picture of the poor,
Demand a song——The Muse can give no more.

Fled are those times, if e'er such times were seen,
When rustic poets prais'd their native green;
No shepherds now in smooth alternate verse,
10 Their country's beauty or their nymphs' rehearse;
Yet still for these we frame the tender strain,
Still in our lays fond Corydons[2] complain,
And shepherds' boys their amorous pains reveal,
The only pains, alas! they never feel.

London: Dodsley, 1783.

[1]Of humble origins himself, Crabbe (1754–1832) wrote *The Village* to challenge the idealized portrait of the poor that Oliver Goldsmith painted in his popular poem *The Deserted Village* (1770). Lines 15–18 of this poem were written by Crabbe's friend Samuel Johnson (1709–84), poet, literary critic, essayist, lexicographer, and one of the most distinguished literary figures of the eighteenth century. [ED.]

[2]Corydon is a stock name for love-sick shepherds in classical pastoral poetry, such as Virgil's *Eclogues*. [ED.]

15 On Mincio's banks, in Caesar's bounteous reign,[3]
   If Tityrus found the golden age again,
   Must sleepy bards the flattering dream prolong,
   Mechanic echoes of the Mantuan song?
   From truth and nature shall we widely stray,
20 Where Virgil, not where fancy leads the way?

   Yes, thus the Muses sing of happy swains,
   Because the Muses never knew their pains:
   They boast their peasants' pipes, but peasants now
   Resign their pipes and plod behind the plow;
25 And few amid the rural tribe have time
   To number syllables, and play with rhyme;
   Save honest Duck,[4] what son of verse could share
   The poet's rapture and the peasant's care?
   Or the great labours of the field degrade,
30 With the new peril of a poorer trade?

   From one chief cause these idle praises spring,
   That, themes so easy, few forbear to sing;
   They ask no thought, require no deep design,
   But swell the song and liquefy the line;
35 The gentle lover takes the rural strain,
   A nymph his mistress and himself a swain;
   With no sad scenes he clouds his tuneful prayer,
   But all, to look like her, is painted fair.

   I grant indeed that fields and flocks have charms
40 For him that gazes or for him that farms;
   But when amid such pleasing scenes I trace
   The poor laborious natives of the place,
   And see the mid-day sun, with fervid ray,
   On their bare heads and dewy temples play;
45 While some, with feebler heads and fainter hearts,
   Deplore their fortune, yet sustain their parts:

Mincio: a river in northern Italy, near Mantua, a city near Virgil's birthplace.

Tityrus: a character in Virgil's *Eclogues*.

Mantuan song: a reference to Virgil's pastoral poetry.

fervid: very hot or burning.

[3] Virgil lived during Augustus Caesar's reign (27 B.C.–A.D. 14). [ED.]
[4] Stephen Duck (1705–56) was a self-educated farm laborer who became a successful poet, earning a government pension and the patronage of Queen Caroline. [ED.]

Then shall I dare these real ills to hide
In tinsel trappings of poetic pride?

No, cast by Fortune on a frowning coast,
50 Which can no groves nor happy vallies boast; [5]
Where other cares than those the Muse relates,
And other shepherds dwell with other mates;
By such examples taught, I paint the cot,
As Truth will paint it, and as bards will not:
55 Nor you, ye poor, of letter'd scorn complain,
To you the smoothest song is smooth in vain;
O'ercome by labour and bow'd down by time,
Feel you the barren flattery of a rhyme?
Can poets sooth you, when you pine for bread,
60 By winding myrtles round your ruin'd shed?
Can their light tales your weighty griefs o'erpower,
Or glad with airy mirth the toilsome hour?

Lo! where the heath, with withering brake grown o'er,
Lends the light turf that warms the neighbouring poor;
65 From thence a length of burning sand appears,
Where the thin harvest waves its wither'd ears;
Rank weeds, that every art and care defy,
Reign o'er the land and rob the blighted rye:
There thistles stretch their prickly arms afar,
70 And to the ragged infant threaten war;
There poppies nodding mock the hope of toil,
There the blue bugloss paints the sterile soil;
Hardy and high, above the slender sheaf,
The slimy mallow waves her silky leaf;
75 O'er the young shoot the charlock throws a shade,
And the wild tare clings round the sickly blade;

---

cot: cottage.
myrtles: leaves of the myrtle tree, used as an emblem of love because the myrtle tree was considered sacred to Venus.
brake: an area covered with bushes or brambles.
bugloss: blue-flowered herb.
mallow: herb found in marshes.
charlock: wild mustard.
tare: a noxious weed.

[5] Crabbe based his poem on Aldeburgh, a small, economically depressed seaport on the southeast coast of England, where he grew up. [ED.]

With mingled tints the rocky coasts abound,
And a sad splendour vainly shines around.

So looks the nymph[6] whom wretched arts adorn,
80 Betray'd by man, then left for man to scorn;
Whose cheek in vain assumes the mimic rose,
While her sad eyes the troubled breast disclose;
Whose outward splendour is but Folly's dress,
Exposing most, when most it gilds distress.

85 Here joyless roam a wild amphibious race,
With sullen woe display'd in every face;
Who far from civil arts and social fly,
And scowl at strangers with suspicious eye.

Here too the lawless vagrant of the main
90 Draws from his plow th'intoxicated swain;
Want only claim'd the labour of the day,
But vice now steals his nightly rest away.

Where are the swains, who, daily labour done,
With rural games play'd down the setting sun;
95 Who struck with matchless force the bounding ball,
Or made the pond'rous quoit obliquely fall;
While some huge Ajax, terrible and strong,
Engag'd some artful stripling of the throng,
And foil'd beneath the young Ulysses fell;
100 When peals of praise the merry mischief tell?
Where now are these? Beneath yon cliff they stand,
To show the freighted pinnace where to land;
To load the ready steed with guilty haste,
To fly in terror o'er the pathless waste,
105 Or when detected in their straggling course,
To foil their foes by cunning or by force;
Or yielding part (which equal knaves contest)
To gain a lawless passport for the rest.

---

quoit: a ring of rope used in quoits, a game similar to horseshoes.
Ajax: gigantic Greek hero of the Trojan War who appears in Homer's *Iliad*.
Ulysses: Roman name for Odysseus, who, in the *Iliad*, is awarded Achilles' armor, fatally vexing Ajax, who goes mad and kills himself.
pinnace: a sailing ship.

[6]Despite the realistic nature of his portrait of rural life, Crabbe continues to use the terms of conventional pastoral poetry (e.g., *nymph* and *swain*) for ironic effect. [ED.]

Here wand'ring long amid these frowning fields,
110 I sought the simple life that Nature yields;
Rapine and Wrong and Fear usurp'd her place,
And a bold, artful, surly, savage race;
Who, only skill'd to take the finny tribe,
The yearly dinner, or septennial bribe,
115 Wait on the shore, and as the waves run high,
On the tost vessel bend their eager eye;
Which to their coast directs its vent'rous way,
Theirs, or the ocean's miserable prey.

As on their neighbouring beach yon swallows stand,
120 And wait for favouring winds to leave the land;
While still for flight the ready wing is spread:
So waited I the favouring hour, and fled;
Fled from these shores where guilt and famine reign,
And cry'd, Ah! hapless they who still remain;
125 Who still remain to hear the ocean roar,
Whose greedy waves devour the lessening shore;
Till some fierce tide, with more imperious sway,
Sweeps the low hut and all it holds away;
When the sad tenant weeps from door to door,
130 And begs a poor protection from the poor!

But these are scenes where Nature's niggard hand
Gave a spare portion to the famish'd land;
Hers is the fault, if here mankind complain
Of fruitless toil and labour spent in vain;
135 But yet in other scenes, more fair in view,
Where Plenty smiles—alas! she smiles for few,
And those who taste not, yet behold her store,
Are as slaves that dig the golden ore,
The wealth around them makes them doubly poor:
140 Or will you deem them amply paid in health,
Labour's fair child, that languishes with Wealth?
Go then! and see them rising with the sun,
Through a long course of daily toil to run;
Like him to make the plenteous harvest grow,
145 And yet not share the plenty they bestow;

The yearly dinner: a Christmas dinner often held by landlords for their tenants.
septennial: once every seven years, when parliamentary elections were held.

See them beneath the dog-star's raging heat,[7]
When knees tremble and the temples beat;
Behold them, leaning on their scythes, look o'er
The labour past, and toils to come explore;
150 See them alternate suns and showers exchange,
And hoard up aches and anguish for their age;
Thro' fens and marshy moors their steps pursue,
When their warm pores imbibe the evening dew;
Then own that labour may as fatal be
155 To these thy slaves, as luxury to thee.

Amid this tribe too oft a manly pride
Strives in strong toil the fainting heart to hide;
There may you see the youth of slender frame
Contend with weakness, weariness, and shame;
160 Yet urg'd along, and proudly loth to yield,
He strives to join his fellows of the field;
Till long contending nature droops at last,
Declining health rejects his poor repast,
His cheerless spouse the coming danger sees,
165 And mutual murmurs urge the slow disease.
Yet grant them health, 'tis not for us to tell,
Though the head droops not, that the heart is well;
Or will you urge their homely, plenteous fare,
Healthy and plain and still the poor man's share?
170 Oh! trifle not with wants you cannot feel,
Nor mock the misery of a stinted meal;
Homely not wholesome, plain not plenteous, such
As you who envy would disdain to touch.

Ye gentle souls who dream of rural ease,
175 Whom the smooth stream and smoother sonnet please;
Go! if the peaceful cot your praises share,
Go look within, and ask if peace be there:
If peace be his—that drooping weary sire,
Or theirs, that offspring round their feeble fire,
180 Or hers, that matron pale, whose trembling hand
Turns on the wretched hearth th' expiring brand!

---

you who envy: those of you who entertain a romanticized idea of rural life.

[7] Sirius, the Dog Star, is the brightest star in the sky and was believed to cause excessive heat. [Ed.]

Nor yet can time itself obtain for these
Life's latest comforts, due respect and ease;
For yonder see that hoary swain, whose age
185 Can with no cares except his own engage;
Who, propt on that rude staff, looks up to see
The bare arms broken from the withering tree;
On which, a boy, he climb'd the loftiest bough,
Then his first joy, but his sad emblem now.

190 He once was chief in all the rustic trade,
His steady hand the straitest furrow made;
Full many a prize he won, and still is proud
To find the triumphs of his youth allow'd;
A transient pleasure sparkles in his eyes,
195 He hears and smiles, then thinks again and sighs:
For now he journeys to his grave in pain;
The rich disdain him; nay, the poor disdain;[8]
Alternate masters now their slave command,
And urge the efforts of his feeble hand;
200 Who, when his age attempts its task in vain,
With ruthless taunts, of lazy poor complain.[9]

Oft may you see him when he tends the sheep,
His winter charge, beneath the hillock weep;
Oft hear him murmur to the winds that blow
205 O'er his white locks and bury them in snow;
When rouz'd by rage and muttering in the morn,
He mends the broken hedge with icy thorn:

"Why do I live, when I desire to be
"At once from life and life's long labour free?
210 "Like leaves in spring, the young are blown away,
"Without the sorrows of a slow decay;
"I, like yon wither'd leaf, remain behind;
"Nipt by the frost and shivering in the wind;
"There it abides till younger buds come on,
215 "As I, now all my fellow swains are gone;

---

allow'd: acknowledged.

[8] In other words, not only do the rich disdain not only him, but so do the poor. [ED.]
[9] Compare this portrait of a once vigorous but now decrepit man to that in Wordsworth's "Simon Lee" (64–67). [ED.]

"Then, from the rising generation thrust,
"It falls, like me, unnotic'd to the dust.

"These fruitful fields, these numerous flocks I see,
"Are others' gain, but killing cares to me;
220 "To me the children of my youth are lords,
"Cool in their looks, but hasty in their words;
"Wants of their own demand their care, and who
"Feels his own want and succors others too?
"A lonely, wretched man, in pain I go,
225 "None need my help, and none relieve my woe;
"Then let my bones beneath the turf be laid,
"And men forget the wretch they would not aid!"

Thus groan the old, till, by disease opprest,
They taste a final woe, and then they rest.
230 Theirs is yon house that holds the parish poor,[10]
Whose walls of mud scarce bear the broken door;
There, where the putrid vapours, flagging, play,
And the dull wheel hums doleful through the day;
There children dwell, who know no parents' care;
235 Parents, who know no children's love, dwell there;
Heart-broken matrons on their joyless bed,
Forsaken wives, and mothers never wed;
Dejected widows with unheeded tears,
And crippled age with more than childhood-fears;
240 The lame, the blind, and, far the happiest they!
The moping idiot and the madman gay.

. . . .

---

yon house that holds the parish poor: the parish workhouse in which those who were unable to provide for themselves were confined.

[10] For more on parish workhouses, see the headnote to "Political Backgrounds," page 173. [ED.]

FROM *THE TASK*

A Poem
in Six Books

William Cowper

FROM BOOK I [1]

There often wanders one, whom better days
535 Saw better clad, in cloak of sattin trimm'd
With lace, and hat with splendid ribband bound.
A serving maid was she, and fell in love
With one who left her, went to sea and died.
Her fancy followed him through foaming waves
540 To distant shores, and she would sit and weep
At what a sailor suffers; fancy too
Delusive most where warmest wishes are,
Would oft anticipate his glad return,
And dream of transports she was not to know.
545 She heard the doleful tidings of his death,
And never smil'd again. And now she roams
The dreary waste; there spends the livelong day,
And there, unless when charity forbids,
The livelong night. A tatter'd apron hides,
550 Worn as a cloak, and hardly hides a gown
More tatter'd still; and both but ill conceal
A bosom heaved with never-ceasing sighs.
She begs an idle pin of all she meets,
And hoards them in her sleeve; but needful food,
555 Though press'd with hunger oft, or comelier cloaths,
Though pinch'd with cold, asks never. — Kate is craz'd.

———————

London: Johnson, 1785.

[1] This passage, frequently excerpted, came to be known as "Crazy Kate." [ED.]

THE HAPPY COTTAGE

Anonymous[1]

How serene and how peaceful his mind,
   How contented, how blest is his lot;
No sorrow, no care you will find
   In his happy, his thrice happy cot.

5 He harbours no wish to be great,
   He sighs not for wealth, or for power;
But easy in his low estate,
   He asks not, or wishes for more.

With the lark he does welcome the day,
10   And chearfully joins in his song;
What courtier's so happy and gay,
   As the meadows he passes along.

At ev'ning when labour is o'er,
   With joy he returns to his cot;
15 His fatigue is remember'd no more,
   And ev'ry sad thought is forgot.

His wife and his children he loves
   With a tenderness free from all guilt;
His actions she ever approves,
20   And rewards ev'ry look with a smile.

Then happily passes each day;
   With content and sweet peace ever blest;
His pleasure does more than repay
   His toils e'er he goes to his rest.

25 What lordling can boast of such bliss?
   What mortal who envies him not,
And wishes his days could like his
   Be pass'd in so happy a cot?

New Lady's Magazine (Oct. 1790).

lordling: minor or insignificant lord.

[1] The poem was signed, "A Constant Reader." [ED.]

TAM O' SHANTER

A Tale

Robert Burns

[Burns (1759–96) was born into a lower-class family, but after the publication of Poems, Chiefly in the Scottish Dialect *(1786), became the most celebrated Scottish poet of all time. Burns's famous poem first appeared in print as a footnote to Grose's description of Alloway Church, Ayrshire, prefaced by the following: "This church is also famous for being the place wherein the witches and warlocks used to hold their infernal meetings, or sabbaths, and prepare their magical unctions: here too they used to amuse themselves with dancing to the pipes of the muckle-horned Deel (great-horned Devil). Diverse stories of these horrid rites are still current; one of which my worthy friend Mr. Burns has here favoured me with in verse."*

In his 1816 "A Letter to a Friend of Robert Burns," Wordsworth provides this spirited defense of Burns's poem:

> *Who, but some impenetrable dunce or narrow-minded puritan in the works of art, ever read without delight the picture which he has drawn of the convivial exhalation of the rustic adventurer Tam o' Shanter? The poet fears not to tell the reader at the outset that his hero was a desperate and sottish drunkard, whose excesses were [as] frequent as his opportunities. This reprobate sits down to his cups, while the storm is roaring, and heaven and earth are in confusion; — the night is driven on by song and tumultuous noise — laughter and jest thicken as the beverage improves upon the palate — conjugal fidelity archly bends to the service of general benevolence — selfishness is not absent, but wearing the mask of cordiality — and, while, these various elements of humanity are blended into one proud and happy composition of elated spirits, the anger of the tempest only heightens and sets off the enjoyment within. — I pity him who cannot perceive that, in all this, though there was no moral purpose, there is a moral effect. (*Prose Works *2.124)*

In addition to his obvious delight in the poem's "elated spirits," Wordsworth may also have found in "Tam o' Shanter" a model for the kind of narrative experimentation that he would attempt in Lyrical

---

From *The Antiquities of Scotland by Francis Grose Esq: F. A. S. of London and Perth*. Vol. 2. London: Hooper, 1791.

Ballads. *Just as Burns jumbles together elements from the epic, the humanitarian poem, and the Gothic ballad, Wordsworth would also oscillate wildly between different genres in poems such as "Goody Blake and Harry Gill," "Simon Lee," and "The Idiot Boy." Ed.]*

When chapmen billies leave the street,
And drouthy neebors, neebors meet,
As market-days are wearing late,
And folk begin to tak the gate;
5 While we sit bowsing at the nappy,
And getting fou, and unco happy,
We think na on the long Scots miles,
The waters, mosses, slaps and styles,
That lie between us and our hame,
10 Where sits our sulky, sullen dame,
Gathering her brows, like gathering storm,
Nursing her wrath to keep it warm.

This truth fand honest Tam o' Shanter,
As he frae Ayr ae night did canter;
15 (Auld Ayr, wham ne'er a town surpasses,
For honest men and bonnie lasses).

O Tam! had'st thou but been sae wise,
As taen thy ain wife Kate's advice!
She tauld thee weel, thou was a skellum,
20 A bletherin, blusterin, drunken blellum;

---

chapmen billies: peddlers.
drouthy: thirsty.
neebors: neighbors.
bowsing: drinking.
nappy: ale.
fou: drunk.
unco: very.
mosses: bogs.
slaps: gaps in fences or walls.
fand: found.
frae: from.
Ayr: a town in the county of Ayrshire, thirty miles southwest of Glasgow.
ae: one
ain: own.
skellum: rascal, scoundrel.
bletherin: babbling.
blellum: chatterer, blusterer.

That frae November till October,
Ae market-day thou was na sober;
That ilka melder, wi' the miller,
Thou sat as long as thou had siller
25 That ev'ry naig was ca'd a shoe on,
The smith and thee gat roarin fou on;
That at the L——d's house, ev'n on Sunday,
Thou drank wi' Kirkton Jean till Monday.—
She prophesied that, late or soon,
30 Thou wad be found deep drown'd in Doon;
Or catch'd wi' warlocks in the mirk
By Aloway's old haunted kirk.

　　Ah, gentle dames! it gars me greet,
To think how mony counsels sweet,
35 How mony lengthen'd sage advices,
The husband frae the wife despises!

　　But to our tale:——Ae market-night,
Tam had got planted unco right,
Fast by the ingle bleezing finely,
40 Wi' reamin swats that drank divinely;
And at his elbow, souter Johnie,
His ancient, trusty, drouthy crony;
Tam lo'ed him like a vera brither,
They had been fou for weeks tegither.—
45 The night drave on wi' sangs an' clatter,
And ay the ale was growing better:
The landlady and Tam grew gracious,

---

ilka melder: each grinding of meal.
siller: silver, money.
ev'ry naig was ca'd a shoe on: every time a horse was shod.
Doon: a river in Ayrshire.
Aloway: Alloway, the town in which Burns was born.
kirk: church.
gars me greet: makes me cry.
mony: many.
planted unco right: settled very nicely.
ingle bleezing: fire blazing.
reamin swats: foaming new ale.
souter: shoemaker.
vera brither: very brother.
drave on wi' sangs an' clatter: drove on with songs and chatter.

Wi' favours secret, sweet, and precious:
The souter tauld his queerest stories;
50 The landlord's laugh was ready chorus:
The storm without might rair and rustle,
Tam did na mind the storm a whistle. —
Care, mad to see a man sae happy,
E'en drown'd himsel amang the nappy.
55 As bees flee hame, wi' lades o' treasure,
The minutes wing'd their way wi' pleasure:
Kings may be blest, but Tam was glorious;
O'er a' the ills o' life victorious!

But pleasures are like poppies spread,
60 You seize the flower, its bloom is shed;
Or like the snow falls in the river,
A moment white—then melts for ever;
Or like the borealis race,
That flit ere you can point their place;
65 Or like the rainbow's lovely form,
Evanishing amid the storm. —
Nae man can tether time or tide,
The hour approaches Tam maun ride;
That hour o'night's black arch the key-stane,
70 That dreary hour he mounts his beast in;
And sic a night he taks the road in
As ne'er poor sinner was abroad in.

The wind blew, as 'twad blawn its last;
The rattling showers rose on the blast;
75 The speedy gleams the darkness swallow'd;
Loud, deep, and lang the thunder bellow'd:
That night, a child might understand
The deil had business on his hand.

---

rair: roar.
lades: loads.
borealis: the aurora borealis, or northern lights.
maun: must.
That hour o'night's black arch the key-stane: midnight, i.e., the keystone of night's black arch.
sic: such.
as 'twad blawn: as if it had blown.
deil: devil.

Weel-mounted on his grey meare, Meg,
80 A better never lifted leg,
Tam skelpit on thro' dub and mire,
Despising wind, and rain, and fire:
Whyles holding fast his gude blue bonnet;
Whyles crooning o'er an auld Scots sonnet;
85 Whyles glow'ring round wi' prudent cares,
Lest bogles catch him unawares;
Kirk-Aloway was drawing nigh,
Where ghaists and houlets nightly cry.

By this time he was cross the ford,
90 Where in the snaw the chapman smoor'd;
And past the birks and meikle stane,
Where drunken Charlie brak's neck-bane;
And thro' the whins, and by the cairn,
Where hunters fand the murder'd bairn;
95 And near the tree, aboon the well,
Where Mungo's mither hang'd hersel:
Before him, Doon pours all his floods;
The doubling storm roars thro' the woods;
The light'nings flash from pole to pole;
100 Near, and more near, the thunders roll;
When, glimmering thro' groaning trees,
Kirk-Aloway seem'd in a bleeze;
Thro' ilka bore the beams were glancing,
And loud resounded mirth and dancing.

---

meare: mare.
skelpit: hurried.
dub: puddle.
Whyles: at times.
gude: good.
bogles: ghosts or goblins.
Kirk-Aloway: Aloway Church.
ghaists and houlets: ghosts and young owls.
Where in the snaw the chapman smoor'd: where in the snow the peddler was smothered.
birks and meikle stane: birches and large stone.
brak's neck-bane: broke his neck bone.
whins: furze bushes.
cairn: pile of stones, often used as a monument or tombstone.
bairn: child.
aboon: above.
mither: mother.
ilka bore: each crack.

105   Inspiring, bold John Barleycorn!
      What dangers thou canst make us scorn:
      Wi' tippeny, we fear nae evil;
      Wi' usquebae, we'll face the devil!
      The swats sae ream'd in Tammie's noddle,
110   Fair play, he car'd na deils a boddle:
      But Maggy stood, right sair astonish'd,
      Till by the heel and hand admonish'd,
      She ventur'd forward on the light,
      And, vow! Tam saw an unco sight!

115   Warlocks and witches in a dance,
      Nae cotillion brent new frae France,
      But hornpipes, jigs, strathspeys and reels,
      Put life and mettle in their heels. —
      At winnock-bunker in the East,
120   There sat auld Nick in shape o' beast;
      A tousie tyke, black, grim, and large,
      To gie them music was his charge:
      He screw'd the pipes and gart them skirl,
      Till roof and rafters a' did dirl. —
125   Coffins stood round, like open presses,
      That shaw'd the dead in their last dresses;
      And (by some devilish cantraip slight)
      Each in its cauld hand held a light;
      By which heroic Tam was able

John Barleycorn: the personification of whisky.
tippeny: two-penny ale.
usquebae: whisky.
noddle: head or brain.
he car'd na deils a boddle: he cared very little for devils — a *boddle* was a coin worth one-sixth of an English penny.
sair: sorely.
unco: strange.
brent new: brand new.
strathspeys: a Scottish dance.
At winnock-bunker in the East: on a window seat at the east end of the church.
auld Nick: the devil.
tousie tyke: shaggy dog.
gart them skirl: made them squeal.
dirl: rattle.
presses: furniture for holding clothes.
cantraip slight: magic trick.

130 To note upon the haly table,
    A murderer's banes, in gibbet-airns;
    Twa span-lang, wee, unchristened bairns;
    A thief, new-cutted frae a rape,
    Wi' his last gasp his gab did gape;
135 Five tomahawks, wi' blude red-rusted;
    Five scymitars, wi' murder crusted;
    A garter which a babe had strangled;
    A knife, a father's throat had mangled;
    Whom his ain son of life bereft,
140 The grey hairs yet stack to the heft;
    Wi' mair of horrible and awefu',
    That even to name wad be unlawfu':—

    As Tammie glowr'd, amaz'd, and curious,
    The mirth and fun grew fast and furious:
145 The piper loud and louder blew;
    The dancers quick and quicker flew;
    They reel'd, they set, they cross'd, they cleekit,
    Till ilka Carlin swat and reekit,
    And coost her duddies on the wark,
150 And linkit at it in her sark.—

    Now Tam! O Tam! had thae been queans,
    A' plump and strappin in their teens!
    Their sarks, instead o' creeshie flainen,
    Been snaw-white, seventeen-hunder linen;

---

haly table: the altar.
gibbet-airns: gibbet or gallows irons.
span-lang: the distance from the thumb to the little finger.
rape: rope.
gab: mouth.
blude: blood.
stack: stuck.
to the heft: to the handle.
mair: more.
cleekit: linked arms in dance.
Till ilka Carlin swat and reekit: until each old woman sweated and steamed.
coost her duddies on the wark: threw off her clothes to go about her work, i.e., so that she could dance more easily.
linkit at it in her sark: skipped about in her slip or chemise.
queans: young girls.
Their sarks, instead o' creeshie flainen, / Been snaw-white, seventeen-hunder linen: if their slips had been fine snow-white linen instead of filthy flannel.

155 Thir breeks o' mine, my only pair,
 That ance were plush o' gude blue hair,
 I wad hae gien them off my hurdies
 For ae blink o' the bonie burdies!
 But wither'd beldams, auld and droll,
160 Rigwoodie hags wad spean a foal,
 Loupin an' flingin on a crumock,
 I wonder did na turn thy stomach. —

 But Tam kend what was what fu' brawlie;
 There was ae winsome wench and walie,
165 That night enlisted in the core,
 (Lang after kend on Carrick shore;
 For mony a beast to dead she shot,
 And perish'd mony a bonnie boat,
 And shook baith meikle corn and bear,
170 And kept the country-side in fear) —
 Her cutty-sark o' Paisley harn,
 That while a lassie she had worn,
 In longitude tho' sorely scanty,
 It was her best, and she was vauntie, —
175 Ah! little thought thy reverend graunie,
 That sark she coft for her wee Nannie
 Wi' twa pund Scots ('twas a' her riches),
 Should ever grac'd a dance of witches!

 But here my Muse her wing maun cour,
180 Sic flights are far beyond her power;

Thir breeks: these breeches.
hurdies: buttocks.
ae blink o' the bonie burdies: one look at the pretty girls.
Rigwoodie: withered.
spean: wean.
Loupin an' flingin on a crumock: leaping and jumping on a cane.
kend: knew.
fu' brawlie: full well.
walie: handsome.
core: band of dancers.
meikle corn and bear: much oats and barley.
harn: cloth.
vauntie: vain.
coft: bought.
twa pund Scots: two Scottish pounds.
her wing maun cour: must fold her wing.

To sing how Nannie lap and flang
(A souple jad she was and strang,)
And how Tam stood like ane bewitch'd,
And thought his very een enrich'd:
185 Even Satan glowr'd, and fidg'd fu' fain,
And hotch'd, and blew wi' might and main;
Till first ae caper—syne anither—
Tam lost his reason a' thegither,
And roars out—"Weel done, cutty-sark!"
190 And in an instant all was dark;
And scarcely had he Maggie rallied,
When out the hellish legion sallied.—

As bees bizz out wi' angry fyke,
When plundering herds assail their byke;
195 As open pussie's mortal foes,
When, pop, she starts before their nose;
As eager runs the market-croud,
When "catch the thief!" resounds aloud;
So Maggie rins, the witches follow,
200 Wi' mony an eldritch skreich and hollo.—

Ah Tam! ah Tam! thou'll get thy fairin!
In hell they'll roast thee like a herrin!
In vain thy Kate awaits thy comin,
Kate soon will be a woefu' woman!!!
205 Now, do thy speedy utmost, Meg!
And win the key-stane o' the brig;
There at them thou thy tail may toss,
A running stream they dare na cross!

---

lap and flang: leaped and kicked.
souple jad: supple wench.
een: eyes.
fidg'd fu' fain: twitched with excitement.
hotch'd: jerked about.
syne: then.
a' thegither: altogether.
fyke: fuss or commotion.
byke: hive.
pussie's: hare's.
rins: runs.
Wi' mony an eldritch skreich and hollo: with many a ghastly screech and cry.
fairin: reward—in this case, punishment.
brig: bridge.

But ere the key-stane she could make,
210 The fient a tail she had to shake;
For Nannie, far before the rest,
Hard upon noble Maggy prest,
And flew at Tam with furious ettle,
But little kend she Maggy's mettle!
215 Ae spring brought off her master hale,
But left behind her ain gray tale:
The carlin claught her by the rump,
And left poor Maggy scarce a stump.

Now wha this Tale o' truth shall read,
220 Ilk man and mother's son, take heed:
Whene'er to drink you are inclin'd,
Or cutty-sarks rin in your mind,
Think, ye may buy the joys o'er dear;
Remember Tam o' Shanter's meare!

THE BEGGAR'S PETITION

Anonymous

Pity the sorrows of a poor old man,
Whose trembling limbs have borne him to your door;
Whose days are dwindled to the shortest span:—
Oh, give relief, and Heav'n will bless your store!

5 These tatter'd cloaths my poverty bespeak;
These hoary locks proclaim my lengthen'd years;
And many a sorrow in my grief-worn cheek
Has been the channel to a flood of tears!

Yon house, erected on the rising ground,
10 With tempting aspect drew me from my road;
For Plenty there a residence has found,
And Grandeur a magnificent abode.

Gentleman's Magazine (Sept. 1791).

fient: devil.
ettle: purpose.
claught: caught hold of.
The carlin: the witch.

Hard is the fate of the infirm and poor!
Here, as I crav'd a morsel of their bread,
15   A pamper'd menial drove me from the door,
To seek a shelter in a humbler shed.

Oh, take me to your hospitable dome!
Keen blows the wind, and piercing is the cold!
   Short is my passage to the friendly tomb;
20   For I am poor, and miserably old!

Should I reveal the sources of my grief,
If soft Humanity e'er touch'd your breast,
   Your hands would not withhold the kind relief,
And tears of Pity would not be represt.

25   Heav'n sends misfortunes! why should we repine? —
'Tis Heav'n has brought me to the state you see! —
   And your condition soon may be like mine,
The child of Sorrow, and of Misery!

A little farm was my paternal lot;
30   Then, like the lark, I sprightly hail'd the morn! —
   But, ah! Oppression forc'd me from my cot;
My cattle died, and blighted was my corn.

My daughter, once the comfort of my age,
Lur'd by a villain from her native home,
35   Is cast, abandon'd, on the world's wide stage,
And doom'd in scanty poverty to roam.

My tender wife, sweet soother of my cares,
Struck with sad anguish at the stern decree,
   Fell, ling'ring fell, a victim to Despair,
40   And left the world to wretchedness and me![1]

Pity the sorrows of a poor old man,
Whose trembling limbs have borne him to your door;
   Whose days are dwindled to the shortest span:
Oh, give relief, and Heav'n will bless your store!

---

[1]Compare line 4 of Thomas Gray's "Elegy Written in a Country Churchyard": "And leaves the world to darkness and to me." [ED.]

THE BEGGAR BOY

Anonymous[1]

When the wind whistles loud, with a bleak cutting blast,
And the sleet drizzling cloud is to icicles cast;
When the rattling of coaches each way up and down,
Denote that the idle are once more come to town;
5 When the clink of the pattens sound shrill on the ear,
And the hoarse call of Oisters tells Winter is here:—
Then at the street-corner, cold and ragged is seen,
The poor little Beggar-boy, who the crossing sweeps clean.

He no father has known, and his mother forgot,
10 In his earliest of years, all the ties of her lot;
She dropp'd him a foundling at a wealthy man's door,
Who, *feeling*, consign'd him to the parish, as poor:
There half-starv'd and ill-treated eight summers forlorn,
Till his soul felt the freedom to which he was born.
15 He fled from the work house, and now pensive is seen
The poor little Beggar-boy, who the crossing sweeps clean.

To the world, with true pathos, his tale he oft told,
Where the one had not means, and another was cold,
Whilst the throng pass unheeding, his case none attend,
20 The child of misfortune wants the blessing—a Friend:
Yet scorning to pilfer, sense innate of what's right,
He in some market-shambles abideth the night,
And with old birchen stump all the day still is seen
The poor little Beggar-boy, who the crossing sweeps clean.

25 Then ye who're in affluence, take heed on the Boy,
A small pittance from you unto him is a joy.
He had not been so poor, but the chance of his fate,
And, perhaps, when the troubles attending this state
Shall at last cease with breath, then the earth may afford,
30 A repose unto him, by the man call'd a Lord.
Spare the mite then of pity, where attentive is seen.
The poor little Beggar-boy, who the crossing sweeps clean.

Gentleman's Magazine (Apr. 1794).

pattens: wooden shoes.
Oisters: oysters.

[1] Originally signed "J. H."

PATIENT JOE

Or the Newcastle Collier
Hannah More[1]

Have you heard of a collier of honest renown,
Who dwelt on the borders of Newcastle Town?
His name it was Joseph—you better may know
If I tell you he always was called patient Joe.

5   Whatever betided he thought it was right,
And Providence still he kept ever in sight;
To those who love God, let things turn as they wou'd,
He was certain that all work'd together for good.[2]

He prais'd his Creator whatever befel;
10   How thankful was Joseph when matters went well!
How sincere were his carols of praise for good health,
And how grateful for any increase in his wealth!

In trouble he bow'd him to God's holy will;
How contented was Joseph when matters went ill!
15   When rich and when poor he alike understood
That all things together were working for good.

If the land was afflicted with war, he declar'd,
'Twas a needful correction for sins which *he* shar'd:
And when merciful Heaven bade slaughter to cease,
20   How thankful was Joe for the blessing of peace!

When taxes ran high, and provisions were dear,
Still Joseph declar'd he had nothing to fear;
It was but a trial he well understood,
From Him who made all work together for good.

25   Tho' his wife was but sickly, his gettings but small,
Yet a mind so submissive prepar'd him for all;

From *Cheap Repository for Religious and Moral Tracts*. London: Marshall, 1795.

collier: coal miner.
Newcastle Town: city in northwest England, famous for its coal-mining industry.

[1] Compare More's poem with the Book of Job. [ED.]
[2] Compare Pope, *Essay on Man* 1.292–94: "All partial evil, universal good: / And, spite of pride, in erring reason's spite, / One truth is clear: Whatever is, is right." [ED.]

He liv'd on his gains, were they greater or less,
And the Giver he ceas'd not each moment to bless.

When another child came he received him with joy,
30 And Providence bless'd who had sent him the boy;
But when the child dy'd—said poor Joe I'm content,
For God had a right to recall what he lent.

It was Joseph's ill-fortune to work in a pit
With some who believ'd that profaneness was wit;
35 When disasters befel him much pleasure they show'd,
And laugh'd and said—Joseph, will this work for good?

But ever when these would profanely advance
That *this* happen'd by luck, and *that* happen'd by chance;
Still Joseph insisted no chance could be found,
40 Not a sparrow by accident falls to the ground.[3]

Among his companions who work'd in the pit,
And made him the butt of their profligate wit,
Was idle Tim Jenkins, who drank and who gam'd,
Who mock'd at his Bible, and was not asham'd.

45 One day at the pit his old comrades he found,
And they chatted, preparing to go underground;
Tim Jenkins, as usual, was turning to jest,
Joe's notion—that all things which happen'd were best.

As Joe on the ground had unthinkingly laid
50 His provision for dinner of bacon and bread,
A dog on the watch seiz'd the bread and the meat,
And off with his prey ran with footsteps so fleet.

Now to see the delight that Tim Jenkins exprest!
"Is the loss of thy dinner too, Joe, for the best?"
55 "No doubt on't," said Joe; "but as I must eat,
'Tis my duty to try to recover my meat."

So saying, he followed the dog a long round,
While Tim laughing and swearing went down under ground.
Poor Joe soon return'd, though his bacon was lost,
60 For the dog a good dinner had made at his cost.

---

[3]Compare Matthew 10.29 and Luke 12.6–7. [ED.]

When Joseph came back, he expected a sneer,
But the face of each collier spoke horror and fear;
What a narrow escape hast thou had, they all said,
The pit's fall'n in, and *Tim Jenkins* is dead!

65 How sincere was the gratitude Joseph express'd!
How warm the compassion which glow'd in his breast!
Thus events great and small if aright understood
Will be found to be working together for good.

"When my meat," Joseph cry'd, "was just now stol'n away,
70 And I had no prospect of eating to-day,
How could it appear to a short-sighted sinner,
That my life would be sav'd by the loss of my dinner."

THE STORY OF SINFUL SALLY

Told by Herself
Anonymous

Shewing

*How from being Sally of the Green she was first led to become Sinful
Sally, and afterwards Drunken Sal, and how at last she came to a
most melancholy and almost hopeless End; being therein a Warning
to all young Women both in Town and Country.*

Come each maiden lend an ear,
    Country Lass and London Belle!
Come and drop a mournful tear
    O'er the tale that I shall tell!

5 I that ask your tender pity,
    Ruin'd now and all forlorn,
Once, like you, was young and pretty,
    And as cheerful as the morn.

In yon distant Cottage sitting,
10   Far away from London town,

From *Cheap Repository for Moral and Religious Tracts*. London: Marshall,
1795.

Once you might have seen me knitting
　In my simple Kersey Gown.

Where the little lambkins leap,
　Where the meadow looks so gay,
15 Where the drooping willows weep,
　Simple Sally used to stray.

Then I tasted many a Blessing,
　Then I had an honest fame;
Father Mother me caressing,
20 Smiled and thought me free from blame.

Then, amid my friends so dear,
　Life it speeded fast away;
O, it moves a tender tear,
　To bethink me of the day!

25 From the villages surrounding,
　Ere I well had reach'd Eighteen,
Came to the modest youths abounding,
　All to Sally of the Green.

Courting days were thus beginning,
30 And I soon had prov'd a wife;
O! if I had kept from sinning,
　Now how blest had been my life.

Come each maiden lend an ear,
　Country Lass and London Belle!
35 Come ye now and deign to hear
　How poor sinful Sally fell.

Where the Hill begins inclining,
　Half a furlong from the Road
O'er the village white and shining
40 Stands Sir William's great abode.

Near his meadow I was tripping
　Vainly wishing to be seen,
When Sir William met me skipping,
　And he spoke me on the Green.

Kersey: a coarse woolen cloth.

45 Bid me quit my cloak of scarlet,
     Blam'd my simple Kersey Gown;
   Ey'd me then, so like a Varlet,
     Such as live in London town.

   With his presents I was loaded,
50   And bedeck'd in ribbons gay;
   Thus my ruin was foreboded,
     O, how crafty was his way!

   Vanish'd now from Cottage lowly,
     My poor Parents' hearts I break;
55 Enter on a state unholy,
     Turn a Mistress to a Rake.

   Now no more by morning light
     Up to God my voice I raise;
   Now no shadows of the night
60   Call my thoughts to prayer and praise.

   Hark! a well-known sound I hear!
     'Tis the Church's Sunday Bell;
   No; I dread to venture near:
     No; I'm now a child of Hell.

65 Now I lay my Bible by,
     Chuse that impious book so new
   Love the bold blaspheming lie,
     And that filthy novel too.

   Next to London town I pass
70   (Sinful Sally is my name)
   There to gain a front of brass,
     And to glory in my Shame.

   Powder'd well, and puff'd, and painted,
     Rivals all I there out shine;
75 With skin so white and heart so tainted,
     Rolling in my Chariot fine.

   In the Park I glitter daily,
     Then I dress me for the play,

Varlet: knave, rascal.

Then to masquerade so gaily,
80   See me, see me tear away.

When I meet some meaner Lass
    Then I toss with proud disdain;
Laugh and giggle as I pass,
    Seeming not to know a pain.

85 Still at every hour of leisure
    Something whispers me within,
O! I hate this life of pleasure
    For it is a Life of Sin.

Thus amidst my peals of laughter
90   Horror seizes oft my frame:
Pleasure now—Damnation after,
    And a never dying flame.

Save me, Save me, Lord, I cry
    Save my soul from Satan's chain!—
95 Now I see Salvation nigh,
    Now I turn to Sin again.

Is it then some true Repentance
    That I feel for evil done?
No; 'tis horror of my sentence,
100   'Tis the pangs of Hell begun.

By a thousand ills o'ertaken
    See me now quite sinking down;
'Till so lost and so forsaken,
    Sal is cast upon the town.

105 At the dusk of evening grey
    Forth I step from secret cell;
Roaming like a beast of prey,
    Or some hateful Imp of Hell.

Ah! how many youths so blooming
110   By my wanton looks I've won;
Then by vices all consuming
    Left them ruin'd and undone!

Thus the cruel spider stretches
    Wide his web for every fly;

115 Then each victim that he catches
　　Strait he poisons till he die.

Now no more by conscience troubled,
　　Deep I plunge in every Sin:
True my sorrows are redoubled,
120　　But I drown them all in Gin.

See me next with front so daring
　　Band of ruffian rogues among;
Fighting, cheating, drinking, swearing
　　And the vilest of the throng.

125 Mark that youngest of the thieves;
　　Taught by Sal he ventures further;
What he filches Sal receives,
　　'Tis for Sal he does the murther.

See me then attend my victim
130　　To the fatal Gallows Tree;
Pleas'd to think how I have nick'd him,
　　Made him swing while I am free.

Jack I laughing see depart,
　　While with Dick I drink and sing;
135 Soon again I'll fill the cart,
　　Make this present Lover swing.

But while thus with guilt surprising,
　　Sal pursues her bold career,
See God's dreadful wrath arising,
140　　And the day of vengeance near!

Fierce disease my body seizes,
　　Racking pain afflicts my bones;
Dread of death my spirit freezes,
　　Deep and doleful are my groans.

145 Here with face so shrunk and spotted
　　On the clay-cold ground I lie;
See how all my flesh is rotted,
　　Stop, O Stranger, see me die!

---

murther: murder.
nick'd: cheated.

Conscience, as my breath's departing,
150   Plunges too his arrow deep,
With redoubled fury starting
    Like some Giant from his sleep.

In this Pit of Ruin lying,
    Once again before I die,
155 Fainting, trembling, weeping, sighing,
    Lord to thee I'll lift mine eye.

Thou can'st save the vilest Harlot,
    Grace I've heard is free and full,
Sins that once were "red as scarlet"
160   Thou canst make as "white as wool."

Savior, whom I've pierc'd so often,
    Deeper still my guilt imprint!
Let thy mighty Spirit soften
    This my harden'd heart of flint!

165 Vain, alas! is all my groaning,
    For I fear the die is cast;
True, thy blood is all-atoning,
    But my day of Grace is past.

Savior! hear me or I perish!
170   None who *lives* is quite undone;
Still a Ray of Hope I'll cherish
    'Till Eternity's begun.

THE WIDOW

Robert Southey[1]

Cold was the night wind, drifting fast the snows fell,
Wide were the downs and shelterless and naked,
When a poor Wanderer struggled on her journey
    Weary and way-sore.

From *Poems, by Robert Southey.* Bristol: Cottle; London: Robinson, 1797.

downs: the range of low ridges in southern England.

[1] Southey (1774–1843) was the friend of both Wordsworth and Coleridge and one of the most famous poets of the age. He was named poet laureate in 1813. For information on the meter of this poem, see note 4 for the *Anti-Jacobin* (310). [Ed.]

5   Drear were the downs, more dreary her reflections;
Cold was the night wind, colder was her bosom!
She had no home, the world was all before her,
      She had no shelter.

Fast o'er the bleak heath rattling drove a chariot,
10 "Pity me!" feebly cried the poor night wanderer.
"Pity me Strangers! lest with cold and hunger
      "Here I should perish.

"Once I had friends, —but they have all forsook me!
"Once I had parents, —they are now in Heaven!
15 "I had a home once—I had once a husband—
      "Pity me Strangers!

"I had a home once—I had once a husband—
"I am a Widow poor and broken-hearted!"
Loud blew the wind, unheard was her complaining,
20   On drove the chariot.

On the cold snows she laid her down to rest her;
She heard a horseman, "pity me!" she groan'd out;
Loud blew the wind, unheard was her complaining,
      On went the horseman.

25 Worn out with anguish, toil and cold and hunger,
Down sunk the Wanderer, sleep had seiz'd her senses;
There, did the Traveller find her in the morning,
      God had release her.

HANNAH

A Plaintive Tale
   Robert Southey

   The coffin, as I cross'd the common lane,
   Came sudden on my view; it was not here
   A sight of every day, as in the streets
   Of the great city; and we paus'd and ask'd
5 Who to the grave was going? it was one,

Monthly Magazine (Oct. 1797).

the world was all before her: see *Paradise Lost* 12.646.

A village girl; they told us she had borne
An eighteen months strange illness; pined away
With such slow wasting as had made the hour
Of Death most welcome. — To the house of mirth
10 We held our way, and, with that idle talk
That passes o'er the mind and is forgot,
We wore away the hour. But it was eve
When homewardly I went, and in the air
Was that cool freshness, that discolouring shade
15 That makes the eye turn inward. Then I heard,
Over the vale, the heavy toll of death
Sound slow, and question'd of the dead again.
It was a very plain and simple tale:
She bore, unhusbanded, a mother's name,
20 And he who should have cherish'd her, far off
Sail'd on the seas, self-exil'd from his home;
For he was poor. Left thus, a wretched one,
Scorn made a mock of her, and evil tongues
Were busy with her name. She had one ill
25 Heavier, neglect, forgetfulness from him
Whom she had lov'd so dearly. Once he wrote,
But only once that drop of comfort came,
To mingle with her cup of wretchedness;
And when his parents had some tidings from him,
30 There was no mention of poor Hannah there;
Or 'twas the cold inquiry, bitterer
Than silence. So she pin'd and pin'd away,
And for herself and baby toil'd and toil'd,
Till she sunk with very weakness. Her old mother
35 Omitted no kind office, and she work'd
Most hard, and with hard working, barely earn'd
Enough to make life struggle. Thus she lay
On the sick bed of poverty, so worn
That she could make no effort to express
40 Affection for her infant: and the child,
Whose lisping love, perhaps, had solac'd her,
With strangest infantine ingratitude,
Shunn'd her as one indifferent. She was past
That anguish — for she felt her hour draw on;

---

the heavy toll of death: literally, the tolling of a church bell to signal a death or a funeral.

45 And 'twas her only comfort now to think
    Upon the grave. "Poor girl!" her mother said,
    "Thou hast suffer'd much!" — "Aye, mother; there is none
    "Can tell what I have suffer'd," she reply'd;
    "But I shall soon be where the weary rest."
50 And she did rest her soon; for it pleased God
    To take her to his mercy.

THE IDIOT [1]

Robert Southey

*The circumstance related in the following ballad happened some years
since in Herefordshire.*

It had pleas'd God to form poor Ned,
    A thing of idiot mind,
Yet to the poor, unreas'ning man
    God had not been unkind.

5 Old Sarah lov'd her helpless child
    Whom helplessness made dear,
And life was happiness to him
    Who had no hope nor fear.

She knew his wants, she understood
10   Each half artic'late call,
And he was ev'ry thing to her
    And she to him was all.

And so for many a year they dwelt,
    Nor knew a wish beside,
15 But age at length on Sarah came,
    And she fell sick and died.

He tried in vain to waken her,
    And call'd her o'er and o'er.

Morning Post and Gazeteeer (30 June 1798).

Herefordshire: formerly a county in western England, now split between Hereford and
Worcester.

[1] Compare this poem with Wordsworth's treatment of a similar type of character in "The
Idiot Boy." [ED.]

They told him she was dead—the sound
20　　To him no import bore.

They clos'd her eyes and shrouded her,
　　And he stood wond'ring by,
And when they bore her to the grave
　　He follow'd silently.

25　They laid her in the narrow house,
　　They sung the fun'ral stave;
But when the fun'ral train dispers'd,
　　He loiter'd by the grave.

The rabble boys who used to jeer
30　　Whene'er they saw poor Ned,
Now stood and watch'd him at the grave,
　　And not a word they said.

They came and went and came again,
　　Till night at last came on,
35　And still he loiter'd by the grave
　　Till all to rest were gone.

And when he found himself alone,
　　He swift remov'd the clay,
And rais'd the coffin up in haste,
40　　And bore it swift away.

And when he reach'd his hut he laid
　　The coffin on the floor,
And with the eagerness of joy
　　He barr'd the cottage door.

45　And out he took his mother's corpse,
　　And plac'd it in her chair,
And then he heapt the hearth and blew
　　The kindling fire with care.

He plac'd his mother in her chair,
50　　And in her wonted place,
And blew the kindling fire that shone
　　Reflected in her face.

---

fun'ral stave: the music for a funeral service.

And pausing now, her hand would feel,
    And now her face behold,
55 "Why, mother, do you look so pale,
    "And why are you so cold?"

It had pleas'd God from the poor wretch
    His only friend to call,
But God was kind to him, and soon
60   In death restor'd him all.

FROM THE *ANTI-JACOBIN*
George Canning and John Hookham Frere[1]

Another principle [of Jacobin poetry] no less devoutly entertained, and no less sedulously disseminated, is the natural and eternal warfare of the Poor and the Rich. In those orders and gradations of Society, which are the natural result of the original difference of talents and of industry among mankind, the Jacobin sees nothing but a graduated scale of violence and cruelty. He considers every rich man as an oppressor, and every person in a lower situation as the victim of avarice, and the slave of aristocratical insolence and contempt. These truths he declares loudly, not to excite compassion, or to soften the consciousness of superiority in the higher, but for the purpose of aggravating discontent in the inferior orders.

A human being, in the lowest state of penury and distress, is a treasure to a reasoner of this cast — He contemplates, he examines, he turns him in every possible light, with a view of extracting from the variety of his wretchedness, new topics of invective against the pride of property. He indeed (if he is a true Jacobin) refrains from *relieving* the object of his compassionate contemplation; as well knowing that every diminution from the general mass of human misery, must proportionably diminish the force of his argument.

This principle is treated at large by many Authors. It is versified in

---

Anti-Jacobin, or Weekly Examiner (27 Nov. 1797).

[1]Canning (1770–1827), who founded the *Anti-Jacobin* (1797–98), and Frere (1769–1846) were Tories who used this platform to ridicule radicals who were publishing in forums such as Coleridge's *Watchman* and Richard Phillips's *Monthly Magazine*. Since English radicals during this time were commonly called "Jacobins" after the most radical faction of the French Revolution, the conservatives Canning and Frere logically named their periodical the *Anti-Jacobin*. The poem that follows, "The Friend of Humanity and the Knife-Grinder," parodies both the meter and the content of Robert Southey's "The Widow" (304–05). [ED.]

Sonnets and Elegies without end. We trace it particularly in a Poem by the same Author[2] from whom we borrowed our former illustration of the Jacobin Doctrine of Crimes and Punishments.[3] In this Poem the pathos of the Matter is not a little relieved by the absurdity of the Metre. We shall not think it necessary to transcribe the whole of it, as our imitation does not pretend to be so literal as in the last instance, but merely aspires to convey some idea of the manner and sentiment of the original. One Stanza, however, we must give, lest we should be suspected of painting from fancy and not from life.

The learned Reader will perceive that the Metre is Sapphic,[4] and affords a fine opportunity for his *scanning* and *proving*, if he has not forgotten them.

Cōld wăs thē nīght wīnd: drīftĭng fāst thĕ snōws fĕll,
Wīde wĕre thē Dōwns, ānd shĕltĕrlĕss ănd nākĕd:
Whēn ă poōr Wānd'rēr strŭgglĕd ōn hĕr joūrnĕy
           Wēarў ănd wāy-sōre.[5]

This is enough: unless the Reader should wish to be informed how

Fāst o'ĕr thē blēak hēath răttlĭng drōve ă Chārĭot;

or how, not long after,

Loūd blĕw thē wīnd, ūnhĕard wăs hĕr cŏmplāinĭng —
           ōn wĕnt thē Hōrsemān.

We proceed to give our Imitation, which is of the *Amoeboean* or *Collocutory* kind.

Amoeboean or **Collocutory** kind: the kind of poem that consists of dialogue.

[2] Southey. [ED.]

[3] In the previous issue of the *Anti-Jacobin,* the editors had mocked Southey's humanitarian poem "Inscription for the Apartment in Chepstow Castle, where Henry Marten, the Regicide, Was Imprisoned Thirty Years" with the parody "Inscription for the Door of the Cell in Newgate where Mrs. Brownrigg, the 'Prentice-cide, Was Confined Previous to Her Execution." Canning and Frere accused "Jacobin poets" such as Southey of attending only to the "*severity of the punishment,* without any reference to the *malignity of the crime*" (69). [ED.]

[4] Sapphic meter, named for the Greek lyric poet Sappho, consists of three lines of eleven syllables followed by a fourth consisting of five. The scansion employed here is based on classical prosody, which distinguishes between long and short syllables, not between stressed and unstressed syllables (as in English prosody), and follows the conventional scansion for Sapphic meter (although Canning and Frere exaggerate the meter for satirical effect). [ED.]

[5] Lines from Southey's poem "The Widow." [ED.]

(Imitation)

SAPPHICS

The Friend of Humanity

and the Knife-grinder

FRIEND OF HUMANITY
"Needy Knife-grinder! whither are you going?
Rough is the road, your Wheel is out of order —
Bleak blows the blast; — your hat has got a hole in't,
          So have your breeches!

5 "Weary Knife-grinder! little think the proud ones,
Who in their coaches roll along the turnpike —
road, what hard work 'tis crying all day 'Knives and
          'Scissars to grind O!'

"Tell me, Knife-grinder, how you came to grind knives?
10 Did some rich man tyrannically use you?
Was it the 'Squire? or Parson of the Parish?
          Or the Attorney?

"Was it the 'Squire, for killing of his Game? or
Covetous Parson, for his Tythes distraining?[6]
15 Or roguish Lawyer, made you lose your little
          All in a law-suit?

"(Have you not read the Rights of Man,[7] by Tom Paine?)
Drops of compassion tremble on my eye-lids,
Ready to fall, as soon as you have told your
20   Pitiful story."

KNIFE-GRINDER
"Story! God bless you! I have none to tell, Sir,
Only last night a-drinking at the Chequers,

---

distraining: seizing property in order to settle a debt.
Chequers: the name of a tavern.

[6]The Friend of Humanity speculates that the Parson has reduced the Knife-grinder to his current level of poverty by forcing him to pay his tithe, the money collected to support the Church. [ED.]
[7] *The Rights of Man* is Thomas Paine's 1791 tract in defense of the French Revolution. For more on Paine and the Revolution controversy, see the headnote to "Political Backgrounds." [ED.]

This poor old hat and breeches, as you see, were
                              Torn in a scuffle.

25 "Constables came up for to take me into
   Custody; they took me before the Justice;
   Justice Oldmixon put me in the parish-
                              Stocks for a Vagrant.

   "I should be glad to drink your Honour's health in
30 A pot of beer, if you will give me Sixpence;
   But for my part, I never love to meddle
                              With Politics, Sir."

FRIEND OF HUMANITY
   "*I* give thee Sixpence! I will see thee damn'd first—
   Wretch! whom no sense of wrongs can rouse to vengeance;
35 Sordid, unfeeling, reprobate, degraded,
                              Spiritless outcast!"
   (Kicks the Knife-grinder, overturns his Wheel, and exits in a transport of
      republican enthusiasm and universal philanthropy.)

THE DEAD BEGGAR
Charlotte Smith

An elegy,
Addressed to a Lady, who was affected at seeing the Funeral of a
nameless Pauper, buried at the Expence of the Parish, in the Church-
Yard at Brighthelmstone, in November 1792.[1]

From *Elegiac Sonnets and Other Poems.* Vol. 2. London: Cadell, 1797.

Brighthelmstone: the ancient name of Brighton, a seaport on the English Channel.

[1] "I have been told that I have incurred blame for having used in this short composition, terms that have become obnoxious to certain persons. Such remarks are hardly worth notice; and it is very little my ambition to obtain the suffrage of those who suffer party prejudice to influence their taste; or of those who desire that because they have themselves done it, every one else should be willing to sell their best birth-rights, the liberty of thought, and of expressing thought, for the *promise* of a mess of pottage.

"It is surely not too much to say, that in a country like ours, where such immense sums are annually raised for the poor, there ought to be some regulation which should prevent any miserable deserted being from perishing through want, as too often happens to such objects as that on whose interment these stanzas were written.

"It is somewhat remarkable that a circumstance exactly similar is the subject of a short poem called the Pauper's Funeral, in a volume lately published by Mr. Southey." [Smith's note.]

Swells then thy feeling heart, and streams thine eye
　O'er the deserted being, poor and old,
Whom cold, reluctant Parish Charity[2]
　Consigns to mingle with his kindred mold?[3]

5　Mourn'st thou, that *here* the time-worn sufferer ends
　Those evil days still threatening woes to come;
Here, where the friendless feel no want of friends,
　Where even the houseless wanderer finds an home!

What tho' no kindred croud in sable forth,
10　And sigh, or seem to sigh, around his bier;
Tho' o'er his coffin with the humid earth
　No children drop the unavailing tear?

Rather rejoice that *here* his sorrows cease,
　Whom sickness, age, and poverty oppress'd;
15　Where Death, the Leveller, restores to peace
　The wretch who living knew not where to rest.

Rejoice, that tho' an outcast spurn'd by Fate,
　Thro' penury's rugged path his race he ran;
In earth's cold bosom, equall'd with the great,
20　Death vindicates the insulted rights of Man.[4]

Rejoice, that tho' severe his earthly doom,
　And rude, and sown with thorns the way he trod,
Now, (where unfeeling Fortune cannot come)
　He rests upon the mercies of his God.

---

kindred: relatives.

[2]See the discussion of the poor laws in the headnote to "Political Backgrounds" in Part Two. [Ed.]

[3]Mold is the soil or dirt of the graveyard. By calling it "kindred mold," Smith is suggesting that the beggar is returning to earth out of which he was formed—as in the phrase "ashes to ashes, dust to dust." [Ed.]

[4]"Death vindicates the insulted rights of Man": This line most likely contains "the terms that have become obnoxious to certain persons" that Smith refers to in her note. It calls to mind two of the key English tracts in defense of the French Revolution: Mary Wollstonecraft's *A Vindication of the Rights of Men* and Thomas Paine's *The Rights of Man*. [Ed.]

THE OLD CUMBERLAND BEGGAR

A Description[1]

> The class of Beggars to which the old man here described belongs, will
> probably soon be extinct. It consisted of poor, and, mostly, old and
> infirm persons, who confined themselves to a stated round in their
> neighborhood, and had certain fixed days, on which, at different
> houses, they regularly received charity; sometimes in money, but
> mostly in provisions.

I saw an aged Beggar in my walk,
And he was seated by the highway side,
On a low structure of rude masonry
Built at the foot of a huge hill, that they
Who lead their horses down the steep rough road
May thence remount at ease. The aged man
Had placed his staff across the broad smooth stone
That overlays the pile, and from a bag
All white with flour the dole of village dames,
He drew his scraps and fragments, one by one,
And scann'd them with a fix'd and serious look
Of idle computation. In the sun,
Upon the second step of that small pile,
Surrounded by those wild unpeopled hills,
He sate, and eat his food in solitude;
And ever, scatter'd from his palsied hand,
That still attempting to prevent the waste,
Was baffled still, the crumbs in little showers
Fell on the ground, and the small mountain birds,

5

10

15

From *Lyrical Ballads, with Other Poems. In Two Volumes.* London: Longman, 1800.

[1] Although this poem was later published in the 1800 edition of *Lyrical Ballads,* it was written in 1798, and so gives considerable insight into Wordsworth's attitudes toward the poor at the time he was writing the poems for the first edition. Cumberland was the county in northern England in which Wordsworth was born and raised; it is now part of Cumbria. In the Fenwick note, Wordsworth says of the poem: "Observed with great benefit to my own heart, when I was a child: written at Racedown and Alfoxden in my 28th year [1798]. The political economists were about that time beginning their war upon mendicity in all its forms, and by implication, if not directly, on Almsgiving too" (Curtis 56). Compare Wordsworth's attitude toward beggars here with Jeremy Bentham's in "Outline of a Work Entitled 'Pauper Management Improved'" (pages 204–10). [ED.]

20 Not venturing yet to peck their destin'd meal,
Approached within the length of half his staff.[2]

Him from my childhood have I known, and then
He was so old, he seems not older now;
He travels on, a solitary man,
25 So helpless in appearance, that for him
The sauntering horseman-traveller does not throw
With careless hand his alms upon the ground,
But stops, that he may safely lodge the coin
Within the old Man's hat; nor quits him so,
30 But still, when he has given his horse the rein
Towards the aged Beggar turns a look,
Sidelong and half-reverted. She who tends
The toll-gate, when in summer at her door
She turns her wheel, if on the road she sees
35 The aged Beggar coming, quits her work,
And lifts the latch for him that he may pass.
The Post-boy when his rattling wheels o'ertake
The aged Beggar, in the woody lane,
Shouts to him from behind, and, if perchance
40 The old Man does not change his course, the Boy
Turns with less noisy wheels to the road-side,
And passes gently by, without a curse
Upon his lips, or anger at his heart.
He travels on, a solitary Man,
45 His age has no companion. On the ground
His eyes are turn'd, and, as he moves along,
They move along the ground; and evermore,
Instead of common and habitual sight
Of fields with rural works, of hill and dale,
50 And the blue sky, one little span of earth
Is all his prospect. Thus, from day to day,
Bowbent, his eyes for ever on the ground,
He plies his weary journey, seeing still,
And never knowing that he sees, some straw,
55 Some scatter'd leaf, or marks which, in one track,
The nails of cart or chariot-wheel have left
Impress'd on the white road, in the same line,

---

[2] Compare lines 1–2 of "Old Man Travelling," a poem that Wordsworth says in the Fenwick notes was "an overflowing from *The Old Cumberland Beggar*." [ED.]

At distance still the same. Poor Traveller!
His staff trails with him, scarcely do his feet
60 Disturb the summer dust, he is so still
In look and motion, that the cottage curs,
Ere he has pass'd the door, will turn away
Weary of barking at him. Boys and girls,
The vacant and the busy, maids and youths,
65 And urchins newly breech'd all pass him by:
Him even the slow-pac'd waggon leaves behind.

But deem not this Man useless. —— Statesmen![3] ye
Who are so restless in your wisdom, ye
Who have a broom still ready in your hands
70 To rid the world of nuisances; ye proud,
Heart-swoln, while in your pride ye contemplate
Your talents, power, or wisdom, deem him not
A burthen of the earth. 'Tis Nature's law
That none, the meanest of created things,
75 Or forms created the most vile and brute,
The dullest or most noxious, should exist
Divorced from good, a spirit and pulse of good,
A life and soul to every mode of being
Inseparably link'd.[4] While thus he creeps
80 From door to door, the Villagers in him
Behold a record which together binds
Past deeds and offices of charity
Else unremember'd,[5] and so keeps alive
The kindly mood in hearts which lapse of years,
85 And that half-wisdom half-experience gives
Make slow to feel, and by sure steps resign
To selfishness and cold oblivious cares.
Among the farms and solitary huts,
Hamlets, and thinly-scattered villages,
90 Where'er the aged Beggar takes his rounds,
The mild necessity of use compels

---

burthen: burden.

[3] In his letter to Charles James Fox, Wordsworth defines the word *statesmen* as "small independent *proprietors* of land" (*Letters* 314). Here, though, he seems to be using the word in its more familiar sense, i.e., "politicians." [ED.]

[4] Compare "The Rime of the Ancyent Marinere," lines 647–50. [ED.]

[5] Compare "Tintern Abbey," lines 35–37. [ED.]

To acts of love; and habit does the work
Of reason, yet prepares that after joy
Which reason cherishes. And thus the soul,
95 By that sweet taste of pleasure unpursu'd,
Doth find itself insensibly dispos'd
To virtue and true goodness.[6] Some there are,
By their good works exalted, lofty minds
And meditative, authors of delight
100 And happiness, which to the end of time
Will live, and spread, and kindle; minds like these,
In childhood, from this solitary being,
This helpless wanderer, have perchance receiv'd,
(A thing more precious far than all that books
105 Or the solicitudes of love can do!)
That first mild touch of sympathy and thought,
In which they found their kindred with a world
Where want and sorrow were. The easy man
Who sits at his own door, and like the pear
110 Which overhangs his head from the green wall,
Feeds in the sunshine; the robust and young,
The prosperous and unthinking, they who live
Shelter'd, and flourish in a little grove
Of their own kindred, all behold in him
115 A silent monitor, which on their minds
Must needs impress a transitory thought
Of self-congratulation, to the heart
Of each recalling his peculiar boons,
His charters and exemptions; and perchance,
120 Though he to no one give the fortitude
And circumspection needful to preserve
His present blessings, and to husband up
The respite of the season, he, at least,
And 'tis no vulgar service, makes them felt.

125 Yet further.——Many, I believe, there are
Who live a life of virtuous decency,
Men who can hear the Decalogue and feel

Decalogue: the Ten Commandments.

[6]Wordsworth's argument here draws upon the associationist psychology of David Hartley. See the discussion of Hartley in the headnote to "Literary and Philosophical Backgrounds" (120–21). [ED.]

No self-reproach, who of the moral law
Establish'd in the land where they abide
130 Are strict observers, and not negligent,
Meanwhile, in any tenderness of heart
Or act of love to those with whom they dwell,
Their kindred, and the children of their blood.
Praise be to such, and to their slumbers peace!
135 —But of the poor man ask, the abject poor,
Go and demand of him, if there be here,
In this cold abstinence from evil deeds,
And these inevitable charities,
Wherewith to satisfy the human soul.
140 No—man is dear to man: the poorest poor
Long for some moments in a weary life
When they can know and feel that they have been
Themselves the fathers and the dealers out
Of some small blessings, have been kind to such
145 As needed kindness, for this single cause,
That we have all of us one human heart.
—Such pleasure is to one kind Being known
My neighbour, when with punctual care, each week
Duly as Friday comes, though pressed herself
150 By her own wants, she from her chest of meal
Takes one unsparing handful for the scrip
Of this old Mendicant, and, from her door
Returning with exhilarated heart,
Sits by her fire, and builds her hope in heav'n.

155 Then let him pass, a blessing on his head!
And while, in that vast solitude to which
The tide of things has led him, he appears
To breathe and live but for himself alone,
Unblam'd, uninjur'd, let him bear about
160 The good which the benignant law of heaven
Has hung around him, and, while life is his,
Still let him prompt the unletter'd Villagers
To tender offices and pensive thoughts.
Then let him pass, a blessing on his head!
165 And, long as he can wander, let him breathe

---

scrip: small bag or satchel
Mendicant: beggar.

The freshness of the vallies, let his blood
Struggle with frosty air and winter snows,
And let the charter'd wind that sweeps the heath
Beat his grey locks against his wither'd face.[7]
170 Reverence the hope whose vital anxiousness
Gives the last human interest to his heart.
May never House, misnamed of industry,[8]
Make him a captive; for that pent-up din,
Those life-consuming sounds that clog the air,
175 Be his the natural silence of old age!
Let him be free of mountain solitudes,
And have around him, whether heard or not,
The pleasant melody of woodland birds.
Few are his pleasures; if his eyes, which now
180 Have been so long familiar with the earth,
No more behold the horizontal sun
Rising or setting, let the light at least
Find a free entrance to their languid orbs.
And let him, *where* and *when* he will, sit down
185 Beneath the trees, or on a grassy bank
Of high-way side, and with the little birds
Share his chance-gather'd meal, and, finally,
As in the eye of Nature he has liv'd,
So in the eye of Nature let him die.

---

[7] Compare "Tintern Abbey," lines 135–38. [ED.]

[8] Wordsworth here refers to the proposals by such reformers as Jeremy Bentham to do away with "outdoor relief"—i.e., supplementing the income of the working poor—and to confine the poor instead within workhouses. During this time, workhouses were euphemistically called "houses of industry." [ED.]

NATURE

In his landmark essay, "Structure and Style in the Greater Romantic Lyric," M. H. Abrams provides a brief but highly instructive history of British nature poetry in order to reveal the ways in which Romantic poets both draw on and diverge from the writings of their predecessors. In particular, he focuses on the tradition of the *local* or *loco-descriptive poem*, which, as Samuel Johnson defines it, is "a species of composition [. . .] of which the fundamental subject is some particular landscape to be poetically described, with the addition of such embellishments as may be supplied by historical retrospection or incidental meditation" (1.50). After surveying a number of the most notable examples of this genre (John Denham's *Coopers Hill*, John Dyer's *Grongar Hill*, and Thomas Gray's "Ode on a Distant Prospect of Eton College"), Abrams demonstrates how Wordsworth and Coleridge—under the influence of William Lisle Bowles's descriptive sonnets—moved the genre in a new direction:

> In local poetry the order of the thoughts is the sequence in which the natural objects are observed; the poet surveys a prospect, or climbs a hill, or undertakes a tour, or follows the course of a stream, and he introduces memories and ideas intermittently, as the descriptive occasion offers. In Bowles' sonnets, the meditation, while more continuous, and highly serious is severely limited by the straitness of the form, and consists mainly of the pensive commonplaces of the typical late-century man of feeling. In the fully developed Romantic lyric, the description is structurally subordinate to the meditation and the meditation is sustained, continuous, and highly serious. Even when the initial impression is of the casual movement of a relaxed mind, retrospect reveals the whole to have been firmly organized around an emotional issue pressing for resolution. (103)

According to Abrams then, the chief difference between the eighteenth-century local poem and the "greater Romantic lyric" is the latter's sense of what Coleridge would later call "organic unity." In contrast to the local poems of Denham, Dyer, and Gray, which consist of a series of political or moral set pieces, Wordsworth's and Coleridge's efforts in this genre work from beginning to end to accomplish a single goal. The three basic sections of Coleridge's "Frost at Midnight" are all stages in the poet's attempts to overcome his initial state of alienation; each detail of "Tintern Abbey" helps prepare for the poet's eventual recognition of his continued kinship with nature: "the nurse, the guide, the guardian of [his] heart, and soul / Of all [his] moral being."

But, as instructive and insightful as Abrams's essay continues to be, recent scholars have argued that these poems may be considerably more political than he suggests. According to Abrams, early examples of the local poem, such as *Coopers Hill,* are built around a "controlling political motif," but later poets turned from politics to focus on "the mental and emotional experience of a specific lyric speaker" (Abrams 87). While this observation does seem to be true of many midcentury poems such as Dyer's *Grongar Hill* and Gray's "Ode on a Distant Prospect of Eton College," it is less convincing when applied to Wordsworth's and Coleridge's nature poetry from the 1790s. Unquestionably, much of "Tintern Abbey" deals with Wordsworth's own "mental and emotional experience," but it seems highly unlikely that he would have dated his poem on the eve of Bastille Day if he did not wish to place it within the context of the French Revolution and its aftermath.[1] And, as Paul Magnuson has argued, even a poem as seemingly apolitical as "Frost at Midnight" assumes a distinctly political character "if it is read within the public context of *Fears in Solitude* and the political debates of the 1790s" (67).

What we attempt to do in this section is to provide a general sense of what English nature poetry was like at the time of *Lyrical Ballads.* In keeping with Abrams's focus, two of our selections are local poems, John Denham's *Coopers Hill* and William Crowe's *Lewesdon Hill.*[2] We have provided *Coopers Hill* in part because, as the original poem in the genre, it helps establish the conventions of the local poem tradition and in part because it is so clearly a model for "Tintern Abbey." Originally composed during the English Civil War, *Coopers Hill* consistently uses the features of the landscape to comment on contemporary events: The ruins of Chertsey Abbey warn against the dangers of religious zeal, while the Thames River serves as both an emblem of moderation and an aesthetic and political ideal:

O could I flow like thee, and make thy streame
My great example, as it is my theme!

---

[1] See Roe, *Wordsworth and Coleridge* 273 and Levinson 16.
[2] Local poems, such as *Coopers Hill* or *Lewesdon Hill,* set on a hill or mountain overlooking an expansive vista are often called *prospect poems.*

Though deep, yet cleare, though gentle, yet not dull,
Strong without rage, without o'er-flowing full. (lines 189–92)

Consequently, when Denham turns from the abbey to the river, it is as if he is receiving guidance from the "book of nature" about how to confront the problems of his age. In *Lewesdon Hill*—a poem that Coleridge cites as one of the early influences on his poetic style—we can see how much more descriptive the local poem became in the course of the eighteenth century (*Biographia* 17–18). Unlike Denham, who rarely devotes more than a line or two to depicting the physical appearance of a particular scene before drawing some moral or political lesson, Crowe begins his poem with over a hundred lines celebrating the natural beauty of Lewesdon's "variegated scene." This is not to say, however, that *Lewesdon Hill* is by any means an apolitical poem since, as in the following pacifistic digression, Crowe also found numerous opportunities to express his own Whiggish views:

And blest are they,
Who in life's toilsome journey may make pause
After a march of glory: yet not such
As rise in causeless war, troubling the world
By their mad quarrel, and in fields of blood
Hail'd victors, thence renown'd, but in high Heaven
Thieves, ruffians, murderers; these find no repose. (lines 240–47)

Another group of poems comes from a subgenre of the local poem that had particular appeal to both Wordsworth and Coleridge, what Mary Jacobus calls the "revisit poem" (113–18). As the name suggests, these poems (represented here by three sonnets: Thomas Warton's "To the River Lodon," William Lisle Bowles's "To the River Itchin, Near Winton," and Coleridge's "To the River Otter") describe an individual's response to a place he had been before and thus allow him to compare his state of mind at two different times in his life. The revisit poem's relevance to "Tintern Abbey" is clear from that poem's very subtitle ("On Revisting the Banks of the Wye"), but this type of poem also demonstrates the increasingly psychological focus of late eighteenth-century nature poetry. Whereas *Coopers Hill* reveals practically nothing about its speaker, Bowles's "To the River Itchin" focuses largely on the poet's own emotional state and personal history.[3]

Most of the remaining selections in this section serve as intertexts for two individual poems in *Lyrical Ballads*: Wordsworth's "Tintern Abbey" and Coleridge's "The Nightingale." In addition to Edward Gardner's "Sonnet Written in Tintern Abbey, Monmouthshire," we have reprinted the

---

[3] See Abrams, "Structure and Style" 90.

chapter from William Gilpin's *Observations on the River Wye*, in which he applies his notion of the picturesque to the abbey and its environs. For Gilpin, the picturesque differs from what Edmund Burke had called "the beautiful" because, while the beautiful refers to those objects "which please the eye in their *natural* state," the picturesque describes "those, which please from some quality, capable of being *illustrated in painting*" (*Three Essays* 3).[4] This unapologetically artificial emphasis of Gilpin's thinking is no less evident in his travel writing:

> The following little work proposes a new object of pursuit; that of not barely examining the face of a country; but of examining it by the rules of picturesque beauty: that of not merely describing; but of adapting the description to the principles of artificial landscape; and of opening the sources of those pleasures, which are derived from the composition. (*Observations* 1–2)

Since Wordsworth brought Gilpin's guidebook along with him on his walking tour to southern Wales, it seems likely that he was responding to it in "Tintern Abbey." Moreover, as Marjorie Levinson has suggested, the passages in Gilpin that detail the intense poverty present in the Wye Valley during this time encourage us to reexamine Wordsworth's representation of "vagrant dwellers in the houseless woods" (30–37).

Readers today associate the Romantics with nature largely because of "Tintern Abbey" and John Keats's "Ode to a Nightingale." But Keats was following in a distinct tradition that *Lyrical Ballads* participates in through Coleridge's somewhat iconoclastic poem "The Nightingale." To demonstrate how startling Coleridge's joyful depiction of the nightingale's song would have seemed to eighteenth-century readers, we have selected a few of the countless celebrations of the nightingale as a "most musical, most melancholy" bird: Charlotte's Smith's "To a Nightingale" and Coleridge's own "Effusion XXIII. To the Nightingale" in which he adopts the very trope that he would ridicule just two years later. Though it is not exactly an intertext, we have also included in this section another nature poem whose literary destiny is closely connected to that of "The Nightingale": Coleridge's "Lewti, or The Circassian's Love Chant." In the first few copies of the Bristol edition

---

[4]In his enormously influential 1757 treatise, *A Philosophical Enquiry into the Origins of our Ideas of the Sublime and Beautiful*, Burke defines *the beautiful* as "that quality, or those qualities in bodies, by which they cause love, or some passion similar to it" and identifies smallness, smoothness, and delicacy as some of its essential qualities (91). Conversely, he characterizes *the sublime* as "whatever is in any sort terrible, or is conversant about terrible objects, or operates in a manner analogous to terror" (39). Its primary qualities include vastness, ruggedness, obscurity, and power.

of *Lyrical Ballads*, it is "Lewti" and not "The Nightingale" that appears; but, because this poem had been previously published in the *Morning Post*, Wordsworth and Coleridge quickly replaced it with "The Nightingale."

FROM *COOPERS HILL*

John Denham[1]

If there be Poets, which did never dreame
Upon Parnassus, nor did tast the streame
Of Helicon,[2] we justly may suppose,
Those made not Poets, but the Poets those.
5 And as Courts make not Kings, but Kings the Court,
So where the Muses and their traine resort,
Parnassus stands; if I can be to thee
A Poet, thou Parnassus art to me.
Nor wonder, if (advantag'd in my flight,
10 By taking wing from thy auspicious height)
Through untrac't waves and ayrie paths I flye,
More boundlesse in my Fancy than my eye:
My eye, which swift as thought contracts the space
That lyes between and first salutes the place
15 Crown'd with that sacred pile, so vast, so high,
That whether 'tis a part of Earth, or sky,
Uncertaine seemes, and may be thought a proud
Aspiring mountain, or a falling cloud,

6th ed. London: Moseley, 1655.

thee: Coopers Hill.
pile: a large building.

[1] Denham (1615–69), an Irish poet, fought for the English crown during the English Civil Wars and was knighted and appointed surveyor-general upon the restoration of the monarchy. The poem first appeared in an unauthorized text in 1642 and went through several editions. The title page of the 1655 edition advertises that it is "Now Printed from a Perfect Copy; And A Corrected Impression." The preface informs the reader, "You have seen this Poem often, and yet never: for, though there have been Five Impressions, this now in your hand is the onely true Copie. Those former were all but meer Repetitions of the same false Transcript, which stole into Print by the Author's long absence from this Great Town." [ED.]

[2] Both Parnassus and Helicon are mountains in Greece that were thought to be sacred to Apollo, god of poetry, and the nine Muses of the various arts. "The streame of Helicon" refers to Hippocrene, whose waters—according to Greek myth—inspired poetic creation. [ED.]

Pauls,[3] the late theme of such a Muse whose flight
20 Has bravely reach't and soar'd above thy height:
Now shalt thou stand, though sword, or time, or fire,
Or zeale more fierce than they, thy fall conspire,
Secure, whilst thee the best of Poets sings,
Preserv'd from ruine by the best of Kings.
25 Under his proud survay the City lyes,
And like a mist beneath a hill doth rise;
Whose state and wealth, the business and the crowd,
Seems at this distance but a darker cloud:
And is to him, who rightly things esteems,
30 No other in effect than what it seems:
Where with like hast, though several waies, they run,
Some to undo, and some to be undone;
While luxury, and wealth, like war and peace,
Are each the others ruine, and increase;
35 As Rivers lost in Seas some secret veine
Thence reconveighs, there to be lost again.
Oh happinesse of sweet retir'd content!
To be at once secure, and innocent.

Windsor the next (where Mars with Venus dwells,
40 Beauty with strength) above the valley swells
Into my eye, and doth it self present
With such an easie and unforc't ascent,
That no stupendious precipice denyes
Accesse, no horror turnes away our eyes:
45 But such a Rise, as doth at once invite
A pleasure, and a reverence from the sight.
Thy mighty Masters Embleme, in whose face
Sate meeknesse, heightned with Majestick Grace.
Such seems thy gentle height, made onely proud
50 To be the basis of that pompous load,
Then which, a Nobler weight no Mountain Bears,
But Atlas only that supports the Sphears.
When Natures hand this ground did thus advance,

---

the best of Kings: Charles I.
Windsor: Windsor Castle in which Mars (Charles I) and Venus (his queen, Henrietta Maria) reside.
Atlas: in Greek mythology, the Titan who supports the sky on his shoulders.

[3] "Master Waller." [original note.] Denham refers here to Edmund Waller's (1606–87) 1645 poem "Upon His Majesty's Repairing of Paul's" — i.e., St. Paul's Cathedral in London. [ED.]

'Twas guided by a wiser power than Chance;
55 Mark't out for such a use, as if 'twere meant
T'invite the builder, and his choice prevent.
Nor can we call it choice, when what we chuse,
Folly, or blindness only could refuse.
A Crown of such Majestick towrs doth Grace
60 The Gods great Mother, when her heavenly race
Doe homage to her, yet she cannot boast
Amongst that numerous, and Celestial hoast,
More Heros than can Windsor, nor doth Fames
Immortall booke record more noble names.
65 Not to look back so far, to whom this Ile
Owes the first Glory so brave a pile,
Whether to Caesar, Albanact, or Brute,
The Brittish Arthur, or the Danish Knute,
(Though this of old no lesse content did move,
70 Than when for Homers birth seven Cities strove)
(Like him in birth, thou should'st be like in Fame,
As thine his fate, if mine had been his Flame)
But whosoere it was, Nature design'd
First a brave place, and then as brave a minde.
75 Not to recount those severall Kings, to whom
It gave a Cradle, or to whom a Tombe,
But thee (great *Edward*) and thy greater sonne,[4]
(The lillies which his Father wore, he wonne)[5]
And thy Bellona,[6] who the Consort came
80 Not onely to thy bed, but to thy Fame,
She to thy Triumph led one Captive King,

---

prevent: anticipate.
The Gods great Mother: Cybele or Rhea, the mother of Zeus.
Ile: isle — i.e., England.
Caesar: Julius Caesar who invaded England in 55 and 56 B.C.
Brute: the grandson of the Trojan warrior Aeneas and the legendary founder of London; Albanact was one of his sons.
Knute: Canute, king of England and Denmark in the eleventh century.

[4] "Edward the 3. and the black Prince." [original note.]
[5] "The lillies which his Father wore, he wonne" refers to Edward the Black Prince, who was largely responsible for his father's victories over France — the lily or fleur-de-lis being the emblem of the royal family of France. [ED.]
[6] "Queene Philippa." [original note.] Bellona was the Roman goddess of war, and, by linking Queen Phillipa with her, Denham alludes to the queen's exhortation of the British troops before a decisive battle against the Scots (the Battle of Neville's Cross). [ED.]

And brought that sonne, which did the second bring.[7]
Then didst thou found that Order (whither love,
Or victory thy Royall thoughts did move)
85 Each was a noble cause, and nothing lesse,
Than the designe, has been the great successe:
Which forraigne Kings, and Emperors esteeme
The second Honour to their Diadem.
Had thy great destiny but given thee skill,
90 To know as well, as power to act her will,
That from those Kings, who then thy captives were,
In after-times should spring a Royall paire,
Who should possesse all that thy mighty power,
Or thy desires more mighty, did devoure;
95 To whom their better Fate reserves what ere
The Victor hopes for, or the Vanquisht feare;
That blood, which thou and thy great Grandsire shed,
And all that since these sister Nations bled,
Had bin unspilt, had happy *Edward* known
100 That all the blood he spilt had been his own.
When he that Patron chose, in whom are joyn'd
Souldier and Martyr, and his arms confin'd
Within the Azure Circle, he did seem
But to foretel, and prophecie of him,
105 Who to his Realms that Azure round hath joyn'd,
Which Nature for their bound at first design'd.
That bound, which to the Worlds extreamest ends,
Endlesse itselfe, its liquid arms extends;
He, who not needs that Embleme which we paint,
110 But is himself the Souldier and the Saint.
Here should my wonder dwell, and here my praise,
But my fixt thoughts my wandring eye betrays,

Order: the Order of the Garter—an order of knighthood modeled on King Arthur's legendary Knights of the Round Table, founded by Edward III in 1344.
Royall paire: Charles I and Henrietta Maria.
Patron: St. George—the seat of the Order of the Garter is St. George's Chapel at Windsor Castle.
Azure Circle: the insignia of the Order of the Garter.
him: Charles I.

[7] "The Kings of France & Scotland." [original note.] Scottish King David II was captured at the Battle of Neville's Cross; French King John II was captured by the Black Prince at the Battle of Poitiers. [ED.]

Viewing a neighboring hill, whose top of late
A Chappel crown'd, till in the Common Fate,
115 The adjoyning Abby[8] fell (may no such storme
Fall on our times, where ruine must reform.)
Tell me (my Muse) what monstrous dire Offence,
What crime could any Christian incense
To such a rage? was't Luxury? or lust?
120 Was he so temperate, so chast, so just?
Were these their crimes? they were his own much more:
But wealth is Crime enough to him that's poor,
Who having spent the Treasures of his Crown,
Condemns their Luxury to feed his own.
125 And yet this Act, to varnish o'er the shame
Of sacriledge, must bear devotions name.
No Crime so bold, but would be understood
A reall, or at least a seeming good.
Who fear not to do ill, yet fears the Name,
130 And free from Conscience, is a slave to Fame.
Thus he the Church at once protects, and spoyles:[9]
But Princes swords are sharper then their styles.
And thus to th'ages past he makes amends,
Their Charity destroyes, their Faith defends.
135 Then did Religion in a lazie Cell,
In empty, airie contemplation dwell;
And like the block, unmoved lay: but ours,
As much too active, like the storke devours.[10]
Is there no temperate Region can be knowne,
140 Betwixt their Frigid, and our Torrid Zone?
Could we not wake from that Lethargicke Dreame,
But to be restlesse in a worse extreame?
And for that Lethargy was there no cure,
But to be cast into a Calenture?

Calenture: a tropical fever.

[8] Abbey: Chertsey Abbey on St. Anne's Hill—destroyed at the command of Henry VIII after his break with the Catholic Church. [ED.]

[9] For his book against Martin Luther, Pope Leo X granted Henry VIII the title of Defender of the Faith; a little more than a decade later, he would break with Rome and declare himself the head of the English Church. [ED.]

[10] These lines refer to Aesop's fable in which a nation of frogs asks the gods for a king. First, they are given a log for their king, but they complain when the log does nothing. Then they are given a stork, but it devours them. [ED.]

145 Can knowledge have no bound, but must advance
So farre, to make us wish for ignorance?
And rather in the darke to grope our way,
Then led by a false guide to erre by day?
Who sees these dismall heaps, but would demand,
150 What barbarous Invader sackt the land?
But when he heares, no Goth, no Turk did bring
This desolation, but a Christian King;
When nothing, but the Name of Zeale appears
'Twixt our best actions and the worst of theirs,
155 What does he think our Sacriledge would spare,
When such th'effects of our devotions are?
Parting from thence 'twixt anger, shame, and feare,
Those for what's past, and this for what's too neare: [11]
My eye descending from the Hill, survaies
160 Where *Thames* amongst the wanton vallies strayes.
Thames, the most lov'd of all the Oceans sonnes,
By his old Sire, to his imbraces runnes,
Hasting to pay his tribute to the Sea,
Like mortall life to meet Eternity.
165 Though with those streames he no resemblance hold,
Whose foame is Amber, and their Gravell Gold; [12]
His genuine, and lesse guilty wealth t'explore,
Search not his bottom, but survey his shore;
Ore which he kindly spreads his spacious wing,
170 And hatches plenty for th'ensuing Spring.
Nor them destroyes it with too fond a stray,
Like Mothers which their Infants overlay.
Nor with a suddain and impetuous wave,
Like profuse Kings, resumes the wealth he gave.
175 No unexpected inundations spoyle
The mowers hopes, nor mock the plowmans toyle:
But Godlike his unwearied Bounty flows;
First loves to do, then loves the Good he does.
Nor are his Blessings to his banks confin'd,

---

[11] Denham's contemplation of Chertsey Abbey causes him to think about the religious controversies of his own time and the conflict between the royalist and parliamentary factions that would lead to the English Civil War (1642–49). [ED.]

[12] Rivers such as the Po in northern Italy were thought to be rich in amber, and numerous rivers (e.g., the Pactolus in what is now Turkey) were famous for the gold that washed up on their banks. [ED.]

180 But free, and common, as the Sea or Wind;
     When he to boast, or to disperse his stores
     Full of the tributes of his gratefull shores,
     Visits the World, and in his flying towers
     Brings home to us, and makes both Indies ours;
185 Finds wealth where 'tis, bestows it where it wants,
     Cities in deserts, woods in Cities plants.
     So that to us no thing, no place is strange,
     While his fayre bosome is the worlds exchange.
     O could I flow like thee, and make thy streame
190 My great example, as it is my theme!
     Though deep, yet cleare, though Gentle, yet not dull,
     Strong without rage, without o'er-flowing full.
     Here[13] Nature, whether more intent to please
     Us, or her selfe, with strange varieties,
195 (For things of wonder give no lesse delight
     To the wise Maker's, then beholder's sight.
     Though these delights from severall causes move,
     For so our children, thus our friends we love)
     Wisely she knew, the harmony of things,
200 As well as that of sounds, from discords springs.
     Such was the discord, which did first disperse
     Forme, order, beauty through the Universe;
     While drynesse moysture, coldnesse heat resists,
     All that we have, and that we are, subsists.
205 While the steepe horrid roughnesse of the Wood
     Strives with the gentle calmenesse of the flood.
     Such huge extreames when Nature doth unite,
     Wonder from thence results, from thence delight.[14]
     The streame is so transparent, pure, and cleare,
210 That had the selfe-enamour'd youth[15] gaz'd here,
     So fatally deceiv'd he had not been,
     While he the bottome, not his face had seene.
     But his proud head the ayery Mountaine hides
     Among the Clouds; his shoulders, and his sides

---

flying towers: tall sailing ships.

[13] "The Forrest." [Original note.]

[14] At this point, Denham makes explicit the idea of *concordia discors* (a harmony between opposites) that Earl Wasserman identifies as the organizing principle of *Coopers Hill* (57). [ED.]

[15] "Narcissus." [Original note.]

215 A shady mantle cloaths; his curled brows
   Frowne on the Gentle streame, which calmly flows,
   While winds and stormes his lofty forhead beat:
   The common fate of all that's high, or great.
   Low at his foot a spacious plaine is plac't,
220 Between the mountaine and the streame imbrac't:
   Which shade and shelter from the Hill derives,
   While the kind river wealth and beauty gives;
   And in the mixture of all these appears
   Variety, which all the rest indears.

   . . . .

SONNET IX

TO THE RIVER LODON

Thomas Warton[1]

   Ah! what a weary race my feet have run,
      Since first I trod thy banks with alders crown'd,
      And thought my way was all through fairy ground,
      Beneath thy azure sky, and golden sun:
5 Where first my muse to lisp her notes begun!
      While pensive memory traces back the round,
      Which fills the varied interval between;
      Much pleasure, more of sorrow, marks the scene.
   Sweet native stream! those skies and suns so pure
10   No more return, to chear my evening road!
      Yet still one joy remains, that not obscure,
   Nor useless, all my vacant days have flow'd,
      From youth's gay dawn to manhood's prime mature;
      Nor with the Muse's laurel unbestowed.[2]

From *Poems*. London: Becket, 1777.

alders: shrubs or trees that grow in cool, moist regions.

[1] Warton (1728–90), a professor of poetry at Oxford, was named poet laureate in 1785. The Lodon River, now called the Chet, flows through Norfolk, England, Warton's native region. [ED.]
[2] The laurel wreath traditionally is a symbol of poetic achievement. [ED.]

FROM *OBSERVATIONS ON THE RIVER WYE*
William Gilpin[1]

SECTION IV

As we left Monmouth, the banks, on the left, were, at first, low; but on both sides they soon grew steep, and woody; varying their shapes, as they had done the day before. The most beautiful of these scenes is in the neighbourhood of St. Breval's castle; where the vast, woody declivities, on each hand, are uncommonly magnificent. The castle is at too great a distance to make any object in the view.

The weather was now serene: the sun shone; and we saw enough of the effect of light, in the exhibitions of this day, to regret the want of it before.

During the whole course of our voyage from Ross, we had scarce seen one corn-field. The banks of the Wye consist, almost entirely either of wood, or of pasturage; which I mention as a circumstance of peculiar value in landscape. Furrowed-lands, and waving-corn, however charming in pastoral poetry, are ill-accommodated to painting. The painter never desires the hand of art to touch his grounds. — But if art *must* stray among them — if it *must* mark out the limits of property, and turn them to the uses of agriculture; he wishes, that these limits may be as much concealed as possible; and that the lands they circumscribe, may approach, as nearly as may be, to nature — that is, that they may be pasturage. Pasturage not only presents an agreeable surface: but the cattle, which graze it, add great variety, and animation to the scene.

The Meadows, below Monmouth, which run shelving from the hills to the water-side, were particularly beautiful, and well-inhabited. Flocks of sheep were every where hanging on their green steeps; and herds of cattle occupying the lower grounds. We often sailed past groups of them laving their sides in the water; or retiring from the heat under sheltered banks:

vallem, amnemq; tenebant.[2]

Observations on the River Wye, and Several Parts of South Wales, etc. Relative Chiefly to Picturesque Beauty; Made in the Summer of the Year 1770. London: Blamire, 1782.

Monmouth: a city in southern Wales.

[1] Gilpin (1724–1804), a schoolmaster, vicar, artist, and aesthetician, developed the influential concept of the picturesque (defined on page 323). [ED.]

[2] They held the valley and the river. [ED.]

In this part of the river, which now begins to widen, we were often entertained with light vessels gliding past us. Their white sails passing along the sides of the hills were very picturesque.

In many places also the views were varied by the prospect of bays, and harbours in miniature; where little barks lay moored, taking in ore, and other commodities from the mountains. These vessels, designed plainly for rougher water, than they at present incountered, shewed us, without any geographical knowledge, that we approached the sea.

From Monmouth we reached, by a late breakfast-hour, the noble ruin of *Tintern-abbey*; which belongs to the Duke of Beaufort; and is esteemed, with its appendages, the most beautiful and picturesque view on the river.

Castles, and abbeys have different situations, agreeable to their respective uses. The castle, meant for defence, stands boldly on the hill: the abbey, intended for meditation, is hid in the sequestered vale.

> *Ah! happy thou*, if one superior rock
> Rear on its brow, the shivered fragment huge
> Of some old Norman fortress: happier far,
> Ah then most happy, if thy vale below
> Wash, with the crystal coolness of its rills,
> Some mould'ring abbey's ivy-vested wall.[3]

Such is the situation of Tintern-abbey. It occupies a gentle eminence in the middle of a circular valley, beautifully screened on all sides by woody hills; through which the river winds its course; and the hills, closing on its entrance, and on its exit, leave no room for inclement blasts to enter. A more pleasing retreat could not easily be found. The woods, and glades intermixed; the winding of the river; the variety of the ground; the splendid ruin, contrasted with the objects of nature; and the elegant line formed by the summits of the hills, which include the whole; make all together a very inchanting piece of scenery. Every thing around breathes an air so calm, and tranquil; so sequestered from the commerce of life, that it is easy to conceive, a man of warm imagination, in monkish times, might have been allured by such a scene to become an inhabitant of it.

No part of the ruins of Tintern is seen from the river, except the abbey-church. It has been an elegant Gothic pile; but it does not make that appearance as a *distant* object, which we expected. Though the parts are

---

screened: flanked or surrounded. *Screen* is a technical term referring to the side sections of a landscape that set off the central portion.

[3] Gilpin quotes from the first book of *The English Garden* (1771; lines 380–85) by William Mason (1725–97). [ED.]

beautiful, the whole is ill-shaped. No ruins of the tower are left, which might give form, and contrast to the walls, and buttresses, and other inferior parts. Instead of this, a number of gabel-ends hurt the eye with their regularity;[4] and disgust it by the vulgarity of their shape. A mallet judiciously used (but who durst use it?) might be of service in fracturing some of them; particularly those of the cross isles, which are not only disagreeable in themselves, but confound the perspective.

But were the building ever so beautiful, incompassed as it is with shabby houses, it could make no appearance from the river. From a stand near the road, it is seen to more advantage.

But if Tintern-abbey be less striking as a *distant* object, it exhibits, on a *nearer* view (when the whole together cannot be seen, but the eye settles on some of its nobler parts) a very inchanting piece of ruin. Nature has now made it her own. Time has worn off all traces of the rule: it has blunted the sharp edges of the chisel; and broken the regularity of opposing parts. The figured ornaments of the east-window are gone; those of the west-window are left. Most of the other windows, with their principal ornaments, remain.

To these are superadded the ornaments of time. Ivy, in masses uncommonly large, has taken possession of many parts of the wall; and gives a happy contrast to the grey-coloured stone, of which the building is composed. Nor is this undecorated. Mosses of various hues, with lichens, maiden-hair, penny-leaf, and other humble plants, overspread the surface; or hang from every joint, and crevice. Some of them were in flower, others only in leaf; but, all together, they give those full-blown tints, which add the richest finishing to a ruin.

Such is the beautiful appearance, which Tintern-abbey exhibits on the *outside*, in those parts, where we can obtain a near view of it. But when we enter it, we see in it most perfection: at least, if we consider it as an independent object, unconnected with landscape. The roof is gone: but the walls, and pillars, and abutments, which supported it, are intire. A few of the pillars indeed have given way; and here, and there, a piece of the facing on the wall: but in correspondent parts, one always remains to tell the story. The pavement is obliterated: the elevation of the choir is no longer visible: the whole area is reduced to one level; cleared of rubbish; and covered with neat turf, closely shorn; and interrupted with nothing, but the noble columns, which formed the isles, and supported the tower.

When we stood at one end of this awful piece of ruin; and surveyed the whole in one view—the elements of air, and earth, its only covering, and

---

[4]Roughness and irregularity are hallmarks of Gilpin's notion of the picturesque; therefore, he longs to take a mallet to those overly regular sections of the Abbey. [ED.]

pavement; and the grand, and venerable remains, which terminated both —
perfect enough to form the perspective; yet broken enough to destroy the
regularity; the eye was above measure delighted with the beauty, the greatness, and the novelty of the scene. More picturesque it certainly would have
been, if the area, unadorned, had been left with all its rough fragments of
ruin scattered round; and bold was the hand that removed them: yet as the
outside of the ruin, which is the chief object of *picturesque curiosity*, is still
left in all its wild, and native rudeness; we excuse — perhaps we approve —
the neatness, that that is introduced within. It *may* add to the *beauty* of the
scene — to its *novelty* it undoubtedly *does*.

Among other things in this scene of desolation, the poverty and wretchedness of the inhabitants were remarkable. They occupy little huts, raised
among the ruins of the monastery; and seem to have no employment, but
begging: as if a place, once devoted to indolence, could never again become
the seat of industry. As we left the abbey, we found the whole hamlet at the
gate, either openly soliciting alms; or covertly, under the pretence of carrying us to some part of the ruins, which each could shew; and which was far
superior to any thing, which could be shewn by any one else. The most lu-
crative occasion could not have excited more jealousy, and contention.

One poor woman we followed, who had engaged to shew us the monk's
library. She could scarce crawl; shuffling along her palsied limbs, and meagre, contracted body, by the help of two sticks. She led us, through an old
gate, into a place overspread with nettles and briars; and pointing to the
remnant of a shattered cloister, told us, that was the place. It was her own
mansion. All indeed she meant to tell us, was the story of her own wretchedness; and all she had to shew us, was her own miserable habitation. We did
not expect to be interested: but we found we were. I never saw so loathsome
a human dwelling. It was a cavity, loftily vaulted, between two ruined walls;
which streamed with various-coloured stains of unwholsome dews. The
floor was earth; yielding, through moisture, to the tread. Not the merest
utensil, or furniture of any kind, appeared, but a wretched bedstead, spread
with a few rags, and drawn into the middle of the cell, to prevent its receiving the damp, which trickled down the walls. At one end was an aper-
ture; which served just to let in light enough to discover the wretchedness
within. — When we stood in the midst of this cell of misery; and felt the
chilling damps, which struck us in every direction, we were rather surprised, that the wretched inhabitant was still alive; than that she had only
lost the use of her limbs.

The country about Tintern-abbey hath been described as a solitary,
tranquil scene: but its immediate environs only are meant. Within half a
mile of it are carried on great iron-works; which introduce noise and bustle into these regions of tranquility.

The ground, about these works, appears from the river to consist of grand woody hills, sweeping, and intersecting each other, in elegant lines. They are a continuation of the same kind of landscape, as that about Tintern-abbey; and are fully equal to it.

As we still descend the river, the same scenery continues. The banks are equally steep, winding, and woody; and in some parts diversified by prominent rocks, and ground finely broken, and adorned.

But one great disadvantage began here to invade us. Hitherto the river had been clear, and splendid; reflecting the several objects on its banks. But its waters now became ouzy, and discoloured. Sludgy banks too appeared, on each side; and other symptoms, which discovered the influence of a tide.

SONNET III

TO A NIGHTINGALE

Charlotte Smith[1]

Poor melancholy bird, that all night long
   Tell'st to the moon thy tale of tender woe;
   From what sad cause can such sweet sorrow flow,
And whence this mournful melody of song?

5 Thy poet's musing fancy would translate
   What mean the sounds that swell thy little breast,
   When still at dewy eve thou leavest thy nest,
Thus to the listening night to sing thy fate.

Pale Sorrow's victims wert thou once among,
10 Tho' now releas'd in woodlands wild to rove,
   Or hast thou felt from friends some cruel wrong,
Or diedst thou martyr of disastrous love?
Ah! songstress sad! that such my lot might be,
To sigh and sing at liberty—like thee!

From *Elegiac Sonnets and Other Essays*. 2nd ed. London: Dodsley, 1784.

[1] Adapted from Petrarch. In modern editions of Petrarch's *Canzoniere*, the sonnet Smith adapts here is canzone 311, appearing in the second part of the series, which describes Petrarch's grief over the death of his beloved Laura. [ED.]

FROM *LEWESDON HILL*

A Poem

  William Crowe[1]

Up to thy summit, Lewesdon, to the brow
Of yon proud rising, where the lonely thorn
Bends from the rude South-east, with top cut sheer
By his keen breath, along the narrow track
5 By which the scanty-pastured sheep ascend
Up to thy furze-clad summit, let me climb;
My morning exercise; and thence look round
Upon the variegated scene, of hills,
And woods, and fruitful vales, and villages
10 Half-hid in tufted orchards,[2] and the sea
Boundless, and studded thick with many a sail.

  Ye dew-fed vapours, nightly balm, exhaled
From earth, young herbs and flowers, that in the morn
Ascend as incense to the Lord of day,
15 I come to breathe your odours; while they float
Yet near this surface, let me walk embathed
In your invisible perfumes, to health
So friendly, nor less grateful to the mind,
Administring sweet peace and cheefulness.

20 How changed is thy appearance, beauteous hill![3]
Thou hast put off thy wintry garb, brown heath
And russet fern, thy seemly-colour'd cloak

Oxford: Clarendon, 1788.

furze-clad: covered with furze, an evergreen shrub.

[1] Crowe (1745–1829) was the rector of Stoke Abbey in Dorset. As he notes in the Advertisement, Lewesdon Hill "is situated in the western part of Dorsetshire"—about three miles from Racedown Lodge where Wordsworth lived from 1795–97. "This choice of a Subject," he goes on to say, "to which the Author was led by his residence near the spot, may seem perhaps to confine him to topics of mere rural and local description. But he begs leave here to inform the Reader that he has advanced beyond those narrow limits to something more general and important." [ED.]

[2] Compare "Tintern Abbey," line 11: "These plots of cottage ground, these orchard tufts." [ED.]

[3] Compare "Tintern Abbey," lines 66–68: "And so I dare to hope / Though changed no doubt, from what I was, when first / I came among these hills." Whereas Crowe describes the effect of seasonal changes to Lewesdon Hill, Wordsworth focuses on the emotional and psychological changes that had taken place within himself. [ED.]

To bide the hoary frosts and dripping rains
Of chill December, and art gaily robed
25 In livery of the spring: upon thy brow
A cap of flowery hawthorn, and thy neck
Mantled with new-sprung furze and spangles thick
Of golden bloom: nor lack thee tufted woods
Adown thy sides: Tall oaks of lusty green,
30 The darker fir, light ash, and the nesh tops
Of the young hazel join, to form thy skirts
In many a wavy fold of verdant wreath.
So gorgeously hath Nature drest thee up
Against the birth of May; and, vested so,
35 Thou dost appear more gracefully array'd
Than Fashion's worshippers; whose gaudy shews,
Fantastical as are a sick man's dreams,
From vanity to costly vanity
Change ofter than the moon. Thy comely dress,
40 From sad to gay returning with the year,
Shall grace thee still till Nature's self shall change.

These are the beauties of thy woodland scene
At each return of spring: yet some delight
Rather to view the change; and fondly gaze
45 On fading colours, and the thousand tints
Which Autumn lays upon the varying leaf.
I like them not; for all their boasted hues
Are kin to Sickliness: mortal Decay
Is drinking up their vital juice; that gone,
50 They turn to sear and yellow. Should I praise
Such false complexions, and for beauty take
A look consumption-bred? As soon, if gray
Were mixt in young Louisa's tresses brown,
I'd call it beautiful variety,
55 And therefore doat on her. Yet I can spy
A beauty in that fruitful change, when comes
The yellow Autumn and the hopes o'the year
Brings on to golden ripeness; nor dispraise
The pure and spotless form of that sharp time,
60 When January spreads a pall of snow

---

nesh: soft.
consumption-bred: caused by consumption, i.e., tuberculosis.

O'er the dead face of th'undistinguish'd earth.
Then stand I in the hollow comb beneath
And bless this friendly mount the weather sends
My reed-roof'd cottage, while the wintry blast
65 From the thick north comes howling: till the Spring
Return, who leads my devious steps abroad,
To climb, as now, to Lewesdon's airy top.

    Above the noise and stir of yonder fields
Uplifted, on this height I feel the mind
70 Expand itself in wider liberty.
The distant sounds break gently on my sense,
Soothing to meditation: so methinks,
Even so, sequester'd from the noisy world,
Could I wear out this transitory being
75 In peaceful contemplation and calm ease.
But conscience, which still censures on our acts,
That awful voice within us, and the sense
Of an hereafter, wake and rouse us up
From such unshaped retirement; which were else
80 A blest condition on this earthly stage.
For who would make his life a life of toil
For wealth, o'er balanced with a thousand cares;
Or power, which base compliance must uphold;
Or honour, lavish'd most on courtly slaves;
85 Or fame, vain breath of a misjuding world;
Who for such perishable gaudes would put
A yoke upon his free unbroken spirit,
And gall himself with trammels and the rubs
Of this world's business; so he might stand clear
90 Of judgment and the tax of idleness
In that dread audit, when his mortal hours
(Which now with soft and silent stealth pace by)
Must all be counted for? But, for this fear,
And to remove, according to our power,
95 The wants and evils of our brother's state,
'Tis meet we justle with the world; content,

---

comb: coombe, a small, narrow valley among the hills.
devious: without a definite course, wandering.
gaudes: trinkets.
justle: jostle.

If by our sovereign Master we be found
At last not profitless: for worldly meed,
Given or witheld, I deem of it alike.[4]

.   .   .   .

But hark! the village clock strikes nine; the chimes
440 Merrily follow, tuneful to the sense
Of the pleased clown attentive, while they make
False-measured melody on crazy bells.
O wondrous Power! of modulated sound!
Which like the air (whose all-obedient shape
445 Thou makest thy slave) canst subtilly pervade
The yielded avenues of sense, unlock
The close affections, by some fairy path
Winning an easy way through every ear,
And with thine unsubstantial quality
450 Holding in mighty chains the hearts of all;
All, but some cold and sullen-temper'd spirits,
Who feel no touch of sympathy or love.

Yet what is music, and the blended power
Of voice with instruments of wind and string?
455 What but an empty pageant of sweet noise?
Tis past: and all that it has left behind
Is but an echo dwelling in the ear
Of the toy-taken fancy, and beside
A void and countless hour in life's brief day.

460 But ill accords my verse with the delights
Of this gay month: and see the Villagers
Assembling jocund in their best attire
To grace this genial morn. Now I descend
To join the worldly croud; perchance to talk,
465 To think, to act as they: then all these thoughts,
That lift th' expanded heart above this spot
To heavenly musing, these shall pass away
(Even as this goodly prospect from my view)
Hidden by near and earthly-rooted cares.

---

meed: reward.
clown: rustic, peasant.

[4] Much of the above verse-paragraph echoes Hamlet's famous "To be or not to be" speech
(3.1.55–87). [ED.]

470 So passeth human life; our better mind
  Is as a sunday's garment, then put on
  When we have nought to do; but at our work
  We wear a worse for thrift. Of this enough:
  To-morrow for severer thought; but now
475 To breakfast, and keep festival to-day.

SONNET II
William Lisle Bowles[1]

Languid, and sad, and slow from day to day,
  I journey on, yet pensive turn to view
  (Where rich landscape gleams with softer hue)
The streams, and vales, and hills, that steal away.
5 So fares it with the children of the earth:
  For when life's goodly prospect opens round,
  Their spirits beat to tread that fairy ground,
Where every vale sounds to the pipe of mirth.
But them, vain hope, and easy youth beguiles,
10 And soon a longing look, like me, they cast
  Back o'er the pleasing prospect of the past:
Yet fancy points where still far onward smiles
  Some sunny spot, and her fair colouring blends,
  Till cheerless on their path the night descends.

From *Sonnets, Written Chiefly on Picturesque Spots, during a Tour*. Bath: Cruttwell, 1789.

[1] Bowles (1762–1850) was the vicar of Bremhill and canon of Salisbury Cathedral. His sonnets first appeared anonymously in 1789 as *Fourteen Sonnets, Elegiac and Descriptive, Written during a Tour;* the advertisement prefacing the sonnets claims that they "were found in a Traveler's Memorandum-Book." Their popularity warranted immediately a second edition that corrected the many printing errors in the first edition. They are chiefly remembered today because of their influence on the young Coleridge, who was so "enthusiastically delighted and inspired" by them that he transcribed forty copies of Bowles's book by hand to give to his friends as gifts. [ED.]

SONNET IX

TO THE RIVER ITCHIN

NEAR WINTON[1]

William Lisle Bowles

Itchin, when I behold thy banks again,
    Thy crumbling margin, and thy silver breast,
    On which the self-same tints still seem to rest,
Why feels my heart the shiv'ring sense of pain?
5   Is it—that many a summer's day has past
Since, in life's morn, I carol'd on thy side?
Is it—that oft, since then, my heart has sigh'd,
    As Youth, and Hope's delusive gleams, flew fast?
Is it—that those, who circled on thy shore,
10 Companions of my youth, now meet no more?
    Whate'er the cause, upon thy banks I bend
Sorrowing, yet feel such solace at my heart,
    As at meeting some long-lost friend
From whom, in happier hours, we wept to part.

SONNET XIX

NETLEY ABBEY

William Lisle Bowles

Fallen pile! I ask not what has been thy fate,—
    But when the weak winds, wasted from the main,
    Through each lone arch, like spirits that complain,
Come mourning to my ear, I meditate
5   On this world's passing pageant, and on those
Who once, like thee, majestic and sublime
Have stood; till bow'd beneath the hand of time,
    Or hard mishap, at their sad evening's close,
    Their bold and beauteous port has sunk forlorn:

From *Sonnets, Written Chiefly on Picturesque Spots, during a Tour*. Bath: Cruttwell, 1789.

[1] Bowles was clearly influenced by the sonnet "To the River Lodon" by his Oxford tutor Thomas Warton (331). [ED.]

From *Sonnets, Written Chiefly on Picturesque Spots, during a Tour*. Bath: Cruttwell, 1789.

10 Yet wearing still a charm, that age and cares
　Cou'd ne'er subdue, decking the silver hairs
　　Of sorrow—as with short-liv'd gleam the morn
　Illumines, whilst it weeps, the rested tower
　That lifts its forehead grey, and smiles beneath the shower.

EFFUSION XXIII

TO THE NIGHTINGALE

Samuel Taylor Coleridge

　Sister of love-lorn Poets, Philomel![1]
　How many Bards in city garret pent,[2]
　While at their window they with downward eye
　Mark the faint Lamp-beam on the kennell'd mud,
5 And listen to the drowsy cry of Watchmen,
　(Those hoarse unfeather'd Nightingales of Time!)
　How many wretched Bards address *thy* name,
　And Hers, the full-orb'd Queen, that shines above.
　But I *do* hear thee, and the high bough mark,
10 Within whose mild moon-mellow'd foliage hid
　Thou warblest sad thy pity-pleading strains.
　O! have I listen'd, till my working soul,
　Wak'd by those strains to thousand phantasies,
　Absorb'd hath ceas'd to listen! Therefore oft,
15 I hymn thy name: and with a proud delight
　Oft will I tell thee, Minstrel of the Moon!
　"Most musical, most melancholy"[3] Bird!
　That all thy soft diversities of tone,
　Tho' sweeter far than the delicious airs
20 That vibrate from a white-arm'd Lady's harp,
　What time the languishment of lonely love

From *Poems on Various Subjects, by S. T. Coleridge, Late of Jesus College, Cambridge*. London: Robinsons; Bristol: Cottle, 1796.

Philomel: from *Philomela* (literally, "lover of song"), the Greek word for nightingale.
kennell'd: in a gutter.

[1] For the myth of Philomela, see the note to Coleridge's "The Nightingale" (48). [ED.]
[2] Compare with line 57 of "Frost at Midnight" (234). [ED.]
[3] Line 62 from John Milton's *Il Penseroso* (1645); see note 2 to Coleridge's "The Nightingale" in *Lyrical Ballads*. [ED.]

Melts in her eye, and heaves her breast of snow,
Are not so sweet, as is the voice of her,
My Sara—best belov'd of human Kind!
25 When breathing the pure soul of Tenderness
She thrills me with the Husband's promis'd name![4]

SONNET IV
TO THE RIVER OTTER [1]
Samuel Taylor Coleridge

Dear native Brook! wild streamlet of the West!
　　How many various-fated Years have past,
　　What blissful and what anguish'd hours, since last
I skimm'd the smooth thin stone along thy breast,
5　　Numbering its light leaps! Yet so deep imprest
　　Sink the sweet scenes of Childhood, that mine eyes
I never shut amid the sunny blaze,
　　But strait with all their tints thy waters rise,
Thy crossing plank, thy margin's willowy maze,
10　　And bedded sand that vein'd with various dyes,
　　Gleam'd thro' thy bright transparence to the gaze!
　　Visions of Childhood! oft have ye beguil'd
Lone Manhood's cares, yet waking fondest sighs,
　　Ah! that once more I were a careless Child!

From *Poems, by S. T. Coleridge, Second Edition. To Which Are Now Added Poems by Charles Lamb and Charles Lloyd.* Bristol: Cottle; London: Robinsons, 1797.

strait: straight, immediately.

[4] See note 1 to "Effusion XXXV" in "Literary and Philosophical Backgrounds" (156). [ED.]
[1] The poem appears in the series entitled "Sonnets, Attempted in the Manner of the Rev. W. L. Bowles." The Otter River flows through Devon near Coleridge's birthplace. [ED.]

LEWTI

or the Circassian's Love Chant [1]
Samuel Taylor Coleridge

At midnight, by the stream I rov'd
To forget the form I lov'd.
Image of Lewti! from my mind
Depart; for Lewti is not kind.
5   The moon was high, the moonlight gleam
   And the shadow of a star
Heav'd upon Tamaha's stream;
   But the rock shone brighter far.
The rock half-shelter'd from my view,
10 By pendent boughs of tressy yew.
So shines my Lewti's forehead fair,
Gleaming thro' her sable hair.
Image of Lewti! from my mind
Depart; for Lewti is not kind.

15 I saw the white waves, o'er and o'er,
Break against the distant shore.
All at once they broke in light:
I heard no murmur of their roar,
Nor ever I beheld them flowing,
20 Neither coming, neither going;
But only saw them, o'er and o'er,
Break against the curved shore;
Now disappearing from the sight,
Now twinkling regular and white,
25 And Lewti's smiling mouth can shew
As white and regular a row.
Nay, treach'rous image! from my mind
Depart; for Lewti is not kind.

Morning Post and Gazeteer (13 Apr. 1798).

Tamaha: a river in Circassia.
tressy: hairlike.

[1] Adapted from Wordsworth's "Beauty and Moonshine," this poem first appeared under the pseudonym "Nicias Erythraeus" in the *Morning Post* and then in early Bristol editions of *Lyrical Ballads* (see page 18); Wordsworth and Coleridge quickly replaced it with Coleridge's "The Nightingale." Circassia is a region in southern Russia (or Belarus), bordering on the Black Sea. [ED.]

I saw a cloud of palest hue,
30   Onward to the moon it pass'd.
Still brighter and more bright it grew,
With floating colours not a few,
    Till it reach'd the moon at last.
Then the cloud was wholly bright,
35 With a rich and amber light;
And so with many a hope I seek,
    And with such joy I find my Lewti;
And even so my pale wan cheek
    Drinks in as deep a flush of beauty!
40 Nay, treach'rous image! leave my mind,
If Lewti never will be kind.

The little cloud—it floats away,
    Away it goes—away so soon!
Alas! it has no pow'r to stay:
45 Its hues are dim, its hues are grey—
    Away it passes from the moon.
How mournfully it seems to fly,
    Ever fading more and more,
To joyless regions of the sky—
50   And now 'tis whiter than before,
As white as my poor cheek will be,
    When, Lewti! on my couch I lie,
A dying man, for love of thee.
Nay, treach'rous image! leave my mind—
55 And yet thou didst not look unkind!

    I saw a vapour in the sky,
    Thin and white and very high.
I ne'er beheld so thin a cloud—
    Perhaps the breezes that can fly
60   Now below, and now above,
Have snatch'd aloft the lawny shroud
    Of Lady fair, that died for love:
    For Maids, as well as Youths, have perish'd
    From fruitless love, too fondly cherish'd!
65   Nay, treach'rous image! leave my mind—
    For Lewti never will be kind;

---

lawny: made of lawn, a thin linen or cotton fabric.

This hand should make his life blood flow,
That ever scorn'd my Lewti so!

   I cannot chuse but fix my sight
70   On that small vapour, thin and white!
   So thin, it scarcely, I protest,
      Bedims the star that shines behind it:
   And pity dwells in Lewti's breast,
      Alas! if I knew how to find it.
75   And O! how sweet it were, I wist,
      To see my Lewti's eyes to-morrow
   Shine brightly thro' as thin a mist
      Of pity and repentant sorrow!
  Nay, treach'rous image! leave my mind —
80 Ah, Lewti! why art thou unkind?

   Hush! my heedless feet from under
      Slip the crumbling banks for ever;
   Like echoes to a distant thunder,
      They plunge into the gentle river:
85   The river-swans have heard my tread,
   And startle from their reedy bed.
   O beauteous birds! methinks ye measure
      Your movements to some heav'nly tune!
   O beauteous birds! 'tis such a pleasure
90   To see you move beneath the moon;
   I would, it were your true delight
   To sleep by day and wake all night.
   I know the place where Lewti lies,
   When silent night has clos'd her eyes —
95   It is a breezy jasmin bow'r,
      The Nightingale sings o'er her head;
   Had I the enviable pow'r
      To creep unseen with noiseless tread,
   Then should I view her bosom white,
100 Heaving lovely to my sight,
   As those two swans together heave
   On the gently swelling wave.
   O that she saw me in a dream,

---

wist: know.
methinks: it seems to me.

And dreamt that I had died for care!
105 All pale and wasted I would seem,
    Yet fair withal, as spirits are.
I'd die indeed, if I might see
Her bosom heave, and heave for me!
Sooth, gentle image! sooth my mind!
110   To-morrow Lewti may be kind.

SONNET WRITTEN IN TINTERN ABBEY, MONMOUTHSHIRE

Edward Gardner [1]

Admiring stranger, that with ling'ring feet,
    Enchain'd by wonder, pauses on this green;
Where thy enraptur'd sight the dark woods meet,
    Ah! rest awhile, and contemplate the scene.

5 These hoary pillars clasp'd by ivy round,
    This hallow'd floor by holy footsteps trod,
The mould'ring choir by spreading moss embrown'd,
    Where fasting saints devoutly hymn'd their God.

Unpitying Time, with slow but certain sweep,
10   Has laid, alas! Their ancient splendour low:
Yet here let Pilgrims, while they muse and weep,
    Think on the lesson that from hence may flow.
Like theirs, how soon may be the tott'ring state
Of man,—the temple of a shorter date.

From *Miscellanies in Prose and Verse, by Edward Gardner*. Vol. 2. Bristol: Biggs, 1798.

Monmouthshire: a county in southern Wales.

[1] Gardner (fl. 1770–98) was a poet and essayist.

Part Three

REACTIONS TO *LYRICAL BALLADS*

CONTEMPORARY REVIEWS

Reactions to *Lyrical Ballads* are ongoing. The scope of this edition, however, limits us to considering only the more immediate responses—no less significant considering that they would condition the reception of Romanticism for the next two hundred years. To help readers understand that legacy, we have provided selections from the book's first critics: the reviewers who panned or praised it, the poets who pursued or parodied it, and the authors themelves, who continued to ponder its poetic enterprise.

When reading the contemporary reviews of *Lyrical Ballads,* one might be astonished by how generally unimpressed most of the reviewers seem to have been—not that they were blatantly offended but rather that they seem on the whole ambivalent and uninterested. If this was a revolutionary text, we might expect reviewers to recognize this fact and celebrate it, or to recognize and then excoriate it. If it was not, the reviewers might indicate whose poetry Wordsworth and Coleridge were copying and then curse their dullness. Of the initial reviews, only a brief notice in the *Monthly Mirror* recognizes the book's reaction against the popular literature of Sensibility: "Instead of the pompous and high-sounding phraseology of the *Della Cruscan school,* [the author of *Lyrical Ballads*] has produced sentiments of feeling and sensibility, expressed without affectation, and in the language of nature." [1] The reviewer adds his view that *Lyrical Ballads* is a welcome stylistic innovation that might "correct that depraved taste, occasioned by an incessant *importation* from the press of *sonnets* and other poems"—no doubt a reference to the popularity of Charlotte Smith and her imitators, among them William Lisle Bowles, whose sonnets Coleridge greatly admired. Oddly enough, the reviewer was particularly taken with "Lines Left

---

[1] See Robert Merry's "To Anna Matilda" (pages 153–56) and the headnote to "Literary and Philosophical Backgrounds" in Part Two. Since the book was published anonymously, the reviewers generally assume single authorship.

upon a Seat in a Yew-Tree," writing nothing about the more experimental poems in *Lyrical Ballads.*

What seems particularly striking is how misunderstood the book was in 1798 through 1800. The ultra-conservative *Anti-Jacobin Review,* for instance, which dubbed itself a "Monthly Political and Literary Censor," praised the volume for its "genius, taste, elegance, wit, and imagery of the most beautiful kind," while describing its supposed author as "classic and accomplished," indicating that the reviewer found in the book conservative values and high literary cachet—priase that no doubt would have befuddled Wordsworth and Coleridge considerably. Another reviewer from the conservative *British Critic* commends the book despite sensing not so much a liberal agenda but an anti-providential worldview that still manages not to detract from the beauty of the poetry.

Ironically, those periodicals that seem to have shared many of Wordsworth and Coleridge's political views were the ones whose reviewers seemed least impressed. The left-leaning *Monthly Magazine,* in which Taylor's translations of Bürger appeared and to which the two poets planned to submit "The Ancyent Marinere," had little to say about the volume, praising it overall but panning the poem begun with them in mind. Even the *Analytical Review,* published by Joseph Johnson, the radical who published Coleridge's *Fears in Solitude* volume, found the book to be mediocre. The most noteworthy reactions against the book came from two generally liberal magazines, the *Monthly Review* and the *Critical Review.* Of the original reviews, Dr. Charles Burney's, which appeared in the *Monthly Review,* is certainly the most engaging. Though Burney objects to the volume's claims to include "*poetry,*" he finds much to enjoy in the "sentiments" it contains. The *Critical Review*'s reception of *Lyrical Ballads* is the most surprising: its reviewer Robert Southey shared many of the poets' political and literary views—not to mention that he was friend to Wordsworth and brother-in-law to Coleridge—but nonetheless he composed the most damning review of them all.

FROM THE *CRITICAL REVIEW*
Robert Southey

The majority of these poems, we are informed in the advertisement, are to be considered as experiments.

"They were written chiefly with a view to ascertain how far the language of conversation in the middle and lower classes of society is adapted to the purposes of poetic pleasure."

Critical Review 24 (1798).

Of these experimental poems, the most important is the Idiot Boy, the story of which is simply this. Betty Foy's neighbour Susan Gale is indisposed; and no one can conveniently be sent for the doctor but Betty's idiot boy. She therefore puts him upon her poney, at eight o'clock in the evening, gives him proper directions, and returns to take care of her sick neighbour. Johnny is expected with the doctor by eleven; but the clock strikes eleven, and twelve, and one, without the appearance either of Johnny or the doctor. Betty's restless fears become insupportable; and she now leaves her friend to look for her idiot son. She goes to the doctor's house, but hears nothing of Johnny. About five o'clock, however, she finds him sitting quietly upon his feeding poney. As they go home they meet old Susan, whose apprehensions have cured her, and brought her out to seek them; and they all return merrily together.

Upon this subject the author has written nearly five hundred lines. With what spirit the story is told, our extract will evince.[. . .] [1]

No tale less deserved the labour that appears to have been bestowed upon this. It resembles a Flemish picture in the worthlessness of its design and the excellence of its execution. From Flemish artists we are satisfied with such pieces: who would not have lamented if Corregio or Rafaelle had wasted their talents in painting Dutch boors or the humours of a Flemish wake? [2]

The other ballads of this kind are as bald in story, and are not so highly embellished in narration. With that which is entitled the Thorn, we were altogether displeased. The advertisement says, it is not told in the person of the author, but in that of some loquacious narrator. The author should have recollected that he who personates tiresome loquacity becomes tiresome himself. The story of a man who suffers the perpetual pain of cold, because an old woman prayed that he might never be warm is perhaps a good story for a ballad, because it is a well-known tale: but is the author certain that it is "*well-authenticated*"? and does not such an assertion promote the popular superstition of witchcraft?

In a very different style of poetry is the Rime of the Ancyent Marinere; a ballad (says the advertisement) "professedly written in imitation of the *style,* as well as of the spirit of the elder poets." We are tolerably conversant with the early English poets and can discover no resemblance whatever, except in antiquated spelling and a few obsolete words. This piece appears to

---

[1] Southey quotes lines 322–401. [ED.]

[2] Raphael (1483–1520) and Correggio (1494–1534) were two of the greatest painters of the Italian Renaissance. Southey here draws upon the frequently observed contrast between the grandeur of Italian art and the relative banality of Dutch and Flemish art. While Italian artists typically devoted themselves to the sublime religious and mythological subjects, Dutch and Flemish painters often painted scenes of lower-class life. [ED.]

us perfectly original in style as well as in story. Many of the stanzas are laboriously beautiful; but in connection they are absurd or unintelligible. Our readers may exercise their ingenuity in attempting to unriddle what follows.[. . .] [3]

We do not sufficiently understand the story to analyze it. It is a Dutch attempt at German sublimity. Genius has here been employed in producing a poem of little merit.

With pleasure we turn to the serious pieces, the better part of the volume. The Foster-Mother's Tale is in the best style of dramatic narrative. The Dungeon and the Lines upon the Yew-tree Seat are beautiful. The tale of the Female Vagrant is written in the stanza, not the style, of Spenser.[4] We extract a part of this poem.[. . .] [5]

Admirable as the poem is, the author seems to discover still superior powers in the Lines written near Tintern Abbey. On reading this production, it is impossible not to lament that he should ever have condescended to write such pieces as the Last of the Flock, the Convict, and most of the ballads. In the whole range of English poetry, we scarcely recollect any thing superior to a part of the following passage.[. . .] [6]

The "experiment," we think, has failed, not because the language of conversation is little adapted to "the purposes of poetic pleasure," but because it has been tried upon uninteresting subjects. Yet every piece discovers genius; and, ill as the author has frequently employed his talents, they certainly rank him with the best of living poets.

FROM THE *NEW LONDON REVIEW*
Anonymous

As this volume has some pretension to originality, it is peculiarly an object of critical examination; the writer professes that "the majority of the poems are to be considered as *experiments*." It is our duty to state his views, and to estimate his execution.

He says, "these poems were written chiefly with a view to ascertain how far *the language of conversation,* in the *middle* and *lower* classes of society, is adapted to the purposes of poetic pleasure." That there should ever have been a doubt upon this subject in the mind of a man of taste, is not a little

---

New London Review (January 1799).

[3] Southey quotes lines 301–22. [ED.]
[4] The Spenserian stanza is a nine-line stanza form, rhyming ababbcbcc and ending in an iambic hexameter. [ED.]
[5] Lines 91–180 follow. [ED.]
[6] Lines 65–111 follow. [ED.]

surprising. The language of *conversation,* and that too of the *lower classes,* can never be considered as the language of *poetry.* What is to affect the imagination, must at least address itself to the imagination; and the imagination has its peculiar style. It is chiefly objected to French poetry, that in general, it is the language of conversation; this is not strictly true; but because it is frequently nothing more than elegant; because it is at times divested of poetical diction; of the colourings, the freshness, and the graces of poetry; men of taste in Europe have universally depreciated its claim to the honours of genuine poetry.

Our author, conscious of his paradox, and of the feelings of his readers, adds that "they will often look round for poetry, and enquire by what species of courtesy these attempts can be permitted to assume that title." We really sympathise with the forlorn reader; but our author, to moderate his despair, offers a singular consolation; he assures us, that we have no settled notion of what poetry is. These are his words, "It is desirable that they should not suffer the *solitary word,* poetry, *a word* of very *disputed meaning,* to stand in the way of their gratification." Nothing can be more ludicrous than this ingenious request of our author, excepting its grave refutation. If the writer of these poems will, for a moment, dismiss his jocular paradox (and we almost suspect that some of these poems were intended merely as lusory effusions) we trust to his cultivated taste, and his poetical acquirements, to tell us *what is poetry.* He will find no difficulty in resolving the question, by comparing Dryden with D'Urfey, Pope with Pomfret, and Waller with Walsh.[1]

Our author must have had very unsettled notions of what we are to understand by the term poetical simplicity. He is not singular in this unhappy indecision of taste; we have had a multitude of rhimers who have looked into the earliest efforts of the art, for their models; and seem to have thought, that rudeness was synonymous to simplicity. Bishop Percy's publication of the Reliques of Ancient Poetry has been the fertile mother of a numerous and meagre race of *stanza-enditers.*

We may distinguish a *simple* style from a style of *simplicity.* By a simple style we may suppose a colloquial diction, debased by inelegance, and gross by familiarity. Simplicity is a manner of expression, facile, pure, and always elegant. Simplicity will not detract from the elevation of the thoughts, nor

---

lusory: written in a playful style.
stanza-enditers: literally stanza writers; here, a pejorative term for hack poets.

[1] John Dryden (1631–1700), English playwright, critic, and poet; Thomas Durfey (1653–1723), English-French poet and comedian; Alexander Pope (1688–1744), English poet; John Pomfret (1667–1702), English poet and clergyman; Edmund Waller (1606–87), English poet; William Walsh (1663–1708), English poet and mentor to Pope. [ED.]

injure the beauty of the composition. The arch-critic of France felt and marked the distinction, in these happy lines.

> Quoique vouse ecrivez, evitez la bassesse,
> Le *stile le moins noble* a pourtant sa *noblesse.*
>
> ART. POET. C.1[2]

The simple style has all the squalid nakedness of a beggar, and simplicity the lovely nudity of a grace.

> *Thoughtless of beauty* she is beauty's self!
>
> THOMSON[3]

Our criticism is so just that our poet seems to have felt its truth, while he was employed in its violation; and so far from these poems being entirely written in the eccentric principle he proposes, we shall find that he has many exquisite thoughts exquisitely expressed. If ever he disgusts by the meagreness and poverty of his composition, it is precisely where, aiming at simplicity, he copies the rudest effusions of our vulgar ballads. So far indeed from obtaining that simplicity to which he pretends, we, at times, have wished that he were somewhat *more* simple. Among his irregular verses, we are often surprised with beautiful expression, and sometimes displeased with a turgid obscurity, which evidently shews that our poet found it impossible to keep the imagination alive, in the creeping measures of his *conversation verses.* In the first ballad, entitled "The Rime of the Ancyent Marinere," the following stanza is a dark enigma. It is a moonlight scene, where the inimitable expression of Shakespeare was floating in the recollection of the writer.

> The rock shone bright, the kirk no less
>   That stands above the rock;
> The moon-light *steeped in silentness*
>   The steady weather-cock.[4]

Our poet more happily describes the morning sun, at sea, in the "Female Vagrant." [. . .][5]

This is a very elegant passage, and there are many such, but while the reader will admire these, he cannot but smile, as he perceives how easily the poet forgets the principle he lays down in his preface.

---

[2] Lines 79–80 from Canto I of *L'Art poétique* (1674) by Nicholas Boileau (1636–1711), "the arch-critic of France" referred to above. The lines may be translated as follows: "When you write familiarly, avoid baseness; the least noble style has nonetheless its nobility." Boileau was one of the most influential Neoclassical critics. [ED.]

[3] James Thomson (1700–48), popular English nature poet. [ED.]

[4] Lines 503–06. The reviewer's italics refer to Shakespeare's frequent use of the expression to be "steeped in" something. [ED.]

[5] The reviewer quotes lines 138–44. [ED.]

Our limits will not permit us to offer the reader many specimens of that simplicity, in which, in our opinion, the author has egregiously failed. If such passages as the following find admirers, the writer is fortunate; for they never cost him any labour in the composition.[. . .][6]

The greater part of this volume is not composed in this in-artificial and anti-poetical manner. Some of the poems are so far removed from the rudeness they affect, that their entire texture is brilliant and rich, and there are many passages of perfect beauty. Our poet seems to want nothing, but more fortunate topics than those he has, at times, unhappily selected. We hope that, by this time, he is convinced of the failure of these "*Experiments*"; but we recommend them to the curious as the failures of a man of genius. We take our leave of the writer, in the words of Boileau.

Prenez mieux votre ton. Soyez simple avec d'art,
Sublime sans orgueil, agreeable sans fard.[7]

FROM THE *MONTHLY REVIEW*
Charles Burney [1]

The author of these ingenious compositions presents the major part of them to the public as *experiments;* since they were written, as he informs us in the *advertisement* prefixed, "chiefly with a view to ascertain how far the language of conversation in the middle and lower classes of society is adapted to the purposes of poetic pleasure."

Though we have been extremely entertained with the fancy, the facility, and (in general) the sentiments, of these pieces, we cannot regard them as *poetry*, of a class to be cultivated at the expence of a higher species of versification, unknown in our language at the time when our elder writers, whom this author condescends to imitate, wrote their ballads. —Would it not be degrading poetry, as well as the English language, to go back to the barbarous and uncouth numbers of Chaucer? Suppose, instead of modernizing the old bard, that the sweet and polished measures, on lofty subjects, of Dryden, Pope, and Gray, were to be transmuted into the dialect and versification of the xivth century? Should we be gainers by the retrogradation? *Rust*

Monthly Review (June 1799).

[6]The reviewer quotes lines 29–32 and 45–48 of "Goody Blake and Harry Gill." [ED.]
[7]"Get a better grasp of your tone. Be simple in your art: grand without arrogance, pleasing without artifice" from *L'Art Poétique* 1. 101–02. [ED.]

[1]Burney (1726–1814) was a music historian, composer, and critic. He was the father of the novelist Fanny Burney. [ED.]

is a necessary quality to a counterfeit old medal: but, to give artificial rust to modern poetry, in order to render it similar to that of three or four hundred years ago, can have no better title to merit and admiration than may be claimed by any ingenious forgery. None but savages have submitted to eat acorns after corn was found. — We will allow that the author before us has the art of cooking his acorns well, and that he makes a very palatable dish of them for *jours maigres:* but, for festivals and *gala* days,

> *Multos castra juvant, & liuo tubae*
> *Permistus sonitus.*[2]

We have had pleasure in reading the *reliques of antient poetry,* because it was antient; and because we were surprised to find so many beautiful thoughts in the rude numbers of barbarous times. These reasons will not apply to *imitations* of antique versification. — We will not, however, dispute any longer about names; the author shall style his rustic delineations of low-life, *poetry,* if he pleases, on the same principle on which Butler is called a poet, and Teniers a painter:[3] but are doggrel verses of the one equal to the sublime numbers of a Milton, or are the Dutch boors of the other to be compared with the angels of Raphael or Guido?[4] — When we confess that our author has had the art of pleasing and interesting in no common way by his natural delineation of human passions, human characters, and human incidents, we must add that these effects were not produced by the *poetry:* — we have been as much affected by pictures of misery and unmerited distress, in *prose.* The elevation of soul, when it is lifted into the higher regions of imagination, affords us a delight of a different kind from the sensation which is produced by the detail of common incidents. For this fact, we have better authority than is to be found in the writings of most critics: we have it in a poet himself, whose award was never (till now) disputed:

> The poet's eye, in a fine frenzy rolling,
> Doth glance from heaven to earth, from earth to heav'n;

---

jours maigres: lean days.

[2] "Military camps and the sound of the trumpet mixed with that of the clarion bring joy to many men," from Horace's *Odes* 1.1.23–24. [ED.]

[3] Samuel Butler (1613–80), English poet and author of *Hudibras* (1663), written in doggerel as a burlesque on the English Civil Wars; David Teniers (1610–90), Flemish painter known for his genre paintings — i.e., paintings of everyday life.

[4] Guido Reni (1575–1642), Italian painter of the Baroque period. This reviewer essentially draws the same distinction between Flemish and Italian art that Southey makes in his discussion of "The Idiot Boy" (353) to suggest that the low subject matter of *Lyrical Ballads* inevitably compromises the volume's dignity.

And, as imagination bodies forth
The forms of things unknown, the poet's pen
Turns them to shape, and gives to aery nothing
A local habitation and a name.

SHAKESPEARE[5]

Having said thus much on the *genus,* we now come more particularly to the *species.*

The author's first piece, the *Rime of the ancyent marinere,* in imitation of the *style* as well as of the spirit of the elder poets, is the strangest story of a cock and a bull that we saw on paper: yet, though it seems a rhapsody of unintelligible wildness and incoherence, (of which we do not perceive the drift, unless the joke lies in depriving the wedding guest of his share of the feast,) there are in it poetical touches of an exquisite kind.

The Dramatic Fragment, if it intends anything, seems meant to throw disgrace on the savage liberty preached by some modern *philosophes.*

The *Yew-Tree* seems a seat for *Jean Jacques;* while the reflections on the subject appear to flow from a more pious pen.

The Nightingale sings a strain of true and beautiful poetry; — Miltonic, yet original; reflective, and interesting, in an uncommon degree.[. . .][6]

The Female Vagrant is an agonizing tale of individual wretchedness; highly coloured, though, alas! but too probable. Yet, as it seems to stamp a general stigma on all military transactions, which were never more important in free countries than at the present period, it will perhaps be asked whether the hardships described never happen during revolution, or in a nation subdued? The sufferings of individuals during war are dreadful: but is it not better to try to prevent them from becoming general, or to render them transient by heroic and patriotic efforts, than to fly to them for ever?

Distress from poverty and want is admirably described, in the "*true story of Goody Blake, and Harry Gill:*" but are we to imagine that Harry was bewitched by Goody Blake? The hardest heart must be softened into pity for the poor old woman; — and yet, if all the poor are to help themselves, and supply their wants from the possessions of their neighbours, what imaginary wants and real anarchy would it not create? Goody Blake should have been relieved out of the *two millions* annually allowed by the state to the poor of this country, not by the plunder of an individual.

Jean Jacques: Rousseau.

[5] *A Midsummer Night's Dream* 5.1.12–17. [ED.]
[6] The review quotes "The Nightingale" in its entirety. [ED.]

Lines on the first mild day of March abound with beautiful sentiments from a polished mind.

Simon Lee, the old Huntsman, is the portrait, admirably painted, of every huntsman who, by toil, age, and infirmities, is rendered unable to guide and govern his canine family.

Anecdote for Fathers. Of this the dialogue is ingenious and natural: but the object of the child's choice, and the inferences, are not quite obvious.

We are seven—innocent and pretty infantine prattle.

On an *early Spring.* The first stanza of this little poem seems unworthy of the rest, which contain reflections truly pious and philosophical.

The Thorn. All our author's pictures, in colouring, are dark as those of Rembrandt or Spanioletto.

The last of the Flock is more gloomy than the rest. We are not told how the wretched hero of this piece became so poor. He had, indeed, ten children: but so have many cottagers; and ere the tenth child is born, the eldest began to work, and help, at least, to maintain themselves. No oppression is pointed out; nor are any means suggested for his relief. If the author be a wealthy man, he ought not to have suffered this poor peasant to part with *the last of the flock.* What but an Agrarian law can prevent poverty from visiting the door of the indolent, injudicious, extravagant, and, perhaps, vicious? and is it certain that rigid equality of property as well as of laws could remedy this evil?

The Dungeon. Here candour and tenderness for criminals seem pushed to excess. Have not jails been built on the humane Mr. Howard's plan, which have almost ruined some counties, and which look more like palaces than habitations for the perpetrators of crimes?[7] Yet, have fewer crimes been committed in consequence of the erection of those magnificent structures, at an expence which would have maintained many in innocence and comfort out of a jail, if they have been driven to theft by want?

The mad Mother; admirable painting! in Michael Angelo's bold and masterly manner.

The Idiot Boy leads the reader on from anxiety to distress, and from distress to terror, by incidents and alarms which, though of the most mean and ignoble kind, interest, frighten, and terrify, almost to torture, during the perusal of more than a hundred stanzas.

Lines written near Richmond—literally *"most musical, most melancholy!"*

Expostulation and Reply. The author tells us that "these lines, and those which follow, arose out of conversation with a friend who was somewhat

---

[7] John Howard (1726–1790), English philanthropist and prison reformer. [ED.]

unreasonably attached to books of moral philosophy." These two pieces will afford our readers an opportunity of judging of the author's poetical talents, in a more modern and less gloomy style than his Ballads.[...] [8]

The Old Man traveling, a Sketch, finely drawn: but the termination seems pointed against the war; from which, however, we are now no more able to separate ourselves, than Hercules was to free himself from the shirt of Nessus.[9] The old traveller's son might have died by disease.

Each ballad is a tale of woe. The style and versification are those of our antient ditties: but much polished, and more constantly excellent. In old songs, we have only a fine line or stanza now and then; here we meet with few that are feeble;—but it is *poesie larmoiante.* The author is more plaintive than Gray himself.[10]

The Complaint of a forsaken Indian Woman: another tale of woe! of the most afflicting and harrowing kind. The want of humanity here falls not on wicked Europeans, but on the innocent Indian savages, who enjoy unlimited freedom and liberty, unbridled by kings, magistrates, or laws.

The Convict. What a description! and what misplaced commiseration, on one condemned by the laws of his country, which he had confessedly violated! We do not comprehend the drift of lavishing that tenderness and compassion on a criminal, which should be reserved for virtue in unmerited misery and distress, suffering untimely death from accident, injustice, or disease.

Lines written near Tintern Abbey—The reflections of no common mind; poetical, beautiful, and philosophical: but somewhat tinctured with gloomy, narrow, and unsociable ideas of seclusion from the commerce of the world: as if men were born to live in woods and wilds, unconnected with each other! Is it not to education and the culture of the mind that we owe the raptures which the author so well describes, as arising from the view of beautiful scenery, and sublime objects of nature enjoyed in tranquillity, when contrasted with the artificial machinery and "busy hum of men" in a city? The savage sees none of the beauties which this author describes. The convenience of food and shelter, which vegetation affords him, is all his concern; he thinks not of its picturesque beauties, the course of rivers, the

---

poesie larmoiante: sniveling poetry.

[8] The review gives the complete text of "Expostulation and Reply" and "The Tables Turned." [ED.]

[9] Hercules was killed when he put on a robe coated with the blood of the Centaur Nessus. When he tried to remove the robe, it clung to him, tearing his flesh off. [ED.]

[10] Perhaps a reference to Gray's mournful "Sonnet on the Death of Mr. Richard West," which Wordsworth discusses in the 1802 Preface to *Lyrical Ballads* (397–98). [ED.]

height of mountains, etc. He has no *dizzy raptures* in youth; nor does he listen in maturer age "to the still sad music of humanity."

So much genius and originality are discovered in this publication, that we wish to see another from the same hand, written on more elevated subjects and in a more cheerful disposition.

FROM THE *BRITISH CRITIC*
Anonymous

The attempt made in this little volume is one that meets our cordial approbation; and it is an attempt by no means unsuccessful. The endeavour of the author is to recall our poetry, from the fantastical excess of refinement, to simplicity and nature. The account of this design, and its probable effects upon modern readers, is so very sensibly given in the Introduction, that we shall insert the passage at large.[. . .] [1]

We fully agree with the author, that the true notion of poetry must be sought among the poets, rather than the critics; and we will add that, unless a critic is a poet also, he will generally make but indifferent work in judging of the effusions of Genius. In the collection of poems subjoined to this introduction, we do not often find expressions that we esteem too familiar, or deficient in dignity; on the contrary, we think that in general the author has succeeded in attaining that judicious degree of simplicity, which accommodates itself with ease even to the sublime. It is not by pomp of words, but by energy of thought, that sublimity is most successfully achieved; and we infinitely prefer the simplicity, even of the most unadorned tale in this volume, to all the meretricious frippery of the *Darwinian*[2] taste.

The Poem of "the Ancyent Marinere," with which the collection opens, has many excellencies and many faults; the beginning and the end are striking and well-conducted; but the intermediate part is too long, and has, in some places, a kind of confusion of images, which loses all effect, from not being quite intelligible. The author, who is confidently said to be Mr. Coleridge, is not correctly versed in the old language, which he undertakes to employ. "Noises of a *swound*," p. 9, and "broad as a *weft*," p. 11, are both nonsensical; but the ancient style is so well imitated, while the antiquated words are so very few, that the latter might with advantage be entirely removed without any detriment to the effect of the Poem. The opening of the

---

British Critic (Oct. 1799).

[1] The review quotes the Advertisement. [ED.]
[2] A reference to the highly ornate poetry of Erasmus Darwin (1731–1802), such as *The Loves of the Plants* (1789). [ED.]

Poem is admirably calculated to arrest the reader's attention, by the well-imagined idea of the Wedding Guest, who is held to hear the tale, in spite of his efforts to escape. The beginning of the second canto, or fit, has much merit, if we except the very unwarrantable comparison of the Sun to that which no man can conceive: — "like God's own head," a simile which makes a reader shudder; not with poetic feeling, but with religious disapprobation. The following passage is eminently good.[. . .][3]

The conclusion, as we remarked before, is very good, particularly the idea that the Marinere has periodical fits of agony, which oblige him to relate his marvellous adventure.[. . .][4]

Whether the remaining poems of the volume are by Mr. Coleridge, we have not been informed; but they seem to proceed from the same mind; and in the Advertisement, the writer speaks of himself as of a single person accountable for the whole. It is therefore reasonable to conclude that this is the fact. They all have merit, and many among them a very high rank of merit, which our feelings respecting some parts of the supposed author's character do not authorize or incline us to deny. The Poem on the Nightingale, which is there styled a *conversational Poem,* is very good; but we do not perceive it to be more conversational than Cowper's Task, which is the best poem in that style that our language possesses. "The Female Vagrant" is a composition of exquisite beauty, nor is the combination of events, related in it, out of the compass of possibility; yet we perceive, with regret, the drift of the author in composing it; which is to show the worst side of civilized society, and thus to form a satire against it. But let fanciful men rail as they will at the evils which no care can always prevent, they can have no dream more wild than the supposition, that any human wisdom can possibly exclude all evils from a state which divine Providence has decreed, for reasons the most wise, to be a state of suffering and of trial. The sufferers may be changed, by infinite revolutions, but sufferers there will be, till Heaven shall interfere to change the nature of our tenure upon earth. From this beautiful Poem, partly on account of its apparent design, and partly because the loss of the connection would destroy much of its effect, we shall make no extract.

The story of "Goody Blake and Harry Gill" is founded, the Introduction tells us, "on a well-authenticated fact which happened in Warwickshire." Yet it is a miracle; and modern miracles can seldom be admitted, without some degree of credulity, or a very uncommon weight of evidence. One of the simplest stories in the book is that entitled "We are Seven"; yet he must be a very fastidious reader who will deny that it has great beauty and feeling.

---

[3] The review quotes lines 99–118. [ED.]
[4] The review quotes lines 619–23. [ED.]

The tale of "the Thorn" has many beauties; nor can we pass without notice "the Mad Mother," or the long and familiar tale of "the Idiot Boy," which, though it descends quite to common life, is animated by much interest, and told with singular felicity. One more Poem we shall particularly notice for its pathos, and shall indeed insert the whole. The imagery of it is in many instances new, and is introduced with admirable effect.[. . .] [5]

The purchasers of this little volume will find that, after all we have said, there are poems, and passages of poems, which we have been obliged to pass over, that well deserve attention and commendation; nor does there appear any offensive mixture of enmity to present institutions, except in one or two instances, which are so unobtrusive as hardly to deserve notice.

---

[5] "The Complaint of a Forsaken Indian Woman" appears in its entirety. [ED.]

POETIC RESPONSES

In his review of *Lyrical Ballads,* poet Robert Southey writes that Wordsworth and Coleridge's experiment "has failed," criticizing the poems that they had called "lyrical ballads" while praising the more conventional "other poems," particularly "Tintern Abbey." [1] Southey did not dislike ballads; in fact, he participated actively in the ballad revival, but his aesthetic standards for the ballad form were more narrative than those of Wordsworth, who stresses "feeling" over "situation." Southey finds the subjects "uninteresting" and, judging from his own ballads, wanted them to be more overtly moral and didactic.

His campaign against *Lyrical Ballads* continued, most obviously in his 1799 *Poems.* Here, Southey's goals in his series entitled "English Eclogues" seemingly echo Wordsworth's Advertisement to *Lyrical Ballads:* "How far poems requiring almost a colloquial plainness of language may accord with the public taste I am doubtful.[. . .] I have endeavoured to make them true to nature." But the specific poems that directly respond to poems from *Lyrical Ballads* show how Southey's practice differs from Wordsworth's. One of the "English Eclogues," "The Witch" (not included here), is an attempt to counter what Southey found objectionable in "Goody Blake and Harry Gill," that is, what he saw as Wordsworth's promotion of "the popular superstition of witchcraft." Rather than endow the poor old woman with supernatural powers, Southey demystifies the witch figure by having the compassionate curate of a rural village disabuse a farmer and his son of such a prejudice. The curate admonishes them:

And crooked with her years, without a child
Or friend in her old age, 'tis hard indeed
To have her very miseries made her crimes!
I met her but last week in that hard frost

---

[1] See Southey's review (352–54).

That made my young limbs ache, and when I ask'd
What brought her out in the snow, the poor old woman
Told me that she was forced to crawl abroad
And pick the hedges, just to keep herself
From perishing with cold, because no neighbour
Had pity on her age; and then she cried,
And said the children pelted her with snow-balls,
And wish'd that she were dead. (78–101)

With such a description—an inevitable comparison to Wordsworth's Goody Blake—Southey clearly intends also to make the poor woman a sympathetic figure and thereby to make his readers more aware of the conditions of real people in similar circumstances. Also noteworthy is Southey's formal distinction "eclogue," a classical form associated with pastoral depictions of idealized country life, which makes this commonplace tale all the more bitterly ironic.

The Southey selections that follow in this section develop comparisons to specific poems from *Lyrical Ballads*. "The Sailor, Who Had Served in the Slave Trade" is an elaborate reworking of Coleridge's "Ancyent Marinere," one of the poems that Southey found most troubling in the book. Similarly, in "The Mad Woman" (published the following year), he so explicitly responds to "The Thorn" that the infanticide in his ballad shares the same first name as Wordsworth's Martha Ray. All in all, Southey's poetic responses to *Lyrical Ballads* share a common distaste for what he perceived to be the evasion of social responsibility and the obfuscation of political indignation. As Stuart Curran puts it, Southey's responses to *Lyrical Ballads* show that he was pioneering "the new realism that [would] impel English poetry into the nineteenth century" and a keener sense of social conditioning and class conflict in poetry ("Mary Robinson" 24–26). One might even say that, to Southey, the *Lyrical Ballads* were not radical enough in their politics, however radical they may have been in their aesthetics.[2]

Another significant poetic response came from Mary Robinson, a noted poet whom both Coleridge and Southey knew personally. Some readers may be surprised that, as Wordsworth completed the poems for the new second volume, he briefly considered dropping the title *Lyrical Ballads* altogether because of a competing volume by the more established Robinson. Dorothy Wordsworth writes that "Mrs. Robinson has claimed the title and is about publishing a volume of *Lyrical Tales*" (*Early Years* 297). Significantly, Dorothy Wordsworth considers Robinson's title, *Lyrical Tales,* as

---

[2]For more on Southey's responses to *Lyrical Ballads,* see Christopher Smith's "Robert Southey and the Emergence of *Lyrical Ballads.*"

synonymous with *Lyrical Ballads*. Robinson was greatly esteemed by Coleridge, who exchanged poems with her (including an early version of "Kubla Khan" that she responded to in verse sixteen years before its first publication). Robinson experimented widely with meter and stanza patterns, and Coleridge recognized that she had a keen ear for the technicalities of versification (*Letters* 1.576). It is therefore not surprising that she was intrigued by the formal paradox implied in the title of Wordsworth and Coleridge's volume and used it as a guiding principle for her 1800 volume.[3] The poems in *Lyrical Tales* are not directly imitative of any of the *Lyrical Ballads*, although such poems as "The Haunted Beach" and "The Poor, Singing Dame" have strong intertextual connections to "The Rime of the Ancyent Marinere" and "Goody Blake and Harry Gill." Robinson's poems have less irony and ambiguity than Wordsworth's or Coleridge's, thus accounting for their relative obscurity in the twentieth century; but they are vivid and powerful and show an eagerness to engage the two male poets in their own arena that is both grateful and fiercely competitive. As Curran points out, Robinson's *Lyrical Tales* shares with *Lyrical Ballads* and Southey's *Poems* a concern for the poor, the disenfranchised, and the socially displaced; but she informs the poems with an outlook that has been shaped by her own frequently victimized position as a woman in society. She makes her point by showing all the more pathetically that "marginality [is] the normal condition of life" (Curran, "Mary Robinson" 30).

Despite Robinson's tribute and some encouraging reviews, Wordsworth—especially after the publication of the 1800 Preface to *Lyrical Ballads*—became increasingly the target of ridicule among those who either misunderstood or disapproved of his poetic program. One hilarious example of the derision Wordsworth endured is the 1801 burlesque "Barham-Downs, or Goody Grizzle and Her Ass," subtiteld "A Lyrical Ballad, in the Present Fashionable Stile." Since Southey's and Robinson's adaptations were hardly "fashionable," the subtitle is both an identification of Wordsworth as the target and an expression of anxiety that such drivel might yet become, to use Hazlitt's phrase, "the spirit of the age." The parody is also a good excuse for some scatological humor at Wordsworth's expense. A less playful poetic attack on Wordsworth and Coleridge is Richard Mant's *Simpliciad,* which takes issue with the two poets (and with Southey) for degrading simplicity into childlike prattle and for seeking to reform the established codes of literary taste. The misapprehension of Romanticism as a reaction against Neoclassicism, moreover, begins with Mant, who rather unfairly

---

[3] See the headnote to "The Ballad Revival" in Part Two.

calls Wordsworth and Coleridge the founders of a new "Anti-classical" school of poetry. But Mant's fury surely indicates how much the authors of *Lyrical Ballads* had raised the literary stakes.

THE SAILOR,
WHO HAD SERVED
IN THE SLAVE TRADE [1]

Robert Southey

In September, 1798, a Dissenting Minister of Bristol discovered a Sailor in the neighbourhood of that City, groaning and praying in a hovel. The circumstance that occasioned his agony of mind is detailed in the annexed Ballad, without the slightest addition or alteration. By presenting it as a Poem the story is made more public, and such stories ought to be made as public as possible.

He stopt,—it surely was a groan
    That from the hovel came!
He stopt and listened anxiously
    Again it sounds the same.

5 It surely from the hovel comes!
    And now he hastens there,
And thence he hears the name of Christ
    Amidst a broken prayer.

He entered in the hovel now,
10 A sailor there he sees,
His hands were lifted up to Heaven
    And he was on his knees.

Nor did the Sailor so intent
    His entering footsteps heed,
15 But now the Lord's prayer said, and now
    His half-forgotten creed.

Poems. Vol. 2. Bristol: Biggs; London: Longman, 1799.

[1] This poem appeared in a section entitled "Ballads." Although England's participation in the slave trade did not end until 1807, it was very much a subject of debate throughout the 1790s. Here, Southey adapts the verse form of Coleridge's "Rime of the Ancyent Marinere"—as well as its focus on the psychology of guilt—to address this issue in a very direct and unambiguous manner. [ED.]

And often on his Saviour call'd
 With many a bitter groan,
In such heart-anguish as could spring
20 From deepest guilt alone.

He ask'd the miserable man
 Why he was kneeling there,
And what the crime had been that caus'd
 The anguish of his prayer.

25 Oh I have done a wicked thing!²
 It haunts me night and day,
And I have sought this lonely place
 Here undisturb'd to pray.

I have no place to pray on board
30 So I came here alone,
That I might freely kneel and pray,
 And call on Christ and groan.

If to the main-mast head I go,
 The wicked one is there,
35 From place to place, from rope to rope,
 He follows every where.

I shut my eyes,—it matters not—
 Still still the same I see,—
And when I lie me down at night
40 'Tis always day with me.

He follows follows every where,
 And every place is Hell!
O God—and I must go with him
 In endless fire to dwell.

45 He follows follows every where,
 He's still above—below,
Oh tell me where to fly from him!
 Oh tell me where to go!

But tell me, quoth the Stranger then,
50 What this thy crime hath been,

---

²Compare "The Rime of the Ancyent Marinere," line 89: "And I had done an hellish thing." [ED.]

So haply I may comfort give
    To one that grieves for sin.

O I have done a cursed deed
    The wretched man replies,
55 And night and day and every where
    'Tis still before my eyes.

I sail'd on board a Guinea-man
    And to the slave-coast went;
Would that the sea had swallowed me
60   When I was innocent!

And we took in our cargo there,
    Three hundred negroe slaves,
And we sail'd homeward merrily
    Over the ocean waves.

65 But some were sulky of the slaves
    And would not touch their meat,
So therefore we were forced by threats
    And blows to make them eat.

One woman sulkier than the rest
70   Would still refuse her food, —
O Jesus God! I hear her cries —
    I see her in her blood!

The Captain made me tie her up
    And flog while he stood by,
75 And then he curs'd me if I staid
    My hand to hear her cry.

She groan'd, she shriek'd — I could not spare
    For the Captain he stood by —
Dear God! that I might rest one night
80   From that poor woman's cry!

She twisted from the blows — her blood
    Her mangled flesh I see —
And still the Captain would not spare —
    Oh he was worse than me!

Guinea-man: a ship used for the slave trade.

85 She could not be more glad than I
    When she was taken down,
  A blessed minute—'twas the last
    That I have ever known!

  I did not close my eyes that night,
90   Thinking what I had done;
  I heard her groans and they grew faint
    About the rising sun.

  She groan'd and groan'd, but her groans grew
    Fainter at morning tide,
95 Fainter and fainter still they came
    Till at the noon she died.

  They flung her overboard;—poor wretch
    She rested from her pain,—
  But when—o Christ! o blessed God!
100   Shall I have rest again!

  I saw the sea close over her,
    Yet she was still in sight;
  I see her twisting every where;
    I see her day and night.

105 Go where I will, do what I can
    The wicked one I see—
  Dear Christ have mercy on my soul,
    O God deliver me!

  Tomorrow I set sail again
110   Not to the Negroe shore—
  Wretch that I am I will at least
    Commit that sin no more.

  O give me comfort if you can—
    Oh tell me where to fly—
115 And bid me hope, if there be hope,
    For one so lost as I.

  Poor wretch, the stranger he replied,
    Put thou thy trust in heaven,
  And call on him for whose dear sake
120   All sins shall be forgiven.

This night at least is thine, go thou
    And seek the house of prayer,
There shalt thou hear the word of God
    And he will help thee there!

THE MAD WOMAN

Robert Southey

*The circumstance on which the following Ballad is founded happened
not many years ago in Bristol.*

The Traveller's hands were white with cold,
    The Traveller's lips were blue,
Oh! glad was he when the village Church
    So near was seen in view!

5   He hasten'd to the village Inn,
    That stood the Church-door nigh —
There sat a Woman on a grave,
    And he could not pass her by.

Her feet were bare, and on her breast
10   Thro' rags did the winter blow,
She sat with her face towards the wind,
    And the grave was cover'd with snow.

Is there never a christian in the place,
    To her the Traveller cried,
15   Who will let thee, this cold winter time,
    Sit by his fire side?

I have fire in my head, she answered him,
    I have fire in my heart also;
And there will be no winter time
20   In the place where I must go!

A curse upon thee, man,
    For mocking me! she said;
And he saw the woman's eyes, like one
    In a fever-fit, were red.

25   And when he to the inn door came,
    And the host his greeting gave,

He ask'd who that mad woman was
    Who sat upon the grave.

God in his mercy, quoth the host,
30   Forgive her for her sin;
For heavy is her crime, and strange
    Her punishment hath been.

She was so pale and meagre-ey'd,
    As scarcely to be known,
35 When to her mother she return'd
    From service in the town.

She seldom spake, she never smil'd,
    What ail'd her no one knew,
But every day more meagre-pale,
40   And sullen sad she grew.

It was upon last Christmas eve,
    As we sat around the hearth,
And every soul but Martha's
    Was full of Christmas mirth.

45 She sat, and look'd upon the fire,
    That then so fiercely shone,
She look'd into it earnestly,
    And we heard a stifled groan.

And she shook like a dying wretch,
50   In a convulsive fit;
And up she rose, and in the snow,
    Went out on a grave to sit.

We follow'd her, and to the room
    Besought her to return;
55 She groan'd and said, that in the fire,
    She saw her Baby burn.

And in her dreadful madness then
    To light her murder came,
How secretly from every eye
60   Nine months she hid her shame;

And how she slew the wretched babe
    Just as he sprung to light,
And in the midnight fire consum'd
    His little body quite.

65 Would I could feel the winter wind,
    Would I could feel the snow!
I have fire in my head, poor Martha cried,
    I have fire in my heart also.

So there from morn till night she sits —
70   Now God forgive her sin!
For heavy is her crime, and strange
    Her punishment hath been.

THE POOR, SINGING DAME

Mary Robinson [1]

Beneath an old wall, that went round an old Castle,
    For many a year, with brown ivy o'erspread;
A neat little Hovel, its lowly roof raising,
    Defied the wild winds that howl'd over its shed:
5 The turrets, that frown'd on the poor simple dwelling,
    Were rock'd to and fro, when the Tempest would roar,
And the river, that down the rich valley was swelling,
    Flow'd swiftly beside the green step of its door.

The Summer Sun, gilded the rushy-roof slanting,
10   The bright dews bespangled its ivy-bound hedge
And above, on the ramparts, the sweet Birds were chanting,
    And wild buds thick dappled the clear river's edge.
When the Castle's rich chambers were haunted, and dreary,
    The poor little Hovel was still, and secure;
15 And no robber e'er enter'd, or goblin or fairy,
    For the splendours of pride had no charms to allure.

The Lord of the Castle, a proud, surly ruler,
    Oft heard the low dwelling with sweet music ring:
For the old Dame that liv'd in the little Hut chearly,
20   Would sit at her wheel, and would merrily sing: [2]

From *Lyrical Tales*. London: Longman; Bristol: Biggs, 1800.

[1] Robinson (1758–1800) was a successful actress, poet, and novelist; her novel *Walsingham* (1797) was a best seller; in 1800, she succeeded Robert Southey as poetry editor for the *Morning Post*. Coleridge thought highly of her poetry, calling her "a woman of undoubted genius" (*Letters* 1.562). [ED.]

[2] Compare "Goody Blake and Harry Gill," lines 39–40: "Then at her door the *canty* dame / Would sit, as any linnet gay." [ED.]

When with revels the Castle's great Hall was resounding,
   The Old Dame was sleeping, not dreaming of fear;
And when over the mountains the Huntsmen were bounding
   She would open her wicket, their clamours to hear.

25 To the merry-ton'd horn, she would dance on the threshold,
   And louder, and louder, repeat her old Song:
And when Winter its mantle of Frost was displaying
   She caroll'd, undaunted, the bare woods among:
She would gather dry Fern, ever happy and singing,
30   With her cake of brown bread, and her jug of brown beer,
And would smile when she heard the great Castle-bell ringing,
   Inviting the Proud—to their prodigal chear.

Thus she liv'd, ever patient and ever contented,
   Till Envy the Lord of the Castle possess'd,
35 For he hated that Poverty should be so chearful,
   While care could the fav'rites of Fortune molest;
He sent his bold yeoman with threats to prevent her,
   And still would she carol her sweet roundelay;
At last, an old Steward, relentless he sent her—
40   Who bore her, all trembling, to Prison away!

Three weeks did she languish, then died, broken-hearted,
   Poor Dame! how the death-bell did mournfully sound!
And along the green path six young Bachelors bore her,
   And laid her, for ever, beneath the cold ground!
45 And the primroses pale, 'mid the long grass were growing,
   The bright dews of twilight bespangled her grave
And morn heard the breezes of summer soft blowing
   To bid the fresh flow'rets in sympathy wave.

The Lord of the Castle, from that fatal moment
50   When poor Singing Mary was laid in her grave,
Each night was surrounded by Screech-owls appalling,
   Which o'er the black turrets their pinions would wave!
On the ramparts that frown'd on the river, swift flowing,
   They hover'd, still hooting a terrible song,
55 When his windows would rattle, the Winter blast blowing,
   They would shriek like a ghost, the dark alleys among!

Whenever he wander'd they followed him crying,
   At dawnlight, at Eve, still they haunted his way!
When the Moon shone across the wide common, they hooted,
60   Nor quitted his path, till the blazing of day.

His bones began wasting, his flesh was decaying,[3]
 And he hung his proud head, and he perish'd with shame;
And the tomb of rich marble, no soft tear displaying,
 O'ershadows the grave, of the Poor Singing Dame!

THE HAUNTED BEACH

Mary Robinson

Upon a lonely desart Beach
 Where the white foam was scatter'd,
A little shed uprear'd its head
 Though lofty Barks were shatter'd.
5 The Sea-weeds gath'ring near the door,
 A somber path display'd;
And, all around, the deaf'ning roar,
Re-echo'd on the chalky shore,
 By the green billows made.

10 Above, a jutting cliff was seen
 Where Sea Birds hover'd, craving;
And all around, the craggs were bound
 With weeds—for ever waving.
And here and there, a cavern wide
15 Its shad'wy jaws display'd;
And near the sands, at ebb of tide,
A shiver'd mast was seen to ride
 Where the green billows stray'd.

And often, while the moaning wind
20 Stole o'er the Summer Ocean,
The moonlight scene was all serene,
 The waters scarce in motion:
Then, while the smoothly slanting sand
 The tall cliff wrapp'd in shade,
25 The Fisherman beheld a band
Of Spectres, gliding hand in hand—
 Where the green billows play'd.

From *Lyrical Tales.* London: Longman; Bristol: Biggs, 1800.

Barks: boats.

[3] Compare "Goody Blake and Harry Gill," line 117: "And Harry's flesh it fell away."

And pale their faces were, as snow,
   And sullenly they wander'd:
30 And to the skies with hollow eyes
   They look'd as though they ponder'd.
And sometimes, from their hammock shroud,
   They dismal howlings made,
And while the blast blew strong and loud
35 The clear moon mark'd the ghastly croud,
   Where the green billows play'd!

And then, above the haunted hut
   The Curlews screaming hover'd;
And the low door with furious roar
40   The frothy breakers cover'd.
For, in the Fisherman's lone shed
   A murder'd Man was laid,
With ten wide gashes in his head
And deep was made his sandy bed
45   Where the green billows play'd.

A Shipwreck'd Mariner was he,
   Doom'd from his home to sever;
Who swore to be thro' wind and sea
   Firm and undaunted ever!
50 And when the wave resistless roll'd,
   About his arm he made
A packet rich of Spanish gold,
And, like a British sailor, bold,
   Plung'd, where the billows play'd!

55 The Spectre band, his messmates brave
   Sunk in the yawning ocean,
While to the mast he lash'd him fast
   And brav'd the storm's commotion.
The winter moon, upon the sand
60   A silv'ry carpet made,
And mark'd the Sailor reach the land,
And mark'd his murd'rer wash his hand
   Where the green billows play'd.

Curlews: wading birds.
packet: a small boat that carries passengers and goods.

And since that hour the Fisherman
65 Has toil'd and toil'd in vain!
For all the night, the moony light
    Gleams on the spectr'd main!
And when the skies are veil'd in gloom,
    The Murd'rer's liquid way
70 Bounds o'er the deeply yawning tomb,
And flashing fires the sands illume,
    Where the green billows play!

Full thirty years his task has been,
    Day after day more weary;
75 For Heav'n design'd, his guilty mind
    Should dwell on prospects dreary.
Bound by a strong and mystic chain,
    He has not pow'r to stray;
But, destin'd mis'ry to sustain,
80 He wastes, in Solitude and Pain—
    A loathsome life away.

BARHAM-DOWNS,

OR GOODY GRIZZLE AND HER ASS

A Lyrical Ballad
in the Present Fashionable Stile

Anonymous[1]

One winter, at the close of day,
    Her eggs and butter sold,
Dame Grizzle took her homeward way,
    Amidst the rain and cold.

5 O'er Barham-Downs, of martial fame,[2]
    Her homeward way did pass:
Good lack! so poor was she, and lame,
    She rode upon an ass!

European Magazine 40 (Sept. 1801).

[1] This anonymous poem was signed facetiously by "Rusticus." [ED.]
[2] During the twelfth and thirteenth centuries, Barham Down was used twice as a military camp to guard against invasions from France. [ED.]

The patient beast along did creep,
10   A basket on each side;
O'er which the dame, her seat to keep,
    Sat with her legs astride.

The load was great, the load was great,
    For Grizzle she was big;
15 One basket loaded was with meat,
    And t'other with a pig.

The load was great, the road was rough,
    And much the Ass did strain;
And Grizzle, with a broom-stick tough,
20   Increased the poor thing's pain.

It came to pass, it came to pass,
    Oh tale of wond'rous dole!
That Goody Grizzle and her Ass
    Fell plump into a hole.

25 All in a hole, all in a hole,[3]
    Down, down they tumbled plump,
And Grizzle's nose, alas, poor soul!
    Lay close to Dapple's rump.

The Ass he kick'd, the Ass he bray'd,
30   The woman loud did squall;
For much was Gammer Griz afraid,
    And painful was the fall.

Oh woe on woe! for as she lay
    Upon the Ass's back,
35 Struggling in vain to get away,
    She heard a dreadful crack!

And first she thought her poor, poor Ass,
    Was yielding up his breath;
"And oh! (she cried) alas! alas!
40   *His* death will be *my* death."

And then she thought it was a ghost,
    Now prone, on each occasion,

Gammer: old woman (contracted form of *grandmother*).

[3] Compare "The Rime of the Ancyent Mariner," line 224: "Alone, alone, all all alone."

To come from Pluto's realms per post,[4]
  And charm the British nation.

45 She thought it was a modern sprite,
    And long'd to see it pass:
"Come, Ghost! (she cried, with all her might)
  "Come! help me and my Ass."

But ah! it was nor ghost nor groan!
50   It was a rumbling roar;
A kind of broken-winded tone
    She ne'er had heard before.

It was—it was—oh, sad mishap!
    The Ass in "doleful dumps,"
55 With whoop whoop whoop, and clap clap clap
    Was thund'ring out his trumps!

Not wind alone, ah lack-a-day,
    Burst forth at each explosion!
Six quarts of half-digested hay
60   Composed the od'rous lotion!

And o'er poor Grizzle's face it flew,
    And o'er poor Grizzle's neck!
Half-choaked, she turned herself askew,
    And lay upon her back!

65 Ah poor! ah, poor afflicted ass!
    He strained—to change his station;
But every strain he made, alas!
    Increased his crepitation!

In what a plight was Grizzle's mind!
70   The Ass her sides did kick,
And his eruptions from behind,
    Oh, made her *vastly* sick!

Her patience gone, the poor, poor dame,
    Tho' much she loved the creature,
75 Enraged by fear, and pain, and shame,
    Oft curst his ventilator.

---

crepitation: crackling.

[4]Pluto was the classical god of the underworld, also known as Hades; the joke is a play on the "lower regions," or the lower part of the ass, from which the sound came.

She opened her eyes to look around,
    And look around did she;
She oped her eyes, and looked around,
80   But nothing could she see!

It was so dark, it was so dark,
    That, even in the sky,
Of light, oh! not a single spark
    Could Gammer Grizzle spy!

85 The Ass he bray'd with horrid sound;
    Dame Grizzle loud did howl;
The rain it rattled on the ground;
    The thunder it did growl;

When lo! a Heaven-directed swain,
90   His mastiff dog before,
Trudging from Canterburia's plain
    To Dover's sea-laved shore,

Passed near the spot where Grizzle lay,
    And eke her ass so strong:
95 A lantern shed its friendly ray
    To guide his steps along.

He saw the hole, he saw the ass,
    He heard the woman bawl;
Not yet unfeeling did he pass,
100   But saved her — Ass and all!

He led her to a neighbouring inn,
    Her drooping soul to cheer,
Where Grizzle she got drunk with gin,
    And he got drunk with beer.

105 The Jack-Ass too, dear, suffering beast!
    Was led into a stall,
Where he enjoyed of hay a feast,
    And soon forgot his fall.

And still the luckless hole is seen,
110   Where Griz and Dapple fell;
And still the lotion marks the green,
    And still retains its smell;

---

eke: also.

And still is heard, in winter hoar,
    When night has banish'd day,
115 Poor Dapple's fundamental roar,
    And eke his fearful bray.

And still does Pity wander there,
    Her leisure hours to pass,
And still relate the wild despair
120 Of Grizzle and her Ass.

For tho' Dame Grizzle did not die,
    Nor yet her Ass so strong,
Their tale deserves a tender sigh,
    And eke a tender song.

FROM *THE SIMPLICIAD*
Richard Mant[1]

Should Wyatt[2] spurn whate'er of fair and grand,[3]
Or Grecian grace or Gothic spirit plann'd,
His pow'rs on pasteboard trifles to employ,
The nick-nack semblance of a baby-toy:
5 Or Flaxman[4] bid the sculptur'd marble wear
A vacant simper and a clownish stare;

The Simpliciad; A Satirico-Didactic Poem. Containing Hints for the Scholars of the New School Suggested by Horace's Art of Poetry, and Improved by a Contemplation of the Works of the First Masters. London: Stockdale, 1808.

fundamental: pertaining to the fundament, i.e., the anus.

[1] In the prose introduction to *The Simpliciad,* the Reverend Richard Mant (1776–1848) sarcastically credits Wordsworth, Southey, and Coleridge with founding the "Anticlassical School" by which he means a type of poetry that blatantly disregards the established rules concerning poetic "subject, ideas, diction, and metre." Although claiming that he will create an "Art of Poetry" for this new school, Mant concludes by lamenting the "degradation of [the poets'] genius" and deprecating "the propagation of [their] perverted taste." [ED.]

[2] James Wyatt (1746–1813), English architect best known for designing the Neoclassical London Parthenon and the Gothic Fonthill Abbey. [ED.]

[3]   Humano capiti cervicem pictor equimam
        Jungere sit velit, &c.

[Mant's note.] Here Mant quotes the opening lines of Horace's *Ars Poetica:* "If a painter should choose to join a horse's neck with a human head." [ED.]

[4] John Flaxman (1755–1826), English Neoclassical sculptor. [ED.]

Who but would laugh the artist's skill to scorn?
Who but his prostituted art would mourn?
And will you then the smile, the sigh refuse,
10 Daughter of heav'n to see the high-soul'd Muse
Condemn'd in leading strings to pipe, and cry,
And lisp the accents of the nursery;
Or clad in gipsy-rags, with rustic air
To whine with beggars, and with felons swear?

. . . .

Thus subject, image, language, metre cull,
290 Spite of resisting genius, you'll be dull:
But to th' abyss of bathos would you creep,
Unfailing source of ridicule or sleep,
For themes of sorrow marshal all your art,
And plant your whole artillery at the heart.
295   Now the gruff farmer's dozing conscience wake,[5]
With tale of Harry Gill and Goody Blake.
Poor Goody Blake, and cruel Harry Gill!
She stole his hedges, and he used her ill,
And now his teeth they chatter, chatter, still.
300 Now rouse maternal fears for Betty Foy,[6]
Her lamblike pony, and her idiot boy;
Who went to fetch the Doctor, but he staid
Beside the water, while the pony fed,
Took the pale moon-beam for the sun, nor knew
305 The cock's shrill clarion from the owl's to-whoo!
Let Pity now the one-eyed huntsman[7] wail,
Whose legs are wither'd, and whose ancles swell,
Plumb-coated, cherry-cheek'd Old Simon Lee!

. . . .

---

bathos: ridiculously unsuccessful attempt at pathos or at gravitas.

[5] Mant's note here quotes the opening four lines of "Goody Blake and Harry Gill." [ED.]
[6] "Her history, whether true or not does not appear, occupies thirty pages of the same volume. Johnny's answer to his mother's question where he had been all night, what he had heard, and what he had seen, is contained in the following lines, which may serve as a sample for their four hundred and fifty brethren." [Mant's note.] Mant goes on to quote the final stanza of "The Idiot Boy." [ED.]
[7] Mant's note here quotes lines 9–16, 33–36, and 67–68 of "Simon Lee." [ED.]

REACTIONS OF WORDSWORTH
AND COLERIDGE

Having thus presented the sometimes scathing responses to *Lyrical Ballads* by their contemporaries, we felt it only fair to let the volume's two authors defend themselves. The later reactions of Wordsworth and Coleridge no doubt were influenced by Wordsworth's taking charge of the book and Coleridge's diminished influence on it. The 1800 *Lyrical Ballads* was very much Wordsworth's venture: his additions of his own poetry more than doubled the size of the collection, now expanded to two volumes.

It is fair to say that Wordsworth prepared this second edition with his own reputation in mind. Wordsworth went so far as to write notes that answer some of Robert Southey's criticisms, which his friend had so publicly articulated in the *Critical Review*. He apologizes for the eccentricities of "The Ancyent Marinere," attributing it to his "friend," and asserts the validity of the perspective of "The Thorn," attempting to answer the unanswerable reminder of Southey that "he who personates tiresome loquacity becomes tiresome himself." In response to the general bewilderment over Coleridge's major contribution, Wordsworth further demoted "The Ancyent Marinere" by replacing it as the first poem with "Tintern Abbey" and moving it to the end of the first volume, effectively burying it in the middle of the book.

We have not included Coleridge's revision for the 1800 edition, "The Ancient Mariner: A Poet's Reverie," in which he modernized much of the language, offering instead the more thoroughly retailored "Rime of the Ancient Mariner" from Coleridge's 1817 volume, *Sibylline Leaves*. Consider, however, how the subtitle "A Poet's Reverie" shifts from the emphasis away from the Mariner himself to the psychology of the poet. This important change was in keeping with Coleridge's interest in the unconscious mind and dreams, as exemplified by other poems he wrote at the end of the eighteenth century, such as "Christabel" and "Kubla Khan."

Wordsworth's new poems — most of which were written during his dismal year in Goslar, Germany — have much in common with their 1798 predecessors, but they reveal little of the giddiness of "The Idiot Boy" and far less of the wild experimenation with narrative technique that he employed in "The Thorn" and "Simon Lee." Even when they deal with the poor, the politics of these new poems seem safer and less overtly liberal. They may elicit sympathy for the disadvantaged and comment on specific social policy, but they show none of the outrage of "The Female Vagrant" or "The Convict," and — as the vast of amount of commentary on "The Old Cumberland Beggar" demonstrates — their exact political stance remains rather elusive.[1] Since the 1798 *Lyrical Ballads* is the main focus of this edition, we feel that the new poems in the second volume are better suited for a book devoted to Wordsworth's poetry because they reveal much more about his development as a poet than they do about the original collaboration and its context.

Our major inclusion from the later editions of *Lyrical Ballads* is Wordsworth's famous Preface with its appendix on poetic diction, texts that we feel read very differently when they appear as they do here alongside the contemporary reviews and poetic responses to the first edition of *Lyrical Ballads.* Even though the Preface was first published in 1800 and then expanded for the 1802 edition, readers often forget that it was not designed as a blueprint for the 1798 edition. Rather it was an apologia written after the fact in which Wordsworth attempts to clear up what he believed were common misconceptions about his intentions and about the nature of the poems he had written. Much like the poems from the 1800 edition, the Preface has a greater sense of gravitas and a loftier sense of purpose in its poetic program than does the 1798 Advertisement. Whereas the Advertisement focuses on the *modus operandi* of that specific volume of poems, the Preface is much more universal in its claims: "In spite of difference of soil and climate, of language and manners, of laws and customs, in spite of things silently gone out of mind and things violently destroyed, the Poet binds together by passion and knowledge the vast empire of human society, as it is spread *over the whole earth,* and *over all time*" (emphasis added). Consequently, the Preface's poetic philosophy is in many ways more representative of the poetry Wordsworth was writing in 1800 and 1802 than it is of what he was attempting in the original edition.

As Coleridge's account of *Lyrical Ballads* in his 1816 *Biographia Literaria* reveals, this process of reevaluation accelerated as the years passed. Here — perhaps in an effort to highlight his own contributions to the project — he

---

[1] "The Old Cumberland Beggar" appears in "Rustic and Humanitarian Poetry" in Part Two (314–19).

provides his famous account of how the volume was designed to explore "the two cardinal points of poetry, the power of exciting the sympathy of the reader by a faithful adherence to the truth of nature, and the power of giving the interest of novelty by the modifying colours of imagination." And he uses this opportunity to distance himself from many of the major principles in Wordsworth's Preface. Coleridge had once bragged to Southey that the Preface was "half the child of [his] own brain" (*Letters* 2.830). Now, however, he says flatly that he never agreed with many parts of the Preface, objecting to them "as erroneous in principle, and as contradictory (in appearance at least) both to other parts of the same preface, and to the author's own practice in the greater number of the poems themselves."

But perhaps the best indication of how these two poets' attitudes toward the *Lyrical Ballads* project changed over the course of their careers is their own revisions to the poems from the 1798 edition. The 1832 version of "Simon Lee," for instance, transforms what was once a wildly disorienting poem into something not all that different from a typical humanitarian poem. No longer does it jump frantically back and forth between past and present, but now recounts Simon's tale in a simple, easy to follow, and largely sentimental fashion. Moreover, the phrase that Wordsworth adds as a transition between these two sections — "But, oh the heavy change!" — signals a dramatic shift in tone and strategy. As nearly all nineteenth-century readers would have recognized, Wordsworth here alludes to Milton's "Lycidas," thereby accomplishing two goals at once. On the one hand, the reference confers dignity upon his subject by associating this ballad with one of the oldest and most respected of all poetic genres, the pastoral elegy. On the other hand, it is equally honorific to the poet himself, linking him with the great tradition of Western verse. Just as Virgil, Spenser, and Milton all wrote pastoral poetry in their youth, Wordsworth seemingly has written "Simon Lee" to prepare himself for his later epic verse. Consequently, he pares away most of the jollity and irreverence of the earlier version, leaving only those elements that will reinforce the high seriousness of his later poetic program. Wordsworth was a very different poet at age sixty-two than he was at age twenty-eight; the revision of "Simon Lee" certainly reflects this change.

An even more extreme example is Coleridge's 1817 version of "The Rime of the Ancient Mariner," which not only eliminates most of the archaic spellings that identify the 1798 version as a Gothic ballad but also adds marginal glosses that seem to lend credence to the very supernatural events that were so ambiguous in the original text. As with "Simon Lee," the effect is to make the poem far more conventional and orthodox — a rather pious Christian allegory instead of an uncompromising analysis of a guilt-ridden imagination. Coleridge himself recognized the heavy-handedness of the poem's message, which was only exacerbated by the notes: when the poet

Anna Letitia Barbauld complained that the poem was beautiful but lacked a moral, Coleridge replied that "the only fault in the poem is that there is *too much!* In a work of such pure imagination I ought not to have stopped to give reasons for things, or inculcate humanity to beasts" (*Table Talk* 273). Even though this remark applies equally well to both the 1798 and 1817 versions of "The Ancient Mariner," Coleridge implicitly acknowledges the superiority of the less-didactic text and suggests that, perhaps, the glosses are a parody of himself. Readers might therefore consider whether the notes lead them to an interpretation of the poem that they would not otherwise have had. We have provided both versions so that readers may decide for themselves which they prefer.

NOTE TO "THE THORN"
William Wordsworth[1]

This Poem ought to have been preceded by an introductory Poem, which I have been prevented from writing by never having felt myself in a mood when it was probable that I should write it well. — The character which I have here introduced speaking is sufficiently common. The Reader will perhaps

---

Lyrical Ballads, with Other Poems. Vol. 1. 2nd ed. London: Longman, 1800.

[1] This note appears to have been prompted by the criticism of this poem in reviews such as Robert Southey's in the *Critical Review*. But it apparently only provoked Francis Jeffrey, who in his review of George Crabbe's *Poems* (*Edinburgh Review* [April 1808]) attacks the explanatory note as much as he does the poem itself:

> A pathetic tale of guilt or superstition may be told, we are apt to fancy, by the poet himself, in his general character of poet, with full as much effect as by any other person. An old nurse, at any rate, or a monk or parish clerk, is always at hand to give grace to such a narration. None of these, however, would satisfy Mr. Wordsworth. He has written a long poem of this sort, in which he thinks it indispensably necessary to apprise the reader, that he has endeavoured to represent the language and sentiments of a particular character— of which character, he adds, 'the reader will have a general notion, if he has ever known a man, *a captain of a small trading vessel,* for example, who being *past the middle age of life,* has retired upon an *annuity, or small independent income,* to some *village* or country town, of which he was *not a native,* or in which he had not been accustomed to live!'
>
> Now, we must be permitted to doubt whether, among all the readers of Mr. Wordsworth (few or many), there is a single individual who has had the happiness of knowing a person of this very peculiar description; or who is capable of forming any sort of conjecture of the particular disposition and turn of thinking which such a combination of attributes would be apt to produce. To us, we will confess, the *annonce* appears as ludicrous and absurd as it would be in the author of an ode or epic to say, "Of this piece the reader will necessarily form a very erroneous judgement unless he is apprised that it was written by a pale man in a green coat—sitting cross-legged on an oaken stool—with a scratch on his nose, and a spelling dictionary on the table." [ED.]

have a general notion of it, if he has ever known a man, a Captain of a small trading vessel for example, who being past the middle age of life, had retired upon an annuity or small independent income to some village or country town of which he was not a native, or in which he had not been accustomed to live. Such men having little to do become credulous and talkative from indolence; and from the same cause, and other predisposing causes by which it is probable that such men may have been affected, they are prone to superstition. On which account it appeared to me proper to select a character like this to exhibit some of the general laws by which superstition acts upon the mind. Superstitious men are almost always men of slow faculties and deep feelings; their minds are not loose but adhesive; they have a reasonable share of imagination, by which word I mean the faculty which produces impressive effects out of simple elements; but they are utterly destitute of fancy, the power by which pleasure and surprize are excited by sudden varieties of situation and by accumulated imagery.[2]

It was my wish in this poem to shew the manner in which such men cleave to the same ideas; and to follow the turns of passion, always different, yet not palpably different, by which their conversation is swayed. I had two objects to attain: first, to represent a picture which should not be unimpressive yet consistent with the character that should describe it, secondly, while I adhered to the style in which such persons describe, to take care that words, which in their minds are impregnated with passion, should likewise convey passion to Readers who are not accustomed to sympathize with men feeling in that manner or using such language. It seemed to me that this might be done by calling in the assistance of Lyrical and rapid Metre. It was necessary that the Poem, to be natural, should in reality move slowly; yet I hoped, that, by the aid of the metre, to those who should at all enter into the spirit of the Poem, it would appear to move quickly. The Reader will have the kindness to excuse this note as I am sensible that an introductory Poem is necessary to give this Poem its full effect.

Upon this occasion, I will request permission to add a few words closely connected with The Thorn and many other Poems in these Volumes. There is a numerous class of readers who imagine that the same words cannot be repeated without tautology: this is a great error: virtual tautology is much oftener produced by using different words when the meaning is exactly the same. Words, a Poet's words more particularly, ought to be weighed in the balance of feeling and not measured by the space which they occupy upon

---

tautology: needless repetition of an idea.

[2]Compare these definitions of the imagination and fancy with Coleridge's (421).

paper. For the Reader cannot be too often reminded that Poetry is passion: it is the history or science of feelings: now every man must know that an attempt is rarely made to communicate impassioned feelings without something of an accompanying consciousness of the inadequateness of our own powers, or the deficiencies of language. During such efforts there will be a craving in the mind, and as long as it is unsatisfied the Speaker will cling to the same words, or words of the same character. There are also various other reasons why repetition and apparent tautology are frequently beauties of the highest kind. Among the chief of these reasons is the interest which the mind attaches to words, not only as symbols of the passion, but as *things,* active and efficient, which are of themselves part of the passion. And further, from a spirit of fondness, exultation, and gratitude, the mind luxuriates in the repetition of words which appear successfully to communicate its feelings. The truth of these remarks might be shewn by innumerable passage from the Bible and from the impassioned poetry of every nation.

Awake, awake Deborah: awake, awake, utter a song:
  Arise Barak, and lead thy captivity captive, thou Son of Abinoam.

At her feet he bowed, he fell, he lay down:
  at her feet he bowed, he fell;
  where he bowed there he fell down dead.

Why is his Chariot so long in coming?
Why tarry the Wheels of his Chariot?

              —Judges, Chap. 5th. Verses 19th, 27th, and part of 28th.
—See also the whole of that tumultuous and wonderful Poem.

NOTE TO "THE ANCIENT MARINER"
William Wordsworth

I cannot refuse myself the gratification of informing such Readers as may have been pleased with this Poem, or with any part of it, that they owe their pleasure in some sort to me; as the Author was himself very desirous that it should be suppressed. This wish had arisen from a consciousness of the defects of the Poem, and from a knowledge that many persons had been much displeased with it. The Poem of my Friend has indeed great defects; first, that the principal person has no distinct character, either in his profession of Mariner, or as a human being who having been long under the controul

----

From *Lyrical Ballads, with Other Poems.* Vol. 1. 2nd ed. London: Longman, 1800.

of supernatural impressions might be supposed himself to partake of something supernatural: secondly, that he does not act, but is continually acted upon: thirdly, that the events having no necessary connection do not produce each other; and lastly, that the imagery is somewhat too laboriously accumulated. Yet the Poem contains many delicate touches of passion, and indeed the passion is every where true to nature; a great number of the stanzas present beautiful images, and are expressed with unusual felicity of language; and the versification, though the metre is itself unfit for long poems, is harmonious and artfully varied, exhibiting the utmost powers of that metre, and every variety of which it is capable. It therefore appeared to me that these several merits (the first of which, namely that of the passion, is of the highest kind,) gave to the Poem a value which is not often possessed by better Poems. On this account I requested of my Friend to permit me to republish it.

PREFACE [TO *LYRICAL BALLADS* (1802)]
William Wordsworth

The first Volume of these Poems has already been submitted to general perusal. It was published, as an experiment, which, I hoped, might be of some use to ascertain, how far, by fitting to metrical arrangement a selection of the real language of men[1] in a state of vivid sensation, that sort of pleasure and that quantity of pleasure may be imparted, which a Poet may rationally endeavour to impart.

I had formed no very inaccurate estimate of the probable effect of those Poems: I flattered myself that they who should be pleased with them would read them with more than common pleasure: and, on the other hand, I was well aware, that by those who should dislike them they would be read with more than common dislike. The result has differed from my expectation in this only, that I have pleased a greater number, than I ventured to hope I should please.

For the sake of variety, and from a consciousness of my own weakness, I was induced to request the assistance of a Friend, who furnished me with the Poems of the *Ancient Mariner,* the *Foster-Mother's Tale,* the *Nightingale,* and the Poem entitled *Love.*[2] I should not, however, have requested this assistance, had I not believed that the Poems of my Friend would in a great

---

From *Lyrical Ballads, with Pastoral and Other Poems, in Two Volumes.* Vol. 1. 3rd ed. London: Longman, 1802.

[1] the real language of men: Compare this phrase with its equivalent in the 1798 Advertisement: "the language of conversation in the middle and lower classes of society." [ED.]
[2] "Love" is the one Coleridge poem added to the 1800 edition of *Lyrical Ballads.* [ED.]

measure have the same tendency as my own, and that, though there would be found a difference, there would be found no discordance in the colours of our style; as our opinions on the subject of poetry do almost entirely coincide.

Several of my Friends are anxious for the success of these Poems from a belief, that, if the views with which they were composed were indeed realized, a class of Poetry would be produced, well adapted to interest mankind permanently, and not unimportant in the multiplicity, and in the quality of its moral relations: and on this account they have advised me to prefix a systematic defence of the theory, upon which the poems were written. But I was unwilling to undertake the task, because I knew that on this occasion the Reader would look coldly upon my arguments, since I might be suspected of having been principally influenced by the selfish and foolish hope of *reasoning* him into an approbation of these particular Poems: and I was still more unwilling to undertake the task, because, adequately to display my opinions, and fully to enforce my arguments, would require a space wholly disproportionate to the nature of a preface. For to treat the subject with the clearness and coherence, of which I believe it susceptible, it would be necessary to give a full account of the present state of the public taste in this country, and to determine how far this taste is healthy or depraved; which, again, could not be determined, without pointing out, in what manner language and the human mind act and re-act on each other, and without retracing the revolutions, not of literature alone, but likewise of society itself. I have therefore altogether declined to enter regularly upon this defence; yet I am sensible, that there would be some impropriety in abruptly obtruding upon the Public, without a few words of introduction, Poems so materially different from those, upon which general approbation is at present bestowed.

It is supposed, that by the act of writing in verse an Author makes a formal engagement that he will gratify certain known habits of association; that he not only thus apprizes the Reader that certain classes of ideas and expressions will be found in his book, but that others will be carefully excluded. This exponent or symbol held forth by metrical language must in different areas of literature have excited very different expectations: for example, in the age of Catullus, Terence, and Lucretius and that of Statius or Claudian; [3] and in our own country, in the age of Shakespeare and Beaumont

---

[3] Catullus (c. 87–54 B.C.), Roman lyric poet; Terence (c. 185–159 B.C.), Roman comic playwright; Lucretius (c. 98–55 B.C.), Roman philosophical poet; Statius (c. A.D. 45–96), Roman epic poet; Claudian (c. A.D. 395–404), Roman epic poet. [ED.].

and Fletcher, and that of Donne and Cowley, or Dryden, or Pope.[4] I will not take upon me to determine the exact import of the promise which by the act of writing in verse an Author, in the present day, makes to his Reader; but, I am certain, it will appear to many persons that I have not fulfilled the terms of an engagement thus voluntarily contracted. They who have been accustomed to the gaudiness and inane phraseology of many modern writers, if they persist in reading this book to its conclusion, will, no doubt, frequently have to struggle with feelings of strangeness and aukwardness: they will look round for poetry, and will be induced to inquire by what species of courtesy these attempts can be permitted to assume that title. I hope therefore the Reader will not censure me, if I attempt to state what I have proposed to myself to perform; and also (as far as the limits of a preface will permit) to explain some of the chief reasons which have determined me in the choice of my purpose: that at least he may be spared any unpleasant feeling of disappointment, and that I myself may be protected from the most dishonorable accusation which can be brought against an Author, namely, that of an indolence which prevents him from endeavouring to ascertain what is his duty, or, when his duty is ascertained, prevents him from performing it.

The principal object, then, which I proposed to myself in these Poems was to chuse incidents and situations from common life, and to relate or describe them, throughout, as far as was possible, in a selection of language really used by men; and, at the same time, to throw over them a certain colouring of imagination, whereby ordinary things should be presented to the mind in an unusual way; and, further, and above all, to make these incidents and situations interesting by tracing in them, truly though not ostentatiously, the primary laws of our nature: chiefly, as far as regards the manner in which we associate ideas in a state of excitement. Low and rustic life was generally chosen because, in that condition, the essential passions of the heart find a better soil in which they can attain their maturity, are less under restraint, and speak a plainer and more emphatic language; because in that condition of life our elementary feelings co-exist in a state of greater simplicity, and, consequently, may be more accurately contemplated, and more forcibly communicated; because the manners of rural life germinate

---

[4]In other words, Wordsworth distinguishes (1) an age of English Renaissance drama: Shakespeare (1564–1616), Francis Beaumont (c. 1584–1616), and John Fletcher (1579–1625), with whom Beaumont frequently collaborated; (2) following Samuel Johnson's distinction, an age of seventeenth-century "metaphysical" poets: John Donne (1572–1631) and Abraham Cowley (1618–67); (3) an age of Dryden, during the Restoration (1660–1700), featuring John Dryden (1631–1700), poet laureate; and (4) an age of Pope, with Alexander Pope (1688–1744) as the preeminent poet. [ED.]

from those elementary feelings; and, from the necessary character of rural occupations, are more easily comprehended, and are more durable; and lastly, because in that condition the passions of men are incorporated with the beautiful and permanent forms of nature. The language, too, of these men is adopted (purified indeed from what appear to be its real defects, from all lasting and rational causes of dislike or disgust) because such men hourly communicate with the best objects from which the best part of language is originally derived; and because, from their rank in society and the sameness and narrow circle of their intercourse, being less under the influence of social vanity they convey their feelings and notions in simple and unelaborated expressions. Accordingly, such a language, arising out of repeated experience and regular feelings, is a more permanent, and a far more philosophical language, than that which is frequently substituted for it by Poets, who think that they are conferring honour upon themselves and their art, in proportion as they separate themselves from the sympathies of men, and indulge in arbitrary and capricious habits of expression, in order to furnish food for fickle tastes, and fickle appetites, of their own creation.[5]

I cannot, however, be insensible of the present outcry against the triviality and meanness both of thought and language, which some of my contemporaries have occasionally introduced into their metrical compositions;[6] and I acknowledge, that this defect, where it exists, is more dishonorable to the Writer's own character than false refinement or arbitrary innovation, though I should contend at the same time that it is far less pernicious in the sum of its consequences. From such verses the Poems in these volumes will be found distinguished at least by one mark of difference, that each of them has a worthy *purpose*. Not that I mean to say, that I always began to write with a distinct purpose formally conceived; but I believe that my habits of meditation have so formed my feelings, as that my descriptions of such objects as strongly excite those feelings will be found to carry along with them a *purpose*. If in this opinion I am mistaken, I can have little right to the name of a Poet. For all good poetry is the spontaneous overflow of powerful feelings: but though this be true, Poems to which any value can be attached, were never produced on any variety of subjects but by a man, who being possessed of more than usual organic sensibility, had also thought long and deeply. For our continued influxes of feeling are modified and directed by our thoughts, which are indeed the representatives of all our past feelings;

---

[5] "It is worth while here to observe that the affecting parts of Chaucer are almost always expressed in language pure and universally intelligible even to this day." [Wordsworth's note.]

[6] As the reviews in the *Critical Review, New London Review,* and *Monthly Review* reveal, this was also a common criticism of *Lyrical Ballads.* [ED.]

and, as by contemplating the relation of these general representatives to each other we discover what is really important to men, so, by the repetition and continuance of this act, our feelings will be connected with important subjects, till at length, if we be originally possessed of much sensibility, such habits of mind will be produced, that, by obeying blindly and mechanically the impulses of those habits, we shall describe objects, and utter sentiments, of such a nature and in such connection with each other, that the understanding of the being to whom we address ourselves, if he be in a healthful state of association, must necessarily be in some degree enlightened, and his affections ameliorated.[7]

I have said that each of these poems has a purpose. I have also informed my Reader what this purpose will be found principally to be: namely to illustrate the manner in which our feelings and ideas are associated in a state of excitement. But, speaking in language somewhat more appropriate, it is to follow the fluxes and refluxes of the mind when agitated by the great and simple affections of our nature. This object I have endeavoured in these short essays to attain by various means; by tracing the maternal passion through many of its more subtle windings, as in the poems of the *Idiot Boy* and the *Mad Mother*; by accompanying the last struggles of a human being, at the approach of death, cleaving in solitude to life and society, as in the Poem of the *Forsaken Indian*; by shewing, as in the Stanzas entitled *We Are Seven*, the perplexity and obscurity which in childhood attend our notion of death, or rather our utter inability to admit that notion; or by displaying the strength of fraternal, or to speak more philosophically, of moral attachment when early associated with the great and beautiful objects of nature, as in *The Brothers*; or, as in the *Incident of Simon Lee*, by placing my Reader in the way of receiving from ordinary moral sensations another and more salutary impression than we are accustomed to receive from them. It has also been part of my general purpose to attempt to sketch characters under the influence of less impassioned feelings, as in the *Two April Mornings*, the *Fountain*, the *Old Man Travelling*, the *Two Thieves*, &c. characters of which the elements are simple, belonging rather to nature than to manners, such as exist now, and will probably always exist, and which from their constitution may be distinctly and profitably contemplated. I will not abuse the indulgence of my Reader by dwelling longer upon this subject; but it is proper that I should mention one other circumstance which distinguishes these Poems from the popular Poetry of the day; it is this, that the feeling

---

[7]This is one of the many passages in the Preface in which the influence of David Hartley's associationist psychology is visible. See the selections from Hartley in "Literary and Philosophical Backgrounds" in Part Two. [ED.]

therein developed gives importance to the action and situation, and not the action and situation to the feeling. My meaning will be rendered perfectly intelligible by referring my Reader to the Poems entitled *Poor Susan* and the *Childless Father*, particularly to the last Stanza of the latter Poem.[8]

I will not suffer a sense of false modesty to prevent me from asserting, that I point my Reader's attention to this mark of distinction, far less for the sake of these particular Poems than from the general importance of the subject. The subject is indeed important! For the human mind is capable of being excited without the application of gross and violent stimulants; and he must have a very faint perception of its beauty and dignity who does not know this, and who does not further know, that one being is elevated above another, in proportion as he possesses this capability. It has therefore appeared to me, that to endeavour to produce or enlarge this capability is one of the best services in which, at any period, a Writer can be engaged; but this service, excellent at all times, is especially so at the present day. For a multitude of causes, unknown to former times, are now acting with a combined force to blunt the discriminating powers of the mind, and unfitting it for all voluntary exertion to reduce it to a state of almost savage torpor. The most effective of these causes are the great national events which are daily taking place, and the encreasing accumulation of men in cities, where the uniformity of their occupations produces a craving for extraordinary incident, which the rapid communication of intelligence hourly gratifies. To this tendency of life and manners the literature and theatrical exhibitions of the country have conformed themselves. The invaluable works of our elder writers, I had almost said the works of Shakespeare and Milton, are driven into neglect by frantic novels, sickly and stupid German Tragedies, and deluges of idle and extravagant stories in verse.[9] —When I think upon this degrading thirst after outrageous stimulation, I am almost ashamed to have spoken of the feeble effort with which I have endeavoured to counteract it; and, reflecting upon the magnitude of the general evil, I should be

---

[8] "Two Brothers," "Two April Mornings," "The Fountain," "The Two Thieves," "Poor Susan," and "The Childless Father" are all poems that Wordsworth added to the 1800 edition of *Lyrical Ballads*. [ED.]

[9] Wordsworth refers to the popularity of German dramas translated and staged during the 1790s and of ballads by such poets as Gottfried August Bürger (see "The Ballad Revival" in Part Two) and Johann Gottfried Herder (1744–1803) —which represent an early form of German Romanticism called "Sturm und Drang," from the title of a play by Maximillian Klinger (1752–1831). The "frantic novels" to which he refers are most likely such Gothic novels as Ann Radcliffe's *The Mysteries of Udolpho* (1794) or Matthew Gregory Lewis's *The Monk* (1796), both of which were extremely popular. [ED.]

oppressed with no dishonorable melancholy, had I not a deep impression of certain inherent and indestructible qualities of the human mind, and likewise of certain powers in the great and permanent objects that act upon it which are equally inherent and indestructible; and did I not further add to this impression a belief, that the time is approaching when the evil will be systematically opposed, by men of greater powers, and with far more distinguished success.

Having dwelt thus long on the subjects and aim of these Poems, I shall request the Reader's permission to apprize him of a few circumstances relating to their *style,* in order, among other reasons, that I may not be censured for not having performed what I never attempted. The Reader will find that personifications of abstract ideas rarely occur in these volumes; and, I hope, are utterly rejected as an ordinary device to elevate the style, and raise it above prose. I have proposed to myself to imitate, and, as far as is possible, to adopt the very language of men; and assuredly such personifications do not make any natural or regular part of that language. They are, indeed, a figure of speech occasionally prompted by passion, and I have made use of them as such; but I have endeavoured utterly to reject them as a mechanical device of style, or as a family language which Writers in metre seem to lay claim to by prescription. I have wished to keep my Reader in the company of flesh and blood, persuaded that by so doing I shall interest him. I am, however, well aware that others who pursue a different track may interest him likewise; I do not interfere with their claim, I only wish to prefer a different claim of my own. There will also be found in these volumes little of what is usually called poetic diction; I have taken as much pains to avoid it as others ordinarily take to produce it; this I have done for the reason already alleged, to bring my language near to the language of men, and further, because the pleasure which I have proposed to myself to impart is of a kind very different from that which is supposed by many persons to be the proper object of poetry. I do not know how without being culpably particular I can give my Reader a more exact notion of the style in which I wished these poems to be written than by informing him that I have at all times endeavoured to look steadily at my subject; consequently, I hope that there is in these Poems little falsehood of description, and that my ideas are expressed in language fitted to their respective importance. Something I must have gained by this practice, as it is friendly to one property of all good poetry, namely, good sense; but it has necessarily cut me off from a large portion of phrases and figures of speech which from father to son have long been regarded as the common inheritance of Poets. I have also thought it expedient to restrict myself still further, having abstained from the use of many expressions, in themselves proper and beautiful, but which have been foolishly repeated by bad Poets, till such feelings of disgust are connected with them as it is scarcely possible by any art of association to overpower.

If in a Poem there should be found a series of lines, or even a single line, in which the language, though naturally arranged and according to the strict laws of metre, does not differ from that of prose, there is a numerous class of critics, who, when they stumble upon these prosaisms as they call them, imagine that they have made a notable discovery, and exult over the Poet as over a man ignorant of his own profession. Now these men would establish a canon of criticism which the Reader will conclude he must utterly reject, if he wishes to be pleased with these volumes. And it would be a most easy task to prove to him, that not only the language of a large portion of every good poem, even of the most elevated character, must necessarily, except with reference to the metre, in no respect differ from that of good prose, but likewise that some of the most interesting parts of the best poems will be found to be strictly the language of prose, when prose is well written. The truth of this assertion might be demonstrated by innumerable passages from almost all the poetical writings, even of Milton himself. I have not space for much quotation; but, to illustrate the subject in a general manner, I will here adduce a short composition of Gray,[10] who was at the head of those who by their reasonings have attempted to widen the space of separation betwixt Prose and Metrical composition, and was more than any other man curiously elaborate in the structure of his own poetic diction.

In vain to me the smiling mornings shine,
And reddening Phoebus lifts his golden fire:
The birds in vain their amorous descant join,
Or chearful fields resume their green attire:
These ears alas! for other notes repine;
A different object do these eyes require;
My lonely anguish melts no heart but mine;
And in my breast the imperfect joys expire;
Yet Morning smiles the busy race to cheer,
And new-born pleasure brings to happier men;
The fields to all their wonted tribute bear;
To warm their little loves the birds complain.

Phoebus: a classical epithet for Apollo, god of the sun, used as a personification of the sun.

[10]Thomas Gray (1716–71), Age of Sensibility poet, best known for his "Elegy Written in a Country Churchyard" (1751). [ED.]

I fruitless mourn to him that cannot hear
And weep the more because I weep in vain.[11]

It will easily be perceived that the only part of this Sonnet which is of any value is the lines printed in Italics: it is equally obvious, that, except in the rhyme, and in the use of the single word "fruitless" for fruitlessly, which is so far a defect, the language of these lines does in no respect differ from that of prose.

By the foregoing quotation I have shewn that the language of Prose may yet be well adapted to Poetry; and I have previously asserted that a large portion of the language of every good poem can in no respect differ from that of good Prose. I will go further. I do not doubt that it may be safely affirmed, that there neither is, nor can be, any essential difference between the language of prose and metrical composition. We are fond of tracing the resemblance between Poetry and Painting, and, accordingly, we call them Sisters: but where shall we find bonds of connection sufficiently strict to typify the affinity betwixt metrical and prose composition? They both speak by and to the same organs; the bodies in which both of them are clothed may be said to be of the same substance, their affections are kindred and almost identical, not necessarily differing even in degree; Poetry sheds no tears "such as Angels weep,"[12] but natural and human tears;[13] she can boast of no celestial Ichor that distinguishes her vital juices from those of prose; the same human blood circulates through the veins of them both.

If it be affirmed that rhyme and metrical arrangement of themselves constitute a distinction which overturns what I have been saying on the strict affinity of metrical language with that of prose, and paves the way for other artificial distinctions which the mind voluntarily admits, I answer that the language of such Poetry as I am recommending is, as far as is possible, a selection of the language really spoken by men; that this selection, wherever it is made with true taste and feeling, will of itself form a distinction far greater than would at first be imagined, and will entirely separate

---

Ichor: blood of the gods.

[11] Gray's "Sonnet on the Death of Mr. Richard West" was published posthumously in 1775. [ED.]

[12] *Paradise Lost* 1.630. [ED.]

[13] "I here use the word 'Poetry' (though against my own judgment) as opposed to the word Prose, and synonomous with metrical composition. But much confusion has been introduced into criticism by this contradistinction of Poetry and Prose, instead of the more philosophical one of Poetry and Matter of fact, or Science. The only strict antithesis to Prose is Metre; nor is this, in truth, a *strict* antithesis; because lines and passages of metre so naturally occur in writing prose, that it would be scarcely possible to avoid them, even were it desirable." [Wordsworth's note.]

the composition from the vulgarity and meanness of ordinary life; and, if metre be superadded thereto, I believe that a dissimilitude will be produced altogether sufficient for the gratification of a rational mind. What other distinction would we have? Whence is it to come? And where is it to exist? Not, surely, where the Poet speaks through the mouths of his characters: it cannot be necessary here, either for elevation of style, or any of its supposed ornaments: for, if the Poet's subject be judiciously chosen, it will naturally, and upon fit occasion, lead him to passions the language of which, if selected truly and judiciously, must necessarily be dignified and variegated, and alive with metaphors and figures. I forbear to speak of an incongruity which would shock the intelligent Reader, should the Poet interweave any foreign splendour of his own with that which the passion naturally suggests: it is sufficient to say that such addition is unnecessary. And, surely, it is more probable that those passages, which with propriety abound with metaphors and figures, will have their due effect, if, upon other occasions where the passions are of a milder character, the style also be subdued and temperate.

But, as the pleasure which I hope to give by the Poems I now present to the Reader must depend entirely on just notions upon this subject, and, as it is in itself of the highest importance to our taste and moral feelings, I cannot content myself with these detached remarks. And if, in what I am about to say, it shall appear to some that my labour is unnecessary, and that I am like a man fighting a battle without enemies, I would remind such persons, that, whatever may be the language outwardly holden by men, a practical faith in the opinions which I am wishing to establish is almost unknown. If my conclusions are admitted, and carried as far as they must be carried if admitted at all, our judgments concerning the works of the greatest Poets both ancient and modern will be far different from what they are at present, both when we praise, and when we censure: and our moral feelings influencing, and influenced by these judgments will, I believe, be corrected and purified.

Taking up the subject, then, upon general grounds, I ask what is meant by the word Poet? What is a Poet? To whom does he address himself? And what language is to be expected from him? He is a man speaking to men: a man, it is true, endued with more lively sensibility, more enthusiasm and tenderness, who has a greater knowledge of human nature, and a more comprehensive soul, than are supposed to be common among mankind; a man pleased with his own passions and volitions, and who rejoices more than other men in the spirit of life that is in him; delighting to contemplate similar volitions and passions as manifested in the goings-on of the Universe, and habitually impelled to create them where he does not find them. To these qualities he has added a disposition to be affected more than other men by absent things as if they were present; an ability of conjuring up in

himself passions, which are indeed far from being the same as those produced by real events, yet (especially in those parts of the general sympathy
which are pleasing and delightful) do more nearly resemble the passions
produced by real events, than any thing which, from the motions of their
own minds merely, other men are accustomed to feel in themselves;
whence, and from practice, he has acquired a greater readiness and power
in expressing what he thinks and feels, and especially those thoughts and
feelings which, by his own choice, or from the structure of his own mind,
arise in him without immediate external excitement.

But, whatever portion of this faculty we may suppose even the greatest
Poet to possess, there cannot be a doubt but that the language which it will
suggest to him, must, in liveliness and truth, fall far short of that which is
uttered by men in real life, under the actual pressure of those passions, certain shadows of which the Poet thus produces, or feels to be produced, in
himself. However exalted a notion we would wish to cherish of the character of a Poet, it is obvious, that, while he describes and imitates passions, his
situation is altogether slavish and mechanical, compared with the freedom
and power of real and substantial action and suffering. So that it will be the
wish of the Poet to bring his feelings near to those of the persons whose feelings he describes, nay, for short spaces of time perhaps, to let himself slip
into an entire delusion, and even confound and identify his own feelings
with theirs; modifying only the language which is thus suggested to him,
by a consideration that he describes for a particular purpose, that of giving
pleasure. Here, then, he will apply the principle on which I have so much
insisted, namely, that of selection; on this he will depend for removing what
would otherwise be painful or disgusting in the passion; he will feel that
there is no necessity to trick out or to elevate nature: and, the more indus-
triously he applies this principle, the deeper will be his faith that no words,
which his fancy or imagination can suggest, will be to be compared with
those which are the emanations of reality and truth.

But it may be said by those who do not object to the general spirit of
these remarks, that, as it is impossible for the Poet to produce upon all occasions language as exquisitely fitted for the passion as that which the real
passion itself suggests, it is proper that he should consider himself as in the
situation of a translator, who deems himself justified when he substitutes
excellences of another kind for those which are unattainable by him; and
endeavours occasionally to surpass his original, in order to make some
amends for the general inferiority to which he feels that he must submit.
But this would be to encourage idleness and unmanly despair. Further, it
is the language of men who speak of what they do not understand; who talk
of Poetry as of a matter of amusement and idle pleasure; who will converse
with us as gravely about a *taste* for Poetry, as they express it, as if it were a

thing as indifferent as a taste for Rope-dancing, or Frontiniac or Sherry. Aristotle, I have been told, hath said, that Poetry is the most philosophic of all writing:[14] it is so: its object is truth, not individual and local, but general, and operative; not standing upon external testimony, but carried alive into the heart by passion; truth which is its own testimony, which gives strength and divinity to the tribunal to which it appeals, and receives them from the same tribunal. Poetry is the image of man and nature. The obstacles which stand in the way of the fidelity of the Biographer and Historian, and of their consequent utility, are incalculably greater than those which are to be encountered by the Poet, who has an adequate notion of the dignity of his art. The Poet writes under one restriction only, namely, that of the necessity of giving immediate pleasure to a human Being possessed of that information which may be expected from him, not as a lawyer, a physician, a mariner, an astronomer or a natural philosopher, but as a Man. Except this one restriction, there is no object standing between the Poet and the image of things; between this, and the Biographer and Historian there are a thousand.

Nor let this necessity of producing immediate pleasure be considered as a degradation of the Poet's art. It is far otherwise. It is an acknowledgment of the beauty of the universe, an acknowledgment the more sincere because it is not formal, but indirect; it is a task light and easy to him who looks at the world in the spirit of love: further, it is a homage paid to the native and naked dignity of man, to the grand elementary principle of pleasure, by which he knows, and feels, and lives, and moves. We have no sympathy but what is propagated by pleasure: I would not be misunderstood; but wherever we sympathize with pain it will be found that the sympathy is produced and carried on by subtle combinations with pleasure. We have no knowledge, that is, no general principles drawn from the contemplation of particular facts, but what has been built up by pleasure, and exists in us by pleasure alone. The Man of Science, the Chemist and Mathematician, whatever difficulties and disgusts they may have had to struggle with, know and feel this. However painful may be the objects with which the Anatomist's knowledge

---

Frontiniac: a sweet French wine.

[14] In chapter 9 of *The Art of Poetry,* Aristotle writes:

> The difference between the historian and the poet is not that the one writes in prose and the other in verse; the work of Herodotus might be put into verse, and in this metrical form it would be no less a kind of history than it is without metre. The difference is that the one tells of what happened, the other of the kinds of things that might happen. For this reason poetry is something more philosophical and more worthy of serious attention than history; for while poetry is concerned with universal truths, history treats of particular facts. (43–44) [ED.]

is connected, he feels that his knowledge is pleasure; and where he has no pleasure he has no knowledge. What then does the Poet? He considers man and the objects that surround him as acting and re-acting upon each other, so as to produce an infinite complexity of pain and pleasure; he considers man in his own nature and in his ordinary life as contemplating this with a certain quantity of immediate knowledge, with certain convictions, intuitions, and deductions which by habit become of the nature of intuitions; he considers him as looking upon this complex scene of ideas and sensations, and finding every where objects that immediately excite in him sympathies which, from the necessities of his nature, are accompanied by an overbalance of enjoyment.[15]

To this knowledge which all men carry about with them, and to these sympathies in which without any other discipline than that of our daily life we are fitted to take delight, the Poet principally directs his attention. He considers man and nature as essentially adapted to each other, and the mind of man as naturally the mirror of the fairest and most interesting qualities of nature. And thus the Poet, prompted by this feeling of pleasure which accompanies him through the whole course of his studies, converses with general nature with affections akin to those, which, through labour and length of time, the Man of Science has raised up in himself, by conversing with those particular parts of nature which are the objects of his studies. The knowledge both of the Poet and the Man of Science is pleasure; but the knowledge of the one cleaves to us as a necessary part of our existence, our natural and unalienable inheritance; the other is a personal and individual acquisition, slow to come to us, and by no habitual and direct sympathy connecting us with our fellow-beings. The Man of Science seeks truth as a remote and unknown benefactor; he cherishes and loves it in his solitude: the Poet, singing a song in which all human beings join with him, rejoices in the presence of truth as our visible friend and hourly companion. Poetry is the breath and finer spirit of all knowledge; it is the impassioned expression which is in the countenance of all Science. Emphatically may it be said of the Poet, as Shakespeare hath said of man, "that he looks before and after."[16] He is the rock of defence of human nature; an upholder and preserver, carrying every where with him relationship and love. In spite of difference of soil and climate, of language and manners, of laws and customs, in spite of things silently gone out of mind and things violently destroyed,

---

[15] Compare this passage with the excerpts from Adam Smith's *The Theory of Moral Sentiments* and David Hartley's *Observations on Man* in "Literary and Philosophical Backgrounds" in Part Two. [ED.]

[16] Compare *Hamlet* 4.4.36–39. [ED.]

the Poet binds together by passion and knowledge the vast empire of human society, as it is spread over the whole earth, and over all time. The objects of the Poet's thoughts are every where; though the eyes and senses of man are, it is true, his favorite guides, yet he will follow wheresoever he can find an atmosphere of sensation in which to move his wings. Poetry is the first and last of all knowledge—it is as immortal as the heart of man. If the labours of men of Science should ever create any material revolution, direct or indirect, in our condition, and in the impressions which we habitually receive, the Poet will sleep then no more than at present, but he will be ready to follow the steps of the man of Science, not only in those general indirect effects, but he will be at his side, carrying sensation into the midst of the objects of the Science itself. The remotest discoveries of the Chemist, the Botanist, or Mineralogist, will be as proper objects of the Poet's art as any upon which it can be employed, if the time should ever come when these things shall be familiar to us, and the relations under which they are contemplated by the followers of these respective Sciences shall be manifestly and palpably material to us as enjoying and suffering beings. If the time should ever come when what is now called Science, thus familiarized to men, shall be ready to put on, as it were, a form of flesh and blood, the Poet will lend his divine spirit to aid the transfiguration, and will welcome the Being thus produced, as a dear and genuine inmate of the household of man.— It is not not, then, to be supposed that any one, who holds that sublime notion of Poetry which I have attempted to convey, will break in upon the sanctity and truth of his pictures by transitory and accidental ornaments, and endeavour to excite admiration of himself by arts, the necessity of which must manifestly depend upon the assumed meanness of his subject.

What I have thus far said applies to Poetry in general; but especially to those parts of composition where the Poet speaks through the mouths of his characters; and upon this point it appears to have such weight that I will conclude, there are few persons, of good sense, who would not allow that the dramatic parts of composition are defective, in proportion as they deviate from the real language of nature, and are coloured by a diction of the Poet's own, either peculiar to him as an individual Poet, or belonging simply to Poets in general, to a body of men who, from the circumstance of their compositions being in metre, it is expected will employ a particular language.[17]

It is not, then, in the dramatic parts of composition that we look for this distinction of language; but still it may be proper and necessary where the

---

[17] Here Wordsworth may have in mind Joanna Baillie's 1798 "Introductory Discourse," which had also emphasized the need for naturalistic dialogue in dramatic writing. See pages 164–66. [ED.]

Poet speaks to us in his own person and character. To this I answer by referring my Reader to the description which I have before given of a Poet. Among the qualities which I have enumerated as principally conducting to form a Poet, is implied nothing differing in kind from other men, but only in degree. The sum of what I have there said is, that the Poet is chiefly distinguished from other men by a greater promptness to think and feel without immediate external excitement, and a greater power in expressing such thoughts and feelings as are produced in him in that manner. But these passions and thoughts and feelings are the general passions and thoughts and feelings of men. And with what are they connected? Undoubtedly with our moral sentiments and animal sensations, and with the causes which excite these; with the operations of the elements and the appearances of the visible universe; with storm and sun-shine, with the revolutions of the seasons, with cold and heat, with loss of friends and kindred, with injuries and resentments, gratitude and hope, with fear and sorrow. These, and the like, are the sensations and objects which the Poet describes, as they are the sensations of other men, and the objects which interest them. The Poet thinks and feels in the spirit of the passions of men. How, then, can his language differ in any material degree from that of all other men who feel vividly and see clearly? It might be *proved* that it is impossible. But supposing that this were not the case, the Poet might then be allowed to use a peculiar language, when expressing his feelings for his own gratification, or that of men like himself. But Poets do not write for Poets alone, but for men. Unless therefore we are advocates for that admiration which depends upon ignorance, and that pleasure which arises from hearing what we do not understand, the Poet must descend from this supposed height, and, in order to excite rational sympathy, he must express himself as other men express themselves. To this it may be added, that while he is only selecting from the real language of men, or, which amounts to the same thing, composing accurately in the spirit of such selection, he is treading upon safe ground, and we know what we are to expect from him. Our feelings are the same with respect to metre; for, as it may be proper to remind the Reader, the distinction of metre is regular and uniform, and not like that which is produced by what is usually called poetic diction, arbitrary, and subject to infinite caprices upon which no calculation whatever can be made.[18] In the one case, the Reader is utterly at the mercy of the Poet respecting what imagery or diction he may choose to connect with the passion, whereas, in the other, the metre obeys certain laws, to which the Poet and Reader both

---

[18] See the Appendix on poetic diction (412–16). [ED.]

willingly submit because they are certain, and because no interference is made by them with the passion but such as the concurring testimony of ages has shewn to heighten and improve the pleasure which co-exists with it.

It will now be proper to answer an obvious question, namely, why, professing these opinions, have I written in verse? To this, in addition to such answer as is included in what I have already said, I reply in the first place, because, however I may have restricted myself, there is still left open to me what confessedly constitutes the most valuable object of all writing whether in prose or verse, the great and universal passions of men, the most general and interesting of their occupations, and the entire world of nature, from which I am at liberty to supply myself with endless combinations of forms and imagery. Now, supposing for a moment that whatever is interesting in these objects may be as vividly described in prose, why am I to be condemned, if to such description I have endeavoured to superadd the charm which, by the consent of all nations, is acknowledged to exist in metrical language? To this, by such as are unconvinced by what I have already said, it may be answered, that a very small part of the pleasure given by Poetry depends upon the metre, and that it is injudicious to write in metre, unless it be accompanied with the other artificial distinctions of style with which metre is usually accompanied, and that by such deviation more will be lost from the shock which will be thereby given to the Reader's associations, than will be counterbalanced by any pleasure which he can derive from the general power of numbers. In answer to those who still contend for the necessity of accompanying metre with certain appropriate colours of style in order to the accomplishment of its appropriate end, and who also, in my opinion, greatly under-rate the power of metre in itself, it might perhaps, as far as relates to these Poems, have been almost sufficient to observe, that poems are extant, written upon more humble subjects, and in a more naked and simple style than I have aimed at, which poems have continued to give pleasure from generation to generation. Now, if nakedness and simplicity be a defect, the fact here mentioned affords a strong presumption that poems somewhat less naked and simple are capable of affording pleasure at the present day; and, what I wished *chiefly* to attempt, at present, was to justify myself for having written under the impression of this belief.

But I might point out various causes why, when the style is manly, and the subject of some importance, words metrically arranged will long continue to impart such a pleasure to mankind as he who is sensible of the extent of that pleasure will be desirous to impart. The end of Poetry is to produce excitement in co-existence with an overbalance of pleasure. Now, by the supposition, excitement is an unusual and irregular state of the mind;

ideas and feelings do not in that state succeed each other in accustomed order. But, if the words by which this excitement is produced are in themselves powerful, or the images and feelings have an undue proportion of pain connected with them, there is some danger that the excitement may be carried beyond its proper bounds. Now the co-presence of something regular, something to which the mind has been accustomed in various moods and in a less excited state, cannot but have great efficacy in tempering and restraining the passion by an intertexture of ordinary feeling, and of feeling not strictly and necessarily connected with the passion. This is unquestionably true, and hence, though the opinion will at first appear paradoxical, from the tendency of metre to divest language in a certain degree of its reality, and thus to throw a sort of half consciousness of unsubstantial existence over the whole composition, there can be little doubt but that more pathetic situations and sentiments, that is, those which have a greater proportion of pain connected with them, may be endured in metrical composition, especially in rhyme, than in prose. The metre of the old Ballads is very artless; yet they contain many passages which would illustrate this opinion, and, I hope, if the following Poems be attentively perused, similar instances will be found in them. This opinion may be further illustrated by appealing to the Reader's own experience of the reluctance with which he comes to the re-perusal of the distressful parts of Clarissa Harlowe, or the Gamester.[19] While Shakespeare's writings, in the most pathetic scenes, never act upon us as pathetic beyond the bounds of pleasure — an effect which, in a much greater degree than might at first be imagined, is to be ascribed to small, but continual and regular impulses of pleasurable surprise from the metrical arrangement. —On the other hand (what it must be allowed will much more frequently happen) if the Poet's words should be incommensurate with the passion, and inadequate to raise the Reader to a height of desirable excitement, then, (unless the Poet's choice of his metre has been grossly injudicious) in the feelings of pleasure which the Reader has been accustomed to connect with metre in general, and in the feeling, whether chearful or melancholy, which he has been accustomed to connect with that particular movement of metre, there will be found something which will greatly contribute to impart passion to the words, and to effect the complex end which the Poet proposes to himself.

If I had undertaken a systematic defence of the theory upon which these poems are written, it would have been my duty to develope the various causes upon which the pleasure received from metrical language depends.

---

[19] Clarissa Harlowe is the heroine of Samuel Richardson's epistolary novel *Clarissa, or The History of a Young Lady* (1747–49); *The Gamester* (1753) is a tragedy by Edward Moore. Both are prose works. [ED.]

Among the chief of these causes is to be reckoned a principle which must be well known to those who have made any of the Arts the object of accurate reflection; I mean the pleasure which the mind derives from the perception of similitude in dissimilitude. This principle is the great spring of the activity of our minds, and their chief feeder. From this principle the direction of the sexual appetite, and all the passions connected with it take their origin: It is the life of our ordinary conversation; and upon the accuracy with which similitude in dissimilitude, and dissimilitude in similitude are perceived, depend our taste and our moral feelings. It would not have been a useless employment to have applied this principle to the consideration of metre, and to have shewn that metre is hence enabled to afford much pleasure, and to have pointed out in what manner that pleasure is produced. But my limits will not permit me to enter upon this subject, and I must content myself with a general summary.

I have said that Poetry is the spontaneous overflow of powerful feelings: it takes its origin from emotion recollected in tranquillity: the emotion is contemplated till by a species of reaction the tranquillity gradually disappears, and an emotion, kindred to that which was before the subject of contemplation, is gradually produced, and does itself actually exist in the mind. In this mood successful composition generally begins, and in a mood similar to this it is carried on; but the emotion, of whatever kind and in whatever degree, from various causes is qualified by various pleasures, so that in describing any passions whatsoever, which are voluntarily described, the mind will upon the whole be in a state of enjoyment. Now, if Nature be thus cautious in preserving in a state of enjoyment a being thus employed, the Poet ought to profit by the lesson thus held forth to him, and ought especially to take care, that whatever passions he communicates to his Reader, those passions, if his Reader's mind be sound and vigorous, should always be accompanied with an overbalance of pleasure. Now the music of harmonious metrical language, the sense of difficulty overcome, and the blind association of pleasure which has been previously received from works of rhyme or metre of the same or similar construction, an indistinct perception perpetually renewed of language closely resembling that of real life, and yet, in the circumstance of metre, differing from it so widely, all these imperceptibly make up a complex feeling of delight, which is of the most important use in tempering the painful feeling which will always be found intermingled with powerful descriptions of the deeper passions. This effect is always produced in pathetic and impassioned poetry; while, in lighter compositions, the ease and gracefulness with which the Poet manages his numbers are themselves confessedly a principal source of the gratification of the Reader. I might perhaps include all which it is *necessary* to say upon this subject by affirming, what few persons will deny, that, of two descriptions, either of passions, manners, or characters, each of them equally well executed, the one in prose and the other in verse, the verse will be read a hundred times where the prose is read once. We see that Pope by the power of verse alone, has contrived to render the plainest common sense interesting, and even frequently to invest it with the appearance of passion.[20] In consequence of these convictions I related in metre the Tale of *Goody Blake and Harry Gill*, which is one of the rudest of this collection. I wished to draw attention to the truth that the power of the human imagination is sufficient to produce such changes even in our physical nature as might almost appear miraculous. The truth is an important one; the fact (for it is a *fact*) is a valuable illustration of it. And I have the satisfaction of knowing that it has been communicated to many hundreds of people who would never have heard of it, had it not been narrated as a Ballad, and in a more impressive metre than is usual in Ballads.

Having thus explained a few of the reasons why I have written in verse, and why I have chosen subjects from common life, and endeavoured to bring my language near to the real language of men, if I have been too minute in pleading my own cause, I have at the same time been treating a subject of general interest; and it is for this reason that I request the Reader's permission to add a few words with reference solely to these particular poems, and to some defects which will probably be found in them. I am sensible that my associations must have sometimes been particular instead of general, and that, consequently, giving to things a false importance, sometimes from diseased impulses I may have written upon unworthy subjects; but I am less apprehensive on this account, than that my language may frequently have suffered from those arbitrary connections of feelings and ideas with particular words and phrases, from which no man can altogether protect himself. Hence I have no doubt, that, in some instances, feelings even of the ludicrous may be given to my Readers by expressions which appeared to me tender and pathetic. Such faulty expressions, were I convinced they were faulty at present, and that they must necessarily continue to be so, I would willingly take all reasonable pains to correct. But it is dangerous to make these alterations on the simple authority of a few individuals, or even of certain classes of men; for where the understanding of an Author is not convinced, or his feelings altered, this cannot be done without great injury to himself: for his own feelings are his stay and support, and, if he sets them aside in one instance, he may be induced to repeat this act till his mind loses all confidence in itself, and becomes utterly debilitated. To this it may be added, that the Reader ought never to forget that he is himself exposed to

---

[20] See Pope's preface to *An Essay on Man* (239–40). [ED.]

the same errors as the Poet, and perhaps in a much greater degree: for there can be no presumption in saying, that it is not probable he will be so well acquainted with the various stages of meaning through which words have passed, or with the fickleness or stability of the relations of particular ideas to each other; and above all, since he is so much less interested in the subject, he may decide lightly and carelessly.

Long as I have detained my Reader, I hope he will permit me to caution him against a mode of false criticism which has been applied to Poetry in which the language closely resembles that of life and nature. Such verses have been triumphed over in parodies of which Dr. Johnson's Stanza is a fair specimen.

> I put my hat upon my head,
> And walk'd into the Strand,
> And there I met another man
> Whose hat was in his hand.

Immediately under these lines I will place one of the most justly admired stanzas of the "Babes in the Wood."

> These pretty Babes with hand in hand
> Went wandering up and down;
> But never more they saw the Man
> Approaching from the Town.[21]

In both these stanzas the words, and the order of the words, in no respect differ from the most unimpassioned conversation. There are words in both, for example, "the Strand," and "the Town," connected with none but the most familiar ideas; yet the one stanza we admit as admirable, and the other as a fair example of the superlatively contemptible. Whence arises this difference? Not from the metre, not from the language, not from the order of the words; but the *matter* expressed in Dr. Johnson's stanza is contemptible. The proper method of treating trivial and simple verses to which Dr. Johnson's stanza would be a fair parallelism is not to say, this is a bad kind of poetry, or this is not poetry; but this wants sense; it is neither interesting in itself, nor can *lead* to any thing interesting; the images neither originate in that same state of feeling which arises out of thought, nor can excite thought or feeling in the Reader. This is the only sensible manner of

---

[21] "The Children in the Wood," popularly known as "The Babes in the Wood," appeared in Thomas Percy's *Reliques of Ancient English Poetry* (1765); Samuel Johnson's lines parody the poetry in Percy's collection. See the discussion of Percy's *Reliques* in "The Ballad Revival" in Part Two. [ED.]

dealing with such verses: Why trouble yourself about the species till you have previously decided upon the genus? Why take pains to prove that an Ape is not a Newton when it is self-evident that he is not a man? [22]

I have one request to make of my Reader, which is, that in judging these Poems he would decide by his own feelings genuinely, and not by reflection upon what will probably be the judgment of others. How common is it to hear a person say, "I myself do not object to this style of composition or this or that expression, but to such and such classes of people it will appear mean or ludicrous." This mode of criticism, so destructive of all sound unadulterated judgment, is almost universal: I have therefore to request, that the Reader would abide independently by his own feelings, and that if he finds himself affected he would not suffer such conjectures to interfere with his pleasure.

If an Author by any single composition has impressed us with respect for his talents, it is useful to consider this as affording a presumption, that, on other occasions where we have been displeased, he nevertheless may not have written ill or absurdly; and, further, to give him so much credit for this one composition as may induce us to review what has displeased us with more care than we should otherwise have bestowed upon it. This is not only an act of justice, but in our decisions upon poetry especially, may conduce in a high degree to the improvement of our own taste: for an *accurate* taste in poetry, and in all the other arts, as Sir Joshua Reynolds [23] has observed, is an *acquired* talent, which can only be produced by thought and a long continued intercourse with the best models of composition. This is mentioned, not with so ridiculous a purpose as to prevent the most inexperienced Reader from judging for himself, (I have already said that I wish him to judge for himself;) but merely to temper the rashness of decision, and to suggest, that, if Poetry be a subject on which much time has not been bestowed, the judgment may be erroneous; and that in many cases it necessarily will be so.

I know that nothing would have so effectually contributed to further the end which I have in view as to have shewn of what kind the pleasure is, and how that pleasure is produced, which is confessedly produced by metrical composition essentially different from that which I have here endeavoured to recommend: for the Reader will say that he has been pleased by such

---

[22] Compare this paragraph with Robert Southey's remarks in the *Critical Review,* in which he argues that the Lyrical Ballads experiment has failed "because it has been tried upon uninteresting subjects." [ED.]

[23] Sir Joshua Reynolds (1723–92), noted English portrait painter and first president of the Royal Academy. [ED.]

composition; and what can I do more for him? The power of any art is limited; and he will suspect, that, if I propose to furnish him with new friends, it is only upon condition of his abandoning his old friends. Besides, as I have said, the Reader is himself conscious of the pleasure which he has received from such composition, composition to which he has peculiarly attached the endearing name of Poetry; and all men feel an habitual gratitude, and something of an honorable bigotry for the objects which have long continued to please them: we not only wish to be pleased, but to be pleased in that particular way in which we have been accustomed to be pleased. There is a host of arguments in these feelings; and I should be the less able to combat them successfully, as I am willing to allow, that, in order entirely to enjoy the Poetry which I am recommending, it would be necessary to give up much of what is ordinarily enjoyed. But, would my limits have permitted me to point out how this pleasure is produced, I might have removed many obstacles, and assisted my Reader in perceiving that the powers of language are not so limited as he may suppose; and that it is possible that poetry may give other enjoyments, of a purer, more lasting, and more exquisite nature. This part of my subject I have not altogether neglected; but it has been less my present aim to prove, that the interest excited by some other kinds of poetry is less vivid, and less worthy of the nobler powers of the mind, than to offer reasons for presuming, that, if the object which I have proposed to myself were adequately attained, a species of poetry would be produced, which is genuine poetry; in its nature well adapted to interest mankind permanently, and likewise important in the multiplicity and quality of its moral relations.

From what has been said, and from a perusal of the Poems, the Reader will be able clearly to perceive the object which I have proposed to myself: he will determine how far I have attained this object; and, what is a much more important question, whether it be worth attaining; and upon the decision of these two questions will rest my claim to the approbation of the public.

APPENDIX [POETIC DICTION]

William Wordsworth

See Preface, — "by what is usually called Poetic Diction" [404] [1]

As perhaps I have no right to expect from a Reader of an introduction to a volume of Poems that attentive perusal without which it is impossible, imperfectly as I have been compelled to express my meaning, that what I have said in the Preface should throughout be fully understood, I am the more anxious to give an exact notion of the sense in which I use the phrase *poetic diction;* and for this purpose I will here add a few words concerning the origin of the phraseology which I have condemned under that name. — The earliest Poets of all nations generally wrote from passion excited by real events; they wrote naturally, and as men: feeling powerfully as they did, their language was daring, and figurative. In succeeding times, Poets, and men ambitious of the fame of Poets, perceiving the influence of such language, and desirous of producing the same effect, without having the same animating passion, set themselves to a mechanical adoption of those figures of speech, and made use of them, sometimes with propriety, but much more frequently applied them to feelings and ideas with which they had no natural connection whatsoever. A language was thus insensibly produced, differing materially from the real language of men in *any situation.* The Reader or Hearer of this distorted language found himself in a perturbed and unusual state of mind: when affected by the genuine language of passion he had been in a perturbed and unusual state of mind also: in both cases he was willing that his common judgment and understanding should be laid asleep, and he had no instinctive and infallible perception of the true to make him reject the false; the one served as a passport for the other. The agitation and confusion of mind were in both cases delightful, and no wonder if he confounded the one with the other, and believed them both to be produced by the same, or similar causes. Besides, the Poet spoke to him in the character of a man to be looked up to, a man of genius and authority. Thus, and from a variety of other causes, this distorted language was received with admiration; and Poets, it is probable, who had before contented themselves for the most part with misapplying only expressions which at

---

Lyrical Ballads, with Pastoral and Other Poems, in Two Volumes. Vol. 2. 3rd ed. London: Longman, 1802.

[1] Wordsworth here provides the page reference for his quotation. We have done the same. [ED.]

first had been dictated by real passion, carried the abuse still further, and introduced phrases composed apparently in the spirit of the original figurative language of passion, yet altogether of their own invention, and distinguished by various degrees of wanton deviation from good sense and nature.

It is indeed true that the language of the earliest Poets was felt to differ materially from ordinary language, because it was the language of extraordinary occasions; but it was really spoken by men, language which the Poet himself had uttered when he had been affected by the events which he described, or which he had heard uttered by those around him. To this language it is probable that metre of some sort or other was early superadded. This separated the genuine language of Poetry still further from common life, so that whoever read or heard the poems of these earliest Poets felt himself moved in a way in which he had not been accustomed to be moved in real life, and by causes manifestly different from those which acted upon him in real life. This was the great temptation to all the corruptions which have followed: under the protection of this feeling succeeding Poets constructed a phraseology which had one thing, it is true, in common with the genuine language of poetry, namely, that it was not heard in ordinary conversation; that it was unusual. But the first Poets, as I have said, spake a language which though unusual, was still the language of men. This circumstance, however, was disregarded by their successors; they found that they could please by easier means: they became proud of a language which they themselves had invented, and which was uttered only by themselves; and, with the spirit of a fraternity, they arrogated it to themselves as their own. In process of time metre became a symbol or promise of this unusual language, and whoever took upon him to write in metre, according as he possessed more or less of true poetic genius, introduced less or more of this adulterated phraseology into his compositions, and the true and the false became so inseparably interwoven that the taste of men was gradually perverted; and this language was received as a natural language; and, at length, by the influence of books upon men, did to a certain degree really become so. Abuses of this kind were imported from one nation to another, and with the progress of refinement this diction became daily more and more corrupt, thrusting out of sight the plain humanities of nature by a motley masquerade of tricks, quaintnesses, hieroglyphics, and enigmas.

It would be highly interesting to point out the causes of the pleasure given by this extravagant and absurd language; but this is not the place; it depends upon a great variety of causes, but upon none perhaps more than its influence in impressing a notion of the peculiarity and exaltation of the Poet's character, and in flattering the Reader's self-love by bringing him nearer to a sympathy with that character; an effect which is accomplished by unsettling ordinary habits of thinking, and thus assisting the Reader to approach to that perturbed and dizzy state of mind in which if he does not find himself, he imagines that he is *balked* of a peculiar enjoyment which poetry can, and ought to bestow.

The sonnet which I have quoted from Gray, in the Preface, except the lines printed in Italics, consists of little else but this diction, though not of the worst kind; and indeed, if I may be permitted to say so, it is far too common in the best writers, both antient and modern. Perhaps I can in no way, by positive example, more easily give my Reader a notion of what I mean by the phrase *poetic diction* than by referring him to a comparison between the metrical paraphrases which we have of passages in the old and new Testament, and those passages as they exist in our common Translation. See Pope's "Messiah" throughout, Prior's[2] "Did sweeter sounds adorn my flowing tongue," &c. &c. "Though I speak with the tongues of men and of angels," &c. &c. See 1st Corinthians Chapter 13th. By way of immediate example, take the following of Dr. Johnson.

> Turn on the prudent Ant thy heedless eyes,
> Observe her labours, Sluggard, and be wise;
> No stern command, no monitory voice,
> Prescribes her duties, or directs her choice;
> Yet timely provident she hastes away,
> To snatch the blessings of a plenteous day;
> When fruitful Summer loads the teeming plain,
> She crops the harvest and she stores the grain.
> How long, shall sloth usurp thy useless hours,
> Unnerve thy vigour, and enchain thy powers?
> While artful shades thy downy couch enclose,
> And soft solicitation courts repose,
> Amidst the drowsy charms of dull delight,
> Year chases year with unremitted flight,
> Till want now following, fraudulent and slow,
> Shall spring to seize thee, like an ambushed foe.

From this hubbub of words pass to the original, "Go to the Ant, thou Sluggard, consider her ways, and be wise: which having no guide, overseer, or ruler, provideth her meat in the summer, and gathereth her food in the harvest. How long wilt thou sleep, O Sluggard? when wilt thou arise out of thy sleep? Yet a little sleep, a little slumber, a little folding of the hands to

---

[2] Matthew Prior (1664–1721), English diplomat and poet best known for his epigrams and occasional verse. [ED.]

sleep. So shall thy poverty come as one that travaileth, and thy want as an armed man." Proverbs, chap. 6th.

One more quotation and I have done. It is from Cowper's verses supposed to be written by Alexander Selkirk.[3]

> Religion! what treasure untold
> Resides in that heavenly word!
> More precious than silver and gold,
> Or all that this earth can afford.
> But the sound of the church-going bell
> These valleys and rocks never heard
> Ne'er sigh'd at the sound of a knell,
> Or smil'd when a sabbath appear'd.
>
> Ye winds, that have made me your sport,
> Convey to this desolate shore
> Some cordial endearing report
> Of a land I must visit no more.
> My Friends, do they now and then send
> A wish or a thought after me?
> O tell me I yet have a friend
> Though a friend I am never to see.

I have quoted this passage as an instance of three different styles of composition. The first four lines are poorly expressed; some Critics would call the language prosaic; the fact is, it would be bad prose, so bad, that it is scarcely worse in metre. The epithet "church-going" applied to a bell, and that by so chaste a writer as Cowper, is an instance of the strange abuses which Poets have introduced into their language till they and their Readers take them as matters of course, if they do not single them out expressly as objects of admiration. The two lines "Ne'er sigh'd at the sound," &c. are, in my opinion, an instance of the language of passion wrested from its proper use, and, from the mere circumstance of the composition being in metre, applied upon an occasion that does not justify such violent expressions, and I should condemn the passage, though perhaps few Readers will agree with me, as vicious poetic diction. The last stanza is throughout admirably expressed: it would be equally good whether in prose or verse, except that the Reader has an exquisite pleasure in seeing such natural language so naturally connected with metre. The beauty of this stanza tempts me here to add

---

[3] Alexander Selkirk (1676–1721), Scottish sailor whose stay on an uninhabited island provided the model for Daniel Defoe's *Robinson Crusoe* (1719). [ED.]

a sentiment which ought to be the pervading spirit of a system, detached parts of which have been imperfectly explained in the Preface, namely, that in proportion as ideas and feelings are valuable, whether the composition be in prose or in verse, they require and exact one and the same language.

FROM *BIOGRAPHIA LITERARIA*

Or Biographical Sketches of My Literary Life and Opinions

Samuel Taylor Coleridge

CHAPTER XIV

Occasion of the Lyrical Ballads, and the objects originally proposed — Preface to the second edition — The ensuing controversy, its causes and acrimony — Philosophic definitions of a poem and poetry with scholia.

During the first year that Mr. Wordsworth and I were neighbours, our conversations turned frequently on the two cardinal points of poetry, the power of exciting the sympathy of the reader by a faithful adherence to the truth of nature, and the power of giving the interest of novelty by the modifying colours of imagination. The sudden charm, which accidents of light and shade, which moon-light or sun-set diffused over a known and familiar landscape, appeared to represent the practicability of combining both. These are the poetry of nature. The thought suggested itself (to which of us I do not recollect) that a series of poems might be composed of two sorts. In the one, the incidents and agents were to be, in part at least, supernatural; and the excellence aimed at was to consist in the interesting of the affections by the dramatic truth of such emotions, as would naturally accompany such situations, supposing them real. And real in *this* sense they have been to every human being who, from whatever source of delusion, has at any time believed himself under supernatural agency. For the second class, subjects were to be chosen from ordinary life; the characters and incidents were to be such, as will be found in every village and its vicinity, where there is a meditative and feeling mind to seek after them, or to notice them, when they present themselves.

In this idea originated the plan of the "Lyrical Ballads"; in which it was agreed, that my endeavours should be directed to persons and characters

---

London: Fenner, 1817.

scholia: explanatory notes.
cardinal: primary.

supernatural, or at least romantic; yet so as to transfer from our inward nature a human interest and a semblance of truth sufficient to procure for these shadows of imagination that willing suspension of disbelief for the moment, which constitutes poetic faith. Mr. Wordsworth, on the other hand, was to propose to himself as his object, to give the charm of novelty to things of every day, and to excite a feeling analogous to the supernatural, by awakening the mind's attention from the lethargy of custom, and directing it to the loveliness and the wonders of the world before us; an inexhaustible treasure, but for which in consequence of the film of familiarity and selfish solicitude we have eyes, yet see not, ears that hear not, and hearts that neither feel nor understand.[1]

With this view I wrote the "Ancient Mariner," and was preparing among other poems, the "Dark Ladie," and the "Christabel," in which I should have more nearly realized my ideal, than I had done in my first attempt. But Mr. Wordsworth's industry had proved so much more successful, and the number of his poems so much greater, that my compositions, instead of forming a balance, appeared rather an interpolation of heterogeneous matter. Mr. Wordsworth added two or three poems written in his own character, in the impassioned, lofty, and sustained diction, which is characteristic of his genius. In this form the "Lyrical Ballads" were published; and were presented by him as an *experiment*, whether subjects, which from their nature rejected the usual ornaments and extra-colloquial style of poems in general, might not be so managed in the language of ordinary life as to produce the pleasurable interest, which it is the peculiar business of poetry to impart. To the second edition he added a preface of considerable length; in which notwithstanding some passages of apparently a contrary import, he was understood to contend for the extension of this style to poetry of all kinds, and to reject as vicious and indefensible all phrases and forms of style that were not included in what he (unfortunately, I think, adopting an equivocal expression) called the language of *real* life.[2] From this preface, prefixed to poems in which it was impossible to deny the presence of original genius, however mistaken its direction might be deemed, arose the whole long continued controversy. For from the conjunction of perceived power with supposed heresy I explain the inveteracy and in some instances,

---

romantic: in the literal sense of the word, like those appearing in a romance or fanciful story.
inveteracy: persistence.

[1] Compare Isaiah 6.9–10. [ED.]
[2] Wordsworth's actual phrasing is "the real language of men." [ED.]

I grieve to say, the acrimonious passions, with which the controversy has been conducted by the assailants.

Had Mr. Wordsworth's poems been the silly, the childish things, which they were for a long time described as being; had they been really distinguished from the compositions of other poets merely by meanness of language and inanity of thought; had they indeed contained nothing more than what is found in the parodies and pretended imitations of them; they must have sunk at once, a dead weight, into the slough of oblivion, and have dragged the preface along with them. But year after year increased the number of Mr. Wordsworth's admirers. They were found too not in the lower classes of the reading public, but chiefly among young men of strong sensibility and meditative minds; and their admiration (inflamed perhaps in some degree by opposition) was distinguished by its intensity, I might almost say, by its *religious* fervour. These facts, and the intellectual energy of the author, which was more or less consciously felt, where it was outwardly and even boisterously denied, meeting with sentiments of aversion to his opinions, and of alarm at their consequences, produced an eddy of criticism, which would of itself have borne up the poems by the violence, with which it whirled them round and round. With many parts of this preface in the sense attributed to them and which the words undoubtedly seem to authorise, I never concurred; but on the contrary objected to them as erroneous in principle, and as contradictory (in appearance at least) both to other parts of the same preface, and to the author's own practice in the greater number of the poems themselves. Mr. Wordsworth in his recent collection has, I find, degraded this prefatory disquisition to the end of his second volume, to be read or not at the reader's choice. But he has not, as far as I can discover, announced any change in his poetic creed. At all events, considering it as the source of a controversy, in which I have been honoured more than I deserve by the frequent conjunction of my name with his, I think it expedient to declare once for all, in what points I coincide with his opinions, and in what points I altogether differ. But in order to render myself intelligible I must previously, in as few words as possible, explain my ideas, first, of a Poem; and secondly, of Poetry itself, in *kind,* and in *essence.*

The office of philosophical *disquisition* consists in just *distinction*; while it is the privilege of the philosopher to preserve himself constantly aware, that distinction is not division. In order to obtain adequate notions of any truth, we must intellectually separate its distinguishable parts; and this is the technical *process* of philosophy. But having so done, we must then restore them in our conceptions to the unity, in which they actually co-exist; and this is the *result* of philosophy. A poem contains the same elements as a prose composition; the difference therefore must consist in a different combination of them, in consequence of a different object proposed. According to the difference of the object will be the difference of the combination. It is possible, that the object may be merely to facilitate the recollection of any given facts or observations by artificial arrangement; and the composition will be a poem, merely because it is distinguished from composition in prose by metre, or by rhyme, or by both conjointly. In this, the lowest sense, a man might attribute the name of a poem to the well-known enumeration of the days in the several months;

> Thirty days hath September,
> April, June, and November, &c.

and others of the same class and purpose. And as a particular pleasure is found in anticipating the recurrence of sounds and quantities, all compositions that have this charm superadded, whatever be their contents, *may* be entitled poems.

So much for the superficial *form.* A difference of object and contents supplies an additional ground of distinction. The immediate purpose may be the communication of truths; either of truth absolute and demonstrable, as in works of science; or of facts experienced and recorded, as in history. Pleasure, and that of the highest and most permanent kind, may *result* from the *attainment* of the end; but it is not itself the immediate end. In other works the communication of pleasure may be the immediate purpose; and though truth, either moral or intellectual, ought to be the *ultimate* end, yet this will distinguish the character of the author, not the class to which the work belongs. Blest indeed is that state of society, in which the immediate purpose would be baffled by the perversion of the proper ultimate end; in which no charm of diction or imagery could exempt the Bathyllus even of an Anacreon, or the Alexis of Virgil, from disgust and aversion![3]

But the communication of pleasure may be the immediate object of a work not metrically composed; and that object may have been in a high degree attained, as in novels and romances. Would then the mere superaddition of metre, with or without rhyme, entitle *these* to the name of poems? The answer is, that nothing can permanently please, which does not contain in itself the reason why it is so, and not otherwise. If metre be superadded, all other parts must be made consonant with it. They must be such, as to justify the perpetual and distinct attention to each part, which an exact correspondent recurrence of accent and sound are calculated to excite.

---

[3] These are both instances of poetry about homosexual desire. The sixth-century B.C. poet Anacreon sings the praises of Bathyllus's youthful beauty; Virgil's "Second Eclogue" tells of the shepherd Corydon's love for Alexis. [ED.]

The final definition then, so deduced, may be thus worded. A poem is that species of composition, which is opposed to works of science, by proposing for its *immediate* object pleasure, not truth; and from all other species (having *this* object in common with it) it is discriminated by proposing to itself such delight from the *whole,* as is compatible with a distinct gratification from each component *part.*

Controversy is not seldom excited in consequence of the disputants attaching each a different meaning to the same word; and in few instances has this been more striking, than in disputes concerning the present subject. If a man chooses to call every composition a poem, which is rhyme, or measure, or both, I must leave his opinion uncontroverted. The distinction is at least competent to characterize the writer's intention. If it were subjoined, that the whole is likewise entertaining or affecting, as a tale, or as a series of interesting reflections, I of course admit this as another fit ingredient of a poem, and an additional merit. But if the definition sought for be that of a *legitimate* poem, I answer, it must be one, the parts of which mutually support and explain each other; all in their proportion harmonizing with, and supporting the purpose and known influences of metrical arrangement. The philosophic critics of all ages coincide with the ultimate judgement of all countries, in equally denying the praises of a just poem, on the one hand, to a series of striking lines or distichs, each of which absorbing the whole attention of the reader to itself disjoins it from its context, and makes it a separate whole, instead of an harmonizing part; and on the other hand, to an unsustained composition, from which the reader collects rapidly the general result unattracted by the component parts. The reader should be carried forward, not merely or chiefly by the mechanical impulse of curiosity, or by a restless desire to arrive at the final solution; but by the pleasurable activity of mind excited by the attractions of the journey itself. Like the motion of a serpent, which the Egyptians made the emblem of intellectual power; or like the path of sound through the air; at every step he pauses and half recedes, and from the retrogressive movement collects the force which again carries him onward. Precipitandus est *liber* spiritus, says Petronius Arbiter most happily. The epithet, *liber,* here balances the preceding verb; and it is not easy to conceive more meaning condensed in fewer words.

But if this should be admitted as a satisfactory character of a poem, we have still to seek for a definition of poetry. The writings of Plato, and Bishop

---

distichs: units of two lines of verse or couplets.
Precipitandus est *liber* spiritus: "The free spirit must be hurried forward" —the quotation appears in the *Satyricon* by the first-century A.D. Roman satirist Petronius Arbiter.

Taylor,[4] and the Theoria Sacra of Burnet,[5] furnish undeniable proofs that poetry of the highest kind may exist without metre, and even without the contra-distinguishing objects of a poem. The first chapter of Isaiah (indeed a very large proportion of the whole book) is poetry in the most emphatic sense; yet it would be not less irrational than strange to assert, that pleasure, and not truth, was the immediate object of the prophet. In short, whatever *specific* import we attach to the word, poetry, there, will be found involved in it, as a necessary consequence, that a poem of any length neither can be, or ought to be, all poetry. Yet if an harmonious whole is to be produced, the remaining parts must be preserved *in keeping* with the poetry; and this can be no otherwise effected than by such a studied selection and artificial arrangement, as will partake of *one,* though not a *peculiar,* property of poetry. And this again can be no other than the property of exciting a more continuous and equal attention, than the language of prose aims at, whether colloquial or written.

My own conclusions on the nature of poetry, in the strictest use of the word, have been in part anticipated in the preceding disquisition on the fancy and imagination.[6] What is poetry? is so nearly the same question with, what is a poem? that the answer to the one is involved in the solution of the other. For it is a distinction resulting from the poetic genius itself, which sustains and modifies the images, thoughts, and emotions of the poet's own mind. A poet, described in *ideal* perfection, brings the whole soul of man into activity, with the subordination of its faculties to each other, according to their relative worth and dignity. He diffuses a tone, and spirit of unity,

---

[4] Jeremy Taylor (1613–67), author of *The Rule and Exercises of Holy Living* (1650) and *The Rule and Exercises of Holy Dying* (1651). [ED.]

[5] Thomas Burnet (1635?–1715), author of *The Sacred Theory of the Earth* and of *Archaeologiae Philosophicae,* from which Coleridge takes the epigraph to the 1817 version of "The Rime of the Ancient Mariner." [ED.]

[6] In chapter 13, Coleridge writes:

> The Imagination then I consider either as primary, or secondary. The primary Imagination I hold to be the living Power and prime Agent of all human Perception, and as a repetition in the finite mind of the eternal act of creation in the infinite I Am. The secondary I consider as an echo of the former, co-existing with the conscious will, yet still as identical with the primary in the *kind* of its agency, and differing only in *degree,* and in the *mode* of its operation. It dissolves, diffuses, dissipates, in order to re-create; or where this process is rendered impossible, yet still at all events it struggles to idealize and to unify. It is essentially *vital,* even as all objects (*as* objects) are essentially fixed and dead.
>
> Fancy, on the contrary, has no other counters to play with, but fixities and definites. The Fancy is indeed no other than a mode of Memory emancipated from the order of time and space; and blended with, and modified by that empirical phenomenon of the will, which we express by the word Choice. But equally with the ordinary memory it must receive all its materials ready made from the law of association. [ED.]

that blends, and (as it were) *fuses,* each into each, by that synthetic and magical power, to which we have exclusively appropriated the name of imagination. This power, first put in action by the will and understanding, and retained under their irremissive, though gentle and unnoticed, control (*laxis effertur habenis*) reveals itself in the balance or reconciliation of opposite or discordant qualities: of sameness, with difference; of the general, with the concrete; the idea, with the image; the individual, with the representative; the sense of novelty and freshness, with old and familiar objects; a more than usual state of emotion, with more than usual order; judgement ever awake and steady self-possession, with enthusiasm and feeling profound or vehement; and while it blends and harmonizes the natural and the artificial, still subordinates art to nature; the manner to the matter; and our admiration of the poet to our sympathy with the poetry. "Doubtless," as Sir John Davies observes of the soul (and his words may with slight alteration be applied, and even more appropriately to the poetic Imagination):

> Doubtless this could not be, but that she turns
> Bodies to spirit by sublimation strange,
> As fire converts to fire the things it burns,
> As we our food into our nature change.
>
> From their gross matter she abstracts their forms,
> And draws a kind of quintessence from things;
> Which to her proper nature she transforms
> To bear them light, on her celestial wings.
>
> Thus does she, when from individual states
> She doth abstract the universal kinds;
> Which then re-clothed in divers names and fates
> Steal access through our senses to our minds.[7]

Finally, good sense is the body of poetic genius, fancy its drapery, motion its life, and imagination the soul that is every where, and in each; and forms all into one graceful and intelligent whole.

---

laxis effertur habenis: "borne forward with loose reins."

[7] Adapted from John Davies's poem *Nosce Teipsum* (1599). [ED.]

THE RIME OF THE ANCIENT MARINER

In Seven Parts

Samuel Taylor Coleridge

> *Facile credo, plures esse Naturas invisibiles quam visi-*
> *biles in rerum universitate. Sed horum omnium famil-*
> *iam quis nobis enarrabit? et gradus et cognationes et*
> *discrimina et singulorum munera? Quid agunt? quae*
> *loca habitant? Harum rerum notitiam semper ambivit*
> *ingenium humanum, nunquam attigit. Juvat, interea,*
> *non diffiteor, quandoque in animo, tanquam in Tab-*
> *ulâ, majoris et melioris mundi imaginem contemplari:*
> *ne mens assuefecta hodierniae vitae minutiis se contra-*
> *hat nimis, & tota subsidat in pusillas cogitationes. Sed*
> *veritati interea invigilandum est, modusque servan-*
> *dus, ut certa ab incertis, diem a nocte, distinguamus.*
>
> T. *Burnet:* Archaeol. Phil. *p. 68.*[1]

PART THE FIRST

It is an ancient Mariner,
And he stoppeth one of three.
"By thy long grey beard and glittering eye,
"Now wherefore stopp'st thou me?

5   "The Bridegroom's doors are open'd wide,
"And I am next of kin;

*An ancient Mariner
meeteth three
Gallants bidden to
a wedding-feast,
and detaineth one.*

From *Sibylline Leaves: A Collection of Poems.* London: Fenner, 1817.

[1] Thomas Burnet (1635?–1715), Anglican divine, author of *Archaeologiae Philosophicae* (1692). The epigraph from Burnet may be translated as follows: "I find it easy to believe that there are more invisible Natures than visible ones in the universe. But who can say to what family each belongs, what their ranks, relationships, characteristics, and functions are? What do they do? Where do they live? The human mind has always searched for this knowledge but has yet to find it. I do admit, however, that it is good for the human mind to contemplate, as on a tablet, an image of a greater and better world; otherwise the mind becomes too focused on the trivial details of life. At the same time, we must keep searching for truth but with a sense of proportion to enable us to distinguish the certain from the uncertain, day from night." [ED.]

"The guests are met, the feast is set:
May'st hear the merry din."

He holds him with his skinny hand,
10 "There was a ship," quoth he.
"Hold off! unhand me, grey-beard loon!"
Eftsoons his hand dropt he.

The wedding-guest is spellbound by the eye of the old sea-faring man, and constrained to hear his tale.

He holds him with his glittering eye —
The Wedding-Guest stood still,
15 And listens like a three years child:
The Mariner hath his will.

The Wedding-Guest sat on a stone:
He cannot chuse but hear;
And thus spake on that ancient man,
20 The bright-eyed Mariner.

The ship was cheer'd, the harbour clear'd,
Merrily did we drop
Below the kirk, below the hill,
Below the light-house top.

The Mariner tells how the ship sailed southward with a good wind and fair weather, till it reached the line.

25 The Sun came up upon the left,
Out of the sea came he;
And he shone bright, and on the right
Went down into the sea.

Higher and higher every day,
30 Till over the mast at noon —
The Wedding-Guest here beat his breast,
For he heard the loud bassoon.

The wedding-guest heareth the bridal music; but the mariner continueth his tale.

The bride hath paced into the hall,
Red as a rose is she;
35 Nodding their heads before her goes
The merry minstrelsy.

The Wedding-Guest he beat his breast,
Yet he cannot chuse but hear;
And thus spake on that ancient man,
40 The bright-eyed Mariner.

The ship drawn by a storm toward the south pole.

And now the Storm-Blast came, and he
Was tyrannous and strong:

Eftsoons: at once.

He struck with his o'ertaking wings,
And chased south along.

45 With sloping masts and dipping prow,
As who pursued with yell and blow
Still treads the shadow of his foe
And forward bends his head,
The ship drove fast, loud roar'd the blast,
50 And southward aye we fled.

And now there came both mist and snow,
And it grew wonderous cold:
And ice, mast-high, came floating by,
As green as emerald.

55 And through the drifts the snowy clift
Did send a dismal sheen:
Nor shapes of men nor beasts we ken—
The ice was all between.

The land of ice, and
of fearful sounds,
where no living
thing was to be seen.

The ice was here, the ice was there,
60 The ice was all around:
It crack'd and growl'd, and roar'd and howl'd,
Like noises in a swound!

At length did cross an Albatross:
Thorough the fog it came;
65 As if it had been a Christian soul,
We hailed it in God's name.

Till a great sea-bird,
called the Albatross,
came through the
snow-fog, and was
received with great
joy and hospitality.

It ate the food it ne'er had eat,
And round and round it flew.
The ice did split with a thunder-fit;
70 The helmsman steer'd us through!

And a good south wind sprung up behind;
The Albatross did follow,
And every day, for food or play,
Came to the Mariner's hollo! [2]

And lo! the Albatross
proveth a bird of
good omen, and fol-
loweth the ship as it
returned northward,
through fog and
floating ice.

---

[2] Some editors emend the phrase "Mariner's hollo" to make it plural possessive, "Mariners' hollo"; the printed text of 1817 is singular as reprinted here. [ED.]

75 In mist or cloud, on mast or shroud,
It perch'd for vespers nine;
Whiles all the night, through fog-smoke white,
Glimmered the white Moon-shine.

The ancient Mariner inhospitably killeth the pious bird of good omen.

"God save thee, ancient Mariner!
80 From the fiends, that plague thee thus! —
Why look'st thou so?" — With my cross-bow
I shot the Albatross!

PART THE SECOND

The Sun now rose upon the right:
Out of the sea came he,
85 Still hid in mist, and on the left
Went down into the sea.

And the good south wind still blew behind,
But no sweet bird did follow,
Nor any day for food or play
90 Came to the mariners' hollo! [3]

His shipmates cry out against the ancient Mariner, for killing the bird of good luck.

And I had done an hellish thing,
And it would work 'em woe:
For all averred, I had killed the bird
That made the breeze to blow.
95 Ah wretch! said they, the bird to slay
That made the breeze to blow!

But when the fog cleared off, they justify the same, and thus make themselves accomplices in the crime.

Nor dim nor red, like God's own head,
The glorious Sun uprist:
Then all averred, I had killed the bird
100 That brought the fog and mist.
'Twas right, said they, such birds to slay,
That bring the fog and mist.

The fair breeze continues; the ship enters the Pacific Ocean and sails northward, even till it reaches the Line.

The fair breeze blew, the white foam flew,
The furrow [4] stream'd off free:
105 We were the first that ever burst
Into that silent sea.

---

[3] The 1817 text is plural here. [Ed.]
[4] "In the former edition the line was,

"The furrow follow'd free;

Down dropt the breeze, the sails dropt down,
'Twas sad as sad could be;
And we did speak only to break
110 The silence of the sea!

All in a hot and copper sky,
The bloody Sun, at noon,
Right up above the mast did stand,
No bigger than the Moon.

115 Day after day, day after day,
We stuck, nor breath nor motion;
As idle as a painted ship
Upon a painted ocean.

Water, water, every where,
120 And all the boards did shrink;
Water, water, every where,
Nor any drop to drink.

The very deep did rot: O Christ!
That ever this should be!
125 Yea, slimy things did crawl with legs
Upon the slimy sea.

About, about, in reel and rout
The death-fires danced at night;
The water, like a witch's oils,
130 Burnt green, and blue and white.

And some in dreams assured were
Of the spirit that plagued us so:
Nine fathom deep he had followed us
From the land of mist and snow.

135 And every tongue, through utter drought,
Was withered at the root;
We could not speak, no more than if
We had been choked with soot.

A spirit had followed
them; one of the in-
visible inhabitants
of this planet, neither
departed souls nor
angels; concerning
whom the learned
Jew, Josephus, and
the Platonic Con-
stantinopolitan,
Michael Psellus, may
be consulted. They
are very numerous,
and there is no cli-
mate or element
without one or more.

"but I had not been long on board a ship, before I perceived that
this was the image as seen by a spectator from the shore, or
from another vessel. From the ship itself the *Wake* appears like
a brook flowing off from the stern." [Coleridge's note.]

The shipmates, in their sore distress, would fain throw the whole guilt on the ancient Mariner: in sign whereof they hang the dead sea-bird round his neck.

Ah! well a-day! what evil looks
140 Had I from old and young!
Instead of the cross, the Albatross
About my neck was hung.

PART THE THIRD

There passed a weary time. Each throat
Was parched, and glazed each eye.
145 A weary time! a weary time!
How glazed each weary eye,
When looking westward, I beheld
A something in the sky.

The ancient Mariner beholdeth a sign in the element afar off.

At first it seem'd a little speck,
150 And then it seem'd a mist:
It moved and moved, and took at last
A certain shape, I wist.

A speck, a mist, a shape, I wist!
And still it near'd and near'd:
155 As if it dodged a water-sprite,
It plunged and tack'd and veer'd.

At its nearer approach, it seemeth him to be a ship; and at a dear ransom he freeth his speech from the bonds of thirst.

With throat unslack'd, with black lips baked,
We could not laugh nor wail;
Through utter drought all dumb we stood!
160 I bit my arm, I sucked the blood,
And cried, A sail! a sail!

A flash of joy.

With throats unslack'd, with black lips baked,
Agape they heard me call:
Gramercy! they for joy did grin,
165 And all at once their breath drew in,
As they were drinking all.

And horror follows. For can it be a *ship* that comes onward without wind or tide?

See! see! (I cried) she tacks no more!
Hither to work us weal;
Without a breeze, without a tide,
170 She steddies with upright keel!

The western wave was all a-flame.
The day was well nigh done!
Almost upon the western wave
Rested the broad bright Sun;

₁₇₅ When that strange shape drove suddenly
Betwixt us and the Sun.

And straight the Sun was flecked with bars,
(Heaven's Mother send us grace!)
As if through a dungeon-grate he peer'd,
₁₈₀ With broad and burning face.

It seemeth him but the skeleton of a ship.

Alas! (thought I, and my heart beat loud)
How fast she nears and nears!
Are those *her* sails that glance in the Sun,
Like restless gossameres!

₁₈₅ Are those *her* ribs through which the Sun
Did peer, as through a grate?
And is that Woman all her crew?
Is that a Death? and are there two?
Is Death that woman's mate?

And its ribs are seen as bars on the face of the setting Sun. The spectre-woman and her death-mate, and no other on board the skeleton-ship.

₁₉₀ *Her* lips were red, *her* looks were free,
Her locks were yellow as gold:
Her skin was as white as leprosy,
The Night-Mair Life-in-Death was she,
Who thicks man's blood with cold.

Like vessel, like crew!

₁₉₅ The naked hulk alongside came,
And the twain were casting dice;
"The game is done! I've won! I've won!"
Quoth she, and whistles thrice.

Death, and Life-in-Death have diced for the ship's crew, and she (the latter) winneth the ancient Mariner.

A gust of wind sterte up behind
₂₀₀ And whistled through his bones;
Through the holes of his eyes and the hold of his mouth,
Half whistles and half groans.[5]

The Sun's rim dips; the stars rush out:
At one stride comes the dark;
₂₀₅ With far-heard whisper, o'er the sea,
Off shot the spectre-bark.

We listen'd and look'd sideways up!
Fear at my heart, as at a cup,

[5]The errata page for the 1817 volume indicates that this stanza was meant to be canceled. Since it appears to represent a reaction by Death to his mate's winning, we reprint the stanza as it appeared in the original as a textual curiosity. [ED.]

My life-blood seem'd to sip!
210 The stars were dim, and thick the night,
The steersman's face by his lamp gleam'd white;
From the sails the dew did drip—

At the rising of the Moon,

Till clombe above the eastern bar
The horned Moon, with one bright star
215 Within the nether tip.

One after another,

One after one, by the star-dogged Moon
Too quick for groan or sigh,
Each turn'd his face with a ghastly pang,
And curs'd me with his eye.

His shipmates drop down dead;

220 Four times fifty living men,
    (And I heard nor sigh nor groan)
With heavy thump, a lifeless lump,
They dropped down one by one.

But Life-in-Death begins her work on the ancient Mariner.

The souls did from their bodies fly,—
225 They fled to bliss or woe!
And every soul, it passed me by,
Like the whiz of my Cross-Bow!

PART THE FOURTH

The wedding-guest feareth that a spirit is talking to him;

"I fear thee, ancient Mariner!
I fear thy skinny hand!
230 And thou art long, and lank, and brown,
As is the ribbed sea-sand.[6]

"I fear thee and thy glittering eye,
And thy skinny hand, so brown."—

But the ancient Mariner assureth him of his bodily life, and proceedeth to relate his horrible penance.

Fear not, fear not, thou Wedding-Guest!
235 This body dropt not down.

Alone, alone, all, all alone,
Alone on a wide wide sea!
And never a saint took pity on
My soul in agony.

---

[6]"For the two last lines of this stanza, I am indebted to Mr. Wordsworth. It was on a delightful walk from Nether Stowey to Dulverton, with him and his sister, in the Autumn of 1797, that this Poem was planned, and in part composed." [Coleridge's note.]

240 The many men, so beautiful!
And they all dead did lie:
And a thousand thousand slimy things
Lived on; and so did I.

He despiseth the
creatures of the calm,

I look'd upon the rotting sea,
245 And drew my eyes away;
I look'd upon the rotting deck,
And there the dead men lay.

And envieth that
they should live, and
so many lie dead.

I look'd to Heaven, and tried to pray:
But or ever a prayer had gusht,
250 A wicked whisper came, and made
My heart as dry as dust.

I closed my lids, and kept them close,
And the balls like pulses beat;
For the sky and the sea, and the sea and the sky
255 Lay, like a load, on my weary eye,
And the dead were at my feet.

The cold sweat melted from their limbs,
Nor rot nor reek did they:
The look with which they look'd on me
260 Had never pass'd away.

But the curse liveth
for him in the eye of
the dead men.

An orphan's curse would drag to Hell
A spirit from on high;
But oh! more horrible than that
Is a curse in a dead man's eye!
265 Seven days, seven nights, I saw that curse,
And yet I could not die.

The moving Moon went up the sky,
And no where did abide:
Softly she was going up,
270 And a star or two beside.

In his loneliness and
fixedness, he yearn-
eth towards the jour-
neying Moon, and
the stars that still so-
journ, yet still move
onward; and every
where the blue sky
belongs to them, and
is their appointed
rest, and their native
country, and their
own natural homes,
which they enter

unannounced, as lords that are certainly expected, and yet there is a silent joy at their arrival.	Her beams bemock'd the sultry main, Like April hoar-frost spread; But where the ship's huge shadow lay, The charmed water burnt alway 275 A still and awful red.
By the light of the Moon he beholdeth God's creatures of the great calm.	Beyond the shadow of the ship, I watch'd the water-snakes: They moved in tracks of shining white, And when they reared, the elfish light 280 Fell off in hoary flakes.
	Within the shadow of the ship I watch'd their rich attire: Blue, glossy green, and velvet black, They coiled and swam; and every track 285 Was a flash of golden fire.
Their beauty and their happiness.	O happy living things! no tongue Their beauty might declare: A spring of love gusht from my heart,
He blesseth them in his heart.	And I blessed them unaware! 290 Sure my kind saint took pity on me, And I blessed them unaware.
The spell begins to break.	The self same moment I could pray; And from my neck so free The Albatross fell off, and sank 295 Like lead into the sea.

PART THE FIFTH

Oh Sleep! it is a gentle thing,
Belov'd from pole to pole!
To Mary Queen the praise be given!
She sent the gentle sleep from Heaven,
300 That slid into my soul.

By the grace of the holy Mother, the ancient Mariner is refreshed with rain.	The silly buckets on the deck, That had so long remained, I dreamt that they were filled with dew; And when I awoke, it rained.

305 My lips were wet, my throat was cold,
My garments all were dank;
Sure I had drunken in my dreams,
And still my body drank.

I moved, and could not feel my limbs:
310 I was so light—almost
I thought that I had died in sleep,
And was a blessed ghost.

And soon I heard a roaring wind:
It did not come anear;
315 But with its sound it shook the sails,
That were so thin and sere.

The upper air burst into life!
And a hundred fire-flags sheen,
To and fro they were hurried about;
320 And to and fro, and in and out,
The wan stars danced between.

And the coming wind did roar more loud,
And the sails did sigh like sedge;
And the rain poured down from one black cloud;
325 The Moon was at its edge.

The thick black cloud was cleft, and still
The Moon was at its side:
Like waters shot from some high crag,
The lightning fell with never a jag,
330 A river steep and wide.

The loud wind never reached the ship,
Yet now the ship moved on!
Beneath the lightning and the Moon
The dead men gave a groan.

335 They groan'd, they stirr'd, they all uprose,
Nor spake, nor moved their eyes;
It had been strange, even in a dream,
To have seen those dead men rise.

The helmsman steered, the ship moved on;
340 Yet never a breeze up blew;
The mariners all 'gan work the ropes,
Where they were wont to do:

He heareth sounds, and seeth strange sights and commotions in the sky and the element.

The bodies of the ship's crew are inspirited, and the ship moves on;

They raised their limbs like lifeless tools —
We were a ghastly crew.

345 The body of my brother's son,
Stood by me, knee to knee:
The body and I pulled at one rope,
But he said nought to me.

But not by the souls of the men, nor by daemons of earth or middle air, but by a blessed troop of angelic spirits, sent down by the invocation of the guardian saint.

"I fear thee, ancient Mariner!"
350 Be calm, thou Wedding-Guest!
'Twas not those souls that fled in pain,
Which to their corses came again,
But a troop of spirits blest:

For when it dawned — they dropped their arms,
355 And clustered round the mast;
Sweet sounds rose slowly through their mouths,
And from their bodies passed.

Around, around, flew each sweet sound,
Then darted to the Sun;
360 Slowly the sounds came back again,
Now mixed, now one by one.

Sometimes a-dropping from the sky
I heard the sky-lark sing;
Sometimes all little birds that are,
365 How they seem'd to fill the sea and air
With their sweet jargoning!

And now 'twas like all instruments,
Now like a lonely flute;
And now it is an angel's song,
370 That makes the Heavens be mute.

It ceased; yet still the sails made on
A pleasant noise till noon,
A noise like of a hidden brook
In the leafy month of June,
375 That to the sleeping woods all night
Singeth a quiet tune.

Till noon we quietly sailed on,
Yet never a breeze did breathe:
Slowly and smoothly went the ship,
380 Moved onward from beneath.

Under the keel nine fathom deep,
From the land of mist and snow,
The spirit slid: and it was he
That made the ship to go.
385 The sails at noon left off their tune,
And the ship stood still also.

The Sun, right up above the mast,
Had fixt her to the ocean;
But in a minute she 'gan stir,
390 With a short uneasy motion —
Backwards and forwards half her length
With a short uneasy motion.

Then like a pawing horse let go,
She made a sudden bound:
395 It flung the blood into my head,
And I fell down in a swound.

How long in that same fit I lay,
I have not to declare;
But ere my living life returned,
400 I heard and in my soul discerned
Two Voices in the air.

"Is it he?" quoth one, "Is this the man?
By him who died on cross,
With his cruel bow he laid full low,
405 The harmless Albatross.

"The spirit who bideth by himself
In the land of mist and snow,
He loved the bird that loved the man
Who shot him with his bow."

410 The other was a softer voice,
As soft as honey-dew:
Quoth he, "The man hath penance done,
And penance more will do."

The lonesome spirit from the south-pole carries on the ship as far as the line, in obedience to the angelic troop, but still requireth vengeance.

The Polar Spirit's fellow daemons, the invisible inhabitants of the element, take part in his wrong; and two of them relate, one to the other, that penance long and heavy for the ancient Mariner hath been accorded to the Polar Spirit, who returneth southward.

PART THE SIXTH

FIRST VOICE
But tell me, tell me! speak again,
415 Thy soft response renewing —

What makes that ship drive on so fast?
What is the Ocean doing?

SECOND VOICE
Still as a slave before his lord,
The Ocean hath no blast;
420 His great bright eye most silently
Up to the Moon is cast—

If he may know which way to go;
For she guides him smooth or grim.
See, brother, see! how graciously
425 She looketh down on him.

The Mariner hath been cast into a trance; for the angelic power causeth the vessel to drive northward, faster than human life could endure.

FIRST VOICE
But why drives on that ship so fast,
Without or wave or wind?

SECOND VOICE
The air is cut away before,
And closes from behind.

430 Fly, brother, fly! more high, more high!
Or we shall be belated:
For slow and slow that ship will go,
When the Mariner's trance is abated.

The supernatural motion is retarded; the Mariner awakes, and his penance begins anew.

I woke, and we were sailing on
435 As in a gentle weather:
'Twas night, calm night, the Moon was high;
The dead men stood together.

All stood together on the deck,
For a charnel-dungeon fitter:
440 All fixed on me their stony eyes,
That in the Moon did glitter.

The pang, the curse, with which they died,
Had never passed away:
I could not draw my eyes from theirs,
445 Nor turn them up to pray.

The curse is finally expiated.

And now this spell was snapt: once more
I viewed the ocean green.

And looked far forth, yet little saw
Of what had else been seen—

450 Like one, that on a lonesome road
Doth walk in fear and dread,
And having once turn'd round, walks on,
And turns no more his head;
Because he knows, a frightful fiend
455 Doth close behind him tread.

But soon there breathed a wind on me,
Nor sound nor motion made:
Its path was not upon the sea,
In ripple or in shade.

460 It raised my hair, it fanned my cheek
Like a meadow-gale of spring—
It mingled strangely with my fears,
Yet it felt like a welcoming.

Swiftly, swiftly flew the ship,
465 Yet she sailed softly too:
Sweetly, sweetly blew the breeze—
On me alone it blew.

Oh! dream of joy! is this indeed
The light-house top I see?
470 Is this the hill? is this the kirk?
Is this mine own countree?

And the ancient
Mariner beholdeth
his native country.

We drifted o'er the harbour-bar,
And I with sobs did pray—
O let me be awake, my God!
475 Or let me sleep alway.

The harbour-bay was clear as glass,
So smoothly it was strewn!
And on the bay the moonlight lay,
And the shadow of the moon.

480 The rock shone bright, the kirk no less,
That stands above the rock:
The moonlight steeped in silentness
The steady weathercock.

The angelic spirits
leave the dead
bodies,

And the bay was white with silent light,
485 Till rising from the same,
Full many shapes, that shadows were,
In crimson colours came.

And appear in their
own forms of light.

A little distance from the prow
Those crimson shadows were:
490 I turned my eyes upon the deck—
Oh, Christ! what saw I there!

Each corse lay flat, lifeless and flat,
And, by the holy rood!
A man all light, a seraph-man,
495 On every corse there stood.

This seraph-band, each waved his hand:
It was a heavenly sight!
They stood as signals to the land,
Each one a lovely light:

500 This seraph-band, each waved his hand,
No voice did they impart—
No voice; but oh! the silence sank
Like music on my heart.

But soon I heard the dash of oars;
505 I heard the Pilot's cheer;
My head was turn'd perforce away,
And I saw a boat appear.

The Pilot, and the Pilot's boy,
I heard them coming fast:
510 Dear Lord in Heaven! it was a joy
The dead men could not blast.

I saw a third—I heard his voice:
It is the Hermit good!
He singeth loud his godly hymns
515 That he makes in the wood.
He'll shrieve my soul, he'll wash away
The Albatross's blood.

PART THE SEVENTH

This Hermit good lives in that wood
Which slopes down to the sea.
520 How loudly his sweet voice he rears!
He loves to talk with marineres
That come from a far countree.

He kneels at morn and noon and eve —
He hath a cushion plump:
525 It is the moss that wholly hides
The rotted old oak-stump.

The Skiff-boat near'd: I heard them talk,
"Why this is strange, I trow!
Where are those lights so many and fair,
530 That signal made but now?"

"Strange, by my faith!" the Hermit said —
"And they answered not our cheer!
The planks looked warped! and see those sails,
How thin they are and sere!
535 I never saw aught like to them,
Unless perchance it were

"Brown skeletons of leaves that lag
My forest-brook along;
When the ivy-tod is heavy with snow,
540 And the owlet whoops to the wolf below,
That eats the she-wolf's young."

"Dear Lord! it hath a fiendish look —
(The Pilot made reply)
I am a-feared" — "Push on, push on!"
545 Said the Hermit cheerily.

The boat came closer to the ship,
But I nor spake nor stirred;
The boat came close beneath the ship,
And straight a sound was heard.

550 Under the water it rumbled on,
Still louder and more dread:
It reach'd the ship, it split the bay;
The ship went down like lead.

The Hermit of the Wood,

Approacheth the ship with wonder.

The ship suddenly sinketh.

The ancient Mariner
is saved in the Pilot's
boat.

Stunned by that loud and dreadful sound,
555 Which sky and ocean smote,
Like one that hath been seven days drown'd
My body lay afloat;
But swift as dreams, myself I found
Within the Pilot's boat.

560 Upon the whirl, where sank the ship,
The boat spun round and round;
And all was still, save that the hill
Was telling of the sound.

I moved my lips—the Pilot shrieked
565 And fell down in a fit;
The holy Hermit raised his eyes,
And prayed where he did sit.

I took the oars: the Pilot's boy,
Who now doth crazy go,
570 Laughed loud and long, and all the while
His eyes went to and fro.
"Ha! ha!" quoth he, "full plain I see,
The Devil knows how to row."

And now, all in my own countree,
575 I stood on the firm land!
The Hermit stepped forth from the boat,
And scarcely he could stand.

The ancient Mariner
earnestly entreateth
the Hermit to
shrieve him; and
the penance of life
falls on him.

"O shrieve me, shrieve me, holy man!"
The Hermit crossed his brow.
580 "Say quick," quoth he, "I bid thee say—
What manner of man art thou?"

Forthwith this frame of mine was wrench'd
With a woeful agony,
Which forced me to begin my tale;
585 And then it left me free.

And ever and anon
throughout his
future life an agony
constraineth him to
travel from land
to land,

Since then, at an uncertain hour,
That agony returns;
And till my ghastly tale is told,
This heart within me burns.

590 I pass, like night, from land to land;
I have strange power of speech;

That moment that his face I see,
I know the man that must hear me:
To him my tale I teach.

595 What loud uproar bursts from that door!
The wedding-guests are there:
But in the garden-bower the bride
And bride-maids singing are:
And hark the little vesper bell,
600 Which biddeth me to prayer!

O Wedding-Guest! this soul hath been
Alone on a wide wide sea:
So lonely 'twas, that God himself
Scarce seemed there to be.

605 O sweeter than the marriage-feast,
'Tis sweeter far to me,
To walk together to the kirk
With a goodly company! —

To walk together to the kirk,
610 And all together pray,
While each to his great Father bends,
Old men, and babes, and loving friends,
And youths and maidens gay!

Farewell, farewell! but this I tell
615 To thee, thou Wedding-Guest!
He prayeth well, who loveth well
Both man and bird and beast.

And to teach by his
own example, love
and reverence to all
things that God
made and loveth.

He prayeth best, who loveth best
All things both great and small;
620 For the dear God who loveth us
He made and loveth all.

The Mariner, whose eye is bright,
Whose beard with age is hoar,
Is gone; and now the Wedding-Guest
625 Turned from the bridegroom's door.

He went like one that hath been stunned,
And is of sense forlorn:
A sadder and a wiser man,
He rose the morrow morn.

SIMON LEE

The Old Huntsman
With an Incident
in Which He Was Concerned[1]

William Wordsworth

In the sweet shire of Cardigan,
Not far from pleasant Ivor-hall,
An Old Man dwells, a little man,
'Tis said he once was tall.
5   Full five-and-thirty years he lived
A running Huntsman merry;
And still the centre of his cheek
Is blooming as a cherry.

No man like him the horn could sound,
10   And hill and valley rang with glee
When Echo bandied, round and round,
The halloo of Simon Lee.
In those proud days, he little cared
For husbandry or tillage;
15   To blither tasks did Simon rouse
The sleepers of the village.

He all the country could outrun,
Could leave both man and horse behind;
And often, ere the chase was done,
20   He reeled and was stone-blind.
And still there's something in the world
At which his heart rejoices;
For when the chiming hounds are out,
He dearly loves their voices!

25   But, oh the heavy change![2]—bereft
Of health, strength, friends, and kindred, see!
Old Simon to the world is left
In liveried poverty.

The Poetical Works of William Wordsworth. Vol. 3. London: Longman, 1832.

[1]"Simon Lee" appeared in later editions of Wordsworth's poems as part of a series entitled *Poems of Sentiment and Reflection.* [ED.]
[2]From Milton, "Lycidas" line 37. [ED.]

His Master's dead, — and no one now
30   Dwells in the Hall of Ivor;
Men, dogs, and horses, all are dead;
He is the sole survivor.

And he is lean and he is sick;
His body, dwindled and awry,
35   Rests upon ankles swoln and thick;
His legs are thin and dry.
One prop he has, and only one,
His Wife, an aged woman,
Lives with him, near the waterfall,
40   Upon the village Common.

Beside their moss-grown hut of clay,
Not twenty paces from the door,
A scrap of land they have, but they
Are poorest of the poor.
45   This scrap of land he from the heath
Enclosed when he was stronger;
But what avails it now, the land
Which he can till no longer?

Oft, working by her Husband's side,
50   Ruth does what Simon cannot do;
For she, with scanty cause for pride,
Is stouter of the two.
And, though you with your utmost skill
From labour could not wean them,
55   Alas! 'tis very little — all
Which they can do between them.

Few months of life has he in store
As he to you will tell,
For still, the more he works, the more
60   Do his weak ancles swell.
My gentle Reader, I perceive
How patiently you've waited,
And now I fear that you expect
Some tale will be related.

65   O Reader! had you in your mind
Such stores as silent thought can bring,
O gentle Reader! you would find
A tale in every thing.

What more I have to say is short,
70 And you must kindly take it:
It is no tale; but, should you *think*,
Perhaps a tale you'll make it.

One summer-day I chanced to see
This Old Man doing all he could
75 To unearth the root of an old tree,
A stump of rotten wood.
The mattock tottered in his hand;
So vain was his endeavour,
That at the root of the old tree
80 He might have worked for ever.

"You're overtasked, good Simon Lee,
Give me your tool," to him I said;
And at the word right gladly he
Received my proffered aid.
85 I struck, and with a single blow
The tangled root I severed,
At which the poor Old Man so long
And vainly had endeavoured.

The tears into his eyes were brought,
90 And thanks and praises seemed to run
So fast out of his heart, I thought
They never would have done.
—I've heard of hearts unkind, kind deeds
With coldness still returning;
95 Alas! the gratitude of men
Hath oftener left me mourning.

WORDSWORTH AND COLERIDGE:
CHRONOLOGY

1770   William Wordsworth is born (April 7), Cockermouth, Cumberland, second son of John and Anne Wordsworth.

1771   Dorothy Wordsworth is born (December 25), Cockermouth, Cumberland, only daughter of John and Anne Wordsworth.

1772   Samuel Taylor Coleridge is born (October 21), Ottery St. Mary, Devonshire, youngest son of the Rev. John and Anne Coleridge.

1778   Wordsworth attends Hawkshead Grammar School in Lancashire (until 1787); Dorothy Wordsworth is sent to live in Halifax with grandparents.

1782   Gilbert Poor Law reform bill is enacted; Coleridge attends Christ's Hospital in London (until 1791) and studies Greek and Latin.

1783   William Pitt is named Prime Minister.

1784   Charlotte Smith's *Elegiac Sonnets* is published.

1787   Wordsworth enters St. John's College, Cambridge (until 1791) and publishes his first poem, "Sonnet on Seeing Miss Helen Maria Williams Weep at a Tale of Distress."

1789   Wordsworth vacations with Dorothy Wordsworth and Mary Hutchinson at Penrith; with the fall of the Bastille, the French Revolution begins (July 14); Coleridge reads sonnets of William Lisle Bowles and decides to become a poet.

1790   Wordsworth visits France, Switzerland, and Italy; Jacobins come to power in France; Louis XVI accepts new constitution; French royal family is arrested while attempting to flee the country; Edmund Burke's *Reflections on the Revolution in France* and Mary Wollstonecraft's *A Vindication of the Rights of Men* are published.

1791   Wordsworth takes a bachelor's degree without distinction and returns to France in November; Coleridge enters Jesus College, Cambridge, on a scholarship (until 1793).

1792   Wordsworth meets Annette Vallon in Orléans, France; September Massacres occur in France; French monarchy is abolished; Wordsworth returns to England in October; Louis XVI is condemned to death for treason; Wordsworth and Annette Vallon's daughter, Anne-Caroline, is born in December; Wordsworth returns to England.

1793   Louis XVI is executed on January 23; France declares war on Great Britain, Holland, and Spain; Wordsworth visits Tintern Abbey in Wales; Wordsworth visits radicals in London; William Godwin's *Political Justice* is published; Coleridge enlists in the King's Light Dragoons as "Silas Tomkyn Comberbache."

1794   Wordsworth and Dorothy Wordsworth visit the Lake District together; Coleridge is discharged from the army and becomes friends with Robert Southey; Coleridge and Southey plan "Pantisocracy"; Coleridge returns to Cambridge but leaves without a degree.

1795   Speenhamland system of poor relief adopted in some Southern and Midlands counties; Wordsworth inherits £900; he and Dorothy Wordsworth settle at Racedown in Dorset, with Basil Montagu, Jr., as his ward; Coleridge lives with Southey in Bristol; Wordsworth and Coleridge meet; Coleridge marries Sara Fricker (October 4) and settles with her in Clevedon and then in Bristol, where he gives lectures.

1796   Coleridge plans the political periodical the *Watchman* (ten issues) and publishes *Poems on Various Subjects* and a pamphlet of *Sonnets from Various Authors;* Coleridge begins taking opium for relief from painful back spasms; Coleridge's first son, Hartley, is born; Coleridge and family move to Nether Stowey.

1797   Pitt's poor law bill fails; Coleridge writes *Osorio;* William Taylor's translations of Gottfried Bürger are published; Wordsworth and Dorothy Wordsworth settle at Alfoxden in Somerset; Coleridge visits Alfoxden in June; Coleridge and Wordsworth plan *Lyrical Ballads;* Coleridge begins writing "Rime of the Ancyent Marinere," "Christabel," and "Kubla Khan."

1798   Dorothy Wordsworth begins her journals; plans are underway for Joseph Cottle to publish *Lyrical Ballads;* Coleridge publishes *Fears in Solitude* and prepares to become a Unitarian minister;

Wordsworth and Dorothy Wordsworth visit Tintern Abbey in July; Coleridge receives an annuity from the Wedgwood estate; Wordsworth, Dorothy Wordsworth, and Coleridge leave for Goslar, Germany; *Lyrical Ballads, with a Few Other Poems* is published anonymously.

1799 Coleridge studies German philosophy and literature at University of Göttingen; Wordsworth begins writing *The Prelude* for Coleridge; Wordsworth and Dorothy Wordsworth return to England and settle at Dove Cottage, Grasmere (until 1808); Coleridge returns to Nether Stowey and falls in love with Sara Hutchinson, sister of Wordsworth's future wife, Mary Hutchinson; Coleridge contributes to the *Morning Post.*

1800 Coleridge and family settle near Dove Cottage at Greta Hall, Keswick.

1801 The second edition of *Lyrical Ballads,* with additional poems and preface by Wordsworth, is published in January (1800 is the date on title page).

1802 Wordsworth begins writing sonnets; he and Dorothy Wordsworth visit Annette Vallon and daughter at Calais; Wordsworth arranges for annual child-support payments and marries Mary Hutchinson on October 4; Coleridge writes "Dejection: An Ode"; *Lyrical Ballads, with Pastoral and Other Poems* (third edition with expanded preface) is published.

1803 Wordsworth, Dorothy Wordsworth, and Coleridge tour Scotland.

1804 Napoleon is crowned emperor; Coleridge works as secretary to the British High Commissioner and, in increasingly poor health, tours the Mediterranean region.

1805 Wordsworth's brother John dies in a shipwreck, inspiring "Elegiac Stanzas"; Wordsworth publishes the final edition of *Lyrical Ballads.*

1807 Wordsworth publishes *Poems in Two Volumes,* including "Elegiac Stanzas," "Resolution and Independence," and "Ode [Intimations of Immortality]"; Coleridge separates from wife and children and moves to London.

1809 Coleridge starts the moral, literary, and philosophical journal the *Friend;* Coleridge lives with the Wordsworths briefly at Allan Bank.

1810 Wordsworth and Coleridge become estranged due to Wordsworth's criticism of Coleridge's opium addiction; Coleridge moves to London.

1811   The Prince of Wales becomes regent due to George III's incapacitation; Wordsworth and family move to the Rectory, Grasmere; Coleridge works as a journalist in London and gives lectures on literature.

1813   Wordsworth appointed distributor of stamps for Westmoreland; Wordsworth and family move to Rydal Mount, near Grasmere; Coleridge lectures on Shakespeare in Bristol.

1814   Wordsworth publishes *The Excursion.*

1815   Allies led by Wellington defeat Napoleon at Waterloo; Wordsworth publishes *Poems* and *The White Doe of Rylstone.*

1816   Coleridge resides with Dr. James Gillman for treatment of his opium addiction, publishes *Christabel; Kubla Khan, A Vision; The Pains of Sleep.*

1817   Coleridge publishes *Biographia Literaria* and *Sibylline Leaves,* including the revised "Rime of the Ancient Mariner."

1818   Coleridge lectures on literature and philosophy.

1819   Wordsworth publishes *Peter Bell* and *Benjamin the Waggoner.*

1820   Prince Regent becomes George IV; Wordsworth publishes *The River Duddon;* the Wordsworths tour Europe.

1824   Coleridge publishes the theological treatise *Aids to Reflection.*

1828   Wordsworth and Coleridge reconcile and tour the Rhine valley together; Coleridge publishes *Poetical Works.*

1832   First Reform Bill is passed.

1834   Coleridge dies on July 25 of congestive heart failure.

1835   Wordsworth publishes *Yarrow Revisited, and Other Poems.*

1837   Queen Victoria ascends to the throne.

1842   Wordsworth publishes his final volume, *Poems Chiefly of Early and Late Years;* Wordsworth resigns position as stamp distributor, earning a government pension.

1843   Wordsworth succeeds Robert Southey as poet laureate and dictates a series of notes about his poetry to family friend Isabella Fenwick.

1850   Wordsworth dies on April 23 after an attack of pleurisy; Mary Wordsworth publishes *The Prelude.*

WORKS CITED

Abrams, M. H. *A Glossary of Literary Terms.* 6th ed. Fort Worth: Harcourt Brace Jovanovich, 1993.

———. "Structure and Style in the Greater Romantic Lyric." *The Correspondent Breeze: Essays on English Romanticism.* New York: Norton, 1984. 76–108.

Aristotle. "The Art of Poetry." *Classical Literary Criticism.* Trans. T. S. Dorsch. London: Penguin, 1965.

Brett, R. L., and A. R. Jones, eds. *Lyrical Ballads.* 2nd ed. London: Routledge, 1991.

Burke, Edmund. *A Philosophical Enquiry into the Origins of our Ideas of the Sublime and Beautiful.* Ed. James T. Boulton. 1967. Oxford: Blackwell, 1990.

———. *Reflections on the Revolution in France.* Ed. Conor Cruise O'Brien. London: Penguin, 1986.

Burns, Robert. *Poems and Songs.* Ed. James Kinsley. Oxford: Oxford UP, 1969.

Butler, James, and Karen Green, eds. *Lyrical Ballads, and Other Poems, 1797–1800.* By William Wordsworth. Ithaca: Cornell UP, 1992.

Butler, Marilyn, ed. *Burke, Paine, Godwin, and the Revolution Controversy.* 1984. Cambridge: Cambridge UP, 1994.

Coleridge, Samuel Taylor. *Biographia Literaria.* Vol. 2. Ed. James Engell and W. Jackson Bate. Princeton: Princeton UP, 1983.

———. *Collected Letters of Samuel Taylor Coleridge.* Ed. Earl Leslie Griggs. Oxford: Clarendon, 1956. 6 vols.

———. *Poems on Various Subjects.* London: Robinsons; Bristol: Cottle, 1796.

———. *Poetical Works.* Ed. Ernest Hartley Coleridge. Oxford: Clarendon, 1912.

———. *Table Talk.* Ed. Carl Woodring. Vol. 1. Princeton: Princeton UP, 1990. 2 vols.

Cowherd, Raymond G. *Political Economists and the English Poor Laws: A Historical Survey of the Influence of Classical Economists on the Formation of Social Welfare Policy.* Athens: Ohio UP, 1977.

Curran, Stuart. "Mary Robinson's *Lyrical Tales* in Context." *Re-Visioning Romanticism: British Women Writers, 1776–1837.* Ed. Carol Shiner Wilson and Joel Haefner. Philadelphia: U of Pennsylvania P, 1994. 17–35.

———. *Poetic Form and British Romanticism.* New York: Oxford UP, 1986.

Curtis, Jared, ed. *The Fenwick Notes of William Wordsworth.* London: Bristol Classical P, 1993.

Darbishire, Helen. *The Poet Wordsworth.* Oxford: Clarendon, 1950.

Eden, Frederick Morton. *The State of the Poor: A History of the Labouring Classes in England, with Parochial Reports.* Ed. A. G. L. Rogers. 1929. New York: Blom, 1971.

Foxon, D. F. "The Printing of *Lyrical Ballads,* 1798." *Library* 5th ser. 9 (1954): 221–41.

Frye, Northrop. "Towards Defining an Age of Sensibility." *ELH* 23 (1956): 144–52.

Gifford, William. *The Baviad and Maeviad.* 1791, 1795. London: Cobbett, 1799.

Gill, Stephen. *William Wordsworth: A Life.* 1989. Oxford: Oxford UP, 1990.

Gilpin, William. *Observations on the River Wye.* London: Blamire, 1782.

———. *Three Essays: On Picturesque Beauty, On Picturesque Travel, and On Sketching Landscape.* 3rd ed. London: Cadell, 1808.

Glen, Heather. *Vision and Disenchantment: Blake's Songs and Wordsworth's Lyrical Ballads.* Cambridge: Cambridge UP, 1983.

Godwin, William. *Enquiry Concerning Political Justice and Its Influence on Modern Morals and Happiness.* 1798. Ed. Isaac Kramnick. 1976. London: Penguin, 1985.

———. *An Enquiry Concerning the Principles of Political Justice, and Its Influence on General Virtue and Happiness.* London: Robinson, 1793.

Goldsmith, Oliver. *The Deserted Village: A Poem.* London: Griffin, 1770.

Harrison, Gary. *Wordsworth's Vagrant Muse: Poetry, Poverty and Power.* Detroit: Wayne State UP, 1994.

Hazlitt, William. *Lectures on the English Poets; The Spirit of the Age, or Contemporary Portraits.* London: Dent, 1967.

———. *My First Acquaintance with Poets.* 1823. Oxford: Woodstock, 1993.

———. "On the Character of Rousseau." Ed. P. P. Howe. Vol. 4. *The Collected Works of William Hazlitt.* London: Dent, 1931. 21 vols.

Hume, David. *A Treatise of Human Nature.* Ed. L. A. Selby-Bigge. 1888. Oxford: Clarendon, 1951.

Jacobus, Mary. *Tradition and Experiment in Wordsworth's* Lyrical Ballads *(1798).* Oxford: Clarendon, 1976.

Johnson, Samuel. *Lives of the English Poets.* London: Dent, 1968. 2 vols.

Jordan, John E. *Why the* Lyrical Ballads? *The Background, Writing, and Character of Wordsworth's 1798* Lyrical Ballads. Berkeley: U of California P, 1976.

Koch, Mark. "Utilitarian and Reactionary Arguments for Almsgiving in Wordsworth's 'The Old Cumberland Beggar.'" *Eighteenth-Century Life* 13 (1989): 18–33.

Legouis, Emile. *The Early Life of William Wordsworth, 1770–1798.* 1897. London: Dent, 1932.

Levinson, Marjorie. *Wordsworth's Great Period Poems: Four Essays.* Cambridge: Cambridge UP, 1986.

Lindop, Grevel. *A Literary Guide to the Lake District.* London: Chatto, 1993.

Locke, John. *An Essay Concerning Human Understanding.* Oxford: Clarendon, 1975.

Longinus. *On the Sublime.* Classical Literary Criticism. London: Penguin, 1965.

Magnuson, Paul. *Reading Public Romanticism.* Princeton: Princeton UP, 1998.

Mayo, Robert. "The Contemporaneity of the *Lyrical Ballads.*" *PMLA* 69 (1954): 486–522.

McGann, Jerome. *The Poetics of Sensibility: A Revolution in Literary Style.* Oxford: Clarendon, 1996.

———. *The Romantic Ideology: A Critical Investigation.* Chicago: U of Chicago P, 1983.

Milton, John. *The Riverside Milton.* Ed. Roy Flannagan. Boston: Houghton, 1998.

Paine, Thomas. *The Rights of Man.* London: Penguin, 1984.

The Parliamentary History of England from the Earliest Period to the Year 1803. Vol. 32. London: Longman, 1818.

Parrish, Stephen Maxfield. *The Art of the* Lyrical Ballads. Cambridge: Harvard UP, 1973.

Percy, Thomas. *Reliques of Ancient English Poetry: Consisting of Old Heroic Ballads, Songs, and Other Pieces of Our Earlier Poets (Chiefly of the Lyric Kind) Together with Some Few of Later Date.* 2nd ed. Vol. 2. London: Dodsley, 1767.

Pope, Alexander. *Complete Poetical Works.* Ed. Herbert Davis. Oxford: Oxford UP, 1983.

Poynter, J. R. *Society and Pauperism.* Oxford: Oxford UP, 1969.

Price, Richard. "A Discourse on the Love of Our Country." *Political Writings.* Ed. D. O. Thomas. Cambridge: Cambridge UP, 1991. 176–96.

Reed, Mark L. "Wordsworth, Coleridge, and the 'Plan' of the *Lyrical Ballads.*" *University of Toronto Quarterly* 34 (1965): 238–53.

Roe, Nicholas. *Wordsworth and Coleridge: The Radical Years.* Oxford: Clarendon, 1988.

Rousseau, Jean-Jacques. "Discourse on the Arts and Sciences." *The Basic Political Writings.* Trans. Donald A. Cress. Indianapolis: Hackett, 1978.

Ruggles, Thomas. *The History of the Poor: Their Rights, Duties, and the Laws Respecting Them.* London: Deighton, 1793.

Shakespeare, William. *The Riverside Shakespeare.* Ed. G. Blakemore Evans. 2nd ed. Boston: Houghton Mifflin, 1997.

Sheats, Paul D. *The Making of Wordsworth's Poetry, 1785–1798.* Cambridge: Harvard UP, 1973.

Smith, Christopher. "Robert Southey and the Emergence of *Lyrical Ballads.*" *Romanticism on the Net* 9 (February 1998). 26 May 2000 <http://users.ox.ac.uk/~scat0385/southeyLB.html>.

Sutherland, D. M. G. *France 1789–1815: Revolution and Counterrevolution.* New York: Oxford UP, 1986.

Taylor, William. "Some Account of the Poems of G. A. Bürger." *Monthly Magazine* 2 (March 1796): 117–18.

Townsend, Joseph. *A Dissertation on the Poor Laws.* London: Dilly, 1786.

Trevelyan, G. M. *A Shortened History of England.* 1959. Harmondsworth: Penguin, 1974.

Wasserman, Earl. *The Subtler Language: Critical Readings of Neoclassical and Romantic Poems.* Baltimore: Johns Hopkins UP, 1959.

Williams, John. *Wordsworth: Romantic Poetry and Revolution Politics.* Manchester: Manchester UP, 1989.

Wilson, John. [Letter to William Wordsworth.] *Lyrical Ballads: The Text of the 1789 Edition with the Additional 1800 Poems and the Prefaces.* Ed. R. L. Brett and A. R. Jones. 2nd ed. London: Routledge, 1991. 334–39.

Woodring, Carl. *Politics in the Poetry of Coleridge.* Madison: U of Wisconsin P, 1961.

Wordsworth, Dorothy. *The Journals of Dorothy Wordsworth.* Ed. Mary Moorman. 1958. Oxford: Oxford UP, 1971.

Wordsworth, William. *The Letters of William and Dorothy Wordsworth: The Early Years, 1787–1805.* 2nd ed. Ed. Ernest de Selincourt and Chester L. Shaver. Oxford: Clarendon, 1967.

——. *The Letters of William and Dorothy Wordsworth: The Later Years, 1821–53.* 2nd ed. Ed. Ernest de Selincourt and Alan G. Hill. Oxford: Clarendon, 1978–88. 4 vols.

——. *The Prelude, 1799, 1805, 1850.* Ed. Jonathan Wordsworth, M. H. Abrams, and Stephen Gill. New York: Norton, 1979.

——. *The Prose Works of William Wordsworth.* Ed. W. J. B. Owen and Jane Worthington Symser. Oxford: Clarendon, 1974. 3 vols.

FOR FURTHER READING

TEXTUAL

Brett, R. L., and A. R. Jones, eds. *Lyrical Ballads.* 2nd ed. London: Routledge, 1991.

Butler, James, and Karen Green, eds. *Lyrical Ballads, and Other Poems, 1797–1800.* Ithaca: Cornell UP, 1992.

Coleridge, Ernest Hartley, ed. *Coleridge: Poetical Works.* 1912. London: Oxford UP, 1969.

Foxon, D. F. "The Printing of *Lyrical Ballads,* 1798." Library 5th ser. 9 (1954): 221–41.

Gill, Stephen, ed. *William Wordsworth.* 1984. Oxford: Oxford UP, 1990.

Tetrault, Ronald, and Bruce Graver, eds. *Lyrical Ballads Bicentennary Project.* 19 January 1999. Dalhousie University Electronic Text Centre. 31 October 2000 <http://www.dal.ca/etc/lballads/welcome.html>.

BIOGRAPHICAL

Ashton, Rosemary. *The Life of Samuel Taylor Coleridge: A Critical Biography.* Oxford: Blackwell, 1996.

Bate, Walter Jackson. *Coleridge.* New York: Macmillan, 1968.

Gill, Stephen. *William Wordsworth: A Life.* 1989. Oxford: Oxford UP, 1990.

Holmes, Richard. *Coleridge: Early Visions.* London: Hodder, 1989.

Moorman, Mary. *William Wordsworth: A Biography; The Early Years: 1770–1803.* Oxford: Oxford UP, 1957.

Reed, Mark L. *Wordsworth: The Chronology of the Early Years, 1770–1799.* Cambridge: Harvard UP, 1967.

Roe, Nicholas. *Wordsworth and Coleridge: The Radical Years.* Oxford: Clarendon, 1988.

Willey, Basil. *Samuel Taylor Coleridge.* New York: Norton, 1973.

CRITICAL AND CONTEXTUAL

Bateson, F. W. *Wordsworth, A Re-Interpretation.* 2nd ed. London: Longmans, 1956.

Beer, John. *Coleridge the Visionary.* London: Chatto, 1959.

Bialostosky, Don H. *Making Tales: The Poetics of Wordsworth's Narrative Experiments.* Chicago: U of Chicago P, 1984.

Boehm, Alan. "The 1798 *Lyrical Ballads* and the Poetics of Late Eighteenth-Century Book Production." *ELH* 63 (1996): 453–87.

Chandler, James K. *Wordsworth's Second Nature: A Study of the Poetry and Politics.* Chicago: U of Chicago P, 1984.

Darbishire, Helen. *The Poet Wordsworth.* Oxford: Clarendon, 1950.

Eilenberg, Susan. *Strange Power of Speech: Wordsworth, Coleridge, and Literary Possession.* New York: Oxford UP, 1992.

Fraistat, Neil. *The Poem and the Book: Interpreting Collections of Romantic Poetry.* Chapel Hill: U of North Carolina P, 1985.

Gabler, Jane. "Guardians and Watchful Powers: Literary Satire and *Lyrical Ballads* in 1798." *1798: The Year of the* Lyrical Ballads. Ed. Richard Cronin. New York: St. Martin's, 1998. 203–30.

Gaull, Marilyn. *English Romanticism: The Human Context.* New York: Norton, 1988.

Glen, Heather. *Vision and Disenchantment: Blake's Songs and Wordsworth's Lyrical Ballads.* Cambridge: Cambridge UP, 1983.

Gravil, Richard. "*Lyrical Ballads* (1798): Wordsworth as Ironist." *Critical Quarterly* 24 (1982): 39–57.

Harrison, Gary. *Wordsworth's Vagrant Muse: Poetry, Poverty, and Power.* Detroit: Wayne State UP, 1994.

Hartman, Geoffrey H. *Wordsworth's Poetry 1787–1814.* 1967. New Haven: Yale UP, 1971.

Izenberg, Gerald. "The Politics of Song in Wordsworth's *Lyrical Ballads.*" *Refiguring Revolutions: Aesthetics and Politics from the English Revolution to the Romantic Revolution.* Ed. Kevin Sharpe and Steven N. Zwicker. Berkeley: U of California P, 1998. 116–37, 324–26.

Jacobus, Mary. *Tradition and Experiment in Wordsworth's* Lyrical Ballads. Oxford: Clarendon, 1976.

Jordan, John E. *Why the* Lyrical Ballads? *The Background, Writing, and Character of Wordsworth's 1798* Lyrical Ballads. Berkeley: U of California P, 1976.

Klancher, Jon P. *The Making of English Reading Audiences, 1790–1832.* Madison: U of Wisconsin P, 1987.

Kroeber, Karl. *Romantic Narrative Art.* Madison: U of Wisconsin P, 1960.

Levinson, Marjorie. *Wordsworth's Great Period Poems: Four Essays.* Cambridge: Cambridge UP, 1986.

Liu, Alan. *Wordsworth: The Sense of History.* Stanford: Stanford UP, 1989.

Magnuson, Paul. *Coleridge and Wordsworth: A Lyrical Dialogue.* Princeton: Princeton UP, 1981.

———. *Reading Public Romanticism.* Princeton: Princeton UP, 1998.

Matlak, Richard E. *The Poetry of Relationship: The Wordsworths and Coleridge, 1797–1800.* New York: St. Martin's, 1997.

Mayo, Robert. "The Contemporaneity of the *Lyrical Ballads.*" *PMLA* 69 (1954): 486–522.

McEathron, Scott. "Wordsworth and Coleridge, *Lyrical Ballads.*" *A Companion to Romanticism.* Ed. Duncan Wu. Oxford: Blackwell, 1998. 144–56.

McFarland, Thomas. *Coleridge and the Pantheist Tradition.* Oxford: Clarendon, 1969.

McGann, Jerome J. "The Ancient Mariner: The Meaning of the Meanings." 1981. Rpt. *The Beauty of Inflections: Literary Investigations in Historical Method and Theory.* Oxford: Clarendon, 1988. 135–72.

Murray, Roger N. *Wordsworth's Style: Figures and Themes in the* Lyrical Ballads *of 1800.* Lincoln: U of Nebraska P, 1967.

O'Donnell, Brennan. *The Passion of Meter: A Study of Wordsworth's Metrical Art.* Kent: Kent State UP, 1995.

Parrish, Stephen Maxfield. *The Art of the* Lyrical Ballads. Cambridge: Harvard UP, 1973.

Perry, Seamus. "The *Ancient Mariner* Controversy." *Charles Lamb Bulletin* ns 92 (1995): 208–23.

Reed, Mark L. "Wordsworth, Coleridge, and the 'Plan' of the *Lyrical Ballads.*" *University of Toronto Quarterly* 34 (1965): 238–53.

Richey, William. "The Politicized Landscape of 'Tintern Abbey.'" *Studies in Philology* 95 (1998): 197–219.

Robinson, Daniel. "'Work without Hope': Anxiety and Embarrassment in Coleridge's Sonnets." *Studies in Romanticism* 39 (2000): 81–110.

Roe, Nicholas. *The Politics of Nature: Wordsworth and Some Contemporaries.* New York: St. Martin's, 1992.

Salveson, Christopher. *The Landscape of Memory: A Study of Wordsworth's Poetry.* Lincoln: U of Nebraska P, 1965.

Sheats, Paul D. *The Making of Wordsworth's Poetry, 1785–1798.* Cambridge: Harvard UP, 1973.

Simpson, David. *Wordsworth's Historical Imagination: The Poetry of Displacement.* New York: Methuen, 1987.

Soderholm, James. "Dorothy Wordsworth's Return to Tintern Abbey." *New Literary History* 26 (1995): 309–22.

Spargo, R. Clifton. "Begging the Question of Responsibility: The Vagrant Poor in Wordsworth's 'Beggars' and 'Resolution and Independence.'" *Studies in Romanticism* 39 (2000): 51–80.

Stillinger, Jack. "Wordsworth, Coleridge, and the Shaggy Dog: The Novelty of *Lyrical Ballads* (1798)." *Wordsworth Circle* 31 (2000): 70–76.

Williams, John. *Wordsworth: Romantic Poetry and Revolution Politics.* Manchester: Manchester UP, 1989.

Wolfson, Susan J. "*Lyrical Ballads* and the Language of (Men) Feeling: Wordsworth Writing Women's Voices." *Men Writing the Feminine: Literature, Theory, and the Question of Genders.* Ed. Thaïs E. Morgan. Albany: State U of New York P, 1994. 29–57.

Woodring, Carl. *Wordsworth.* Cambridge: Harvard UP, 1975.

Wordsworth, Jonathan. *William Wordsworth and the Borders of Vision.* Oxford: Clarendon, 1982.